Is — singular
Are — plural

And is used for ~~contractions~~ continuation of a

Because indicates casuality

CliffsNotes®

GED®

CRAM PLAN™

Make sure there is a subject + a verb

Although is usually used At the beginning of a sentence

While has to do with time

CliffsNotes®

GED® CRAM PLAN™

by Murray Shukyn and Dale E. Shuttleworth, Ph.D.

WILEY

Wiley Publishing, Inc.

Editorial	*Composition*
Acquisition Editor: Greg Tubach	**Proofreader:** Melissa D. Buddendeck
Project Editor: Elizabeth Kuball	Wiley Publishing, Inc., Composition Services
Copy Editor: Elizabeth Kuball	
Technical Editors: Tony Bedenikovic, Jane Burstein, Sven Dubie, Scott McDougall, Mary Jane Sterling, and Dario Untama	

CliffsNotes® GED® Cram Plan™

Published by:
Wiley Publishing, Inc.
111 River Street
Hoboken, NJ 07030-5774
www.wiley.com

Library of Congress Control Number: 2011922784
ISBN: 978-0-470-87478-3 (pbk)
ISBN: 978-1-118-01571-1 (ebk)

Printed in the United States of America

10 9 8 7 6 5 4 3 2 1

For general information on our other products and services or to obtain technical support, please contact our Customer Care Department within the U.S. at 877-762-2974, outside the U.S. at 317-572-3993, or fax 317-572-4002.

Wiley also publishes its books in a variety of electronic formats. Some content that appears in print may not be available in electronic books. For more information about Wiley products, please visit our web site at www.wiley.com.

About the Authors

Murray Shukyn is Associate Director of the Training Renewal Foundation. He has been a teacher, author, program designer, curriculum designer, and implementer at the elementary, secondary, and university levels. His involvement with GED stretches over a dozen years, and he has tutored, mentored, and assisted students in reaching their goal of passing the GED test.

Dale E. Shuttleworth, Ph.D., is Executive Director of the Training Renewal Foundation. His career as a community educator has included experience as a teacher, school-community worker, consultant, principal, program coordinator, school superintendent, and university course director.

An author of 10 books and 200 articles in journals and periodicals, he has served as an expert consultant for the Organization for Economic Cooperation and Development (OECD) in Paris and is the recipient of the prestigious Dag Hammerskjold Gold Medal for Excellence in Education.

Acknowledgements

We wish to express our appreciation to Marilyn Shuttleworth, who assisted us in the preparation of this manuscript; the Training Renewal Foundation, for the opportunity to work in the world of the GED; and the late Peter Kilburn, former Canadian GED Administrator, for his inspiration, friendship, and encouragement in introducing us to the potential of the GED to be a source of fulfillment and liberation in the lives and careers of so many adult learners who have dropped out of traditional schooling accreditation systems.

Table of Contents

Introduction

The GED tests are an opportunity for people who haven't finished high school to obtain a certificate from a recognized authority (the American Council on Education), showing that they have the equivalent of a high school diploma. The GED is the only high school equivalency certificate recognized all around the world. A GED certificate is a passport to the world of advancement on the job and an entry into the wonderful world of post-secondary education.

If you're interested in this book, you must have already thought of the advantages of earning a high school equivalency certificate. If you bought this book, you're on your way to taking the tests. The first thing you have to do is determine how long you have to prepare for the GED tests. In many areas of the country, tests are given regularly and you can decide for yourself when you want to take the tests. In some areas, the tests aren't given that often, so you have to decide when you *need* to take the tests. Whether you have one week, one month, or two months to prepare, this book can help you do your best on the GED tests.

About the GED

The GED test challenges your abilities in five main areas, divided into seven sections:

Test Area	Number of Questions	Time Limit
Language Arts, Writing, Part I	50	75 minutes
Language Arts, Writing, Part II	1 essay	45 minutes
Social Studies	50	70 minutes
Science	50	80 minutes
Language Arts, Reading	40	65 minutes
Mathematics, Part I	25	45 minutes
Mathematics, Part II	25	45 minutes

For more information on each of these subject areas, go to www.acenet.edu/Content/NavigationMenu/ged/test/prep/The_Content_Area_Tes.htm and click on each of the sections.

Keep in mind the following tips:

- **You're expected to write an essay from your personal experience within a set time.** The only way to prepare for the essay portion of the test is to begin writing short essays on many topics within the 45 minutes allotted for the essay. You'll probably never guess the topic on the test, so what you're doing is developing the writing skills necessary to produce a short essay in the required time.

  Look at newspaper headlines and write on them. Listen for snippets of conversation and use these as topics. Writing logically and coherently is what matters—not what you write about.

- **The GED Science Test assumes that you have an understanding of scientific terms.** Read as much as you can about science and look up any words you don't understand. Go to http://www.acenet.edu/Content/NavigationMenu/ged/etp/science_test_descrip.htm and enter any of the topics that may be covered into an Internet search engine and read some of the results. If you come across a word that you don't understand, enter the word in a search engine and read the explanation. If you have to do this for most of the words in the article, it's probable too difficult to bother with. Remember that the GED is for students at the end of high school, not graduate students at a university or college. Stick to appropriate articles and you'll develop enough of a scientific vocabulary to read any questions on the test.

- **Part I of the GED Mathematics Test allows you to use a calculator, but it's a specific calculator that will be provided to you.** Go to www.acenet.edu/Content/NavigationMenu/ged/etp/2002_resource.htm and click on Math Videos for information and help in using the calculator provided. (Calculator instructions are also provided in Chapter XVI.) Calculators can only make calculations easier to do—they won't solve problems for you. Learn to use the calculator as a tool, but go through the material in this book to learn how to solve the problems.

- **Some of the mathematics questions require an answer in a different format.** Check out the Alternate Formatting Video at www.acenet.edu/Content/NavigationMenu/ged/etp/2002_resource.htm. These alternate format answers are not difficult to use, but they do require some understanding and familiarity. (For more on grid-in questions, see Chapter XI.)

Go to www.acenet.edu/Content/NavigationMenu/ged/test/prep/Prepare_GED.htm and look at Practice Makes Perfect. Here you'll find many resources, including sample questions and answers.

Where to Take the GED

The GED tests are paper-and-pencil tests that are administered on a regular schedule at various test sites. For a list of the test sites in your area, go to www.acenet.edu/resources/GED/center_locator.cfm and enter your zip code in the search box. You can call the test center and get information on when the tests are given and, more important, how far in advance you have to apply to take the GED. Write down this information.

If you need further information, you can call 800-626-9433 or contact your local GED Testing Administrator by going to www.acenet.edu/Content/NavigationMenu/ged/test/admin.htm.

If you have special needs, consult www.acenet.edu/Content/NavigationMenu/ged/test/Take/Accommodations_Disab.htm. For information about taking the GED in Spanish or French, go to www.acenet.edu/Content/NavigationMenu/ged/test/Take/spanish_french.htm. For information on special editions of the test (given in large print, Braille, and so on), go to www.acenet.edu/Content/NavigationMenu/ged/etp/pros/GED_special_editions.htm.

Double-check with your local GED Testing Administrator about what you may or may not take into the test. The usual rule is that you can take in your clothes and shoes and very little else. For the GED Mathematics Test, a calculator will be supplied for you, as will scratch paper and pencils. Double-check with the administrator to make sure that you don't forget something you need or bring something you don't.

When to Take the GED

Now, you have to figure out when to take the test. Instead of setting a random deadline and trying to fit your studying into that timeframe, start by taking the Diagnostic Test in Chapter I. The Diagnostic Test tests you in the skill areas that appear on the real GED. Take the Diagnostic Test seriously. Stick to the time limits as closely as your watch or clock will let you, never look at an answer until after you've finished the test, and, finally, score your test based on the answers you've written (not what you meant to write). After scoring the test, look at the answers and explanations. Even if you got the question right, make sure that you followed a logical process to do so. If you got the question wrong or guessed at the answer, mark the explanation with an X. This will give you a list of areas that you need to review and spend more time on.

If you got at least 75 percent of the questions correct, you can decide when you want to take the test and follow the appropriate cram plan. If you scored between 50 percent and 75 percent, leave yourself more time for preparation. If you scored less than 50 percent, consider doing more extensive preparation (for example, taking a GED preparation course) before deciding which test date would be best.

Regardless of how you do on the Diagnostic Test, don't take this as a failure. We all learn and remember differently, and some of us just need more preparation than others. The important thing to tell yourself is that you're smart enough to recognize that you need to prepare.

The cram plans in Chapters II through VI will guide your studying. Remember that there are five tests in the GED and there is a different cram plan for each. Select your cram plan according to your results on the diagnostic test and leave time for all five cram plans before taking the test. If you feel you need more time to accomplish the objectives in a particular area, consider adjusting your goals and going to a longer cram plan. If you're comfortable with your progress, continue on the schedule you're on.

GED Scoring

For multiple-choice questions, as well as standard grid-in and coordinate plane grid-in questions in the Mathematics Test, you get 1 point for each question you answer correctly. No points are deducted for skipping a question or for answering a question incorrectly. Your total points on a subject test are then converted to a standard score, ranging from 200 to 800. In order to pass a subject test, you need a standard score of 410. (You can achieve a 410 standard score on an individual subject test by answering roughly 65 percent of the questions correctly.) For the five-test battery, you need an overall average score of 450 to pass.

The essay portion (Part II) of the Language Arts, Writing Test is scored on a scale of 1 to 4, with 1 being the lowest possible score. The essay score accounts for 35 percent of the Writing Test standard score. Two GED Testing Service–certified readers evaluate your essay on the basis of its overall effectiveness. If you do any of the following, you must retake both Parts I and II of the Writing Test:

- Score less than 2.
- Leave the essay blank.
- Write on a topic other than the assigned topic.
- Write illegibly.

For more on what makes an effective essay, see Chapter VII.

About This Book

CliffsNotes GED Cram Plan is your guide to preparing for the GED tests, whether you have one week, one month, or two months to prepare. The Diagnostic Test in Chapter I gives you a sense of where you're starting from—and it helps you figure out how much time you need to prepare. The Diagnostic Test doesn't tell you what your score on the GED might be—instead, it gives you a sense of your strengths and weaknesses so you know where to concentrate your studying.

The cram plans in Chapters II through VI give you specific guidance on what to study when; follow these plans, and you won't run the risk of not studying enough. Chapters VII through XI, the subject chapters, give you the information you need to brush up on each subject. And the Full-Length Practice Tests in Chapters XII through XVI help you assess your progress and continue your study.

This book provides diagnosis, remediation, practice, explanation, and a chance to practice with test questions. It gives you everything except the motivation only *you* can bring to the table. With this combination, you can prepare to take the GED and look forward to a positive outcome.

I. Diagnostic Test

The Diagnostic Test (excluding the essay—Language Arts, Writing, Part II) consists of half-length tests. You'll have the full 45 minutes to write the essay.

The areas covered in this Diagnostic Test are: Language Arts, Reading; Language Arts, Writing, Parts I and II; Mathematics; Science; and Social Studies. Taking these tests can give you a good idea of where to spend the most time in your preparation.

Each question is numbered. For all the tests except Mathematics, you have to choose the best answer out of the five given and fill in the corresponding circle on the answer sheet. For Mathematics, there are three possible types of questions: standard multiple-choice, a coordinate plane grid, and a standard grid. See Chapter XI to understand how to use the two grids. The Mathematics test allows you to use a calculator for part of the actual test, but the Diagnostic Test can be completed without the use of a calculator.

The real GED is marked by a machine, and you can fill in only one circle on your answer sheet. Erasing can present problems to marking machines unless the erasure is complete and clean. Try to make your behavior on this Diagnostic Test as close as possible to the real thing. Observe the time constraints and watch your use of the eraser.

Answer all the questions. There is no deduction for wrong answers, and you get 1 point for each right one. If you need to, guess. The more wrong answers you can eliminate, the better your chances of guessing the correct answer. If you could eliminate four choices, you would stand a 100 percent chance of being correct. Unfortunately, for each choice you cannot eliminate, the odds go down.

Each section of the Diagnostic Test is a separate entity. If you finish one part ahead of schedule, take the time to review your answers or just relax. Do not add the extra time you have to the next test.

For the essay and the Mathematics section, you need scrap paper. Either write in the blank sections of this book or use the scrap paper you have on hand.

The total time for all sections of the Diagnostic Test is 3 hours and 54 minutes.

Test	Number of Questions	Number of Minutes
Language Arts, Writing Part I	25	37
Language Arts, Writing Part II	1 essay	45
Social Studies	25	35
Science	25	40
Language Arts, Reading	20	32
Mathematics	25	45

After you complete the Diagnostic Test, score it and review the answer explanations (especially for any questions you got wrong). To score the essay, check the rubric and the sample essay.

Answer Sheet

CUT HERE

Section 1: Language Arts, Writing Part I	Section 3: Social Studies	Section 4: Science	Section 5: Language Arts, Reading
1 ① ② ③ ④ ⑤	1 ① ② ③ ④ ⑤	1 ① ② ③ ④ ⑤	1 ① ② ③ ④ ⑤
2 ① ② ③ ④ ⑤	2 ① ② ③ ④ ⑤	2 ① ② ③ ④ ⑤	2 ① ② ③ ④ ⑤
3 ① ② ③ ④ ⑤	3 ① ② ③ ④ ⑤	3 ① ② ③ ④ ⑤	3 ① ② ③ ④ ⑤
4 ① ② ③ ④ ⑤	4 ① ② ③ ④ ⑤	4 ① ② ③ ④ ⑤	4 ① ② ③ ④ ⑤
5 ① ② ③ ④ ⑤	5 ① ② ③ ④ ⑤	5 ① ② ③ ④ ⑤	5 ① ② ③ ④ ⑤
6 ① ② ③ ④ ⑤	6 ① ② ③ ④ ⑤	6 ① ② ③ ④ ⑤	6 ① ② ③ ④ ⑤
7 ① ② ③ ④ ⑤	7 ① ② ③ ④ ⑤	7 ① ② ③ ④ ⑤	7 ① ② ③ ④ ⑤
8 ① ② ③ ④ ⑤	8 ① ② ③ ④ ⑤	8 ① ② ③ ④ ⑤	8 ① ② ③ ④ ⑤
9 ① ② ③ ④ ⑤	9 ① ② ③ ④ ⑤	9 ① ② ③ ④ ⑤	9 ① ② ③ ④ ⑤
10 ① ② ③ ④ ⑤	10 ① ② ③ ④ ⑤	10 ① ② ③ ④ ⑤	10 ① ② ③ ④ ⑤
11 ① ② ③ ④ ⑤	11 ① ② ③ ④ ⑤	11 ① ② ③ ④ ⑤	11 ① ② ③ ④ ⑤
12 ① ② ③ ④ ⑤	12 ① ② ③ ④ ⑤	12 ① ② ③ ④ ⑤	12 ① ② ③ ④ ⑤
13 ① ② ③ ④ ⑤	13 ① ② ③ ④ ⑤	13 ① ② ③ ④ ⑤	13 ① ② ③ ④ ⑤
14 ① ② ③ ④ ⑤	14 ① ② ③ ④ ⑤	14 ① ② ③ ④ ⑤	14 ① ② ③ ④ ⑤
15 ① ② ③ ④ ⑤	15 ① ② ③ ④ ⑤	15 ① ② ③ ④ ⑤	15 ① ② ③ ④ ⑤
16 ① ② ③ ④ ⑤	16 ① ② ③ ④ ⑤	16 ① ② ③ ④ ⑤	16 ① ② ③ ④ ⑤
17 ① ② ③ ④ ⑤	17 ① ② ③ ④ ⑤	17 ① ② ③ ④ ⑤	17 ① ② ③ ④ ⑤
18 ① ② ③ ④ ⑤	18 ① ② ③ ④ ⑤	18 ① ② ③ ④ ⑤	18 ① ② ③ ④ ⑤
19 ① ② ③ ④ ⑤	19 ① ② ③ ④ ⑤	19 ① ② ③ ④ ⑤	19 ① ② ③ ④ ⑤
20 ① ② ③ ④ ⑤	20 ① ② ③ ④ ⑤	20 ① ② ③ ④ ⑤	20 ① ② ③ ④ ⑤
21 ① ② ③ ④ ⑤	21 ① ② ③ ④ ⑤	21 ① ② ③ ④ ⑤	
22 ① ② ③ ④ ⑤	22 ① ② ③ ④ ⑤	22 ① ② ③ ④ ⑤	
23 ① ② ③ ④ ⑤	23 ① ② ③ ④ ⑤	23 ① ② ③ ④ ⑤	
24 ① ② ③ ④ ⑤	24 ① ② ③ ④ ⑤	24 ① ② ③ ④ ⑤	
25 ① ② ③ ④ ⑤	25 ① ② ③ ④ ⑤	25 ① ② ③ ④ ⑤	

Section 2: Language Arts, Writing Part II

The answer sheet for Language Arts, Writing Part II can be found on pages 5–6.

Section 6: Mathematics

1 ① ② ③ ④ ⑤
2 ① ② ③ ④ ⑤
3 ① ② ③ ④ ⑤
4 ① ② ③ ④ ⑤
5 ① ② ③ ④ ⑤
6 ① ② ③ ④ ⑤
7 ① ② ③ ④ ⑤

8.

17.

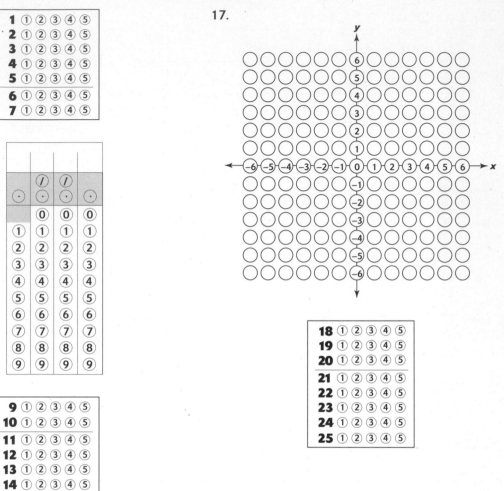

9 ① ② ③ ④ ⑤
10 ① ② ③ ④ ⑤
11 ① ② ③ ④ ⑤
12 ① ② ③ ④ ⑤
13 ① ② ③ ④ ⑤
14 ① ② ③ ④ ⑤
15 ① ② ③ ④ ⑤
16 ① ② ③ ④ ⑤

18 ① ② ③ ④ ⑤
19 ① ② ③ ④ ⑤
20 ① ② ③ ④ ⑤
21 ① ② ③ ④ ⑤
22 ① ② ③ ④ ⑤
23 ① ② ③ ④ ⑤
24 ① ② ③ ④ ⑤
25 ① ② ③ ④ ⑤

Section 2: Language Arts, Writing Part II

For the GED Mathematics Test, you will be provided with a list of mathematical formulas for your reference, like the one provided here.

Formulas	
AREA of a:	
square	Area = side^2
rectangle	Area = length × width
parallelogram	Area = base × height
triangle	Area $= \frac{1}{2} \times$ base $\times$ height
trapezoid	Area $= \frac{1}{2} \times \left(\text{base}_1 + \text{base}_2\right) \times$ height
circle	Area = π × radius^2; π is approximately equal to 3.14
PERIMETER of a:	
square	Perimeter = 4 × side
rectangle	Perimeter = (2 × length) + (2 × width)
triangle	Perimeter = side$_1$ + side$_2$ + side$_3$
CIRCUMFERENCE of a circle	Circumference = π × diameter; π is approximately equal to 3.14
VOLUME of a:	
cube	Volume = edge^3
rectangular solid	Volume = length × width × height
square pyramid	Volume $= \frac{1}{3} \times \left(\text{base edge}\right)^2 \times$ height
cylinder	Volume = π × radius^2 × height; π is approximately equal to 3.14
cone	Volume $= \frac{1}{3} \times \pi \times$ radius$^2 \times$ height; π is approximately equal to 3.14
COORDINATE GEOMETRY	distance between points $= \sqrt{\left(x_2 - x_1\right)^2 + \left(y_2 - y_1\right)^2}$; $\left(x_1, y_1\right)$ and $\left(x_2, y_2\right)$ are two points on a plane slope of a line $= \frac{y_2 - y_1}{x_2 - x_1}$; $\left(x_1, y_1\right)$ and $\left(x_2, y_2\right)$ are two points on the line
PYTHAGOREAN RELATIONSHIP	$a^2 + b^2 = c^2$; a and b are sides, and c is the hypotenuse of a right triangle
MEASURES OF CENTRAL TENDENCY	**mean** $= \frac{x_1 + x_2 + \ldots + x_n}{n}$; where the xs are the values for which a mean is desired, and n is the total number of values for x **median** = the middle value of an odd number of ordered scores, and halfway between the two middle values of an even number of ordered scores
SIMPLE INTEREST	interest = principal × rate × time
DISTANCE	distance = rate × time
TOTAL COST	total cost = (number of units) × (price per unit)

CUT HERE

Section 1: Language Arts, Writing, Part I

Time: 37 minutes

25 questions

Directions: Choose the best answer to each question. Mark your answers on the answer sheet provided.

Questions 1 through 6 refer to the following business letter.

THE TRAINING RENEWAL FOUNDATION
750 Millway Ave., Unit 6
Concord, MA 12345

Ted Tingle
Executive Director
Specialty Coffee Association of America
One World Trade Centre, Suite 1200
Long Beach, CA 96831

March 15, 2010

Dear Mr. Tingle:

(1) With reference to our exchange of e-mail I wish to confirm the following agreement regarding the representation of the Specialty Coffee Association of America (SCAA) by the Training Renewal Foundation (TRF).

(2) SCAA grants TRF an exclusive right for distribution of SCAA's training programs for the period from April 1, 2010, to March 31, 2013, and this agreement shall be renewable if both parties determine that they wish to continue.

(3) TRF will handle the entire registration process including receipt of the fees for all training conducted.

(4) TRF will set the basis fee structure and retain the majority of the fees, while SCAA will receive a sum to offset training manual, promotional and administrative costs.

(5) SCAA will provide master copies of the course description and promotional material.

(6) Hand-outs will consist of SCAAs' Class in a Box training manual, which SCAA will provide.

(7) The training programs will be targeted to all coffee retailers and foodservice operators interested in espresso programs.

(8) SCAA, as well as Coffee Association of America (CAA) members, will be included.

(9) TRF will provide equipment, consumables, and arrange accommodation and transportation for the training programs.

(10) Training program fees will be set by TRF to recover these costs.

(11) TRF will be responsible for selecting and compensating the trainers.

(12) TRF will liaise with the print media, while SCAA will liaise with the electronic media.

(13) TRF will follow the SCAA curriculum and use SCAA training materials for this program.

(14) There will be a joint SCAA/TRF promotion of the program to the retail trade, including non-members of both SCAA and CAA.

(15) We will jointly explore the possibility of introducing TRF's Café Equipment Technician training program (possibly in conjunction with the El Camino College program).

(16) As an SCAA program, we will encourage a joint SCAA/TRF Certificate of Completion.

Looking forward to working together.

Yours sincerely,

Dale E. Shuttleworth, Ph.D.
Executive Director

---

1. Sentence 1: With reference to our exchange of e-mail I wish to confirm the following agreement regarding the representation of the Specialty Coffee Association of America (SCAA) by the Training Renewal Foundation (TRF).

   Which correction should be made to Sentence 1?

   (1) Change <u>wish</u> to <u>want</u>.
   (2) Insert a comma after <u>e-mail</u>.
   (3) Change <u>reference</u> to <u>referance</u>.
   (4) Change <u>following</u> to <u>preceding</u>.
   (5) No correction required.

2. Sentence 2: SCAA grants TRF an exclusive right for distribution of SCAA's training programs for the period from April 1, 2010, to March 31, 2013, and this agreement shall be renewable if both parties determine that they wish to continue.

   Which is the best way to improve this sentence?

   (1) Change <u>an</u> to <u>a</u>.
   (2) Change <u>programs</u> to <u>programmes</u>.
   (3) Change <u>shall</u> to <u>will</u>.
   (4) Change <u>determine</u> to <u>determined</u>.
   (5) Divide it into two sentences by placing a period after <u>2013</u>, deleting <u>and</u>, and capitalizing <u>this.</u>

3. Sentence 3: TRF will handle the entire registration process including receipt of the fees for all training conducted.

   Which improvement should be made to Sentence 3?

   (1) Insert a colon after <u>including</u>.
   (2) Change <u>receipt</u> to <u>reciept</u>.
   (3) Insert a comma after <u>process</u> and after <u>fees</u>.
   (4) Change <u>will</u> to <u>should</u>.
   (5) No correction required.

4. Sentence 4: TRF will set the basis fee structure and retain the majority of the fees, while SCAA will receive a sum to offset training manual, promotional and administrative costs.

   How should Sentence 4 be corrected?

   (1) Change <u>basis</u> to <u>basic</u>.
   (2) Change <u>will</u> to <u>should</u>.
   (3) Change <u>manual</u> to <u>manuel</u>.
   (4) Change <u>offset</u> to <u>off-set</u>.
   (5) No correction required.

5. Sentence 6: Hand-outs will consist of SCAAs' Class in a Box training manual, which SCAA will provide.

How would you improve Sentence 6?

(1) Change <u>Hand-outs</u> to <u>Handouts</u>.
(2) Change <u>SCAAs'</u> to <u>SCAA's</u>.
(3) Remove the comma after <u>manual</u>.
(4) Change <u>will provide</u> to <u>provided</u>.
(5) No change required.

6. Sentence 9: TRF will provide equipment, consumables, and arrange accommodation and transportation for the training programs.

How should Sentence 9 be corrected?

(1) Change <u>will provide</u> to <u>would provide</u>.
(2) Change <u>consumables</u> to <u>consumibles</u>.
(3) Change the comma after <u>equipment</u> to a semicolon.
(4) Change <u>accommodation</u> to <u>accomodation</u>.
(5) No correction required.

Questions 7 through 15 refer to the following passage.

Executive Summary

(1) BETA is a food equipment reconditioning enterprise being organised to meet a growing need in the restaurant and café industry. (2) By year two, BETA would recondition an average of 500 units per year, generating over $1,000,000 in annual revenue and returning almost half a million dollars in salaries to the local economy through the creation of 13 jobs. (3) This should create additional economic benefits as the employees spend in there community. (4) These are conservative estimates based on the best possible information at present.

(5) **Objectives** are as follows:

- (6) to centralize the reconditioning of tired transportable restaurant equipment;
- (7) to develop a new industry in the reconditioning and sale of used transportable restaurant equipment,
- (8) to provide employment and training to a popularity with the ability but not the opportunity.

(9) **Advantages** are as follows:
- (10) BETA creates a new industry in a field ready to expand;
- (11) BETA diverts bio-degradable equipment from the waste stream;
- (12) BETA allowed a new group of entrepreneurs to enter the café business by providing reliable equipment at a lower price point.

---

7. Sentence 1: BETA is a food equipment reconditioning enterprise being organised to meet a growing need in the restaurant and café industry.

Which correction should be made to Sentence 1?

    (1)   Change <u>enterprise</u> to <u>enterprize</u>.
    (2)   Change <u>organised</u> to <u>organized</u>.
    (3)   Insert a colon after <u>meet</u>.
    (4)   Change <u>is</u> to <u>was</u>.
    (5)   No correction required.

8. Sentence 2: By year two, BETA would recondition an average of 500 units per year, generating over $1,000,000 in annual revenue and returning almost half a million dollars in salaries to the local economy through the creation of 13 jobs.

How can Sentence 2 be improved?

    (1)   Remove the comma after <u>two</u>.
    (2)   Change <u>$1,000,000</u> to <u>$1000000</u>.
    (3)   Insert a period after <u>revenue</u>, and begin the new sentence with "Through the creation of 13 jobs, BETA would return . . ."
    (4)   Insert a semicolon after <u>year</u>.
    (5)   No improvement required.

9. Sentence 3: This should create additional economic benefits as the employees spend in there community.

Which correction should be made to Sentence 3?

    (1)   Change <u>employees</u> to <u>employee's</u>.
    (2)   Change <u>benefits</u> to <u>benefit</u>.
    (3)   Change <u>spend</u> to <u>spends</u>.
    (4)   Change <u>there</u> to <u>their</u>.
    (5)   No correction required.

10. Sentence 4: These are conservative estimates based on the best possible information at present.

How can Sentence 4 be improved?

    (1)   Change <u>at present</u> to <u>presently available</u>.
    (2)   Change <u>best</u> to <u>better</u>.
    (3)   Change <u>are</u> to <u>is</u>.
    (4)   Change <u>conservative</u> to <u>conservation</u>.
    (5)   No improvement required.

11. Sentence 6: to centralize the reconditioning of tired transportable restaurant equipment;

What changes should be made to Sentence 6?

(1) Change <u>centralize</u> to <u>centralise</u>.
(2) Change <u>transportable</u> to <u>transported</u>.
(3) Change <u>reconditioning</u> to <u>conditioning</u>.
(4) Change <u>restaurant</u> to <u>restaurant's</u>.
(5) No change required.

12. Sentence 7: to develop a new industry in the reconditioning and sale of used transportable restaurant equipment,

Which corrections are required to Sentence 7?

(1) Change <u>transportable</u> to <u>transported</u>.
(2) Change the comma after <u>equipment</u> to a semicolon.
(3) Change <u>reconditioning</u> to <u>reconditioned</u>.
(4) Change <u>new</u> to <u>knew</u>.
(5) Insert a comma after <u>reconditioning</u>.

13. Sentence 8: to provide employment and training to a popularity with the ability but not the opportunity.

Which improvement should be made to Sentence 8?

(1) Change <u>with</u> to <u>without</u>.
(2) Change <u>not</u> to <u>knot</u>.
(3) Change <u>employment</u> to <u>employability</u>.
(4) Change <u>popularity</u> to <u>population</u>.
(5) No improvement required.

14. Sentence 11: BETA diverts bio-degradable equipment from the waste stream;

Which change should be made to Sentence 11?

(1) Change <u>bio-degradable</u> to <u>biodegradable</u>.
(2) Change <u>diverts</u> to <u>diverted</u>.
(3) Change <u>stream</u> to <u>streem</u>.
(4) Change <u>waste</u> to <u>waist</u>.
(5) No change required.

15. Sentence 12: BETA allowed a new group of entrepreneurs to enter the café business by providing reliable equipment at a lower price point.

    How can Sentence 12 be corrected?

    (1) Change point to pointer.
    (2) Change by to buy.
    (3) Change allowed to allows.
    (4) Change reliable to unreliable.
    (5) Change entrepreneurs to entreprenors.

Questions 16 through 25 refer to the following passage.

Your Résumé

(1) Your résumé is a commercial for you and the information should make a potential employer want to hire you. (2) All the information you want a potential employer to know about you should appear in a well organized, readable manner.

1. **Personal Identification**
(3) The first section should identify you, and include: (a) your name, (b) your complete address, (c) your telephone number.
(4) There is no need to include sex, age, martial status, or nationality. (5) If someone is screening applicants by any of these criteria, which is against the law, he or she is discriminating against people.
(6) It is unusual to include your Social Security card, but this must be provided if you are hired.

2. **Educational Background**
(7) You should list your educational background starting with the most recent school. (8) Each educational listing should include enough information to identify the school and specify your accomplishments.

3. **Work History**
(9) You should list all of the jobs you have had, beginning at the most recent.
(10) Include enough information to identify completely your present and former employers.
(11) Include the tasks you were required to do, and skills acquired. (12) Make sure to include the name of a supervisor and a current phone number.
(13) Always check the accuracy of the names and addresses of the listings before you hand it out to people.
(14) Volunteer jobs should be included, but the voluntary aspect of the job should be noted.

---

16. Sentence 1: Your résumé is a commercial for you and the information should make a potential employer want to hire you.

    Which is the best way to improve this sentence?

    (1) Change Your to You're.
    (2) Change is to was.
    (3) Change hire to higher.
    (4) Place a comma between you and and.
    (5) No improvement required.

17. Sentence 2: All the information you want a potential employer to know about you should appear in a well organized, readable manner.

    Which correction does this sentence require?

    (1) Change want to wanted.
    (2) Place a hyphen between well and organized.
    (3) Change should to would.
    (4) Change organized to organised.
    (5) No correction required.

18. Sentence 3: The first section should identify you, and include: (a) your name, (b) your complete address, (c) your telephone number.

    How should Sentence 3 be improved?

    (1) Change the commas after name and address to semicolons.
    (2) Remove the comma after you.
    (3) Change telephone to telefone.
    (4) Change section to sector.
    (5) Remove the period after number.

19. Sentence 4: There is no need to include sex, age, martial status, or nationality.

    Which correction should be made to Sentence 4?

    (1) Change There to Their.
    (2) Change is to was.
    (3) Change martial to marital.
    (4) Change no to know.
    (5) No correction required.

20. Sentence 5: If someone is screening applicants by any of these criteria, which is against the law, he or she is discriminating against people.

    How can this sentence be improved?

    (1) Change someone to anyone.
    (2) Change criteria to criterion.
    (3) Change the first is to was.
    (4) Change discriminating to descriminating.
    (5) Place which is against the law after people not after criteria.

21. Sentence 6: It is unusual to include your Social Security card, but this must be provided if you are hired.

    How can this sentence be improved?

    (1) Change your to you're.
    (2) Change card to number.
    (3) Change must to would.
    (4) Remove the comma after card.
    (5) Change is to are.

22. Sentence 7: You should list your educational background starting with the most recent school.

    Which correction is required for Sentence 7?

    (1) Change should to would.
    (2) Change educational to education.
    (3) Change recent to resent.
    (4) Change most to more.
    (5) No correction required.

23. Sentence 8: Each educational listing should include enough information to identify the school and specify your accomplishments.

    Which correction should be made to Sentence 8?

    (1) Change accomplishments to acomplishments.
    (2) Change your to you're.
    (3) Change each to all.
    (4) Change listing to listening.
    (5) No correction required.

24. Sentence 9: You should list all of the jobs you have had, beginning at the most recent.

    What change should be made to Sentence 9?

    (1) Change should to could.
    (2) Change have had to had had.
    (3) Remove of after all.
    (4) Change at to with.
    (5) No change required.

25. Sentence 10: Include enough information to identify completely your present and former employers.

How can Sentence 10 be improved?

(1) Change <u>present</u> to <u>presence</u>.
(2) Change <u>former</u> to <u>future</u>.
(3) Replace <u>enough</u> with <u>complete</u> and omit <u>completely</u>.
(4) Change <u>your</u> to <u>you're</u>.
(5) Change <u>enough</u> to <u>enuff</u>.

IF YOU FINISH BEFORE TIME IS CALLED, CHECK YOUR WORK ON THIS
SECTION ONLY. DO NOT WORK ON ANY OTHER SECTION IN THE TEST.

Section 2: Language Arts, Writing, Part II

Time: 45 minutes

1 essay

Look at the box on the following page. In the box, you find your assigned topic and the letter of that topic.

You must write only on the assigned topic.

You have 45 minutes to write on your assigned essay topic. If you have time remaining in this test period after you complete your essay, you may return to the multiple-choice section. Do not return the Language Arts, Writing test booklet until you finish both Parts I and II of the Language Arts, Writing Test.

On the GED, two evaluators will score your essay according to its overall effectiveness. Their evaluation will be based on the following features:

- Well-focused main points
- Clear organization
- Specific development of your ideas
- Control of sentence structure, punctuation, grammar, word choice, and spelling

Remember: You must complete both the multiple-choice questions (Part I) and the essay (Part II) to receive a score on the Language Arts, Writing Test.

To avoid having to repeat both parts of the test, be sure to observe the following rules:

- Before you begin writing, jot notes or outline your essay on the sheets provided.
- For your final copy, write legibly in ink so that the evaluators will be able to read your writing.
- Write on the assigned topic. If you write on a topic other than the one assigned, you won't receive a score for the Language Arts, Writing Test.
- Write your essay on the lined pages of the separate answer sheet booklet (for study purposes, you can use the lined pages provided in this book). Only the writing on these pages will be scored.

Note that if you do not pass one portion of the Language Arts, Writing Test, you must take both parts over again.

Topic A

Many people enjoy a hobby or special interest in their spare time.

Write an essay that encourages someone else to enjoy a hobby or special interest. Use your personal experiences, knowledge gained, relationships formed, and so on to develop your ideas.

Part II is a test to determine how well you can use written language to explain your ideas.

In preparing for your essay, you should take the following steps:

- Read the directions and the topic carefully.
- Plan your essay before you write. Use the scratch paper provided to make any notes. These notes will be collected but not scored.
- Before you turn in your essay, reread what you have written and make any changes that will improve your essay.

Your essay should be long enough to develop the topic adequately.

IF YOU FINISH BEFORE TIME IS CALLED, CHECK YOUR WORK ON THIS SECTION ONLY. DO NOT WORK ON ANY OTHER SECTION IN THE TEST.

Section 3: Social Studies

Time: 35 minutes

25 questions

Directions: Choose the best answer to each question. Mark your answers on the answer sheet provided.

Questions 1 through 5 refer to the following excerpt from U.S. History For Dummies, *2nd Edition, by Steve Wiegand, copyright 2009 by Wiley Publishing, Inc. Reprinted with permission of John Wiley & Sons, Inc.*

Christopher Columbus: Dream Salesman

Christopher Columbus was born in Genoa, Italy, in 1451, the son of a weaver. In addition to running a successful map-making business with his brother, Bartholomew, Columbus was a first-class sailor. He also became convinced that his ticket to fame and fortune depended on finding a western route to the Indies.

Starting in the 1470s, Columbus and his brother began making the rounds of European capitals, looking for ships and financial backing for his idea. His demands were exorbitant. In return for his services, Columbus wanted the title of Admiral of the Oceans, 10 percent of all the loot he found, and the ability to pass governorship of every country he discovered to his heirs.

The rulers of England and France said no thanks, as did some of the city-states that made up Italy. The king of Portugal also told him to take a hike. So in 1486, Columbus went to Spain. Queen Isabella listened to his pitch, and she, like the other European rulers, said no. But she did appoint a commission to look into the idea and decided to put Columbus on the payroll in the meantime.

The meantime stretched out for six years. Finally, convinced she wasn't really risking much because chances were that he wouldn't return, Isabella gave her approval in January 1492. Columbus was on his way.

Partly because of error and partly because of wishful thinking, Columbus estimated the distance to the Indies at approximately 2,500 miles, which was about 7,500 miles short. But after a voyage of about five weeks, he and his crews, totalling 90 men, did find land at around 2 a.m. on October 12, 1492. It was an island in the Bahamas, which he called San Salvador. The timing of the discovery was good; it came even as the crews of the *Nina, Pinta,* and *Santa Maria* were muttering about a mutiny.

1. How did Columbus hope to gain fame and fortune?

    (1) By becoming a weaver
    (2) By becoming a successful map-maker
    (3) By becoming a first-class sailor
    (4) By finding a route to the Indies
    (5) By becoming a famous chef

2. Why did Columbus have trouble financing his voyage?

    (1) He made exorbitant demands.
    (2) He wanted to be Admiral of the Oceans.
    (3) He wanted 10 percent of the loot.
    (4) He wanted governorships for his heirs.
    (5) He wanted the agreement of all the European capitals.

3. Which country finally agreed to support him?

    (1) England
    (2) France
    (3) Spain
    (4) Portugal
    (5) Italy

4. In which year did Columbus gain approval for his voyage?

    (1) 1451
    (2) 1470
    (3) 1475
    (4) 1489
    (5) 1492

5. Where was San Salvador located?

    (1) In the Indies
    (2) In the Bahamas
    (3) In Jamaica
    (4) In Trinidad
    (5) In Cuba

Questions 6 through 10 refer to the following excerpt from U.S. History For Dummies, *2nd Edition, by Steve Wiegand, copyright 2009 by Wiley Publishing, Inc. Reprinted with permission of John Wiley & Sons, Inc.*

Commanding a Country

In spite of his flaws, Washington was a born leader, one of those men who raised spirits and expectations simply by showing up. He was tall and athletic, an expert horseman and a good dancer. He wasn't particularly handsome—his teeth were bad, and he wasn't proud of his hippopotamus ivory and gold dentures, so he seldom smiled. But he had a commanding presence, and his troops felt they could depend on him. He was also a bit of an actor. Once while reading something to his troops, he donned his spectacles, and then apologized, explaining his eyes had grown dim in the service of his country. Some of his audience wept.

He also had an indomitable spirit. His army was ragged, undisciplined, and undependable, with a staggering average desertion rate of 20 percent. His bosses in Congress were often indecisive, quarrelsome, and indifferent. But Washington simply refused to give up. Just as important, he refused the temptation to try to become a military dictator, which he may easily have done.

One of the reasons many men loved him was that Washington was personally brave, often on the frontlines of battles, and always among the last to retreat. He was also incredibly lucky. In one battle, Washington rode unexpectedly into a group of British soldiers, most of whom fired at him at short range. They all missed.

Above all, Washington was a survivor. He drove the British army crazy (they called him "the old fox" even though he wasn't all that old), never staying to fight battles he was losing, and never fully retreating. He bought his new country time—time to find allies and time to wear down the British will to keep fighting.

6. Which of the following best characterizes George Washington?

   (1) He raised spirits and expectations.
   (2) He was tall and athletic.
   (3) He was an expert horseman.
   (4) He was a good dancer.
   (5) All of the above.

7. How did Washington feel about his dentures?

   (1) His teeth were bad.
   (2) He seldom smiled.
   (3) He wasn't proud.
   (4) He was a bit of an actor.
   (5) He proudly displayed them.

8. Which of the following does NOT describe Washington's troops?

   (1) They had a staggering desertion rate.
   (2) They were indecisive and quarrelsome.
   (3) They had an indomitable spirit.
   (4) They were disciplined and dependable.
   (5) They had a commanding presence.

9. How do we know that Washington was brave?

   (1) He was loved by his men.
   (2) He was among the last to retreat.
   (3) He was incredibly lucky.
   (4) He was an expert horseman.
   (5) He wore down the British.

10. Why did the British call Washington "the old fox"?

   (1) He was a survivor.
   (2) He drove them crazy.
   (3) He never fully retreated.
   (4) He bought his country time.
   (5) All of the above.

Questions 11 through 15 refer to the following excerpt from U.S. History For Dummies, *2nd Edition, by Steve Wiegand, copyright 2009 by Wiley Publishing, Inc. Reprinted with permission of John Wiley & Sons, Inc.*

Transporting America

Unions weren't alone in their aspirations for improving the lives of working-class Americans. In Detroit, a generally unlikable, self-taught engineer named Henry Ford decided that everyone should have an automobile, and, thus, the right to go where they wanted, when they wanted. So, Ford's company made one model—the Model T. You could have it in any color you wanted, Ford said, as long as it was black. And because of his assembly-line approach to putting them together, you could have it relatively cheaply.

Ford's plan was a good one. The price of a Model T dropped from $850 in 1908 to $290 by 1924. As prices dropped, sales went up. Sales went from 10,000 in 1909 to just under a million in 1921. Within two decades, Ford and other car-makers had indelibly changed American life. The average family could now literally get away from it all, which created a new sense of independence and self-esteem. Because of the availability of the automobile, new industries, from tire production to roadside cafes, sprang up. And by the end of the 1920s, it could be persuasively argued that the automobile had become the single most dominant element in the U.S. economy.

When it came to getting from here to there, others were looking up to the skies. In December 1903, two brothers who owned a bicycle shop in Dayton, Ohio, went to Kitty Hawk, North Carolina. There they pulled off the world's first powered, sustained, and controlled flights with a machine they had built. Fearful of losing their patent rights, Orville and Wilbur Wright didn't go public with their airplane until 1908, by which time other inventors and innovators were also making planes. Unlike the automobile, however, the airplane's popularity didn't really take off until after its usefulness was proved in World War I.

11. Henry Ford believed that everyone should

   (1) Join a union
   (2) Be an engineer
   (3) Own an automobile
   (4) Have an improved life
   (5) Have a job

12. What was Ford's greatest contribution to the auto industry?

   (1) The Model T
   (2) The assembly line
   (3) New industries
   (4) The U.S. economy
   (5) Independence and self-esteem

13. How did Ford increase sales of his automobiles?

   (1) By lowering prices
   (2) Through better advertising
   (3) By increasing tire production
   (4) By building roadside cafes
   (5) By fostering a sense of independence

14. What impact did the availability of the automobile have on the U.S. economy?

    (1) It caused the Great Depression.
    (2) It changed American life.
    (3) It led to increased self-esteem.
    (4) It became a dominant element in the economy.
    (5) It encouraged independence.

15. Why did the Wright Brothers become famous?

    (1) They owned a bicycle shop.
    (2) They built a machine.
    (3) They made the first powered, sustained flight.
    (4) They influenced World War I.
    (5) They went to Kitty Hawk.

Questions 16 through 20 refer to the following political cartoon from GED For Dummies, *1st Edition, by Murray Shukyn and Dale E. Shuttleworth, Ph.D., copyright 2003 by Wiley Publishing, Inc. Reprinted with permission of John Wiley & Sons, Inc.*

16. What is the direct impact of a rise in oil prices?

   (1) Sales of SUVs decrease.
   (2) People do more traveling.
   (3) Oil companies lose profit.
   (4) Gasoline prices rise.
   (5) Air-conditioning sales increase.

17. How is the cost of living affected by a rise in oil prices?

   (1) The cost of living falls.
   (2) The cost of living rises.
   (3) The cost of living isn't affected.
   (4) The cost of living controls oil prices.
   (5) The cost of living stays the same.

18. What adjective best describes the characters in the SUV?

   (1) Joyful
   (2) Surprised
   (3) Angry
   (4) Wasteful
   (5) Frightened

19. What phrase does NOT describe the SUV?

   (1) Road hog
   (2) Energy saver
   (3) Gas guzzler
   (4) Monster truck
   (5) Pollution machine

20. What solutions does the cartoon suggest for the energy crisis?

   (1) Lower the heat.
   (2) Boil, not fry.
   (3) Reduce lubrication.
   (4) Buy smaller vehicles.
   (5) All of the above.

Questions 21 through 25 refer to the following excerpt from U.S. History For Dummies, *2nd Edition, by Steve Wiegand, copyright 2009 by Wiley Publishing, Inc. Reprinted with permission of John Wiley & Sons, Inc.*

Big Blow in the Big Easy

On August 23, 2005, a hurricane formed over the Bahamas and headed toward the southeastern United States. Called Katrina, it crossed Florida, picked up strength over the Gulf of Mexico, and made landfall in southeast Louisiana on August 29.

While Katrina's 125-mile-per-hour winds—sending beds flying out of hotel windows—and 10 inches of rain were bad enough, a storm surge of more than 28 feet devastated the Mississippi coastal cities of Gulfport and Biloxi. But the greatest damage was reserved for the region's largest city—New Orleans.

Nicknamed "the Big Easy," most of New Orleans is below sea level. Under Katrina's onslaught, levees supposed to protect the city gave way in more than 50 places, and 80 percent of the city was flooded. While most of New Orleans's 1.2 million residents were evacuated (many to the city of Houston, Texas), thousands either refused to leave or could not.

The disaster claimed more than 1,800 lives and destroyed 200,000 homes. Damage estimates ranged as high as $125 billion, making it the most expensive hurricane in U.S. history. It wasn't until October 11 that the last of the floodwaters were pumped out.

By then, a hurricane of criticism had whipped up over the federal government's response to the disaster. The criticism ranged from condemning the government's slow response in some areas with regard to the evacuation process to providing adequate temporary housing after the storm. There were also charges that the slow response was due, in part, to the fact that many of New Orleans's residents were poor African Americans. Bush's approval ratings sank to the lowest of his presidency—at least to this point.

21. The "Big Easy" refers to which of the following?

    (1) Florida

    (2) Louisiana

    (3) New Orleans

    (4) Houston

    (5) Gulfport

22. What was the result of Hurricane Katrina?

    (1) 125 mile-per-hour winds

    (2) Beds flying out of windows

    (3) 10 inches of rain

    (4) 28-foot surges

    (5) All of the above

23. Why was New Orleans in danger?

    (1) It is located below sea level.
    (2) It is the region's largest city.
    (3) Thousands of residents refused to leave.
    (4) Hundreds of thousands of homes were destroyed.
    (5) All of the above.

24. What was the primary reason that the federal government was criticized?

    (1) Many residents were poor African Americans.
    (2) Bush's approval ratings dropped.
    (3) The evacuation process was slow.
    (4) The federal government was slow to respond.
    (5) The levees broke.

25. How will Katrina be remembered in the United States?

    (1) People were evacuated to Houston.
    (2) It was the most expensive hurricane in U.S. history.
    (3) The floodwaters were pumped out.
    (4) There were $125 billion in damages.
    (5) It caused the flooding of New Orleans.

IF YOU FINISH BEFORE TIME IS CALLED, CHECK YOUR WORK ON THIS
SECTION ONLY. DO NOT WORK ON ANY OTHER SECTION IN THE TEST.

Section 4: Science

Time: 40 minutes

25 questions

Directions: Choose the best answer to each question. Mark your answers on the answer sheet provided.

Question 1 refers to the following passage.

Atoms

Although atoms are really tiny, each atom has even smaller components that make up this miniscule bit of matter. In the center of the atom is the nucleus, composed of protons and neutrons and surrounded by electrons.

1. The center of an atom is called the

    (1) Electron.
    (2) Proton.
    (3) Neutron.
    (4) Nucleus.
    (5) Quark.

Question 2 refers to the following passage.

Matter

All matter is made up of atoms, but atoms are made up of particles called electrons, neutrons, and protons. Because these are all so small that they cannot be seen by any means, at present, there are theories about what they look like and how they behave. The negatively charged electrons form a cloud around the nucleus of the atom. Inside the nucleus are positively charged protons and neutral neutrons. Scientist(s) believe that all the parts of the atom are in constant motion.

2. The negative cloud around the nucleus of the atom is composed of

    (1) Protons.
    (2) Neutrons.
    (3) Electrons.
    (4) Atoms.
    (5) Nucleus.

Questions 3 and 4 are based on the following passage.

Rust

Have you ever picked up an old iron tool and found it covered with a flaky brown substance called rust? Have you ever wondered how it formed there? Rust is formed by a chemical reaction between the iron and the oxygen in the air. The chemical reaction produces ferrous oxide, which is commonly known as rust.

3. What two chemicals combine to form rust?

   (1) Iron and water
   (2) Water and oxygen
   (3) Iron and oxygen
   (4) Iron and hydrogen
   (5) Hydrogen and oxygen

4. What is the chemical name for rust?

   (1) Iron oxygen
   (2) Ferrous oxide
   (3) Ferrous oxygen
   (4) Water
   (5) Rustous oxide

Questions 5 through 7 refer to the following passage.

Newton's First Law of Motion

Alvin's hobby is drag racing. He loves the feel of the car shooting away when he stomps on the accelerator and the sudden jerk when the parachute is deployed to slow him down. Janice, Alvin's friend, was telling him that drag racing is an example of Newton's First Law of Motion. She explained that the car will remain at rest until an unbalanced force acts on it. By depressing the accelerator, Alvin causes the engine to produce an unbalanced force through the rear wheels and the car takes off. Theoretically, the car would keep going forever, but Alvin releases the parachute, which causes an unbalanced force in the opposite direction and the car slows to a stop. Alvin looked at Janice and assured her that it was still fun.

5. Drag racing is an example of

   (1) An outlaw sport.
   (2) A scientific experiment.
   (3) Newton's First Law of Motion.
   (4) Newton's Third Law of Motion.
   (5) Einstein's theory.

6. Why does the parachute slow down the car until it can be stopped?

   (1) It catches a lot of wind.
   (2) It's attached to the brakes.
   (3) It's big enough to cause friction with the road.
   (4) It creates an unbalanced force in the opposite direction of the car's motion.
   (5) It creates an unbalanced force in the direction of the car's motion.

7. What provides the power to accelerate the drag racer forward?

   (1) The motor
   (2) The transmission
   (3) The parachute
   (4) The accelerator
   (5) The brakes

Question 8 refers to the following passage.

Perpetual Motion

The law of conservation of energy says that in an isolated system, the total amount of energy remains constant and, thus, energy cannot be created or destroyed. This really upset Hannah, who wanted to build a perpetual motion machine as her science project.

8. Why should Hannah choose another project?

   (1) There is no such thing as perpetual motion.
   (2) Energy cannot be created and the machine could never produce any additional power.
   (3) The government would not allow it.
   (4) Energy cannot be destroyed, and this machine would destroy energy.
   (5) It would break several laws of physics.

9. Laurie was very patient when he was asked to perform the following experiment: He was given a cube of ice, 6 inches on each side, in a glass container and asked to watch it until it changed its state and then to apply heat until it changed its state again. What would explain the first change of state?

   (1) Ice always melts when you watch it.
   (2) The glass container itself caused the change.
   (3) The heat from the room provided the energy needed to change the state of the ice.
   (4) The effect of reflections in the glass provided enough energy to cause a change in state.
   (5) Magnetic waves from the atmosphere provided the energy for the state change.

Question 10 refers to the following passage.

The Cell

The cell is the smallest and most basic unit of life. Human beings, for example, have about 60 trillion to 100 trillion cells. On the other extreme, bacteria are only one cell and that one cell can infect a human being and make him sick. The size of the cell has nothing to do with its potential. An unfertilized ostrich egg cell is the largest known cell, weighing over 3 pounds, while an average cell weighs about 1 nanogram.

10. According to the passage, what is the weight of an unfertilized ostrich egg cell?

    (1) 1 nanogram
    (2) 1 pound
    (3) 10 trillion nanograms
    (4) 3 pounds
    (5) 2 pounds

Questions 11 and 12 are based on the following passage.

DNA and Heredity

DNA stores the basis of heredity in its genetic code. The DNA molecule is a double helix and is constructed in a way that it is capable of self-replication. All living creatures have cells comprised of DNA. Hereditary traits (called genes) are passed on from generation to generation through the DNA.

Heredity is the transmission of characteristics from one generation to the next. If your parents had red hair or blue eyes, there is a greater chance of your possessing these characteristics. If you have two ears and one nose and your parents had the same, that is part of being a human being and not connected with the transmission of specific traits.

11. Heredity contributes to:

   (1) Children having blue eyes.
   (2) Parents having red hair.
   (3) Parents passing characteristics to their children.
   (4) Giving gifts to your family.
   (5) Children behaving badly.

12. The basis of heredity is stored in the genetic code of

   (1) NaCl
   (2) H_2O
   (3) DNA
   (4) BPA
   (5) HCl

Question 13 is based on the following passage.

Evolution

All species undergo gradual changes in order to be able to survive and reproduce in their environment. In the Animal Kingdom, the environment is often competitive and dangerous, and a life form that is less likely to survive in that environment would leave fewer offspring and, thus, be less likely to pass on the traits to the next generation.

On the other hand, a life form that is better suited genetically to a particular environment would be more likely to mate and reproduce, thus producing offspring with these advantageous traits. Because these traits assisted in their survival, their descendents stand a better chance of inheriting these traits and surviving to reproduce again.

There is a gradual but constant shift toward life forms well adapted to their environment, and this can produce new species that differ from their ancestors.

13. What would a life form have to possess in order to survive in its environment?

   (1) Traits
   (2) Heredity
   (3) Parents
   (4) Adaptability
   (5) Ancestors

14. Have you ever wondered why your friend has red hair and you have black hair? If you look at the members of your friend's family, there are probably a number of people with red hair. In your family, there are probably none, unless someone uses hair dye. Characteristics like hair color are hereditary and can be passed on from generation to generation through your genes.

    What is the means of transmission of characteristics like hair color?

    (1) Hair dye
    (2) Heredity
    (3) Environment
    (4) Neighborhood
    (5) Generations

Questions 15 and 16 are based on the following passage.

Interdependence of Organisms

Living organisms depend on each other for survival. Small fish depend on a supply of plankton for food. Larger fish depend on small fish to provide them with their food. Humans eat larger fish as a source of protein. Humans produce garbage, some of which finds its way into the waterways, providing food to the fish.

Ecosystems are composed of many factors. Among the living factors are the consumers and the producers. Producers, like plants create food through their internal processes. A plant can produce sugars using sunlight and carbon dioxide through a process called photosynthesis; consumers like humans and cows can then eat the plants and survive. Animals that eat only plants are called herbivores, animals that eat meat are called carnivores, and animals that eat both are called omnivores. Thus, plants that produce food through photosynthesis are eaten by herbivores that are eaten by carnivores that produce materials that can be used as fertilizers for the plants.

15. Which of the following are among the living factors of an ecosystem?

    (1) Animals and people
    (2) Plants and soil
    (3) Consumers and producers
    (4) Kind people and beasts
    (5) Plants and animals

16. An herbivore will eat

    (1) Only tasty recipes.
    (2) Only plants.
    (3) Only eggs.
    (4) Parts of dead animals.
    (5) Anything if it's hungry.

Questions 17 and 18 refer to the following passage.

Training a Dog

Alice has a new puppy and wants to train it to sit at her right side on command, but she has no idea how to do it. Her father, who used to train dogs, told her that a famous scientist named B. F. Skinner developed a system of changing the behaviors of animals that might help her. If she gave the dog a treat every time it obeyed the command, the chances of the dog obeying the command increased until it would happen each time.

17. Which scientist developed the system that helped Alice train her puppy?

    (1) Einstein
    (2) Newton
    (3) Skinner
    (4) Abrams
    (5) Galileo

18. How did Alice's father suggest she train her puppy?

    (1) Yell at the puppy when it made a mistake.
    (2) Pick up the puppy and speak softly to it when it did what Alice wanted.
    (3) Ignore the puppy when it made a mistake.
    (4) Give the puppy a treat for doing the correct action.
    (5) Study books by famous scientists.

Questions 19 and 20 are based on the following passage.

Solar Power

Harnessing the sun's energy to do work is an example of solar power, and it has the potential to provide much of the Earth's energy requirements. Using photovoltaic cells, this solar energy can be directly converted into electricity.

The other manner of converting the sun's energy into usable energy is through concentration. If you imagine a giant magnifying glass concentrating the energy from the sun on a point, you get the idea. The point would get so hot that, if it were flammable, it would burst into flames. Concentrating the sun's energy usually requires storage so that the heat can be stored for times when the sun is not shining.

19. Solar power is limited in use because

    (1) It is expensive.
    (2) It cannot be stored when the sun is not shining.
    (3) Appliances are not suited for it.
    (4) The sun doesn't shine constantly.
    (5) There are no meters to measure the usage.

20. Most of us have used solar power without thinking about it. Photovoltaic cells often are used in

    (1) Calculators.
    (2) Washing machines.
    (3) Radios.
    (4) Cars.
    (5) Toasters.

Question 21 refers to the following diagram.

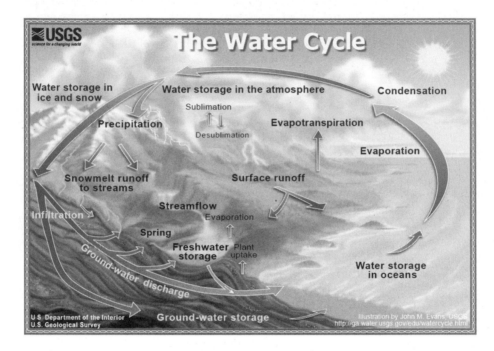

21. Water exists in

    (1) Oceans.
    (2) Ice and snow.
    (3) The atmosphere.
    (4) Springs and streams.
    (5) All of the above.

22. A boater hits a rock at the bottom of a lake he has sailed before because the water level in the lake is very low. According to the diagram, which part of the water cycle is creating this problem?

    (1) Winter storage of ice and snow
    (2) Water storage in oceans
    (3) Ground-water storage
    (4) Thunderstorms
    (5) Dams

Questions 23 through 25 refer to the following passage.

Origins of the Sun and Planets in the Solar System

At first, there was a large cloud of dust and gas rotating through space around the center of the Milky Way (as a result of the Big Bang). This cloud was composed of helium and hydrogen gases. The gas cloud began to contract and rotate, gaining angular speed. This caused it to flatten into a disk, with most of the mass concentrated at the center where it began to heat up.

At the center, these conditions led to the nuclear fusion of hydrogen and helium, thus forming the star we know as the sun. Fragments rotating around this new star began to form bigger and bigger particles, which attracted other particles through gravitational attraction. The planets began to revolve around the sun creating what we know as the solar system.

23. What was the chemical composition of the cloud that was rotating through space around the center of the Milky Way?

    (1) Dust
    (2) Chunks of rock
    (3) Hydrogen and helium
    (4) Oxygen and hydrogen
    (5) Carbon and hydrogen

24. What process formed the star known as the sun?

    (1) Nuclear fusion
    (2) Nuclear fission
    (3) Nuclear bombs
    (4) Nuclear energy
    (5) Nuclear explosion

25. What process caused the particles to gather to form planets?

    (1) Centrifugal force
    (2) Centripetal force
    (3) Magnetism
    (4) Gravitational force
    (5) Brute force

IF YOU FINISH BEFORE TIME IS CALLED, CHECK YOUR WORK ON THIS SECTION ONLY. DO NOT WORK ON ANY OTHER SECTION IN THE TEST.

Section 5: Language Arts, Reading

Time: 32 minutes

20 questions

This test consists of excerpts from fiction and nonfiction. Each excerpt is followed by multiple-choice questions about the reading material. Read each excerpt first and then answer the questions following it.

The purpose question at the beginning of each excerpt gives a reason for reading the material. Use these purpose questions to help focus your reading. You are not required to answer the purpose questions. They are given only to help you concentrate on the ideas presented in the reading material.

Directions: Choose the one best answer to each question.

Questions 1 through 6 refer to the following poem by Sheila Sarah Franschman (2010).

What Is Special about Muir Woods?

Under the worn wooden sign ushering one and all
To wander along the broad plank path
And feast your eyes on the majestic redwoods
Some on earth longer than 1,000 years
Their outer layers bathed in shades of brown and black
Towering above but below the clouds
Gazing now at the branches entwined in lovers' knots
Nature providing the streams meandering through
Feeding the nourishments required to sustain
Through the times
Fog settles on the highest branches
Elevating trees into the heavens above
Small animals dart about the ground cover
And birds choose between plant and branch
The four seasons offer different hues
While spring follows a babbling stream,
Ending in catch basins
And summer opens to sunlight exposing their vulnerability
And their strength
Fall foliage turns to red and yellow,
With a hint of orange
While winter envelopes the landscape
Wearing a coat of white
Vulnerable now
Waiting again for seasons to renew themselves
For people and animals
To wander again along the broad plank path.

1. What is the overall setting for the poem?

   (1) A backyard
   (2) A barn
   (3) A city street
   (4) A forest
   (5) A playground

2. Redwood trees can live as long as

   (1) 400 years.
   (2) 1,000 years.
   (3) 200 years.
   (4) 1,500 years.
   (5) 80 years.

3. When the poet writes, "The four seasons offer different hues," she means that

   (1) Different birds and animals populate the setting each season.
   (2) Leaves change color every season.
   (3) Falling leaves make the streams change color.
   (4) Fog filters the light differently during the winter.
   (5) The colors of the setting change with the seasons.

4. In which seasons does the author describe the setting as "vulnerable"?

   (1) Spring and fall
   (2) Summer and winter
   (3) Fall only
   (4) Winter only
   (5) Not enough information given

5. When someone looks at the foliage in the fall, what predominate color(s) does that person see?

   (1) Green and red
   (2) Red
   (3) Brown and black
   (4) Red and yellow and a bit of orange
   (5) Black

6. What provides the nourishment for the giant trees to grow?

   (1) Nature
   (2) Gardeners
   (3) Park workers
   (4) Animals
   (5) Birds

Questions 7 through 10 are excerpts from the play Easy A? *by Murray Shukyn (2007).*

How Can I Get an A?

Lewis's office at City College; books everywhere; desk heaped with papers and behind it sits Lewis, completely absorbed in his reading. A knock on the door, but Lewis doesn't hear or maybe doesn't pay attention. The door slowly opens, and a female student, Connie, enters the office and stands at the desk.

Connie: I need an A in your course!

Connie, a mediocre student in Lewis's sociology and education course, seems agitated. Her usually well-groomed auburn hair is windblown. Her usually impeccably applied makeup is missing. Her clothing is, as always, immaculate and fashionable as befits the daughter of one of the largest benefactors of City College.

Lewis: I beg your pardon.

Connie: *(with a bit more confidence)* I need an A in your course. Without it, my grade point average falls below scholarship level, and I can't go on to graduate school. Daddy took care of everything else. It's just your course that I need to fix.

Lewis: *(confused)* I don't understand.

Connie: *(fully confident)* Dr. Stephson, I need to go to graduate school. All my brothers did, and in appreciation for their achievement, my parents gave each of them a Porsche, an apartment, and an allowance. I need that car. It's just so cool to arrive at a party in a Porsche. What do I have to do to get an A?

Lewis: It's kind of late in the year to advise you to study harder for the tests or to spend more time on your assignments. I don't have my grade book with me, but I do believe that your average so far is a B–.

Connie: *(becoming agitated)* I don't care about tests, studying, or assignments. This is my life I'm talking about. What do I have to do to get you to give me an A?

Lewis: If you're average in my class, you're probably average in the others. How can you expect to finish with an A average?

Connie: Dr. Stephson, you can't be this naïve. With the money my father pumps into this college, I get special consideration by the staff. I do get A's. My father seems to have forgotten to reach out to you and that means I have to do it. What do you want for me to get an A? What do you need in return? Money? Favors? A promotion? Tell me and it can be arranged. You know who my father is and how generous he can be. What do I have to do to get an A?

Lighting dims as set changes.

7. What seems to be the main reason Connie wants an A in this course?

   (1)   To become the class valedictorian
   (2)   To seem to be better than her brothers
   (3)   To get a Porsche from her father
   (4)   To transfer to Princeton
   (5)   To make her résumé look better

8. Why doesn't Lewis suggest that Connie work harder on her assignments or study harder for the tests?

   (1)   Lewis doesn't think that Connie has the ability to study harder.
   (2)   The rest of the year is packed with parties and other social events.
   (3)   This course only has a final exam.
   (4)   All of Connie's assignments already have been handed in.
   (5)   It is late in the year, and these suggestions would have little effect on the final result.

9. What difference does Connie expect her father's donations to have on her grades?

   (1) Connie expects to be given high grades.
   (2) Connie expects that a building will be named after her father.
   (3) Connie expects the college to give her father an honorary degree.
   (4) Connie expects her father to be introduced as a celebrity at the football games.
   (5) Connie doesn't expect that her father's donations will have any effect on her grades.

10. What effect would a B– in this course have on Connie?

   (1) She would be embarrassed in front of her friends.
   (2) She might have to retake this course in summer school.
   (3) Her self-confidence would decrease.
   (4) Connie would not be able to get into graduate school and, thus, would not get rewarded by her family.
   (5) Her mother would be angry with her.

Questions 11 through 16 refer to the following excerpt from the short story "Rip Van Winkle" by Washington Irving (1819).

Who Was Rip Van Winkle?

In that same village, and in one of these very houses (which, to tell the precise truth, was sadly time-worn and weather-beaten), there lived many years since, while the country was yet a province of Great Britain, a simple good-natured fellow, of the name of Rip Van Winkle. He was a descendant of the Van Winkles who figured so gallantly in the chivalrous days of Peter Stuyvesant, and accompanied him to the siege of Fort Christina. He inherited, however, but little of the martial character of his ancestors. I have observed that he was a simple, good-natured man; he was, moreover, a kind neighbor, and an obedient, henpecked husband. Indeed, to the latter circumstance might be owing that meekness of spirit which gained him such universal popularity; for those men are most apt to be obsequious and conciliating abroad who are under the discipline of shrews at home. Their tempers, doubtless, are rendered pliant and malleable in the fiery furnace of domestic tribulation, and a curtain lecture is worth all the sermons in the world for teaching the virtues of patience and long-suffering. A termagant wife may, therefore, in some respects, be considered a tolerable blessing; and if so, Rip Van Winkle was thrice blessed.

Certain it is that he was a great favorite among all the good wives of the village, who, as usual with the amiable sex, took his part in all family squabbles, and never failed, whenever they talked those matters over in their evening gossipings, to lay all the blame on Dame Van Winkle. The children of the village, too, would shout with joy whenever he approached. He assisted at their sports, made their playthings, taught them to fly kites and shoot marbles, and told them long stories of ghosts, witches, and Indians. Whenever he went dodging about the village, he was surrounded by a troop of them, hanging on his skirts, clambering on his back, and playing a thousand tricks on him with impunity; and not a dog would bark at him throughout the neighborhood.

11. According to the passage where was the village located?

   (1) At Fort Christina
   (2) In a province of Great Britain
   (3) In the Thirteen Colonies
   (4) In New Amsterdam
   (5) Up the Hudson River

12. Which phrase is used to best describe Van Winkle's personality?

   (1) Descended from the Van Winkles
   (2) Gallant and chivalrous
   (3) A good neighbor
   (4) Simple and good-natured
   (5) Disobedient

13. Why was he universally popular?

   (1) He was obsequious and conciliating.
   (2) His martial character was not evident.
   (3) He had a meekness of spirit.
   (4) He was pliant and malleable.
   (5) He was patient and long-suffering.

14. Which phrase does the author use to describe the Van Winkle marriage?

   (1) Tolerable blessing
   (2) Domestic tribulation
   (3) Great favorite
   (4) Happy and loving
   (5) Discipline of shrews

15. How did Van Winkle treat the children of the village?

   (1) He assisted them with sports.
   (2) He made playthings for them.
   (3) He flew kites with them.
   (4) He told them stories.
   (5) All of the above.

16. Who defended Rip Van Winkle in the village?

   (1) The good wives
   (2) The men of the village
   (3) Dame Van Winkle
   (4) The children
   (5) Peter Stuyvesant

Questions 17 through 20 refer to the following business document.

What Was the Partnership Agreement?

Beginning in 1980, Ontario Travel formed an exclusive partnership with Can-Learn International (a division of Can-Learn Limited) to develop, plan, market, and implement educational travel programs with a variety of different constituencies, including school boards, schools, colleges, universities, artistic and cultural interests, trade associations, alumni and senior citizens' organizations, commercial enterprises, professional development groups, and other such affinity groups.

Can-Learn International works with organizational personnel and influences leaders to research and plan custom-designed programs that meet the specific needs and objectives of each program. Can-Learn International assists in marketing such programs and also provides an escort service as required.

Partnering with Can-Learn International, Ontario Travel, as a leading professional travel agency, is responsible for all logistics including accommodations, air, sea, and land arrangements. Ontario Travel also participates with Can-Learn International in the planning, implementation, and marketing of all such programs. Ontario Travel shares any income realized from each of the above programs with Can-Learn International based on a predetermined rate of commission per passenger.

17. What programs does the partnership agreement refer to?

    (1) Professional development
    (2) Citizens' organizations
    (3) Trade associations
    (4) Educational travel
    (5) Organizational personnel

18. What service is NOT mentioned in the partnership agreement?

    (1) Planning
    (2) Retailing
    (3) Marketing
    (4) Developing
    (5) Implementing

19. Which of the following constituencies does the partnership serve?

    (1) School boards
    (2) Alumni organizations
    (3) Universities
    (4) Commercial enterprises
    (5) All of the above

20. How is income to be shared by the partners?

    (1) Equally

    (2) On a sliding scale

    (3) At a predetermined commission rate per passenger

    (4) 75 percent to Ontario Travel, 25 percent to Can-Learn International

    (5) At a fixed amount

IF YOU FINISH BEFORE TIME IS CALLED, CHECK YOUR WORK ON THIS SECTION ONLY. DO NOT WORK ON ANY OTHER SECTION IN THE TEST.

Section 6: Mathematics

Time: 45 minutes

25 questions

Directions: Choose the best answer to each question. Mark your answers on the answer sheet provided.

Completely fill in the bubble corresponding to the correct answer. For the coordinate-plane grid, you may mark only one circle; the circle must represent an *x* and a *y* value, neither of which can be a decimal or a fraction. For the standard grid, enter your answer in the columns in the top row (you can start in any column, provided that your entire answer can be entered), and completely fill in the bubble representing the character under each column. With this grid, no number can be negative, and fractions must be entered as decimals or improper fractions.

On the GED, calculators can be used in only one designated section of the test. For this Diagnostic Test, do not use a calculator.

1. Alvin was shopping for two pairs of jeans. Every store he went to seemed to have a sale. Store A was offering $49.99 jeans for half off; Store B had the same jeans on sale for 50% off; Store C was offering them for "buy one get the second pair free"; and Store D had the same jeans for $25. Where should Alvin buy his jeans to get the best buy?

   (1) Store A.
   (2) Store B.
   (3) Store C.
   (4) Store D.
   (5) It doesn't matter.

2. Liz was getting serious about dieting and wanted to lose 12 pounds before the prom, which was 12 weeks away. If she knew that she was eating an average of 2,000 calories per day and would have to cut her overall intake by 3,500 calories for each pound she wanted to lose, how many calories would she have to cut out of her diet each day to reach her weight-loss goal?

   (1) 42,000
   (2) 500
   (3) 12
   (4) 6,000
   (5) 84

3. Willie bought a new car that was guaranteed to average 36 miles per gallon in the city. For the second fill-up, the cost was $105.35 and the cost per gallon of gasoline was $3.01. If Willie knew how far he had traveled since he had first filled up the gas tank, what arithmetic operation should he use to calculate his average mileage per gallon?

   (1) Addition
   (2) Subtraction
   (3) Multiplication
   (4) Division
   (5) Percentage

4. Georgina went shopping but discovered she had brought only $10 with her. She placed the following items into her shopping cart: bread for $2.49, a gallon of milk for $3.80, butter for $2.49, and a chocolate bar for $1.20. She wanted to make sure that she had enough money to pay for her purchases. She did a quick mental calculation and came up with an answer. What answer did she come up with?

   (1) She probably had enough money.
   (2) She should put the chocolate bar back.
   (3) She should buy a smaller container of milk.
   (4) She should buy a few buns instead of bread.
   (5) She should buy half a pound of butter.

5. Paul was considering redecorating his living room. He measured the longest wall, the shortest wall, and the height of the room and recorded the following measurements:

   Long wall: 22 ft.

   Short wall: 18 ft.

   Height: 9 ft.

   What assumptions can he make about the room, when planning the renovation?

   (1) The two short walls will be parallel.
   (2) The two long walls will be parallel.
   (3) The long wall and the short wall will be perpendicular.
   (4) The outside walls will be perpendicular to the floor.
   (5) All of the above.

Question 6 refers to the following figure.

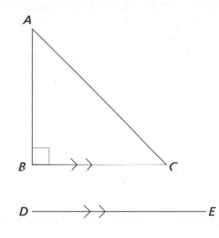

6. Describe the rotation of the triangle required for *BC* to remain parallel to *DE*.

   (1)   45 degrees around *B*
   (2)   90 degrees around *C*
   (3)   135 degrees around *A*
   (4)   180 degrees around *C*
   (5)   45 degrees around *D*

7. In a right triangle with base 30 inches and perpendicular side 20 inches, what is the length of the hypotenuse, in inches, to the nearest inch?

   (1)   34
   (2)   35
   (3)   36
   (4)   37
   (5)   38

8. An acceptable slope for a stairway is 8 inches of rise for each 12 inches of tread or run. A builder wants to build a house with a distance of 9 feet 6 inches between the first floor and the second floor. How many linear feet of room will the stairway occupy on the first floor?

   Record your answer on a standard grid.

9. Georgio wanted to paint the floor in his laundry room. The room measured 25 feet by 12 feet. If the paint he was going to use covered 450 square feet per gallon, how much paint would he use to cover the floor with one coat of paint?

   (1) 1 gallon

   (2) $\frac{1}{2}$ gallon

   (3) $\frac{2}{3}$ gallon

   (4) $\frac{3}{4}$ gallon

   (5) $1\frac{1}{4}$ gallons

10. Sandy knows from experience that she can average 42 miles per hour on the highway between her home and her parents' home. They have invited her to dinner at 5 o'clock sharp to meet some special guests. Sandy calculates that if she leaves at 1:15 p.m., she will arrive on time. How far does Sandy live from her parents?

    (1) 157.5 miles
    (2) 175.5 miles
    (3) 168 miles
    (4) 186.5 miles
    (5) 222.5 miles

11. Kelly and Frank were planning to have a swimming pool built in their backyard. The original dimensions were 60 feet long and 20 feet wide, with an average depth of 4 feet. One contractor said that he would build them a pool that would be 20% larger in surface area. How many more cubic feet of water would the larger pool hold?

    (1) 690
    (2) 960
    (3) 4,800
    (4) 240
    (5) 1,200

Question 12 is based on the following graph.

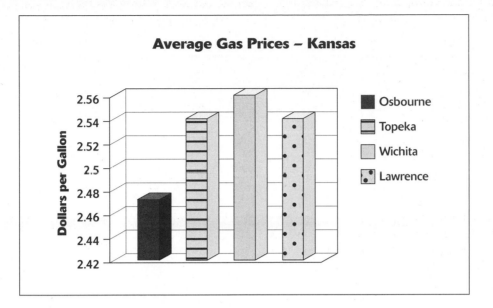

12. From the information in the graph, how much could you save on a 20-gallon fill-up by traveling to the town with the lowest prices?

    (1) $0.09
    (2) $1.80
    (3) $2.56
    (4) $2.47
    (5) $1.56

Questions 13 and 14 are based on the following information.

Surveys were taken regarding television-viewing habits and the penetration of Internet use as a percentage of population. The following results were tabulated.

Hours per Week of Television Viewing	
Country	**Average Hours of Television Viewed per Week**
United Kingdom	26
United States	28
Italy	27
Ireland	23
France	22
Germany	23

Internet Penetration as a Percentage of Population	
Country	Internet Penetration as a Percentage of Population
United Kingdom	74.4
United States	76.3
Italy	51.7
Ireland	67.3
France	69.3
Germany	75.3

13. From the results of the surveys, what conclusions could you reach?

    (1) People who watch a lot of television don't use the Internet a great deal.

    (2) People who use the Internet don't watch television very much.

    (3) Americans watch a lot of television and use the Internet.

    (4) Italians don't like to use the Internet.

    (5) There isn't a lot of television broadcast in French.

14. One of the researchers said in an interview that American children were above average in weight because of the amount of time they spend watching television and using the Internet. How would you evaluate the researcher's statement?

    (1) The researcher was correct.

    (2) The results do not support any such conclusion.

    (3) Anyone who watches a lot of television eats a lot of snacks.

    (4) The researcher was wrong because you shouldn't eat or drink near a computer.

    (5) Commercials on television make you want to eat more.

15. Angela got the following scores on her final exams:

Subject	Score (%)
Geography	91
History	87
Literature	88
Mathematics	72
Science	89

She had hoped for a 90% average and was disappointed in her mathematics score. How many percentage points higher would her mathematics score have to have been for Angela to have gotten her desired average?

    (1) 85.4

    (2) 4.6

    (3) 6.4

    (4) 90

    (5) 23

16. Kelly's 11th-grade social studies class was conducting a political poll to determine the relative popularity of each of the major parties. They asked each person present in the class which party they would vote for in the next election and got the following results:

Democrats: 28

Republicans: 12

Undecided: 3

What conclusion could Kelly reach as a result of her poll?

(1) The Democrats are going to win the next election.
(2) The Republicans are going to win the next election.
(3) Of the 43 people in the class, the majority support the Democrats
(4) Undecided people could swing the vote.
(5) There is not enough information to reach a conclusion.

17. The equation $y = mx + b$ has the slope, m, equal to 1 and passes through the point $P(-1,3)$. Mark the y-intercept on a coordinate plane grid.

18. Donald went shopping for clothes and was offered the following deal during a big sale: He could get 30% off the regular price for trousers, 45% off the regular price for shirts, and 50% off the regular price for overcoats. If he needed four pairs of trousers, six shirts, and one overcoat, write an equation to represent his total if the total spent is represented by T, the regular price of a pair of trousers is represented by P, the regular price of a shirt is represented by S, and the regular price of an overcoat is represented by C.

(1) $T = 4P + 6S + C$
(2) $T = 4(P - 0.3P) + 6(S - 0.45S) + (C - 0.5C)$
(3) $T = 4(P - 0.45P) + 6(S - 0.3S) + 1(C - 0.5C)$
(4) $T = 4(0.45P) + 6(0.3S) + (0.5C)$
(5) $T = 6(P - 0.3P) + 4(S - 0.45S) + (C - 0.5C)$

19. Francis wanted to write a series of equations to represent a group of parallel lines intersecting the y-axis in a sequence of points. What parameter would she have to change for each equation to get the required result?

$y = mx + b$ where m is the slope and b is the y coordinate of the y-intercept.

(1) y
(2) m
(3) x
(4) b
(5) All of the above

20. Andy and a couple of his friends were sitting around watching a documentary about the pyramids in Egypt. Andy wondered how much paint it would take to paint the outside of a pyramid. The program had said that one of the pyramids, said to be that of Sneferu, was 300 feet tall with a square base measuring 470 feet on each side. His friends looked up the formula for finding the lateral surface area of a pyramid and found it to be $A = \dfrac{PL}{2}$, where A is the surface area of the external slopes, P is the base perimeter, and L is the slant height. How many square feet would have to be painted to cover the external slopes of the pyramid?

    (1) 1,880
    (2) 358,234
    (3) 220.900
    (4) 456,543
    (5) 290,206

21. Evaluate the following formula, where $a = 1$, $b = 6$, and $c = 5$.

$$\frac{-b \pm \sqrt{b^2 - 4ac}}{2a}$$

    (1) −5 or −1
    (2) 5 or 1
    (3) $-\dfrac{5}{2}$ or $-\dfrac{1}{2}$
    (4) $-\dfrac{2}{5}$ or $-\dfrac{1}{3}$
    (5) $\dfrac{5}{2}$ or $\dfrac{1}{2}$

22. Solve the following system of equations for x:

    $2x + 3y = 12$
    $3x + 4y = 6$

    (1) $x = 30$
    (2) $x = -15$
    (3) $x = 15$
    (4) $x = -30$
    (5) $x = 48$

23. What effect would doubling the value of c have on E in the equation $E = mc^2$ if the value of m remains constant?

    (1) E would double in value.
    (2) It would have no effect.
    (3) E would be four times its value.
    (4) E would be eight times its value.
    (5) E would be one-half its value.

24. Solve the following equation for d, where $a = 2$, $c = 2$, and $b = 5$.

$$d = \sqrt{b^2 - 4ac}$$

    (1) 1
    (2) 2
    (3) 3
    (4) 4
    (5) 5

25. In the equation $y = mx + b$, how would increasing b by 3 change the value of y if the other variables stay the same?

    (1) y would be 3 times larger.
    (2) y would be one-third of its value.
    (3) y would increase by 3.
    (4) y would decrease by 3.
    (5) y would not change.

IF YOU FINISH BEFORE TIME IS CALLED, CHECK YOUR WORK ON THIS SECTION ONLY. DO NOT WORK ON ANY OTHER SECTION IN THE TEST.

Answer Key

Section 1: Language Arts, Writing Part I

1. (2)	8. (3)	15. (3)	22. (5)
2. (5)	9. (4)	16. (4)	23. (5)
3. (3)	10. (1)	17. (2)	24. (4)
4. (1)	11. (5)	18. (1)	25. (3)
5. (2)	12. (2)	19. (3)	
6. (5)	13. (4)	20. (5)	
7. (2)	14. (1)	21. (2)	

Section 3: Social Studies

1. (4)	8. (4)	15. (3)	22. (5)
2. (1)	9. (2)	16. (4)	23. (1)
3. (3)	10. (5)	17. (2)	24. (4)
4. (5)	11. (3)	18. (4)	25. (2)
5. (2)	12. (2)	19. (2)	
6. (5)	13. (1)	20. (5)	
7. (3)	14. (4)	21. (3)	

Section 4: Science

1. (4)	8. (2)	15. (3)	22. (1)
2. (3)	9. (3)	16. (2)	23. (3)
3. (3)	10. (4)	17. (3)	24. (1)
4. (2)	11. (3)	18. (4)	25. (4)
5. (3)	12. (3)	19. (4)	
6. (4)	13. (4)	20. (1)	
7. (1)	14. (2)	21. (5)	

Section 5: Language Arts, Reading

1. (4)	**6.** (1)	**11.** (2)	**16.** (1)
2. (2)	**7.** (3)	**12.** (4)	**17.** (4)
3. (5)	**8.** (5)	**13.** (3)	**18.** (2)
4. (2)	**9.** (1)	**14.** (2)	**19.** (5)
5. (4)	**10.** (4)	**15.** (5)	**20.** (3)

Section 6: Mathematics

1. (5)	**8.** 14.25	**15.** (5)	**22.** (4)
2. (2)	**9.** (3)	**16.** (3)	**23.** (3)
3. (4)	**10.** (1)	**17.** (0,4)	**24.** (3)
4. (1)	**11.** (2)	**18.** (2)	**25.** (3)
5. (5)	**12.** (2)	**19.** (4)	
6. (4)	**13.** (3)	**20.** (2)	
7. (3)	**14.** (2)	**21.** (1)	

Answer Explanations

Section 1: Language Arts, Writing, Part I

1. **(2)** A comma is required after *e-mail* to separate the introductory section from the main body of the sentence.

2. **(5)** To improve this complex sentence, it is necessary to separate it into two separate sentences: the first dealing with the *right for distribution,* the second describing the terms of the agreement.

3. **(3)** Commas are needed to separate the restrictive clause *including the receipt of fees* from the rest of the sentence.

4. **(1)** This is a spelling error. The sentence refers to the *basic fee structure. Basic* is an adjective modifying fee while *basis* is a noun.

5. **(2)** *SCAA* is singular and requires a singular possessive *(SCAA's),* not the plural possessive *(SCAAs').*

6. **(5)** The sentence is correct, so no changes are needed.

7. **(2)** This is a spelling error. Change *organised* to *organized.*

8. **(3)** To improve this complex sentence, it is necessary to divide it into separate sentences by placing a period after *revenue.* The new sentence should begin with the clause *Through the creation of 13 jobs.*

9. **(4)** The correct word is the possessive adjective *their* not its homonym *there.*

10. **(1)** To improve the meaning of the sentence, it is necessary to change the phrase *at present* to *presently available.*

11. **(5)** The sentence is correct as written. No changes are required.

12. **(2)** This is a punctuation error. The comma after *equipment* should be changed to a semicolon.

13. **(4)** *Population* is the right word because it refers to a number of people. *Popularity* means to be favorably received.

14. **(1)** This is an error in spelling. There should not be a hyphen between *bio* and *degradable.*

15. **(3)** The present tense *allows* is required, not the past tense *allowed.*

16. **(4)** An improvement in punctuation is required by placing a comma after the first *you.*

17. **(2)** To correct a spelling error, place a hyphen between *well* and *organized.*

18. **(1)** Semicolons, not commas, are required after *name* and *address.*

19. **(3)** The adjective modifying status should be *marital,* which refers to marriage. *Martial* is an act of war—not something appropriate for a résumé.

20. **(5)** The clause *which is against the law* should follow *people* not *criteria.* It's the term *discriminating* that is against the law.

21. **(2)** A *Social Security card* would not be submitted with the résumé. It is the *number* that should be referred to here.

22. **(5)** No correction is required for this sentence.

23. **(5)** No correction is required for this sentence.

24. **(4)** *With* is the correct conjunction for use in this sentence because it refers to a sense of belonging, not location.

25. **(3)** Changing *enough* to *complete* gives more specificity to the request for information. You then also delete *completely,* as it is now redundant.

Section 2: Language Arts Writing, Part II

As the test graders read and evaluate your essay, they look for the following:

- Well-focused main points
- Evidence of clear organization
- Specific development of your ideas
- Proper sentence structure
- Correct grammar
- Necessary punctuation
- Appropriate use of words
- Correct spelling

Although every essay will be unique, we provide a sample here to give you a better idea of what the test graders expect to see in your essay. Compare the structure of this essay to yours.

Sample Essay

Hiking is a hobby I can recommend to anyone. Being outdoors, getting exercise, and spending quiet time alone are all facets of hiking that make it unique in today's mostly indoor, sedentary, and yet overly busy life. Many areas—even large cities—offer parks with dirt or grass paths that are perfect for a daily hike.

Hiking gets me outdoors, away from potentially harmful indoor air. Too much time indoors cuts humans off from the sun, which is vital to mental health and can also lead to allergies or other illnesses from too much exposure to chemicals and other products that are trapped indoors. Just an hour per day of hiking can counteract many of the effects of spending too much time indoors.

Hiking is also great exercise, because it works the heart, lungs, and leg muscles without adding stress to the knees and other joints. You can hike in your street clothes (although a good pair of hiking boots is a good idea), so hiking does not require the investment in gear that many forms of exercise do.

Perhaps the best—and most unique—feature of hiking, however, is that it provides solace from our loud, fast-paced, materialistic world. When hiking—even in or near a large, metropolitan area—I see deer, listen to birdsongs, and watch squirrels busy with their work. Without the constant sound of a TV or radio in the background, I can focus on my own thoughts instead of on what is expected by society and promoted by advertisers. While on the trail, I can focus on the natural beauty around me instead of worrying about bills or comparing myself to others. This quiet disconnection from society helps me remember what is important in life.

In short, hiking helps me break free of the workaday world by getting me outside to appreciate nature, encouraging me to exercise, and giving me long periods of restful silence. I recommend hiking to anyone.

After reading through the sample essay once, reread it and answer the following questions about it.

- Is there a series of main points in this essay that clearly relate to the topic? (Underline the main points to check.)

- Does each paragraph have an introductory sentence or thought?
- Does each paragraph have a concluding sentence or thought?
- Are the sentences within each paragraph well organized?
- Are the paragraphs organized in a natural flow from beginning to end? In other words, does each paragraph build on the previous one and lead to the next one?
- Have the ideas in the given topic and the first paragraph been developed throughout the essay?
- Are all the sentences grammatically correct?
- Are all the sentences properly structured?
- Are all the sentences correctly punctuated?
- Are all the words spelled correctly?

As far as this particular sample essay is concerned, a test evaluator probably would have given it a high score because it has all the attributes of a good essay that we list earlier in this section. It isn't perfect, but no one's asking you to write a perfect essay. Look over the list of characteristics that the readers are looking for, and try to determine whether your practice essay satisfies those requirements. Ask a friend to answer these same questions about your essay; then, rewrite your essay until you and your friend can answer yes to every question.

Remember: Your essay shouldn't be just a collection of grammatically correct sentences that flow from beginning to end. Rather, your essay needs to be interesting and even entertaining to read. After all, no one—not even a professional test-grader—wants to read a boring essay!

Section 3: Social Studies

1. **(4)** Columbus hoped to gain fame and fortune by finding a route to the Indies. Although he was the son of a weaver, a successful map maker, and a sailor, none of these is the best answer. We don't know about his cooking skills.

2. **(1)** According to the passage, Columbus was making exorbitant demands of his funders. Admiral of the oceans, loot, and governships are just examples of these demands. European capitals were where he sought funding.

3. **(3)** It was Queen Isabella of Spain who finally gave him support; he was refused by England, France, Portugal, and the Italian states.

4. **(5)** The queen gave her approval in 1492. The other dates are incorrect.

5. **(2)** Columbus named the island in the Bahamas, where he landed, San Salvador. He didn't reach the Indies or the other islands mentioned.

6. **(5)** All the qualities in (1) through (4) contributed to making Washington a born leader.

7. **(3)** The third sentence of the passage clearly states that Washington wasn't proud of his dentures. Although choices (1), (2), and (4) are true, they do not relate to how he felt about his dentures. Choice (5) contradicts the passage.

8. **(4)** According to the passage, Washington's troops could not be described as disciplined and dependable. To the contrary, they were indecisive, quarrelsome, and prone to desertion. They also lacked a commanding presence or an indomitable spirit.

9. **(2)** Washington demonstrated bravery by being among the last to retreat. Though he was loved by his men, rode unexpectantly, and wore down the British, these choices are not the best descriptors of his bravery.

10. **(5)** Choices (1) through (4) all contributed to the British Army's description of Washington as "the old fox."

11. **(3)** Henry Ford believed that everyone should own an automobile. He also may have thought everyone should have a job and an improved life, but none of these is the best answer. Joining a union or being an engineer are irrelevant.

12. **(2)** Ford's greatest contribution to the auto industry was the assembly line. As a result of the assembly line, more workers were employed and gained independence. This method of manufacturing also encouraged new industries, which strengthened the economy.

13. **(1)** Ford was able to sell more automobiles because he introduced cheaper prices. As a result, more tires were produced, roadside cafes opened, and individuals gained greater independence, but these factors don't influence sales. We don't know about his advertising efforts.

14. **(4)** The availability of automobiles became a dominant element in building the U.S. economy. A change in lifestyle, greater self-esteem, and independence were not the most important economic impacts. Cars certainly didn't cause the Great Depression.

15. **(3)** The Wright Brothers were famous for achieving the first powered sustained flight by an aircraft. Owning a bicycle shop, building a machine, or going to Kitty Hawk didn't make them famous. Their invention may have had some influence on World War I, but the Wright Brothers were already famous by the time the war started.

16. **(4)** The rise in oil prices caused an increase in gasoline prices. Other choices—decrease in sales of SUVs and more travel—are not related directly to oil prices. Lost profit and air-conditioning are not relevant choices.

17. **(2)** Higher oil prices cause a rise in the cost of living because many things become more expensive. The other choices are not correct.

18. **(4)** The adjective that best describes the SUV characters is *wasteful*. The other choices—*joyful, surprised, angry,* or *frightened*—are not correct.

19. **(2)** The SUV cannot be described as an *energy saver* due to its poor gasoline mileage. The other terms are much more accurate.

20. **(5)** All the solutions mentioned in choices (1) through (4) could help to solve the energy crisis.

21. **(3)** The third paragraph of the passage specifically states that New Orleans is nicknamed the "Big Easy." The other choices are incorrect.

22. **(5)** Choices (1) through (4) were all results of Hurricane Katrina.

23. **(1)** The major factor that put New Orleans in danger was that it was located below sea level. Thousands of people refusing to leave and the destruction of homes were results, not factors. Being the region's largest city is irrelevant.

24. **(4)** The federal government was slow to respond to the destruction of Katrina. The other choices, while true, were not the primary reason for criticism.

25. **(2)** Katrina will be remembered as the most expensive hurricane, so far, in U.S. history. Flood waters, evacuations, and damage costs were contributing factors to this expense.

Section 4: Science

1. **(4)** The center of the atom is called the nucleus. Read questions and choices carefully because in this question, to a rapid reader, choices (3) and (4) might be easily confused.

2. **(3)** The passage states that the cloud of negatively charged particles surrounding the nucleus is composed of electrons.

3. **(3)** The iron combines with the oxygen to form a new compound, which is commonly called rust.

4. **(2)** The passage states that the chemical name for rust is ferrous oxide.

5. **(3)** As Janice explained, this is an example of Newton's First Law of Motion.

6. **(4)** The parachute creates an unbalanced force in the opposite direction. This is clearly stated in the passage.

7. **(1)** The motor provides the power that propels the drag racer forward.

8. **(2)** For a machine to be useful, it must do something, but according to the passage, energy could not be created; thus, the machine would never produce any additional energy unless it converted some of its energy or matter into this additional energy, and then it would cease to exist as it used up its energy or matter.

9. **(3)** The heat in the room provides the energy required to produce a change of state—in this case, from a solid to a liquid.

10. **(4)** According to the passage, the weight of the egg averages 3 pounds.

11. **(3)** The passage states that heredity is the transmission of characteristics from parents to children.

12. **(3)** The passages states that DNA is the mode of transmission.

13. **(4)** A life form well adapted to its environment stands the greatest chance of survival.

14. **(2)** Heredity is the means of transmission of characteristics from one generation to the next, and hair color is a characteristic or trait.

15. **(3)** The passage states that an ecosystem contains both producers and consumers. If one were missing, the ecosystem would be affected.

16. **(2)** By definition, herbivores eat only plant food.

17. **(3)** The passage mentions that Alice's father told her about Skinner's work with animals.

18. **(4)** Alice's father suggested that she give the puppy a treat for performing the correct behavior. If you want more information on this, look up "conditioning."

19. **(4)** When the sun doesn't shine, there is no source for the power.

20. **(1)** The small dark window in most calculators is a photovoltaic cell, which converts the energy from light into the power to run the calculator. If you need proof of this, cover the cell with your finger and watch the display disappear.

21. **(5)** By carefully looking at the diagram, you'll see that water exists in all these locations.

22. **(1)** If there is insufficient winter storage of ice and snow that will melt into liquid water that feeds the lake, the water level will be low and the boat may hit a rock in the shallower water.

23. **(3)** The correct answer is hydrogen and helium because they're chemical elements. Choice (1) is mentioned in the passage, but dust is not a chemical element.

24. **(1)** The process mentioned in the passage is nuclear fusion. *Nuclear fission* may be a familiar term, but it involves the splitting of the atoms rather than the combining of atoms. Both produce immense amounts of energy but are different processes.

25. **(4)** Gravity provided the attraction to gather the particles into planets, according to the passage. The particles were far enough away from the sun that they were attracted to the planets and not the sun.

Section 5: Language Arts, Reading

1. **(4)** From the description in the first part of the poem (trees, stream, birds, small animals, and so on), you can tell that the setting is a forest. None of the other choices fits the setting described in the poem.

2. **(2)** The poem states that the redwood trees can live longer than 1,000 years. The other choices are factually incorrect. This question is a good example of when skimming can help you find an answer quickly because it's asking for a factual and numeric answer.

3. **(5)** The author describes in detail the changes in color of the setting each season. The other choices may look right, but the poem gives no evidence to support them.

4. **(2)** The author writes, "And summer opens to sunlight exposing their vulnerability" and "While winter envelopes the landscape / Wearing a coat of white / Vulnerable now." The other seasons aren't described in this manner, so you know summer and winter is the answer. Choice (5) is incorrect, because more than enough information is given to answer the question. If you read the question and then skim the poem, you stand a very good chance of efficiently arriving at the right answer.

5. **(4)** The author describes the foliage in the woods as ". . . red and yellow / With a hint of orange." If you have some knowledge of redwood trees, you know that the *wood* is red, not the bark. The other colors may be mentioned in the poem, but they aren't referring to the redwood trees.

6. **(1)** The author says that nature provides the needed nourishment and that the streams carry it to the trees. Although the other choices are feasible, they're incorrect based on the poem. ***Remember:*** You must answer the questions based only on the information given in the passage. Don't let any prior knowledge sway you from this task. The correct answer is always in the passage.

7. **(3)** Connie's main interest in getting an A is that it will get her a Porsche from her father; as she says, "It's just so cool to arrive at a party in a Porsche." The other choices, except for (2), would seem to be typical answers for a student but are not Connie's main concern.

8. **(5)** Toward the end of the year, increasing your grade from a B– to an A is very difficult, because most of the work has already been done. There is no indication of Lewis's thoughts about her abilities and no mention of the course only having a final exam as in choice (3). Nothing in the passage would lead you to choices (2) or (4).

9. **(1)** Connie expects an A as a reward for her father's donations and not for her efforts. Choices (2) and (3) are ways in which a college can honor a major benefactor, but none of these is mentioned in this passage. Choice (5) should be true but is not always the reality; sometimes large donations have an effect on the way people think and act.

10. **(4)** Connie had been expecting certain rewards from her family as soon as she was accepted into graduate school, and this B– would jeopardize her acceptance into graduate school. Choices (1), (2), and (3) might be possible, but the basis for any of them is not found in the passage. Choice (5) is wrong because there is no mention of her mother.

11. **(2)** The village was located "in a province of Great Britain." Fort Christina is not correct; Thirteen Colonies, New Amsterdam, and the Hudson River are not mentioned.

12. **(4)** The phrase used by the author to describe Rip's personality is *simple and good-natured*. Choices (1) and (3) do not relate to his personality. Rip is not described as *disobedient,* but as *obedient and henpecked*. And he is not depicted as *gallant and chivalrous*.

13. **(3)** According to the passage, his "meekness of spirit" was the quality that made him popular. Although he also was pliant and malleable and patient and long-suffering, these are not the best answers. Choices (1) and (2) don't apply to Rip.

14. **(2)** The phrase *domestic tribulation* is used to refer to the Van Winkle marriage. The other choices are incorrect.

15. **(5)** All the activities mentioned in choices (1) through (4) describe Van Winkle's treatment of the children.

16. **(1)** The "good wives" of the village were his best defenders. The men of the village are not mentioned in the passage, and the children, though mentioned, were lesser supporters. Dame Van Winkle and Peter Stuyvesant do not apply.

17. **(4)** According to the passage the agreement refers to "educational travel programs" offered to a variety of constituencies.

18. **(2)** Retailing is the only service not mentioned in the agreement.

19. **(5)** All the constituencies listed in choices (1) through (4) are served by the partnership.

20. **(3)** According to the agreement, the income is to be "based on a predetermined rate of commission per passenger." All other choices are incorrect.

Section 6: Mathematics

1. **(5)** All the discounts and specials will produce the same price; thus, it doesn't matter which store Alvin buys his jeans from as he would pay the same price at each.

2. **(2)** If Liz wanted to lose 12 pounds, she would have to cut $12 \times 3{,}500 = 42{,}000$ calories out of her diet in 12 weeks. Because there are 7 days in a week, she has $7 \times 12 = 84$ days to reach her goal. She would have to cut $42{,}000 \div 84 = 500$ calories out of her diet each day to reach her goal.

   If you wanted to try this problem using mental math, you could look at it this way: Because she wants to lose 12 pounds in 12 weeks, she would have to lose 1 pound per week. To lose 1 pound per week, she would have to cut out 3,500 calories per week or $3{,}500 \div 7 = 500$ calories per day.

3. **(4)** If Alvin knows how far he has traveled on a tankful of gasoline and knows how many gallons he has used, he could find the average miles per gallon by dividing the distance by the fuel consumed. He could calculate the number of gallons of gasoline by dividing the total cost by the price per gallon. Although two operations are required, they are both division.

4. **(1)** If you added up the approximate costs of the items, you would get $2.50 + $4.00 + $2.50 + $1.20 = $10.20, which is more money than she has, but three of the approximations are a little more than the item's actual price (for example, the approximation for milk is a full $0.20 above the real price). The actual total is $9.98.

5. **(5)** In a room, the basic assumptions are all of those stated; otherwise, the building would not be rectangular and the ceiling would be at different heights. If you have difficulty visualizing perpendicular and parallel planes, think of a regular room, and the concept may be easier to visualize.

6. **(4)** Rotating BC 180° around C would provide a line extended from the original BC, which is parallel to DE.

7. **(3)** To find the length of the hypotenuse, you first have to add the squares of the other two sides (900 + 400 = 1,300) and then find the square root of that number. The square root of 1,300 is 36.06, or 36 inches to the nearest inch.

8. **14.25** The slope is calculated by dividing the rise by the run, which is $\frac{8}{12} = \frac{2}{3}$. The rise is 9 feet 6 inches, or 114 inches. Next create the equation $\frac{2}{3} = \frac{114}{run}$. Then $run = \frac{114 \times 3}{2} = \frac{342}{2} = 171$ inches. Converting 171 inches to feet, $\frac{171}{12} = \frac{57}{4} = 14\frac{1}{4} = 14.25$ feet.

Recorded on a standard grid, the answer would look like this:

1	4	.	2	5
	⁄	⁄	⁄	
⊙	⊙	●	⊙	⊙
	⓪	⓪	⓪	⓪
●	①	①	①	①
②	②	②	●	②
③	③	③	③	③
④	●	④	④	④
⑤	⑤	⑤	⑤	●
⑥	⑥	⑥	⑥	⑥
⑦	⑦	⑦	⑦	⑦
⑧	⑧	⑧	⑧	⑧
⑨	⑨	⑨	⑨	⑨

9. **(3)** To find the area, multiply the length by the width, or 25 × 12 = 300 square feet. Because one gallon covers 450 square feet, you would divide the area by the coverage, or $\frac{300}{450} = \frac{2}{3}$. (Divide top and bottom by 150 to simplify the fraction.) Georgio would use $\frac{2}{3}$ gallon of paint.

10. **(1)** If Sandy could leave at 1:15 p.m. and arrive at 5 p.m., she would travel for 3 hours and 45 minutes or 3.75 hours. (Convert 45 minutes to a decimal by dividing it by 60.) She travels an average of 42 miles per hour. To calculate the distance, multiply 3.75 × 42 to get 157.5.

11. **(2)** To calculate the original surface area, multiply the length by the width: 60 × 20 = 1,200. The new pool would be 20 percent larger in surface area, which would be 1,200 × 0.20 = 240 square feet larger. The new surface area would be 1,200 + 240 = 1,440 square feet.

To calculate the volume with the original dimensions, multiply the surface area by the depth: 1,200 × 4 = 4,800 cubic feet.

To calculate the volume with the increased dimensions, multiply 1,440 × 4 = 5,760 cubic feet.

To find the increased volume, subtract the larger volume from the smaller: 5,760 – 4,800 = 960 cubic feet.

The increased surface area would produce an increase in volume of 960 cubic feet.

12. **(2)** The highest price for gas is $2.56 in Wichita and the lowest price for gas is $2.47 in Osbourne. The difference in the price per gallon is $2.56 – $2.47 = $0.09 per gallon. By buying 20 gallons at the lowest price, you would save $20 \times 0.09 = $1.80.

13. **(3)** From the table, the country that watches the most television per week and has the highest penetration of Internet use as a percentage of the population is the United States.

14. **(2)** The rest of the choices may be part of folklore or seem to be logical, but you were asked for an answer supported by the data and neither table mentions food or overeating. The answer for each question should be in the material presented and not be determined by prior knowledge or hearsay.

15. **(5)** Her present average is (91 + 87 + 88 + 72 + 89) = 427. 427 ÷ 5 = 85.4% average. To get an average of 90 percent, she would need a total score of 450 (450 ÷ 5 = 90%). 450 – 427 = 23. So she would have to score 23 more points on her mathematics test to achieve a 90% average.

16. **(3)** The only factual data Kelly gathered was the number of people present in her class that day and their political preference. The sample is too small to make any other conclusion.

17. **(0,4)** Using the equation $y = mx + b$ and substituting $y = 3$, $m = 1$, and solving, the answer would be $b = 3$. The y-intercept would be the point (0,3) on a coordinate plane grid.

Point $P(-1,3)$ has the coordinates, $x = -1$ and $y = 3$. Remember that in writing the coordinates of a point, the first number is the value of x and the second number is the value of y for that point. Use the equation $y = mx + b$ and substitute $x = -1$, $y = 3$, $m = 1$:

$3 = (1)(-1) + b$

$3 = -1 + b$ (Isolate b by adding 1 to both sides.)

$4 = b$

The y-intercept would be the point (0,4) on a coordinate plane grid.

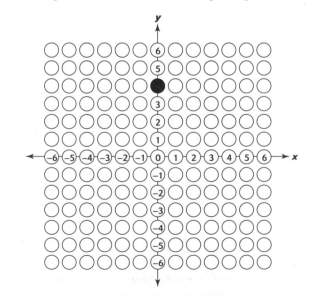

18. **(2)** You could read this equation as follows: The total cost is four times (the regular price of trousers less a 30 percent discount) plus six times (the regular price for shirts less a 45 percent discount) plus the regular price for a coat discounted by 50 percent.

19. **(4)** The slope, m, would need to remain the same if the lines were to be parallel and the y-intercept, b, would have to be different in each equation to produce a sequence of parallel lines.

20. **(2)** This is a problem requiring several steps and would be a good example to use with a calculator. If you look at the formula $A = \frac{PL}{2}$, which calculates the area of the lateral sides, you can calculate the area and the perimeter of the base from the information provided, but calculating the slant height will require another step.

Area of the base = $470 \times 470 = 220,900$ square feet

Perimeter of the base = $2(470 + 470) = 1,880$ feet

To calculate the slant height, you can use the Pythagorean theorem to find the slant height, which would correspond to the hypotenuse of a right triangle formed by the base and the height.

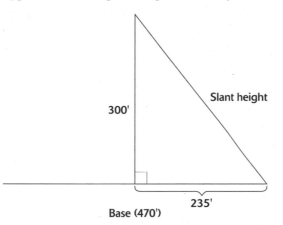

The right-angled triangle would be formed by one-half the width of the base and the height. The reason for using one-half of the width of the base is that the triangle is formed by the height and the base intersecting at 90°, which is halfway across the base. The triangle formed this way is a right-angled triangle.

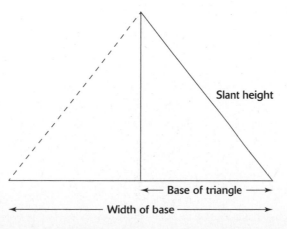

63

To calculate the slant height, (the hypoteneuse of the right-angled triangle), you would have to calculate the square root of $235^2 + 300^2$, which is $235 \times 235 + 300 \times 300 = 55{,}225 + 90{,}000 = 145{,}225$. The square root is one of two numbers that multiply together to form 145,225 as a product. Because both a negative number and a positive number, when squared, would create a positive product, the square root could be either negative or positive. In this question, a negative number would not make sense, and, thus, only the positive square root would be considered. The square root of 145,225 is $\pm$ 381.1, and using only the positive square root, the square root is 381.1.

Substituting in the equation:

$$A = \frac{PL}{2}$$
$$= \frac{(1{,}880)(381.1)}{2}$$
$$= 358{,}234$$

The lateral area that would have to be painted is 358,234 square feet (the base is excluded; the ability to paint the base is severely limited because it is sitting on the ground).

21. **(1)** To evaluate $\dfrac{-b \pm \sqrt{b^2 - 4ac}}{2a} =$, substitute $a = 1$, $b = 6$, and $c = 5$ in the equation:

$$\frac{-b \pm \sqrt{b^2 - 4ac}}{2a} = \frac{-6 \pm \sqrt{6^2 - 4(1)(5)}}{2(1)}$$
$$= \frac{-6 \pm \sqrt{36 - 4(1)(5)}}{2(1)}$$
$$= \frac{-6 \pm \sqrt{16}}{2}$$
$$= \frac{-6 \pm 4}{2}$$
$$= \frac{-10}{2} \text{ or } \frac{-2}{2}$$
$$= -5 \text{ or } -1$$

The answers are –5 or –1.

22. **(4)** To solve this system of equations, you have to eliminate y, which you can do by multiplying the first equation by 4 and the second equation by 3:

$$4(2x + 3y) = 4(12) \rightarrow 8x + 12y = 48$$
$$3(3x + 4y) = 3(6) \rightarrow 9x + 12y = 18$$
$$8x + 12y = 48$$
$$9x + 12y = 18$$

Then subtract the first equation from the second:

$$9x + 12y = 18$$
$$\underline{-8x + 12y = 48}$$
$$x = -30$$

23. **(3)** If c became $2c$, then $(2c)^2$ would become $4c^2$ and E would become four times its value.

24. **(3)** To solve the equation $d = \sqrt{b^2 - 4ac}$, substitute $a = 2$, $b = 5$, and $c = 2$. This will produce $d = \sqrt{5^2 - 4(2)(2)} = 3$.

25. **(3)** If you add 3 to one side of an equation, you must add 3 to the other side to maintain the equality.

II. Language Arts, Writing Cram Plans

Two-Month Cram Plan	
8 weeks before the test	**Study Time:** 5 hours ❑ Take Diagnostic Test (Sections 1 and 2) and review answer explanations. ❑ Note your errors. ❑ Based on your errors, identify difficult topics. These are your targeted topics. ❑ Read Part II instructions regarding the essay in Chapter VII, Section B2. ❑ Write at least one essay this week. ❑ Evaluate your essay using the examples in Chapter VII.

7 weeks before the test	**Study Time:** 4 hours
	❑ **Topic:** Test Strategies – Chapter VII, Section C
	    ❑ Review the material; do the examples.
	    ❑ Check the answer explanations.
	❑ **Topic:** Grammar Review – Chapter VII, Sections D1a to D1g
	    ❑ Review the material; do the examples.
	    ❑ Check the answer explanations.
	❑ Write at least one essay this week.
	❑ Evaluate your essay using the examples in Chapter VII.

6 weeks before the test	**Study Time:** 5 hours
	❑ **Topic:** Grammar Review – Chapter VII, Sections D2a to D2e
	    ❑ Review the material; do the examples.
	    ❑ Check the answer explanations.
	❑ **Topic:** Grammar Review – Chapter VII, Sections D3a to D3d, D4, D5a, and D5b
	    ❑ Review the material; do the examples.
	    ❑ Check the answer explanations.
	❑ Write at least one essay this week.
	❑ Evaluate your essay using the examples in Chapter VII.

5 weeks before the test	**Study Time:** 5 hours
	❑ **Topic:** Grammar Review – Chapter VII, Sections D5, D6, D7, and D8a to D8g
	    ❑ Review the material; do the examples.
	    ❑ Check the answer explanations.
	❑ Write at least one essay this week.
	❑ Evaluate your essay using the examples in Chapter VII.

4 weeks before the test	**Study Time:** 4 hours
	❑ **Topic:** Grammar Review – Chapter VII, Section D8h
	    ❑ Review the material; do the examples.
	    ❑ Check the answer explanations.
	❑ Write at least one essay this week.
	❑ Evaluate your essay using the examples in Chapter VII.

continued

3 weeks before the test	**Study Time:** 4 hours ❏ **Topic:** Types of Questions – A Detailed Look – Chapter VII, Sections B1a to B1bviii 　❏ Review the material; do the examples. 　❏ Check the answer explanations. ❏ **Topic:** Types of Questions — A Detailed Look — Chapter VII, Sections B1ci to B1ciii and B1di to B1diii 　❏ Review the material; do the examples. 　❏ Check the answer explanations. ❏ Write at least one essay this week. ❏ Evaluate your essay using the examples in Chapter VII.
2 weeks before the test	**Study Time:** 3 hours ❏ Take the Practice Test (Chapter XII) and review your answers and the answer explanations at the end of the test. Note those topics that you still need to work on. These are your targeted topics. ❏ Write at least one essay this week. ❏ Evaluate your essay using the examples in Chapter VII.
7 days before the test	**Study Time:** 1.5 hours ❏ **Topic:** Targeted Topics – Review your targeted topics in Chapter VII 　❏ Review the examples and your answers. 　❏ Compare your answers to the answer explanations given.
6 days before the test	**Study Time:** 1.5 hours ❏ Topic: Grammar Review – Chapter VII, Section D1 　❏ Review the material; redo the examples that were targeted. 　❏ Check the answer explanations.
5 days before the test	**Study Time:** 1.5 hours ❏ Topic: Grammar Review – Chapter VII, Sections D2 and D3 　❏ Review the material; redo the examples that were targeted. 　❏ Check the answer explanations.
4 days before the test	**Study Time:** 1.5 hours ❏ Topic: Grammar Review – Chapter VII, Sections D4 to D7 　❏ Review the material; redo the examples that were targeted. 　❏ Check the answer explanations.
3 days before the test	**Study Time:** 1.5 hours ❏ Topic: Grammar Review – Chapter VII, Section D8 　❏ Review the material, redo the examples that were targeted. 　❏ Check the answer explanations.
2 days before the test	**Study Time:** 2 hours ❏ **Topic:** Writing the Essay – Chapter VII, Section B2 　❏ Review the essays you have written. 　❏ Write an essay from a topic of your choice. 　❏ Evaluate your essay using the material in Chapter VII, Section B2.
1 day before the test	❏ Relax . . . you are well prepared for the test. ❏ Have confidence in your ability to do well. ❏ Exercise to help relieve stress and improve sleep.

Morning of the test	**Reminders:**
	❏ Have a good breakfast.
	❏ Take the following with you:
	  ❏ Your admission ticket and photo ID
	  ❏ A watch
	❏ Try to go outside for a few minutes and walk around before the test.
	❏ Most important: Stay calm and confident during the test. Take deep, slow breaths if you feel at all nervous. You can do it!

One-Month Cram Plan

4 weeks before the test	**Study Time:** 5 hours ❏ Take Diagnostic Test (Sections 1 and 2) and review answer explanations. ❏ Note your errors. ❏ Based on your errors, identify difficult topics. These are your targeted topics. ❏ Read Part II instructions regarding the essay in Chapter VII, Section B2. ❏ Write at least one essay this week. ❏ Evaluate your essay using the examples in Chapter VII.

3 weeks before the test	**Study Time:** 2.5 hours
	❏ **Topic:** Types of Questions – A Detailed Look – Chapter VII, Section B
	    ❏ Review the material; do the examples.
	    ❏ Check the answer explanations.
	❏ Write at least one essay this week.
	❏ Evaluate your essay using the examples in Chapter VII.

2 weeks before the test	**Study Time:** 2 hours
	❏ **Topic:** Writing the Essay – Chapter VII, Section B2
	    ❏ Review the essays you have written and the evaluation scheme in the section.
	❏ **Topic:** Test Strategies – Chapter VII, Section C
	    ❏ Review the material.

7 days before the test	**Study Time:** 1.5 hours
	❏ **Topic:** Grammar Review – Chapter VII, Section D1
	    ❏ Review the material; do the examples.
	    ❏ Check the answer explanations.

6 days before the test	**Study Time:** 1.5 hours
	❏ **Topic:** Grammar Review – Chapter VII, Sections D2 to D4
	    ❏ Review the material; do the examples.
	    ❏ Check the answer explanations.

5 days before the test	**Study Time:** 1.5 hours
	❏ **Topic:** Grammar Review – Chapter VII, Sections D5 to D7
	    ❏ Review the material; do the examples.
	    ❏ Check the answer explanations.

4 days before the test	**Study Time:** 1.5 hours
	❏ **Topic:** Grammar Review – Chapter VII, Section D8
	    ❏ Review the material; do the examples.
	    ❏ Check the answer explanations.

3 days before the test	**Study Time:** 3 hours ❏ Take the Practice Test (Chapter XII) and review your answers and the answer explanations at the end of the test. Note those topics that you still need to work on. These are your targeted topics.

2 days before the test	**Study Time:** 2 hours
	❏ **Topic:** Writing the Essay – Chapter VII, Section B2
	    ❏ Review the essays you have written.
	    ❏ Write an essay from a topic of your choice.
	    ❏ Evaluate your essay using the material in Chapter VII, Section B2.

1 day before the test	❏ Relax . . . you are well prepared for the test. ❏ Have confidence in your ability to do well. ❏ Exercise to help relieve stress and improve sleep.

Morning of the test	**Reminders:**
	❏ Have a good breakfast.
	❏ Take the following with you:
	    ❏ Your admission ticket and photo ID
	    ❏ A watch
	❏ Try to go outside for a few minutes and walk around before the test.
	❏ Most important: Stay calm and confident during the test. Take deep, slow breaths if you feel at all nervous. You can do it!

One-Week Cram Plan	
7 days before the test	**Study Time:** 3 hours ❏ Take Diagnostic Test (Sections 1 and 2) and review answer explanations. ❏ Note your errors. ❏ Based on your errors, identify difficult topics. These are your targeted topics.

6 days before the test	**Study Time:** 2 hours
	 ❏ **Topic:** Writing an Essay – Chapter VII, Section B2
	     ❏ Read Part II instructions regarding the essay in Chapter VII, Section B2.
	     ❏ Write at least one essay.
	     ❏ Evaluate your essay using the examples in Chapter VII.

5 days before the test	**Study Time:** 2.5 hours
	 ❏ **Topic:** Types of Questions – Chapter VII, Section B
	     ❏ Review the material; do the examples.
	     ❏ Check the answer explanations.
	 ❏ Write at least one essay.
	 ❏ Evaluate your essay using the examples in Chapter VII.

4 days before the test	**Study Time:** 3.5 hours
	 ❏ **Topic:** Grammar Review – Chapter VII, Section D
	     ❏ Review the material, do the examples.
	     ❏ Check the answer explanations.
	 ❏ Write at least one essay.
	 ❏ Evaluate your essay using the examples in Chapter VII.

3 days before the test	**Study Time:** 3 hours ❏ Take the Practice Test (Chapter XII) and review your answers. Note those topics you still need to work on. These are your targeted topics.

2 days before the test	**Study Time:** 2 hours
	 ❏ Topic: Writing the Essay – Chapter VII, Section B2
	     ❏ Review the essays you have written.
	     ❏ Write an essay from a topic of your choice.
	     ❏ Evaluate your essay using the material in Chapter VII, Section B2.

1 day before the test	❏ Relax . . . you are well prepared for the test. ❏ Have confidence in your ability to do well. ❏ Exercise to help relieve stress and improve sleep.

Morning of the test	**Reminders:**
	 ❏ Have a good breakfast.
	 ❏ Take the following with you:
	     ❏ Your admission ticket and photo ID
	     ❏ A watch
	 ❏ Try to go outside for a few minutes and walk around before the test.
	 ❏ Most important: Stay calm and confident during the test. Take deep, slow breaths if you feel at all nervous. You can do it!

III. Social Studies Cram Plans

	Two-Month Cram Plan
8 weeks before the test	**Study Time:** 3 hours ❑ Take Diagnostic Test (Section 3) and review answer explanations. ❑ Note your errors. ❑ Based on your errors, identify difficult topics. These topics are your targeted topics.
7 weeks before the test	**Study Time:** 3 hours ❑ **Topic:** Test Format – Chapter VIII, Section A ❑ **Topic:** Test Strategies – Chapter VIII, Section C ❑ Review above sections and gain experience reading historical, practical, and visual documents.

6 weeks before the test	**Study Time:** 1.5 hours
	❑ **Topic:** Types of Questions — A Detailed Look – Chapter VIII, Section B
	   ❑ Do the example questions.
	   ❑ Check the answer explanations.
	   ❑ Reread the targeted topics and figure out why you had difficulty with them.

5 weeks before the test	**Study Time:** 1.5 hours
	❑ **Topic:** Comprehension Questions – Chapter VIII, Section B1
	   ❑ Read the material; do the examples.
	   ❑ Check the answer explanations.

4 weeks before the test	**Study Time:** 1.5 hours
	❑ **Topic:** Application Questions – Chapter VIII, Section B2
	   ❑ Read the material; do the examples.
	   ❑ Check the answer explanations.

3 weeks before the test	**Study Time:** 1.5 hours
	❑ **Topic:** Analysis Questions – Chapter VIII, Section B3
	   ❑ Read the material; do the examples.
	   ❑ Check the answer explanations.

2 weeks before the test	**Study Time:** 1.5 hours
	❑ **Topic:** Evaluation Questions – Chapter VIII, Section B4
	   ❑ Read the material; do the examples.
	   ❑ Check the answer explanations.

7 days before the test	**Study Time:** 2 hours ❑ Take the Full-Length Practice Test (Chapter XIII) and review your answers. ❑ Based on your errors on the Practice Test, identify difficult topics and their corresponding sections. Target these sections for extra review.

6 days before the test	**Study Time:** 1.5 hours
	❑ **Topic:** Comprehension Questions
	   ❑ Review example questions, paying special attention to those in error the first time you did them.
	   ❑ Based on your errors on the Practice Test, identify difficult topics and their corresponding sections. Target these sections for extra review.

continued

5 days before the test	**Study Time:** 1.5 hours
	❑ **Topic:** Application Questions
	    ❑ Review example questions paying special attention to those in error the first time you did them.
	    ❑ Based on your errors on the Practice Test, identify difficult topics and their corresponding sections. Target these sections for extra review.

4 days before the test	**Study Time:** 1.5 hours
	❑ **Topic:** Analysis Questions
	    ❑ Review example questions paying special attention to those in error the first time you did them.
	    ❑ Based on your errors on the Practice Test, identify difficult topics and their corresponding sections. Target these sections for extra review.

3 days before the test	**Study Time:** 1.5 hours
	❑ **Topic:** Evaluation Questions
	    ❑ Review example questions paying special attention to those in error the first time you did them.
	    ❑ Based on your errors on the Practice Test, identify difficult topics and their corresponding sections. Target these sections for extra review.

2 days before the test	**Study Time:** 2 hours ❑ Practice Test Review ❑ Based on your errors on the Practice Test, identify difficult topics and their corresponding sections. Target these sections for extra review.
1 day before the test	❑ Relax . . . you are well prepared for the test. ❑ Have confidence in your ability to do well. ❑ Exercise to help relieve stress and improve sleep.

Morning of the test	**Reminders:**
	❑ Have a good breakfast.
	❑ Take the following with you:
	    ❑ Your admission ticket and photo ID
	    ❑ A watch
	❑ Try to go outside for a few minutes and walk around before the test.
	❑ Most important: Stay calm and confident during the test. Take deep, slow breaths if you feel at all nervous. You can do it!

One-Month Cram Plan

4 weeks before the test	**Study Time:** 3 hours ❏ Take Diagnostic Test and review answer explanations. ❏ Note your errors. ❏ Based on your errors, identify difficult topics. These topics are your targeted topics. ❏ Read Test Format — Chapter VIII, Section A. ❏ Read Types of Questions – A Detailed Look – Chapter VIII, Section B. ❏ Reread the targeted topics.
3 weeks before the test	**Study Time:** 3 hours ❏ **Topic:** Test Strategies – Chapter VIII, Section C ❏ Review above section and gain experience reading historical, practical, and visual documents.

2 weeks before the test	**Study Time:** 1.5 hours
	❏ **Topic:** Comprehension Questions – Chapter VIII, Section B1
	   ❏ Read the section and spend extra time on your targeted topics.
	   ❏ Do the example questions.
	   ❏ Check the answer explanations.

7 days before the test	**Study Time:** 1.5 hours
	❏ **Topic:** Application Questions – Chapter VIII, Section B2
	   ❏ Read the section and spend extra time on your targeted topics.
	   ❏ Do the example questions.
	   ❏ Check the answer explanations.

6 days before the test	**Study Time:** 1.5 hours
	❏ **Topic:** Analysis Questions – Chapter VIII, Section B3
	   ❏ Read the section and spend extra time on your targeted topics.
	   ❏ Do the example questions.
	   ❏ Check the answer explanations.

5 days before the test	**Study Time:** 1.5 hours
	❏ **Topic:** Evaluation Questions – Chapter VIII, Section B4
	   ❏ Read the section and spend extra time on your targeted topics.
	   ❏ Do the example questions.
	   ❏ Check the answer explanations.

4 days before the test	**Study Time:** 2 hours ❏ Take the Full-Length Practice Test (Chapter XIII) and review your answers. Note those topics you still need to work on. These are your targeted topics.
3 days before the test	**Study Time:** 2 hours ❏ Practice Test Review ❏ Based on your errors on the Practice Test, identify difficult topics and their corresponding sections. Target these sections for extra review.
2 days before the test	**Study Time:** 1.5 hours ❏ **Topic:** Redo questions that you answered incorrectly on the Practice Test ❏ Check the answer explanations.

continued

1 day before the test	❏ Relax . . . you are well prepared for the test.
	❏ Have confidence in your ability to do well.
	❏ Exercise to help relieve stress and improve sleep.
Morning of the test	**Reminders:**
	❏ Have a good breakfast.
	❏ Take the following with you:
	❏ Your admission ticket and photo ID
	❏ A watch
	❏ Try to go outside for a few minutes and walk around before the test.
	❏ Most important: Stay calm and confident during the test. Take deep, slow breaths if you feel at all nervous. You can do it!

One-Week Cram Plan

7 days before the test	**Study Time:** 3 hours ❑ Take Diagnostic Test (Section 3) and review answer explanations. ❑ Note your errors. ❑ Based on your errors, identify difficult topics. These topics are your targeted topics.

6 days before the test	**Study Time:** 1.5 hours
	❑ **Topic:** Comprehension Questions – Chapter VIII, Section B1
	    ❑ Read the section and spend extra time on your targeted topics.
	    ❑ Do the example questions.
	    ❑ Check the answer explanations.

5 days before the test	**Study Time:** 1.5 hours
	❑ **Topic:** Application Questions – Chapter VIII, Section B2
	    ❑ Read the section and spend extra time on your targeted topics.
	    ❑ Do the example questions.
	    ❑ Check the answer explanations.

4 days before the test	**Study Time:** 1.5 hours
	❑ **Topic:** Analysis Questions – Chapter VIII, Section B3
	    ❑ Read the section and spend extra time on your targeted topics.
	    ❑ Do the example questions.
	    ❑ Check the answer explanations.

3 days before the test	**Study Time:** 1.5 hours
	❑ **Topic:** Evaluation Questions – Chapter VIII, Section B4
	    ❑ Read the section and spend extra time on your targeted topics.
	    ❑ Do the example questions.
	    ❑ Check the answer explanations.

2 days before the test	**Study Time:** 2 hours ❑ Take the Practice Test (Chapter XIII) and review your answer explanations. Note those topics you still need to work on. These are your targeted topics.
1 day before the test	**Study Time:** 1.5 hours ❑ Redo questions that you answered incorrectly on the Practice Test and check the answer explanations.
Night before the test	❑ Relax . . . you are well prepared for the test. ❑ Have confidence in your ability to do well. ❑ Exercise helps to relieve stress and improve sleep.

Morning of the test	**Reminders:**
	❑ Have a good breakfast.
	❑ Take the following with you:
	    ❑ Your admission ticket and photo ID
	    ❑ A watch
	❑ Try to go outside for a few minutes and walk around before the test.
	❑ Most important: Stay calm and confident during the test. Take deep, slow breaths if you feel at all nervous. You can do it!

IV. Science Cram Plans

Two-Month Cram Plan	
8 weeks before the test	**Study Time:** 3 hours ❑ Study vocabulary sections: Chapter IX, Sections C, D1g, D2g, and D3e. ❑ Make note of any terms that you have difficulty understanding and look them up for a fuller explanation. ❑ Take Diagnostic Test (Section 4) and review answer explanations. ❑ Note your errors. ❑ Based on your errors, identify difficult topics. These are your targeted topics.

7 weeks before the test	**Study Time:** 2 hours
	❑ **Topic:** Test Format – Chapter IX, Section A
	  ❑ Read for a general overview.
	❑ **Topic:** Types of Questions – Chapter IX, Section B
	  ❑ Review the material; do the examples.
	  ❑ Check the answer explanations.

6 weeks before the test	**Study Time:** 1.5 hours
	❑ **Topic:** Test Strategies — Chapter IX, Section C.
	  ❑ Read the section.
	❑ **Topic:** Physical Science – Chapter IX, Sections D1a to D1f
	  ❑ Read the material; do the examples.
	  ❑ Check the answer explanations.

5 weeks before the test	**Study Time:** 1.5 hours
	❑ **Topic:** Life Science – Chapter IX, Sections D2a to D2f
	  ❑ Read the material; do the examples.
	  ❑ Check the answer explanations.

4 weeks before the test	**Study Time:** 1 hour
	❑ **Topic:** Earth and Space Science – Chapter IX, Sections D3a to D3d
	  ❑ Read the material; do the examples.
	  ❑ Check the answer explanations.

3 weeks before the test	**Study Time:** 2 hours ❑ **Topic:** General review of targeted sections ❑ Review targeted sections of Chapter IX, paying particular attention to the vocabulary sections.
2 weeks before the test	**Study Time:** 2 hours ❑ Review any new words or terms you have added to the vocabulary sections — Chapter IX, Sections C, D1g, D2g, and D3e. ❑ Take the Practice Test (Chapter XIV) and review your answers. Note those topics that you still need to work on. These are your targeted topics.
7 days before the test	**Study Time:** 1 hour ❑ **Topic:** Physical Science – Chapter IX, Sections D1a to D1c ❑ Review the sections, paying particular attention to your target topics and any questions you had difficulty with.

continued

6 days before the test	**Study Time:** 1 hour ❑ **Topic:** Physical Science – Chapter IX, Sections D1d to D1f ❑ Review the sections, paying particular attention to your target topics and any questions you had difficulty with.
5 days before the test	**Study Time:** 1 hour ❑ **Topic:** Life Science – Chapter IX, Sections D2a to D2c ❑ Review the sections, paying particular attention to your target topics and any questions you had difficulty with.
4 days before the test	**Study Time:** 1 hour ❑ **Topic:** Life Science – Chapter IX, Sections D1d to D1f ❑ Review the sections, paying particular attention to your target topics and any questions you had difficulty with.
3 days before the test	**Study Time:** 1 hour ❑ **Topic:** Earth and Space Science – Chapter IX, Sections D3a and D3b ❑ Review the sections, paying particular attention to your target topics and any questions you had difficulty with.
2 days before the test	**Study Time:** 1 hour ❑ **Topic:** Earth and Space Science – Chapter IX, Sections D3c and D3d ❑ Review the sections paying particular attention to your target topics and any questions you had difficulty with.
1 day before the test	❑ Relax . . . you are well prepared for the test. ❑ Have confidence in your ability to do well. ❑ Exercise to help relieve stress and improve sleep.

Morning of the test	**Reminders:**
	❑ Have a good breakfast.
	❑ Take the following with you:
	  ❑ Your admission ticket and photo ID
	  ❑ A watch
	❑ Try to go outside for a few minutes and walk around before the test.
	❑ Most important: Stay calm and confident during the test. Take deep, slow breaths if you feel at all nervous. You can do it!

One-Month Cram Plan

4 weeks before the test	**Study Time:** 3 hours ❏ Study vocabulary sections: Chapter IX, Sections C, D1g, D2g, and D3e. ❏ Make note of any terms that you have difficulty understanding and look them up for a fuller explanation. ❏ Take Diagnostic Test (Section 4) and review answer explanations. ❏ Note your errors. ❏ Based on your errors, identify difficult topics. These are your targeted topics.

3 weeks before the test	**Study Time:** 1.5 hours
	❏ **Topic:** Test Format — Chapter IX, Section A
	  ❏ Read for a general overview.
	❏ **Topic:** Types of Questions – Chapter IX, Section B
	  ❏ Read to become familiar with the types of questions on the test.
	❏ **Topic:** Test Strategies – Chapter IX, Section C
	  ❏ Read the section.

2 weeks before the test	**Study Time:** 2 hours
	❏ **Topic:** Vocabulary — Chapter IX, Sections C, D1g, D2g, and D3e
	  ❏ Review vocabulary lists and add any words that you have found in your reading.
	❏ **Topic:** Physical Science — Chapter IX, Sections D1a to D1d
	  ❏ Review the sections, paying particular attention to your target topics and any questions you had difficulty with.

7 days before the test	**Study Time:** 2 hours ❏ **Topic:** Physical Science — Chapter IX, Sections D1e and D1f ❏ Review the sections, paying particular attention to your target topics and any questions you had difficulty with.
6 days before the test	**Study Time:** 2 hours ❏ **Topic:** Life Science — Chapter IX, Sections D2a to D2c ❏ Review the sections, paying particular attention to your target topics and any questions you had difficulty with.
5 days before the test	**Study Time:** 2 hours ❏ **Topic:** Life Science — Chapter IX, Sections D2d to D2f ❏ Review the sections, paying particular attention to your target topics and any questions you had difficulty with.
4 days before the test	**Study Time:** 2 hours ❏ **Topic:** Earth and Space Science — Chapter IX, Sections D3a to D3d ❏ Review the sections, paying particular attention to your target topics and any questions you had difficulty with.
3 days before the test	**Study Time:** 2 hours ❏ Review vocabulary sections, including any new words or terms you have added — Chapter IX, Sections C, D1g, D2g, and D3e. ❏ Take the Practice Test (Chapter XIV) and review your answers. Note those topics you still need to work on. These are your targeted topics.

continued

2 days before the test	**Study Time:** 1.5 hours ❑ **Topic:** Types of Questions: Chapter IX, Section B ❑ Reread the section carefully to ensure that you understand the range of questions that you may be asked.
1 day before the test	**Study Time:** 1 hour ❑ **Topic:** Vocabulary: Chapter IX, Sections C, D1g, D2g, and D3e ❑ Reread the vocabulary lists, including any terms that you've added. Make sure that you can use each word in a sentence.
Night before the test	❑ Relax . . . you are well prepared for the test. ❑ Have confidence in your ability to do well. ❑ Exercise to help relieve stress and improve sleep.

Morning of the test	**Reminders:**
	❑ Have a good breakfast.
	❑ Take the following with you:
	   ❑ Your admission ticket and photo ID
	   ❑ A watch
	❑ Try to go outside for a few minutes and walk around before the test.
	❑ Most important: Stay calm and confident during the test. Take deep, slow breaths if you feel at all nervous. You can do it!

One-Week Cram Plan

7 days before the test	**Study Time:** 3 hours ❏ Study vocabulary sections: Chapter IX, Sections C, D1g, D2g, and D3e. ❏ Make note of any terms that you have difficulty understanding and look them up for a fuller explanation. ❏ Take Diagnostic Test (Section 4) and review answer explanations. ❏ Note your errors. ❏ Based on your errors, identify difficult topics. These are your targeted topics.
6 days before the test	**Study Time:** 2 hours ❏ **Topic:** Physical Science – Chapter IX, Section D1 ❏ Review the section, paying particular attention to your target topics and any questions you had difficulty with.
5 days before the test	**Study Time:** 2 hours ❏ **Topic:** Life Science – Chapter IX, Section D2 ❏ Review the section, paying particular attention to your target topics and any questions you had difficulty with.
4 days before the test	**Study Time:** 1 hour ❏ **Topic:** Earth and Space Science – Chapter IX, Section D3 ❏ Review the section, paying particular attention to your target topics and any questions you had difficulty with.
3 days before the test	**Study Time:** 2 hours ❏ Review vocabulary sections, including any new words or terms you have added – Chapter IX, Sections C, D1g, D2g, and D3e. ❏ Take the Practice Test (Chapter XIV) and review your answers. Note those topics you still need to work on. These are your targeted topics.
2 days before the test	**Study Time:** 1 hour ❏ **Topic:** Types of Questions – Chapter IX, Section B ❏ Read to become familiar with the types of questions on the test.
1 day before the test	❏ Relax . . . you are well prepared for the test. ❏ Have confidence in your ability to do well. ❏ Exercise to help relieve stress and improve sleep.

Morning of the test	**Reminders:**
	❏ Have a good breakfast.
	❏ Take the following with you:
	    ❏ Your admission ticket and photo ID
	    ❏ A watch
	❏ Try to go outside for a few minutes and walk around before the test.
	❏ Most important: Stay calm and confident during the test. Take deep, slow breaths if you feel at all nervous. You can do it!

V. Language Arts, Reading Cram Plans

Two-Month Cram Plan	
8 weeks before the test	**Study Time:** 2 hours ❑ Take Diagnostic Test (Section 5) and review answer explanations. ❑ Note your errors. ❑ Based on your errors, identify difficult topics. These topics are your targeted topics.
7 weeks before the test	**Study Time:** 2 hours ❑ **Topic:** Test Format – Chapter X, Section A ❑ **Topic:** Test Strategies – Chapter X, Section C ❑ Review above sections and gain experience reading fiction and nonfiction literary passages.

6 weeks before the test	**Study Time:** 1.5 hours
	❑ **Topic:** Types of Questions – A Detailed Look – Chapter X, Section B
	  ❑ Do the example questions.
	  ❑ Check the answer explanations.
	  ❑ Reread the targeted topics and figure out why you had difficulty with them.

5 weeks before the test	**Study Time:** 1.5 hours
	❑ **Topic:** Comprehension – Chapter X, Section B1
	  ❑ Read the material and do the examples.
	  ❑ Check the answer explanations.

4 weeks before the test	**Study Time:** 1.5 hours
	❑ **Topic:** Application – Chapter X, Section B2
	  ❑ Read the material and do the examples.
	  ❑ Check the answer explanations.

3 weeks before the test	**Study Time:** 1.5 hours
	❑ **Topic:** Analysis – Chapter X, Section B3
	  ❑ Read the material and do the examples.
	  ❑ Check the answer explanations.

2 weeks before the test	**Study Time:** 1.5 hours
	❑ **Topic:** Synthesis – Chapter X, Section B4
	  ❑ Read the material and do the examples.
	  ❑ Check the answer explanations.

7 days before the test	**Study Time:** 1.5 hours ❑ Take the Full-Length Practice Test (Chapter XV) and review your answers. ❑ Based on your errors on the Practice Test, identify difficult topics and their corresponding sections. Target these sections for extra review.

6 days before the test	**Study Time:** 1 hour
	❑ **Topic:** Comprehension — Chapter X, Section B1
	  ❑ Review example questions, paying special attention to those in error the first time you did them.
	  ❑ Based on your errors on the Practice Test, identify difficult topics and their corresponding sections. Target these sections for extra review.

continued

5 days before the test	**Study Time:** 1 hour
	❏ **Topic:** Application — Chapter X, Section B2
	    ❏ Review example questions, paying special attention to those in error the first time you did them.
	    ❏ Based on your errors on the Practice Test, identify difficult topics and their corresponding sections. Target these sections for extra review.

4 days before the test	**Study Time:** 1 hour
	❏ **Topic:** Analysis — Chapter X, Section B3
	    ❏ Review example questions, paying special attention to those in error the first time you did them.
	    ❏ Based on your errors on the Practice Test, identify difficult topics and their corresponding sections. Target these sections for extra review.

3 days before the test	**Study Time:** 1 hour
	❏ **Topic:** Synthesis — Chapter X, Section B4
	    ❏ Review example questions, paying special attention to those in error the first time you did them.
	    ❏ Based on your errors on the Practice Test, identify difficult topics and their corresponding sections. Target these sections for extra review.

2 days before the test	**Study Time:** 2 hours ❏ Practice Test review ❏ Based on your errors on the Practice Test, identify difficult topics and their corresponding sections. Target these sections for extra review.
1 day before the test	❏ Relax . . . you are well prepared for the test. ❏ Have confidence in your ability to do well. ❏ Exercise to help relieve stress and improve sleep.

Morning of the test	**Reminders:**
	❏ Have a good breakfast.
	❏ Take the following with you:
	    ❏ Your admission ticket and photo ID
	    ❏ A watch
	❏ Try to go outside for a few minutes and walk around before the test.
	❏ Most important: Stay calm and confident during the test. Take deep, slow breaths if you feel at all nervous. You can do it!

One-Month Cram Plan	
4 weeks before the test	**Study Time:** 2.5 hours ❑ Take Diagnostic Test (Section 5) and review answer explanations. ❑ Note your errors. ❑ Based on your errors, identify difficult topics. These topics are your targeted topics. ❑ Read Test Format – Chapter X, Section A. ❑ Read Types of Questions – A Detailed Look – Chapter X, Section B. ❑ Reread the targeted topics.
3 weeks before the test	**Study Time:** 3 hours ❑ **Topic:** Test Strategies – Chapter X, Section C. ❑ Review above section and gain experience reading fiction and nonfiction literary passages

2 weeks before the test	**Study Time:** 1.5 hour
	❑ **Topic:** Comprehension – Chapter X, Section B1
	  ❑ Read the section and spend extra time on your targeted topics.
	  ❑ Do the example questions.
	  ❑ Check the answer explanations.

7 days before the test	**Study Time:** 1.5 hours
	❑ **Topic:** Application – Chapter X, Section B2
	  ❑ Read the section and spend extra time on your targeted topics.
	  ❑ Do the example questions.
	  ❑ Check the answer explanations.

6 days before the test	**Study Time:** 1.5 hours
	❑ **Topic:** Analysis – Chapter X, Section
	  ❑ Read the section and spend extra time on your targeted topics.
	  ❑ Do the example questions.
	  ❑ Check the answer explanations.

5 days before the test	**Study Time:** 1.5 hours
	❑ **Topic:** Synthesis – Chapter X, Section B4
	  ❑ Read the section and spend extra time on your targeted topics.
	  ❑ Do the example questions.
	  ❑ Check the answer explanations.

4 days before the test	**Study Time:** 2 hours ❑ Take the Practice Test (Chapter XV) and review your answers. Note those topics you still need to work on. These are your targeted topics.
3 days before the test	**Study Time:** 2 hours ❑ Practice Test review ❑ Based on errors on the Practice Test, identify difficult topics and their corresponding sections. Target those sections for extra review.
2 days before the test	**Study Time:** 1.5 hours ❑ **Topic:** Redo questions that you answered incorrectly on the Practice Test ❑ Check the answer explanations

continued

1 day before the test	❏ Relax . . . you are well prepared for the test. ❏ Have confidence in your ability to do well. ❏ Exercise to help relieve stress and improve sleep.

Morning of the test	**Reminders:**
	❏ Have a good breakfast.
	❏ Take the following with you:
	    ❏ Your admission ticket and photo ID
	    ❏ A watch
	❏ Try to go outside for a few minutes and walk around before the test.
	❏ Most important: Stay calm and confident during the test. Take deep, slow breaths if you feel at all nervous. You can do it!

One-Week Cram Plan	
7 days before the test	**Study Time:** 2 hours ❑ Take Diagnostic Test (Section 5) and review answer explanations. ❑ Note your errors. ❑ Based on your errors, identify difficult topics. These topics are your targeted topics.

6 days before the test	❑ **Study Time:** 1.5 hours
	❑ **Topic:** Comprehension – Chapter X, Section B1
	    ❑ Read the section and spend extra time on your targeted topics.
	    ❑ Do the example questions.
	    ❑ Check the answer explanations.

5 days before the test	**Study Time:** 1.5 hours
	❑ **Topic:** Application – Chapter X, Section B2
	    ❑ Read the section and spend extra time on your targeted topics.
	    ❑ Do the example questions.
	    ❑ Check the answer explanations.

4 days before the test	**Study Time:** 1.5 hours
	❑ **Topic:** Analysis – Chapter X, Section B3
	    ❑ Read the section and spend extra time on your targeted topics.
	    ❑ Do the example questions.
	    ❑ Check the answer explanations.

3 days before the test	**Study Time:** 1.5 hours
	❑ **Topic:** Synthesis – Chapter X, Section B4
	    ❑ Read the section and spend extra time on your targeted topics.
	    ❑ Do the example questions.
	    ❑ Check the answer explanations.

2 days before the test	**Study Time:** 2 hours ❑ Take the Practice Test (Chapter XV) and review your answer explanations. Note those topics you still need to work on. These are your targeted topics.
1 day before the test	**Study Time:** 1.5 hours ❑ Redo questions that you answered incorrectly on the Practice Test and check the answer explanations.
Night before the test	❑ Relax . . . you are well prepared for the test. ❑ Have confidence in your ability to do well. ❑ Exercise to help relieve stress and improve sleep.

Morning of the test	**Reminders:**
	❑ Have a good breakfast.
	❑ Take the following with you:
	    ❑ Your admission ticket and photo ID
	    ❑ A watch
	❑ Try to go outside for a few minutes and walk around before the test.
	❑ Most important: Stay calm and confident during the test. Take deep, slow breaths if you feel at all nervous. You can do it!

VI. Mathematics Cram Plans

	Two-Month Cram Plan
8 weeks before the test	**Study Time:** 3 hours ❏ Take Diagnostic Test (Section 6) and review answer explanations. ❏ Note your errors. ❏ Based on your errors, identify difficult topics. These topics are your targeted topics. ❏ Read Test Format – Chapter XI, Section A.

7 weeks before the test	**Study Time:** 3 hours
	❏ **Topic:** Types of Questions – A Detailed Look – Chapter XI, Section B
	  ❏ Do the example problems.
	  ❏ Check the answer explanations.
	  ❏ Reread the targeted topics and figure out why you had difficulty with them.

6 weeks before the test	**Study Time:** 3 hours
	❏ **Topic:** Review Test Strategies – Chapter XI, Section C
	❏ **Topic:** Begin Math Review: Read introduction – Chapter XI, Section D
	❏ **Topic:** Number Operations and Number Sense – Chapter XI, Sections D1a to D1d
	  ❏ Read the sections and spend extra time on your targeted topics.
	  ❏ Do the example problems.
	  ❏ Check the answer explanations.

5 weeks before the test	**Study Time:** 3 hours
	❏ **Topic:** Number Operations and Number Sense – Chapter XI, Sections D1e to D1m
	  ❏ Read the sections and spend extra time on your targeted topics.
	  ❏ Do the example problems.
	  ❏ Check the answer explanations.

4 weeks before the test	**Study Time:** 2 hours
	❏ **Topic:** Measurement and Geometry – Chapter XI, Sections D2a to D2f
	  ❏ Read the sections and spend extra time on your targeted topics.
	  ❏ Do the example problems.
	  ❏ Check the answer explanations.

3 weeks before the test	**Study Time:** 1 hour
	❏ **Topic:** Data Analysis, Statistics, and Probability – Chapter XI, Sections D3a and D3b
	  ❏ Read the sections and spend extra time on your targeted topics.
	  ❏ Do the example problems.
	  ❏ Check the answer explanations.

2 weeks before the test	**Study Time:** 1 hour
	❏ **Topic:** Algebra, Functions, and Patterns – Chapter XI, Sections D4a to D4g
	  ❏ Read the sections and spend extra time on your targeted topics.
	  ❏ Do the example problems.
	  ❏ Check the answer explanations.

continued

7 days before the test	**Study Time:** 2.5 hours ❏ Take the Practice Test (Chapter XVI) and review your answers. ❏ Based on your errors on the Practice Test, identify difficult topics and their corresponding sections. Target these sections for extra review.

6 days before the test	**Study Time:** 1.5 hours
	❏ **Topic:** Number Operations and Number Sense – Chapter XI, Sections D1a to D1d
	    ❏ Review example problems, paying special attention to those in error the first time you did them.
	    ❏ Based on your errors on the Practice Test, identify difficult topics and their corresponding sections. Target these sections for extra review.

5 days before the test	**Study Time:** 1.5 hours
	❏ **Topic:** Number Operations and Number Sense – Chapter XI, Sections D1e to D1m
	    ❏ Review example problems, paying special attention to those in error the first time you did them.
	    ❏ Based on your errors on the Practice Test, identify difficult topics and their corresponding sections. Target these sections for extra review.

4 days before the test	**Study Time:** 1.5 hours
	❏ **Topic:** Measurement and Geometry – Chapter XI, Sections D2a to D2f
	    ❏ Review example problems, paying special attention to those in error the first time you did them.
	    ❏ Based on your errors on the Practice Test, identify difficult topics and their corresponding sections. Target these sections for extra review.

3 days before the test	**Study Time:** 1 hour
	❏ **Topic:** Data Analysis, Statistics, and Probability – Chapter XI, Sections D3a and D3b
	    ❏ Review example problems, paying special attention to those in error the first time you did them.
	    ❏ Based on your errors on the Practice Test, identify difficult topics and their corresponding sections. Target these sections for extra review.

2 days before the test	**Study Time:** 1 hour
	❏ **Topic:** Algebra. Functions, and Patterns – Chapter XI, Sections D4a to D4g
	    ❏ Review example problems, paying special attention to those in error the first time you did them.
	    ❏ Based on your errors on the Practice Test, identify difficult topics and their corresponding sections. Target these sections for extra review.

1 day before the test	❏ Relax . . . you are well prepared for the test. ❏ Have confidence in your ability to do well. ❏ Exercise to help relieve stress and improve sleep.

Morning of the test	**Reminders:**
	❏ Have a good breakfast.
	❏ Take the following with you:
	    ❏ Your admission ticket and photo ID
	    ❏ A watch
	❏ Try to go outside for a few minutes and walk around before the test.
	❏ Most important: Stay calm and confident during the test. Take deep, slow breaths if you feel at all nervous. You can do it!

One-Month Cram Plan	
4 weeks before the test	**Study Time:** 3 hours ❏ Take Diagnostic Test (Section 6) and review answer explanations. ❏ Note your errors. ❏ Based on your errors, identify difficult topics. These topics are your targeted topics. ❏ Read Test Format – Chapter XI, Section A. ❏ Read Types of Questions – A Detailed Look – Chapter XI, Section B. ❏ Reread the targeted topics.

3 weeks before the test	**Study Time:** 3 hours
	❏ **Topic:** Number Operations and Number Sense – Chapter XI, Sections D1a to D1g
	  ❏ Read the sections and spend extra time on your targeted topics.
	  ❏ Do the example problems.
	  ❏ Check the answer explanations.

2 weeks before the test	**Study Time:** 3 hours
	❏ **Topic:** Number Operations and Number Sense – Chapter XI, Sections D1h to D1m
	  ❏ Read the sections and spend extra time on your targeted topics.
	  ❏ Do the example problems.
	  ❏ Check the answer explanations.

7 days before the test	**Study Time:** 1 hour
	❏ **Topic:** Measurement and Geometry – Chapter XI, Sections D2a to D2d
	  ❏ Read the sections and spend extra time on your targeted topics.
	  ❏ Do the example problems.
	  ❏ Check the answer explanations.

6 days before the test	**Study Time:** 1 hour
	❏ **Topic:** Measurement and Geometry – Chapter XI, Sections D2e and D2f
	  ❏ Read the sections and spend extra time on your targeted topics.
	  ❏ Do the example problems.
	  ❏ Check the answer explanations.

5 days before the test	**Study Time:** 1 hour
	❏ **Topic:** Data Analysis, Statistics, and Probability – Chapter XI, Sections D3a and D3b
	  ❏ Read the sections and spend extra time on your targeted topics.
	  ❏ Do the example problems.
	  ❏ Check the answer explanations.

4 days before the test	**Study Time:** 1 hour
	❏ **Topic:** Algebra, Functions, and Patterns – Chapter XI, Sections D4a to D4g
	  ❏ Read the sections and spend extra time on your targeted topics.
	  ❏ Do the example problems.
	  ❏ Check the answer explanations.

3 days before the test	**Study Time:** 2 hours ❏ Take the Practice Test (Chapter XVI) and review your answers. Note those topics you still need to work on. These are your targeted topics.
2 days before the test	**Study Time:** 1.5 hours ❏ **Topic:** Redo questions that you answered incorrectly on the Practice Test. ❏ Check the answer explanations.

continued

1 day before the test	❏ Relax . . . you are well prepared for the test. ❏ Have confidence in your ability to do well. ❏ Exercise to help relieve stress and improve sleep.

Morning of the test	**Reminders:**
	 ❏ Have a good breakfast.
	 ❏ Take the following with you:
	     ❏ Your admission ticket and photo ID
	     ❏ A watch
	 ❏ Try to go outside for a few minutes and walk around before the test.
	 ❏ Most important: Stay calm and confident during the test. Take deep, slow breaths if you feel at all nervous. You can do it!

One-Week Cram Plan	
7 days before the test	**Study Time:** 2.5 hours ❏ Take Diagnostic Test (Section 6) and review answer explanations. ❏ Note your errors. ❏ Based on your errors, identify difficult topics. These topics are your targeted topics.

6 days before the test	**Study Time:** 3 hours
	❏ **Topic:** Number Operations and Number Sense – Chapter XI, Section D1
	    ❏ Read the section and spend extra time on your targeted topics.
	    ❏ Do the example problems.
	    ❏ Check the answer explanations.

5 days before the test	**Study Time:** 3 hours
	Topic: Measurement and Geometry – Chapter XI, Section D2
	    ❏ Read the section and spend extra time on your targeted topics.
	    ❏ Do the example problems.
	    ❏ Check the answer explanations.

4 days before the test	**Study Time:** 1 hour
	Topic: Data Analysis, Statistics, and Probability – Chapter XI, Section D3
	    ❏ Read the section and spend extra time on your targeted topics.
	    ❏ Do the example problems.
	    ❏ Check the answer explanations.

3 days before the test	**Study Time:** 1 hour
	Topic: Algebra, Functions, and Patterns – Chapter XI, Section D4
	    ❏ Read the section and spend extra time on your targeted topics.
	    ❏ Do the example problems.
	    ❏ Check the answer explanations.

2 days before the test	**Study Time:** 2 hours ❏ Take the Pracvtice Test (Chapter XVI) and review your answer explanations. Note those topics you still need to work on. These are your targeted topics.
1 day before the test	**Study Time:** 1.5 hours ❏ Redo questions that you answered incorrectly on the Practice Test and check the answer explanations.
Night before the test	❏ Relax . . . you are well prepared for the test. ❏ Have confidence in your ability to do well. ❏ Exercise to help relieve stress and improve sleep.

Morning of the test	**Reminders:**
	❏ Have a good breakfast.
	❏ Take the following with you:
	    ❏ Your admission ticket and photo ID
	    ❏ A watch
	❏ Try to go outside for a few minutes and walk around before the test.
	❏ Most important: Stay calm and confident during the test. Take deep, slow breaths if you feel at all nervous. You can do it!

VII. Language Arts, Writing

A. Test Format

The Language Arts, Writing Test measures your ability to use clear and effective English. It is a test of English as it should be written, not as it may be spoken. The Writing Test consists of two parts. Part I has 50 multiple-choice questions to be completed in 75 minutes; these questions test your ability to edit and revise workplace and informational documents. As soon as you complete Part I, you may begin working on Part II.

Part II requires you to write a short essay on an assigned topic. You're asked to present an opinion or an explanation regarding topics that are potentially interesting and meaningful. You have 45 minutes to complete the essay. You are required to write your essay on two lined pages in the answer booklet. Scratch paper is provided for prewriting and drafting. Only the writing on the two pages in the answer booklet will be considered by the scorers.

Scores on both parts are combined to produce a single Language Arts, Writing score.

1. Part I

The 50 multiple-choice questions in Part I of the Language Arts, Writing Test are divided into four sections:

- **Organization:** 7 to 8 questions, or 15 percent
- **Sentence structure:** 15 questions, or 30 percent
- **Usage:** 15 questions, or 30 percent
- **Mechanics:** 12 to 13 questions, 25 percent

2. Part II

The essay portion of the Language Arts, Writing Test, encompasses the following areas:

- Writing
- Editing

B. Types of Questions—A Detailed Look

1. Part I

The four types of multiple-choice questions on the Language Arts test are detailed below, with examples.

a. Organization

Organization questions require you to edit and revise a document by adding, removing, or repositioning sentences. Skills tested include

- Forming new paragraphs as required
- Combining paragraphs to improve documents
- Effective topic sentences and unity/coherence throughout

EXAMPLES:

In the following paragraph, which sentence does NOT belong?

(1) Since 1974, Can-Learn Study Tours has partnered with universities, colleges, school districts, voluntary organizations, and businesses. (2) They provide educational travel programs that meet the needs of their staff and clientele. (3) Financial incentives are important to the bottom line. (4) The programs explore artistic, cultural, historic, and environmental interests. (5) Professional development activities enhance international understanding and boost creativity.

- **(1)** Sentence (1)
- **(2)** Sentence (2)
- **(3)** Sentence (3)
- **(4)** Sentence (4)
- **(5)** Sentence (5)

The correct answer is **(3).** Sentence (3) does not relate to the general theme of educational travel programs and should be deleted from the paragraph.

In the following example, choose a topic sentence with which to begin the following paragraph:

GED is an international testing program for adults who have been unable to complete high school. The tests cover what high school graduates are supposed to know about writing, science, mathematics, social studies, and literature and the arts. They also measure reading comprehension, analytical abilities, writing ability, and other important skills. Since 1942, millions of adults have earned GED diplomas. The GED program is jointly sponsored by the American Council on Education and state, territorial, and provincial departments of education. GED is the acronym for General Educational Development, a testing service for adult high school equivalency.

> Which sentence in the above passage should logically *begin* the paragraph?
>
> **(1)** The tests cover what high school graduates are supposed to know about writing, science, mathematics, social studies, and literature and the arts.
>
> **(2)** The GED program is jointly sponsored by the American Council on Education and state, territorial, and provincial departments of education.
>
> **(3)** Since 1942, millions of adults have earned GED diplomas.
>
> **(4)** GED is the acronym for General Educational Development, a testing service for adult high school equivalency.
>
> **(5)** They also measure reading comprehension, analytical abilities, writing ability, and other important skills.

The correct answer is **(4).** To improve this paragraph, the sentences need to be reorganized in a logical order beginning with sentence (4).

In the following example, place the sentences in logical order.

(1) They are supposed to save trees by using air to dry your hands but the air is heated. (2) Perhaps the only solution is to leave with wet hands and let nature do the drying. (3) Most paper towels today are made from recycled paper and are a long distance from the original trees. (4) Hot-air hand dryers are a scam. (5) Heated air requires energy, and producing energy has a carbon footprint.

> A logical order for these sentences would be
>
> **(1)** 1, 2, 3, 4, 5
> **(2)** 2, 4, 5, 3, 1
> **(3)** 3, 5, 1, 4, 2
> **(4)** 4, 1, 5, 3, 2
> **(5)** 5, 2, 1, 4, 3

The correct answer is **(4).** The best introductory sentence is number 4 and should be the first sentence in the paragraph. This sentence is logically followed by sentence 1. The most logical final sentence is 2. If you look carefully at the answers, after deciding that the most logical introductory sentence is 4, there is only one answer that can be chosen.

b. Sentence Structure

Sentence structure errors involve sentence fragments, comma splices, run-on sentences, improper coordination, improper subordination, dangling modifiers, parallelism, and interrupting phrases.

i. Sentence Fragments

Sentence fragments are the most common sentence structure errors. For example:

John leaving his keys on the coffee table.

This sentence has a subject but not a proper verb. A corrected version is

John left his keys on the coffee table.

Here is another example:

Where the ball? I threw it to you.

The first sentence has no verb. A corrected version is

Where is the ball? I threw it to you.

Here is one more example:

Can't you do right?

This sentence has no object and thus we are not sure what the person spoken to is not doing correctly. A corrected version is

Can't you do anything right?

ii. Comma Splices

Another type of error is a **comma splice.** A comma splice occurs when two independent clauses are joined by a comma rather than a conjunction, a semicolon, or a period. For example:

Peter left the house, he slammed the door.

Some corrected versions are

Peter left the house. He slammed the door.
Peter left the house; he slammed the door.
Peter left the house and slammed the door.

Here is another example:

I turned the key, nothing happened.

Some corrected versions are

> I turned the key. Nothing happened.
> I turned the key; nothing happened.
> I turned the key, but nothing happened.

Here is one more example:

> It was freezing in the kitchen, the windows were all closed.

A corrected version is

> It was freezing in the kitchen even though the windows were all closed.

iii. Run-On Sentences

In a **run-on sentence,** two or more independent clauses (complete sentences) are joined but the necessary conjunction or punctuation is left out. For example:

> John forgot his keys he left them on the coffee table.

Some corrected versions are

> John forgot his keys; he left them on the coffee table.
> John forgot his keys. He left them on the coffee table.

Here is another example:

> I've told you a thousand times, don't exaggerate.

Some corrected versions are

> I've told you a thousand times; don't exaggerate.
> I've told you a thousand times. Don't exaggerate.

Here is one more example:

> Why don't you start your homework, we have to leave early tomorrow?

A corrected version is

> Why don't you start your homework? We have to leave early tomorrow.

iv. Improper Coordination

Improper coordination involves a conjunction error. For example:

> John forgot his keys but left them on the coffee table.

And is used to indicate a continuation of action. A corrected version is

> John forgot his keys and left them on the coffee table.

Here is another example:

> I turned left at the sign although I saw nothing of the trail.

Although is normally used at the beginning of a sentence. *And* indicates a continuation of the action. A corrected version is

> I turned left at the sign and saw nothing of the trail.

Here is one more example:

> Turn off the radio while I can't hear you.

While usually indicates something to do with time. *Because* indicates causality. A corrected version is

> Turn off the radio because I can't hear you.

v. Improper Subordination

Improper subordination involves a subordinating conjunction error. (Some subordinating conjunctions are *after, before, because, since, when,* and *because.*) For example:

> John forgot his car keys when he locked the car.

A corrected version is

> When John locked the car, he forgot his car keys.

Here is another example:

> The dog ran away when I was delayed.

A corrected version is

> When I was delayed, the dog ran away.

Here is one more example:

> The sun had come up before I could start the car.

A corrected version is

> Before I could start the car, the sun had come up.

vi. Dangling Modifiers

Another type of error is the **dangling modifier.** For example:

Having left his keys on the coffee table, the car could not start.

This sentence seems as though "the car" left his keys on the coffee table. A corrected version is

John could not drive his car because he left his keys on the coffee table.

Here is another example:

Barking and running around, my ears hurt from the dog barking

The sentence seems to imply that his ears were barking and running around. A corrected version is

My ears hurt from the dog barking and running around.

Here is one more example:

Falling and piling up on the road my neighbor is complaining about the leaves.

The neighbor is not falling and piling up on the road. A corrected version is

My neighbor is complaining about the leaves falling and piling up on the road.

vii. Parallelism Errors

A **parallelism** error involves two unparallel verbs in the same sentence. For example:

Leaving his keys on the coffee table and having left his wallet in the bedroom, John could not drive his car.

The verbs *leaving* and *have left* are unparallel. A corrected version is:

Having left his keys on the coffee table and his wallet in the bedroom, John could not drive his car.

Here is another example:

Leaving dishes in the sink and having washed them once a week, left the kitchen looking messy.

The verbs *leaving* and *having washed* are unparallel. A corrected version is

Leaving dishes in the sink and washing them once a week left the kitchen looking messy.

Here is one more example:

Looking up the material in several reference books and having written new paragraphs took a lot of time.

Looking up and *having written* are unparallel. A corrected version is

Looking up material in several reference books and writing new paragraphs took a lot of time.

viii. Interrupting Phrases

Any phrase that interrupts the flow of the sentence should be omitted. If the thought is important, it can be restated as a complete sentence. For example:

This music is fantastic—don't you know—and everybody enjoys dancing to it.

The phrase *don't you know* is not needed in this sentence and interrupts the flow.

c. Usage

i. Subject-Verb Agreement

Usage errors may involve subject/verb agreement, verb tense errors, and pronoun agreement errors. Here's an example of a **subject/verb** error:

John and Mary is going to the movies.

The plural subject *John and Mary* requires a plural verb. A corrected version is

John and Mary are going to the movies.

ii. Verb Tense Errors

A **verb tense** error involves using a tense that is not the same as the other verb tenses in the sentence or paragraph. For example:

Peter gets up early, ate his breakfast, and leaves for school.

In this case both *gets* and *leaves* are present tense, while *ate* is past tense. A corrected version is

Peter gets up early, eats his breakfast, and leaves for school.

iii. Pronoun Reference Errors

Pronoun reference errors consist of agreement with antecedents, incorrect relative pronouns, pronoun shift, vague or ambiguous references,

Agreement with antecedents—A pronoun should agree with its antecedent (the noun it refers to). For example:

The players went to the game, and he was the first to leave.

In this case, *players* (the antecedent) is plural, while *he* (the pronoun) is singular. A corrected version is

The players went to the game, and they were the first to leave.

Another example:

Everyone in class was busy reading their material.

Everyone is singular and cannot be followed by the plural pronoun *their*. *Their* should be changed to *his* or *her*.

> Everyone in class was busy reading his material.

Incorrect relative pronouns—Another pronoun reference error involves the incorrect usage of the relative pronoun. The relative pronouns are *who, whom, whose, which, what,* and *that*. For example:

> My brother, which lives in New York, is an engineer.

In this case, the pronoun *which* (used for inanimate objects) should be replaced with the pronoun *who* (used for people). A corrected version is

> My brother, who lives in New York, is an engineer.

Pronoun shift—Pronoun use should be consistent throughout a sentence. For example:

> The teacher gave us a lot of examples to make sure that you could learn about this topic.

In this sentence, the pronouns shift from first person, *us,* to second person, *you.* When you are writing sentences, ensure that your pronouns are consistent. A corrected version is

> The teacher gave us a lot of examples to make sure that we could learn about this topic.

Vague or ambiguous references—A pronoun should refer to a specific noun and not leave the reader wondering what was going on. For example:

> Harry, Joe, and Mohammed went to get ice cream cones and by the look on his face you could tell he was really enjoying the treat.

The two pronouns, *his* and *he,* could refer to any one of the three people named, which is ambiguous and confusing to a reader. A corrected version is

> Harry, Joe, and Mohammed went to get ice cream cones, and by the look on Joe's face you could tell he was really enjoying the treat.

d. Mechanics

Mechanics problems may include capitalization, punctuation, or spelling errors.

i. Capitalization

Capitalization questions require that you understand the correct use of lowercase and capital letters with dates, places, times, titles, proper nouns, and adjectives. How can the following passage be corrected?

> I am pleased to comment on the relationship of our organization to Peta Jackson of the York Square employment Resource center (ERC). Since April 2002, the beatrice institute of technology has partnered with the York Square erc in recruiting candidate for our cafe equipment technician training programs.

To correct this passage, all proper nouns should be capitalized as follows:

> I am pleased to comment on the relationship of our organization to Peta Jackson of the York Square Employment Resource Center (ERC). Since April 2002, the Beatrice Institute of Technology has partnered with the York Square ERC recruiting candidates for our Cafe Equipment Technician training programs.

ii. Punctuation

Punctuation questions cover all kinds of punctuation but especially the use of commas and colons. The comma is used to separate a series of three or more words, phrases, or clauses. The colon is used before a list of items or details.

How can the following sentence be improved?

> These programs have included educational travel programs, which explore the following artistic and cultural interests historic and archaeological themes environmental and wellness experiences and new service patterns.

The sentence can be corrected as follows:

> These programs have included educational travel programs, which explore the following: artistic and cultural interests, historic and archaeological themes, environmental and wellness experiences, and new service patterns.

iii. Spelling

Spelling errors may involve the spelling of possessives, contractions, and *homonyms* (sound-alike words).

Possessives—Possessives show ownership. For example, what change should be made to the following sentence?

> This is an opportunity for adults, who have learned in informal as well as formal venues, to document and assesses there prior learning.

To correct the spelling error, *there* should be replaced by *their*. *Their* is a possessive pronoun (showing belonging) and is required in this sentence.

Contractions—Contractions combine two words, leaving out a letter or letters and replacing them with an apostrophe. How would you correct the following sentence?

> Thank you for you're interest in our new company, which serves the rapidly expanding specialty coffee industry.

To correct this sentence, change *you're* (which means *you are*) to *your*. The pronoun *your* indicates ownership of the new company.

Homonyms—Homonyms are sound-alike words. They may be contractions or possessives, as mentioned earlier, or they may be other words that sound like one another but have different spellings and meanings. For example:

X   This will generate more then $1,000,000.

The correct word to use in this sentence is *than. Than* is used for comparisons, while *then* refers to time sequences. Because this sentence needs a word that indicates a comparison, *than* is the correct answer.

2. Part II

For Part II, your writing and editing skills are tested. Below, we detail the steps to writing and editing an essay, followed by some suggestions for practicing for this portion of the test.

a. Writing

i. Steps to Writing a Passing Essay

1. Read the topic carefully. No credit is given for an essay written on another topic.
2. Plan the main points of the essay: an introduction, the main points, and a conclusion. The main points may need more than one paragraph.
3. Organize the material so it flows from beginning to end.
4. Make sure that the statement of purpose of the essay is contained in the introductory sentence of the first paragraph.
5. Turn the main points into sentences.
6. Reread paragraphs for continuity.
7. Revise material as needed to make sure it's on the topic.
8. Write the final essay.
9. Edit for mistakes in spelling and grammar.

ii. Essay Structure

An effective essay should be organized, with effective text divisions and topic sentences. Your writing also should demonstrate unity and coherence.

Organization—One of the most important aspects of any essay is the organization of the ideas and the sentences that express those ideas. Once you have a list of main points, you have to decide on the order of ideas and which ideas belong together. Putting related ideas together makes dividing the essay into paragraphs a lot easier.

Effective text divisions—Your essay should be divided into paragraphs.

The **first paragraph** is the introduction and should tell the reader what the essay is going to be about. In addition, it should catch the interest of the reader and make them want to read the essay. This can be the hardest paragraph to write and deserves the most attention.

The **last paragraph** is the summary. This should sum up what was said or restate the point of view of the essay. It is the last paragraph to write because you have to know what you're going to summarize.

The **remaining paragraphs** should each contain one main thought and start with an introductory sentence and finish with a summary sentence, which flows into the first sentence of the next paragraph.

Forming new paragraphs—As you look at your rough material for the essay, join material that belongs together. You can do this by numbering the ideas or drawing boxes around related ideas or anything that is quick and keeps related ideas together. Each idea forms the basis for one or more paragraphs. From this point, having decided on the idea that should form the basis for your paragraph, you should write the introductory sentence. Your subpoints can now be put in order so that they flow and advance the topic of your essay. Once this is done, you can write your summary sentence and turn your subpoints into sentences.

Topic sentences—Each paragraph should begin with a topic sentence. It states the main point of the paragraph and draws the reader into the material. Topic sentences have to be the most interesting sentence in the paragraph because they set the tone and define the topic of the paragraph.

Unity and coherence—A good essay is understandable and written about a single topic. If you're asked to write an essay about your favorite animal and you choose a Labrador Retriever, no matter how much you know about elephants, you can't write about them in this essay. Your essay about only Labrador Retrievers as pets would have unity, and if you wrote it in an understandable manner, it would have coherence or consistency. But if you interjected information about elephants into your Labrador Retriever essay, your essay would be disjointed.

b. Editing

After you write an essay or any other document, you come to the most important part of the job: editing. The following steps will help you edit your essay into an even better piece of work.

i. Adding

Read through your essay and your rough notes. Decide if there is any information you should add. The important consideration at this point is whether this additional information will improve the essay. If the information will improve your essay, include it. If not, leave it where it is.

ii. Removing

Would your essay be improved by removing any information, words, or sentences? If there are facts that do not relate to the subject of your essay, leave them out. Your essay should be about one topic and only one topic. If there is anything in the essay about another topic or something that does not add to your essay, leave it out.

[handwritten: Home work write the 71st Topic]

iii. Repositioning

Each paragraph of an essay should flow from beginning to end and the essay itself should flow from beginning to end. If there are sentences that restrict this flow of ideas and are necessary to make the point of the essay, consider moving them. Ask yourself if there is a place in the essay where this sentence would add to the smooth flow of the paragraph. As a final check, make sure that each paragraph aids the smooth flow of ideas from beginning to end. There is nothing wrong with moving words, sentences, or paragraphs to improve the essay.

c. Practice

For practice, write an essay on one of the following topics using the plan suggested above:

- What have you learned from your experiences in the past that should help you in the future? *[handwritten: Finances]*
- How can the education system be improved to better prepare students for life?
- How can we protect the world from the effects of global warming?

When you've completed your essay, you (or a friend) should check it over using the following questions:

- Does the essay focus on the assigned topic?
- Is the statement of purpose of the essay contained in the introductory sentence and paragraph?
- Does the essay flow in an organized manner?
- Do you support your point of view with specific examples?
- Do you always use correct English grammar, spelling, and punctuation?
- Do you use a varied, precise, and appropriate choice of words?
- Is the essay written neatly, and is it easy to read?

If you can answer "yes" to each of these questions, you're well on your way to writing an essay that will reccive at least a passing grade.

C. Test Strategies

Here are some strategies to help you succeed on the Language Arts, Writing Test:

- **Brush up on your grammar skills.** Study Section D at the end of this chapter, in addition to any other grammar handbooks or resources you have available (we list a few suggestions at the beginning of Section D).
- **Read, read, read!** Reading is one of the best ways you can prepare for the Language Arts, Writing Test. Reading literature, magazines, and newspapers can expose you to proper grammar and writing structure.
- **Practice writing.** Start a journal or blog. Write stories.

- **Review the example questions.** There are example questions sprinkled throughout this chapter. Use your hand or a piece of paper to cover the answer and explanation while you're answering the question. After you answer the question, check your answer and, if it's right, read the explanation to reinforce the reasoning. If you got it wrong, read the explanation, reread the question to see where you went wrong, and reread the grammar review material. If you're still struggling with the question, expand your reading until it all makes sense. Additional sample questions can be found online on the GED Web site (www.acenet.edu/Content/NavigationMenu/ged/test/prep/sample_questions.htm).
- **Take the practice test.** Take the full-length Language Arts, Writing Practice Test (Chapter XII). Do so under test conditions, setting a timer. Check your answers and review the explanations.

D. Grammar Review

We've provided this grammar review to help you prepare for the Language Arts, Writing Test. This review will assist you in two ways:

- The material presented here can form the basis of your ability to answer the questions that require corrections.
- In writing your essay, correct grammar is a must; this section provides you with the basic information to write correct sentences.

Please keep in mind that this is a very general review. For additional grammar review, you can visit CliffsNotes.com (www.cliffsnotes.com/writing-grammar-english-study-guides.html) or reference these other great CliffsNotes titles:

CliffsNotes English Grammar Practice Pack
CliffsNotes Verbal Review for Standardized Tests

1. Parts of Speech

a. Nouns

A noun is a word that names a person, place, thing, or idea.

EXAMPLE:

> *The cat was in the house looking for a mouse in the kitchen.*
>
> How many nouns are there in the sentence?
>
> **(1)** 1
> **(2)** 2
> **(3)** 3
> **(4)** 4
> **(5)** 5

The correct answer is **(4).** There are four nouns in the sentence: *cat, house, mouse,* and *kitchen.*

A proper noun names a specific person, place, or thing and begins with a capital letter.

EXAMPLE:

> *I went to visit betty yesterday.*
>
> Change:
>
> **(1)** *y* to *Y* in *yesterday*
> **(2)** *I* to *i*
> **(3)** *b* to *B* in *betty*
> **(4)** *visit* to *visits*
> **(5)** No change needed

The correct answer is **(3)**. *Betty* is a proper noun and should begin with a capital *B*.

b. Pronouns

A pronoun stands in place of a noun in a sentence. You'll encounter several types of pronouns:

- **Personal pronouns:** Stand for nouns that name persons and things.
- **Possessive pronouns:** Indicate ownership and can be used to stand for nouns or used as adjectives. For example:

   His book was on the table beside her.

   His is a possessive pronoun. (*Her* is a personal pronoun in this sentence.)
- **Intensive pronouns:** Can be used to emphasize a noun or another pronoun. For example:

   I myself will fix that tire.

   Myself is an intensive pronoun.
- **Reflexive pronouns:** Look like intensive pronouns but refer back to the subject of the sentence. For example:

   I will fix it myself.

   Myself is a reflexive pronoun in this sentence because it refers back to the subject of the sentence, *I*.
- **Interrogative pronouns:** Used to introduce questions. For example:

   What did you want?

   What is an interrogative pronoun because it is used to introduce a question.
- **Indefinite pronouns:** Stand for unspecified persons or things. For example:

   No one can fix that rotten tire.

   No one is an indefinite pronoun because the noun that it stands for is not specified.
- **Demonstrative pronouns:** Point to nouns. For example:

   That's the garage that can fix the tire.

   That is a demonstrative pronoun because it points to a noun, *garage*.

- **Reciprocal pronouns:** Express the relationship between two or more nouns or pronouns. For example:

    Bill and the mechanic glanced from the flat tire to one another.

    One another is a reciprocal pronoun because it indicates that both *Bill* and the *mechanic* are related in their frustration over the tire.

EXAMPLES:

We often traveled the Grand Canyon on our vacation. No one else seemed to want to hike those trails, but we did and enjoyed each other's company while we were hiking.

How many pronouns are there in total in these sentences?

(1) 4
(2) 7
(3) 9
(4) 8
(5) 5

The correct answer is **(2)**. There are seven pronouns in these sentences: *we* (three times), *no one,* and *each other*. Although we've counted *no one* and *each other* as two words each, if *six* had been one of the answers it could also have been considered correct because *no one* and *each other* could each have been considered as a single pronoun. It's important to read the answers as well as the questions carefully.

What type of pronoun is *no one?*

(1) Personal pronoun
(2) Indefinite pronoun
(3) Reciprocal pronoun
(4) Reflexive pronoun
(5) Possessive pronoun

The correct answer is **(2)**. *No one* is an indefinite pronoun because the person or persons whom it refers to are unspecified.

(1) In order to open the door of the apartment, you should take the key provided by management in your right hand, or your left one if you're left-handed. (2) Stand so that your dominant hand is in front of the lock and insert it into the lock channel. (3) Make sure that the key goes all the way into the cylinder and turn the key clockwise, to the right, until a click is heard. (4) If there is a lot of noise in the hallway, you may miss the click, but be assured that the key can only be turned 45 degrees without forcing it. (5) At this point you may use either hand to turn the door handle clockwise until the door swings open.

Which correction is needed to make the paragraph correct?

(1) Sentence 4 should read: *If there is a lot of noise in the hallway, you may miss the click, but be assured that the key can only be turned 45 degrees without forcing <u>him</u>.*

(2) Sentence 3 should read: *Make sure that the key goes all the way into the cylinder and turn the key counterclockwise, to the right, until a click is heard.*

(3) Sentence 2 should read: *Stand so that your dominant hand is in front of the lock and insert <u>the key</u> into the lock channel.*

(4) Sentence 5: No change

(5) Sentence 1 should read: *In order to open the door of the apartment, you should take the key provided by <u>them</u> in your right hand, or your left one if you're left-handed.*

The correct answer is **(3)**. The pronoun *it* refers back to the noun *hand* and that's incorrect. The noun *key* must be used in the sentence to make sense because most of the paragraph refers to the key. The other changes introduce grammatical errors into sentences that are already correct. For example, choice (1) has the correction of replacing the pronoun *it* referring to the noun *key* with *him*, which is a personal pronoun and should refer to a person.

c. Verbs

i. Verb Forms

Verbs are action words or state-of-being words.

A transitive verb is one that shows action and requires an object; **intransitive verbs** do not require objects in order to be understood. For example:

The cat knocked over the vase.

The verb *knocked* is transitive because it requires the object *vase* to complete it. For example:

The cat fell.

The verb *fell* is intransitive because there is no object, and the sentence makes sense.

A **linking verb** links the subject of the sentence to another word that relates to it. For example:

The cat was sad.

The verb *was* is a linking verb because the subject *cat* is linked to the word *sad.*

A verb also may consist of two words. For example:

The cat didn't have enough to eat.

The verb consists of two words, *didn't* and *have.* In this case, the first word makes the verb negative.

ii. Verb Tense

The tense of a verb tells us when the action takes place.

Present tense of verbs describes actions that take place in the moment. For example:

I am reading this book.

Past tense of verbs describes actions that took place before now. For example:

I read the other book yesterday.

Future tense of verbs describes actions that will take place in the future. For example:

I will read that new book tomorrow.

EXAMPLES:

What is the verb in the following sentence?

The racing car rolled down the steep hill.

(1) Steep
(2) Down
(3) Hill
(4) Racing
(5) Rolled

The correct answer is **(5).** The word *rolled* indicates an action and is, thus, a verb. *Racing* is a form of a verb used as an adjective to modify car.

The next two questions refer to the following passage.

Memo to All Staff

(1) Starting today, all staff members will finish consuming before the start of the business day and prior to going to their work stations. (2) The spilling of coffee on keyboards is creating an unexpected and unnecessary expense, which is starting to decrease our profits. (3) Anyone spilling coffee on his keyboard will be expected to replace it at his won expense. (4) This also applies to water, tea, fruit juices, and any other liquids that can be carried to your workplace.

—Management

What changes must be made to correct Sentence 1?

(1) Replace *Starting* with *Start.*
(2) Insert *coffee* between *consuming* and *before.*
(3) Omit *stations.*
(4) Omit *the start of.*
(5) No changes needed.

The correct answer is **(2).** *Consuming* is a transitive verb and needs an object to complete it. Because the entire memo is about coffee, it would seem reasonable to use *coffee* as the object of the verb.

What changes must be made to correct Sentence 3?

(1) Replace *Anyone* with *Everyone.*
(2) Replace *it* with *him.*
(3) Replace *won* with *own.* ✓
(4) Replace *spilling* with *spilled.*
(5) No changes needed.

The correct answer is **(3).** The word *won* is spelled correctly, but it doesn't make sense in this sentence. If it's replaced with *own,* the sentence makes sense in the context of the memo.

iii. Sequence of Tenses

The verb tenses in a sentence should make sense chronologically. You would never say,

I had to take my dog to the vet today because he will be sick yesterday.

The sequence of events was:

1. The dog got sick.
2. The dog had to be taken to the vet the next day.

The sentence should read:

My dog got sick yesterday and I have to take him to the vet today.

In the corrected sentence, the verb tenses reflect the chronological order of events.

iv. Word Clues to Tense in Sentences

The verb tense in a sentence should make sense according to the clues in the sentence. For example:

"Stop now!" the police officer will shout at the fleeing suspect.

Logically, if the police officer wanted the suspect to stop, the police officer would want the suspect to stop immediately and not some time in the future. The sentence should read:

"Stop now!" the police officer shouted at the suspect.

v. Word Clues to Tense in Paragraphs

The tense of a verb indicates the time an action took place. In a paragraph, the actions indicated should take place in a logical, sequential order. Check over your paragraph to make sure that the tenses indicate the time you want an action to occur.

d. Adjectives

Adjectives modify or describe a noun or pronoun and, by doing so, add information to the sentence. For example:

I saw the red car go by again.

Red is an adjective modifying the noun *car* and adding information to the sentence. We now know that the car is red and not some other color.

EXAMPLES:

Which of the following improves the sentence by adding an adjective?

I love to go out in the woods in late autumn and look at the leaves.

(1) Replace *woods* with *trees.*
(2) Replace *late* with *the.*
(3) Insert *carefully* between *look* and *at.*
(4) Insert *colorful* between *the* and *leaves.*
(5) No changes needed.

The correct answer is **(4)**. Inserting the adjective *colorful* before the noun *leaves* gives us some more information about the leaves. Choice (3) might give you more information, but it does not modify a noun and, thus, is not an adjective.

Which of the following changes would emphasize the experience of being too close to racing cars?

The racing cars sped by and the roar of the engines hurt my ears.

(1) Insert *red* before *cars.*
(2) Insert *slowly* between *cars* and *sped.*
(3) Insert *loud* before *roar.*
(4) Insert *finely tuned* before *engines.*
(5) Insert *cold* before *ears.*

The correct answer is **(3)**. The adjective *loud* emphasizes the sound made by the racing cars as a result of being too close to them. The other choices might make sense but do not answer the question.

Which of the following changes would emphasize the desolation of the cemetery?

The cemetery was bleak and desolate on that autumn day.

(1) Insert *early* before *autumn,*
(2) Insert *sunny* before *day.*
(3) Insert *very* before *bleak.*
(4) Insert *abandoned* before *cemetery.*
(5) Insert *well-kept* before *cemetery.*

The correct answer is **(4)**. Inserting the adjective *abandoned* before *cemetery* gives the reader a mental picture of a desolate place. Choices (2) and (5) would give the opposite image.

e. Adverbs

An adverb modifies a verb, an adjective, or another adverb and gives the reader additional information. For example:

The child screamed constantly.

Constantly is an adverb modifying the verb *screamed* and adding the information that the child had no intention of being quiet.

EXAMPLES:

Which of the following improves the sentence by adding an adverb?

Alvin hurt his leg and had to walk.

(1) Insert *carefully* after *walk*.
(2) Insert *Careless* before *Alvin*.
(3) Replace *his* with *broken*.
(4) Insert *right* between *his* and *leg*.
(5) No changes needed.

The correct answer is **(1)**. *Carefully* is an adverb modifying the verb (infinitive) *to walk* and providing the information as to how he had to walk. *Careless* and *right* are adjectives and do not answer the question.

Which of the following improves the sentence by adding an adverb?

People stayed in their houses as the wind blew across the town.

(1) Insert *mercilessly* before *across*.
(2) Insert *cautious* before *people*.
(3) Insert *happily* after *stayed*.
(4) Insert *gentle* before *wind*.
(5) Insert *empty* before *town*.

The correct answer is **(1)**. The adverb *mercilessly* tells us how the wind was blowing and explains why people would have stayed in their houses. Choices (2), (4), and (5) are adjectives because they modify nouns and could not be considered correct answers to the question even if they improved it. Choice (3) makes little sense in the context of the sentence. Remember to read the questions carefully before deciding on an answer.

> Which of the following improves the sentences by adding an adverb?
>
> *Fishing is a wonderful sport. It gives you a chance to sit in a boat enjoying the scenery for hours on end.*
>
> **(1)** Insert *fly* before *fishing*.
> **(2)** Insert *seldom* before *gives*.
> **(3)** Insert *quietly* after *sit*
> **(4)** Insert *not* before *enjoying*
> **(5)** Insert *many* before *hours*.

The correct answer is **(3)**. *Quietly* modifies the verb *to sit* and explains how you could enjoy the scenery for a long period of time. Choices (2) and (4) are wrong because they change the entire meaning of the sentence. Choices (1) and (5) are adjectives. It is important to understand the difference between adjectives and adverbs. Adjectives modify nouns, while adverbs can modify a verb, an adjective, or another adverb. Read this type of question carefully to make sure what you are being asked.

f. Articles

The is the definite article that indicates one particular thing. For example:

> The horse ran away from the farm in the morning.

Each of the *the*'s is a definite article because it modifies a noun and specifies which of all the things in the world the article refers to. It's a particular horse who ran away from a particular farm at a particular time of day.

A and *an* are indefinite articles, which do not indicate a particular thing. For example:

> Did you leave a book on the table?

A is an indefinite article because it does not refer to a particular book but instead to any book.

EXAMPLE:

> What corrections are needed in this passage?
>
> (1) There is great danger to the personal privacy in allowing governments to monitor and intercept the personal and business e-mails. (2) As the free society, we deserve privacy in our dealings with friends and associates. (3) It is unthinkable that the foreign government would demand to monitor our electronic correspondence. (4) When will we stop allowing the freedoms to slip away?
>
> **(1)** In Sentence 1, replace *the* with *our* between *to* and *personal*.
> **(2)** In Sentence 2, replace *the* with *a* between *As* and *free*.
> **(3)** In Sentence 3, replace *the* with *a* between *that* and *foreign*.
> **(4)** In Sentence 4, replace *the* with *our* between *allowing* and *freedoms*.
> **(5)** All of the above.

The correct answer is **(5)**. This is an excerpt from an editorial and, as such, it makes some specific references and some general references. The articles should reflect this, and some of the articles should be replaced with other adjectives as some grammar books regard articles as a special type of adjective.

In Sentence 1, the sentence should read:

> There is great danger to our personal privacy in allowing governments to monitor and intercept the personal and business e-mails.

Although privacy is a very specific concern, it's a personal concern and *our* makes a better sentence than *the* to indicate this.

Sentence 2 should read:

> As a free society, we deserve privacy in our dealings with friends and associates.

The article should be the indefinite article *a;* although free society is normally considered a definite concept, the sentence talks about it as a general one.

Sentence 3 should read:

> It is unthinkable that a foreign government would demand to monitor our electronic correspondence.

We have to replace the definite article with an indefinite article because the excerpt refers to foreign governments in general and not to a specific foreign government.

Sentence 4 should read:

> When will we stop allowing our freedoms to slip away?

Freedom is a general concept in this context, and *our* is a better choice than *the* to indicate this. When correcting sentences, always consider the meaning of the passage and the context before deciding what changes are needed.

g. Conjunctions

Conjunctions are words that join other words or groups of words in a way that makes the sentence make sense. For example:

> I looked all over the store for you, but I couldn't find you.

But is a coordinating conjunction that joins the two clauses *I looked all over the store for you* and *I couldn't find you* in a way that makes the sentence make sense. Other conjunctions are: *and, for, nor, or, so,* and *yet.*

There are special classes of conjunctions. Subordinating conjunctions make one clause subordinate to another. Examples of subordinating conjunctions are: *after, although, because, since, when,* and *whether.* For example:

> Although I left early, I was still late for the play.

Although is a subordinating conjunction and is used to indicate that the important thought (represented by the main clause) is that I was still late for the play, and the less important idea (represented by a subordinate clause using the conjunction *although*) is that I left early.

Some conjunctions always act in pairs. Examples of these are: *as . . . as; both . . . and; either . . . or; neither . . . nor; not . . . but;* and *not only . . . but also*. For example:

I had neither the time nor the opportunity to shop for groceries.

Neither and *nor* are conjunctions that are always used in pairs.

Sometimes, specific adverbs can act as conjunctions for specific purposes:

Purpose	Example
Addition	Also
Comparison	Similarly
Contrast	However
Emphasis	Namely
Cause and effect	Therefore
Time	Finally

For example:

I enjoyed reading the book; however, I found it much too long.

However is an adverb used as a conjunction here to indicate a contrast between the two clauses. The first clause indicates that the reader enjoyed reading the book, and the second clause indicates that the reader felt that the book was too long.

EXAMPLE:

The following question refers to this passage.

How to Take Apart a Computer

(1) The first thing you must do is to unplug the nonfunctioning computer. (2) Electricity is dangerous and not only will you be faced with sharp edges that can cut your fingers, but if you don't unplug it, you will also be faced with possible electrocution, which would interfere with your plans. (3) There are usually screws on one side of the computer, but if you remove them, the outer case should slip off or expose the inner electronics. (4) Set the outer shell aside. (5) You probably will never need it after dismantling the computer, but you should at least consider recycling it. (6) Inside is the frame containing a lot of electronic stuff or wires. (7) Disconnect all the wires and set them aside, but make sure that you keep them separate because they contain copper, which should be recycled. (8) Before all the wires are removed, take out all the electronic stuff by removing appropriate screws. (9) Don't be worried about damaging anything because at this point when there may be a lot of functioning parts, you probably couldn't reassemble them and the computer didn't work in the first place.

> What changes should be made to make this a better set of instructions?
>
> **(1)** Change Sentence 2 to read: *Electricity is dangerous and not only will you be faced with sharp edges that can cut your fingers, but also, if you don't unplug it, you will be faced with possible electrocution, which would interfere with your plans.*
>
> **(2)** Change Sentence 7 to read: *Disconnect all the wires but set them aside, but make sure that you keep them separate but they contain copper, which should be recycled.*
>
> **(3)** Change Sentence 5 to read: *You probably will never need it after dismantling the computer, yet you should at least consider recycling it.*
>
> **(4)** Change Sentence 1 to read: *The first thing you must do is to unplug the functioning computer.*
>
> **(5)** All of the above.

The correct answer is **(1)**. *Not only* and *but also* are always used together. The original sentence does use them together, but the *also* is so far from the *but* that it make the sentence awkward. The other suggestions make the passage worse.

2. Parts of Sentences

The best way to recognize a correct sentence, or to write one, is to understand how sentences are created.

a. Subject

The subject of a sentence tells us what the sentence is about—a person, place, thing, activity, or idea. For example:

I love baseball.

This sentence is about me, and *I* is the subject of the sentence.

Baseball is my favorite sport.

Here the sentence is about baseball, and *baseball* is the subject of the sentence.

The complete subject is all the words associated with the subject. For example:

Slow, but always exciting, baseball is my favorite sport.

Slow, but always exciting, baseball is the complete subject because it consists of the bare subject, *baseball*, and all the words that modify it. Complete subjects can be used to give more interest to a sentence.

b. Predicate

The predicate tells what the subject is doing or being. For example:

> I wore my favorite jersey to the game.

The subject of the sentence is *I,* and the word that tells what the subject did is *wore,* which is the predicate.

A simple predicate may consist of more than one word. It may have a helper word to show tense. For example:

> The ship had left the dock when I arrived.

The subject of the sentence is *the ship,* and the words that tell what the ship did are *had left,* which is the simple predicate.

A complete predicate consists of all the words in the predicate. For example:

> When I went to the doctor's office, I noticed all the sick people waiting to see him.

The sentence is about *I,* and the word that tells about what *I* did is *noticed* plus *when I went to the doctor's office* (where?), which together form the complete predicate.

c. Object

The word or words that complete the action of the predicate are called the direct object. For example:

> I hung the picture properly, but the wall broke.

The subject of the sentence is *I* and the word that tells what I did is *hung.* The word that answers the question "What did I hang?" is *picture,* which is the direct object.

An indirect object tells to whom or for whom the action of the predicate is performed. For example:

> Harry gave me the book.

The sentence is about *Harry.* The action performed by Harry is giving, and *gave* is the predicate; the object that Harry gave is *the book,* and to whom he gave it is *me.* Therefore, *Harry* is the subject, *the book* is the direct object, and *me* is the indirect object.

In the following examples, identify the part of the sentence of the underlined word.

EXAMPLES:

We all <u>went</u> to the park to watch the squirrels play.

(1) Subject
(2) Predicate
(3) Direct object
(4) Indirect object
(5) Modifier

The correct answer is **(2)**. *Went* is a word that indicates action and is a verb or the predicate of the sentence.

The green <u>book</u> lay on the table unread and unopened.

(1) Subject
(2) Predicate
(3) Direct object
(4) Indirect object
(5) Modifier

The correct answer is **(1)**. *Book* is a noun and the subject of the sentence.

I gave you the <u>basketball</u> after the last game.

(1) Subject
(2) Predicate
(3) Direct object
(4) Indirect object
(5) Modifier

The correct answer is **(3)**. *Basketball* is the word that indicates to what the action was directed and is the direct object. *You* would answer the question "To whom was the action directed?" and is the indirect object, but that is not what the question asked.

How can you go outside on such a <u>cold</u>, wintry day?

(1) Subject
(2) Predicate
(3) Direct object
(4) Indirect object
(5) Modifier

The correct answer is **(5)**. *Cold* is a word that describes the noun *day* and is a modifier.

d. Phrases

A phrase is a group of two or more words that are related to each other. For example:

I stored my CDs in the attic.

The words *in the attic* are related to each other because, together, they form a group of words that tells the reader where the CDs were stored.

Adjective phrases are groups of words that function as an adjective. For example:

Napoleon was a man of action.

Of action is an adjective phrase because it modifies the noun *man*.

Adverb phrases are groups of words that function as adverbs. For example:

Nancy spoke with enthusiasm.

With enthusiasm is an adverb phrase because it modifies the verb *spoke.*

EXAMPLE:

How to Lock Your Apartment Windows

(1) Your apartment has been equipped with the latest developments in windows. (2) Each of your windows consists of two sets of sliding thermal glass with an air space between them. (3) In the open position, they can be easily moved from the inside or the outside. (4) In the closed position, they have an automatic lock that secures them until released by the resident. (5) They cannot be opened in the closed position by people unknown who may have looked into the window, seen something they wanted, and forced it open using a crowbar or other prying device from the outside and glass is easily broken and the management with an office in the building accepts no responsibility for items lost or stolen as a result of entry through broken glass.

In order to improve the passage, you should:

(1) In Sentence 5, move *in the closed position* to the very beginning of the sentence and capitalize the *I* in *in.*

(2) In Sentence 5, put a period after *outside,* omit *and,* and then capitalize *the* before *management.*

(3) In Sentence 5, omit *by people unknown who may have looked into the window, seen something they wanted, and forced it open using a crowbar or other prying device.*

(4) In Sentence 5, omit *with an office in the building.*

(5) All of the above.

The correct answer is **(5).** Sentences should be simple and easy to understand and not full of extra information that really doesn't relate to the topic of the sentence. Moving *in the closed position* to the beginning of the sentence and, of course, capitalizing the *I* in *in* makes the beginning of the sentence easier to read and understand and maintains a parallel structure among sentences 3, 4, and 5, which is common in instructional material. The words, *by people unknown who may have looked into the window, seen something they wanted, and forced it open using a crowbar or other prying device* may be important from a safety and security point of view, but they do nothing to make this sentence easier to read or understand; if they were important to the paragraph, they should have been constructed into separate sentences. *With an office in the building* is a perfectly good phrase, but it adds nothing to the clarity of the sentence; again, if the location of the office is important, it deserves its own sentence.

Remember that in writing your essay, phrases can improve the essay by making it easier to understand, but when they're overused or incorrectly used, they can lower your mark by making the essay difficult to read and understand.

e. Clauses

A clause is a group of related words containing a subject and a verb.

Main clauses can stand alone as sentences with the addition of appropriate punctuation. For example:

My dog barks a lot.

This is a group of words, all about my dog, that contains a subject, *my dog,* and a verb, *barks,* and is a main clause because it expresses a complete thought.

Subordinate clauses depend on a main clause to make the sentence make sense. For example:

The dog that used to live with my sister barks a lot.

That used to live with my sister is a group of words that can't stand alone and is, therefore, a subordinate clause.

A noun clause acts as the subject of a sentence or as an object or a predicate nominative. For example:

Whatever I said should not have upset them.

Whatever I said is a group of words that is used in place of a noun and is, thus, a noun clause.

An adjective clause acts as an adjective. For example:

Autumn, when the leaves are turning colors, is my favorite season.

When the leaves are turning colors is a group of words that modifies a noun *autumn* and is known as an adjective clause.

An adverb clause acts as an adverb. For example:

Frank won before I could show him my best moves.

Before I could show him my best moves is a group of words that modify the verb *won* and is, thus, an adverb clause.

3. Types of Sentences

a. Simple Sentences

Simple sentences consist of only one clause. For example:

I went for a walk.

This sentence consists of only one clause: *I went for a walk.*

b. Compound Sentences

Compound sentences consist of two or more main clauses joined by a coordinating conjunction. For example:

I went for a walk, but it was still drizzling.

In this sentence, there are two main clauses, *I went for a walk* and *it was still drizzling,* each of which is independent and expresses a complete thought.

c. Complex Sentences

Complex sentences consist of one main clause and one or more subordinate clauses. For example:

> I couldn't go for a walk while the rain and wind were blowing across the field.

Here, there is one main clause, *I couldn't go for a walk,* and one subordinate clause, *while the rain and wind were blowing across the field,* which depends on the main clause to give it meaning.

d. Compound-Complex Sentences

Compound-complex sentences consist of two or more main clauses and at least one subordinate clause. For example:

> I went for a walk after the rain stopped, and I discovered that the ground was still very wet.

This sentence has two main clauses, *I went for a walk* and *I discovered that the ground was still very wet,* each of which expresses a complete thought and can stand alone, and one subordinate clause, *after the rain stopped,* which requires the main clauses to make its meaning clearly understood.

4. Voice

Active voice indicates that the subject performs the action of the sentence. For example:

> I listen to my favorite tunes every day.

Passive voice indicates that the subject has the action of the sentence performed on it. For example:

> My favorite tunes are listened to every day.

Avoid the passive voice unless absolutely necessary.

5. Agreement

When writing your paragraph, as well as when correcting sentences, make sure that appropriate words agree with each other.

a. Subject-Verb Agreement

In a proper sentence, the subject agrees with the verb. For example:

> The boys have run away from the bear.

The boys is a plural noun/subject and requires a plural verb/predicate, *have run.* If the subject were singular, the sentence would read: *The boy has run away from the bear.*

b. Pronoun-Antecedent Agreement

Pronouns must agree with the nouns they replace. If a pronoun replaces a singular noun, it should itself be singular. For example:

I brought my fishing rod.

My and *I* are both singular and agree with each other. If the subject were plural, it would read: *We brought our fishing rods.* The plural pronoun *our* agrees with the plural *we.*

6. Pronoun Reference

A pronoun must refer back to a noun. If you write a sentence or a paragraph with pronouns and the reader cannot figure out what the pronouns refer to, you'll quickly lose the reader's interest. For example:

She wrote a letter to her about him that mentioned her but not his best friend.

This sentence has a lot of pronouns that do not refer to any nouns, making the sentence hard to understand.

7. Pronoun Case

Pronouns have a case depending on their function. The **subjective case** indicates that the pronoun is used as the subject of a sentence. For example:

He sat in the chair.

He is a subjective pronoun because it is used as the subject of the verb *sat.*

The **objective case** indicates that the pronoun is the object of a verb or a preposition. For example:

I had to leave without him.

Him is an objective pronoun because it is the object of the preposition *without.*

The **possessive case** indicates that the pronoun indicates ownership. For example:

That is my umbrella.

My is a possessive pronoun since it indicates ownership of the *umbrella.*

8. Correcting Sentences

a. Sentence Fragments

A sentence without a subject or a predicate and/or that does not express a complete thought is considered a sentence fragment. In writing your essay, make sure that each sentence is really a sentence and not a sentence fragment. There are some quick questions you can ask yourself when you're writing to make sure that you haven't left a lot of sentence fragments in your essay.

- Does every one of my sentences have a subject?
- Does every one of my sentences have a verb?
- If I've used clauses in my sentences, is there a main clause for every subordinate clause?
- Can each of my sentences stand alone and make sense?

If you can answer "Yes" to every question, there are no sentence fragments in your essay.

b. Comma Splice and Fused Sentences

i. Comma Splice

If you join two perfectly good but unrelated main clauses or sentences together with a comma, you've created a comma splice and a lot of confusion in the reader's mind. There is no place for comma splices in coherent writing. For example:

> The kite was blowing in the wind, the dog was running around.

These are two good but unrelated sentences. The best way to correct this error is to put a period after *wind,* put a capital *t* on *the,* and end up with two complete sentences.

ii. Fused Sentences

A fused sentence would be:

> The kite was blowing in the wind the dog was running around.

Again, these are two good but unrelated sentences just put together without any punctuation. The correction would be the same as for a comma splice. Put a period after *wind,* put a capital *t* on *the,* and end up with two complete sentences.

c. Misplaced and Dangling Modifiers

Words that modify are meant to give the reader additional information or a clearer picture of what is being written about. Make sure that the word being modified and the modifier are close together, and make sure that a modifier can modify only one word. Don't put in modifiers if they have nothing to modify. For example:

> Feeling a headache coming on, Sally went to her bedroom and looked out the window bright and glowing in the late afternoon sky without a heavy curtain to shade the room.

If you tried to connect the modifiers with what they modified, it might look like this:

> Feeling a headache coming on, Sally went to her bedroom and looked out the window
> <u>bright and glowing in the late afternoon sky</u> <u>without a heavy curtain to shade the room</u>.
>   What does this modify?   What does this modify?

In reading the sentence and answering the questions, you realize that the sentence doesn't make sense in its present form. If it were completely rewritten as follows, it still wouldn't be great literature, but at least the meaning of the words would be clear:

Sally felt a headache coming on and went to her bedroom. She stood and looked out her window, which had no heavy curtain to shade the room. The sun outside shone bright and glowed in the late afternoon sky.

d. Incomplete Sentences

If a sentence has all the requisite parts—subject and predicate—but still does not express a complete thought, it's considered incomplete. For example:

I have always wanted to.

This sentence has a subject, *I*, a predicate *have always wanted to,* and makes no sense. It is incomplete.

Another example:

After I buy a new lure, fishing is always.

This sentence has a subject, *fishing,* and a verb, *is,* but makes no sense. Fishing could be *wonderful, peaceful, productive, awful, boring,* or anything else you wanted to complete this incomplete sentence.

Another example:

After gulping my morning coffee. I ran to the car, key in hand.

The first sentence is incomplete. It has words that go together, but no real verb. *Gulping* may look like a verb because it implies an action, but it isn't. Technically, it is a present participle because it is used as a verb and ends in *-ing*. If we rewrote the sentence as

After gulping my coffee, I ran to the car, key in hand.

it would be correct because *After gulping my coffee* is now used as an introductory phrase.

e. Punctuation

i. End Punctuation

Periods are used to end sentences that tell us something. **Question marks** are used to end sentences that ask questions. **Exclamation points** are used to end sentences that call for emphasis, interjection, or a command.

ii. Commas

Commas prevent the reader from misreading sentences. They're also used

- To join two main clauses with coordinating conjunctions (for example, *and* or *but*)
- After an introductory clause, word, or phrase
- Between items in a list
- Between adjectives (provided that they are separate and equal and modify the same noun)
- To set off a phrase or clause that does not restrict the meaning of the word it modifies
- To set off a noun or noun phrase that renames the noun preceding it

- Before the words *however* and *nevertheless*
- To set off a contrasting phrase or clause
- To set off quotations
- To set off introductory elements (words, phrases, or clauses that begin a sentence)

Commas always come after:

- **Adverbial clauses:** For example:

    Although we read that chapter twice, I still couldn't remember what it was about.
- **Long prepositional phrases:** For example:

    Before Charlotte got up and started to change her clothes, the doorbell rang.
- **Adverbial clauses that seem to modify the entire sentence:** For example:

    On the other hand, Fung did not complete all the questions in the assignment.
- **Any word or phrase that would confuse the reader:** For example:

    Before this summer, reading lists were not posted early

An **appositive** is any information that is added to a sentence that explains a noun or pronoun. An appositive is separated from the rest of the sentence by commas. For example:

Jenny, who tried to empty this cupboard, always ends up with more stuff than she started with.

Commas seem to have enough rules associated with their use to ensure that there is a comma after every word, but if you follow a simple rule, you won't overuse them: Use commas to make the sense of a sentence clear.

Although commas have many uses, they can be overused. In your writing, try to use commas properly, but beware of using so many commas that your sentences are hard to read because of the multiple pauses.

iii. The Semicolon

The most common use for the semicolon is to separate items with internal punctuation in a list.

The semicolon joins independent clauses without the separation created by a period and provides more sophisticated sentences than a series of short simple sentences separated by periods. Semicolons also are used with conjunctive adverbs (such as *therefore, nevertheless, besides, however,* and *otherwise*) to form a closer thought connection. For example:

I studied very hard for this test; however, my cold proved to be a huge distraction while I was writing it.

I believe three things about passing the GED tests: No matter how hard I have to work, it will be worth it; I will be able to apply for that promotion; and no matter how long I live, I will know that this is one of my achievements.

iv. More Punctuation

Apostrophes are used to show possession and to indicate that a letter is missing. **Quotation marks** surround a direct quote.

f. Capitalization

Proper names are always capitalized. For example:

John, Mary, Paul, and Edward decided to go to a show.

Titles are capitalized. For example:

Mr., Mrs., Ms., and Dr.

Months are always capitalized. For example:

June, March, and October

g. Spelling

Spelling can cause the most trouble in essays. If you misspell a word, you'll be marked down. In the first part of the exam, you'll be asked to correct some sentences of which a few will have spelling mistakes. The usual spelling mistakes that you're expected to correct consist of possessives, contractions, and *homonyms* (words that sound alike but are spelled differently).

For example:

Type of Error	Examples	Usage
Possessives	John's Mary's	Belonging to John Belonging to Mary
Contractions	O'clock Wouldn't It's	Contraction for "of the clock" Contraction for "would not" Contraction for "it is"
Homonyms	Here, hear	Please come here and help me lift the parcel. Didn't you hear what I said?
	Aid, aide	I need your aid in tying this parcel. Edwin was studying to become a nurse's aide.
	Fir, fur	The fir tree grew straight and tall. People are finally deciding not to wear fur as a fashion accessory to save the animals.
	Groan, grown	After that bad joke, all I could hear was the audience groan. It's so nice to see you after all these years; you look so grown up.
	Role, roll	Alvin played the role of Edwin in the play. Roll that barrel over here, please.

Let's = Let us (handwritten)

h. Practice

Directions: Correct the following sentences.

---

1. larry went to the dry cleaner every day at the same time to pick up the next day's clean shirt.

   (1) Change *every day* to *daily.*
   (2) Correct the spelling of *cleaner.*
   (3) Capitalize *larry.*
   (4) Change *day's* to *days.*
   (5) No changes necessary.

The correct answer is **(3)**. *Larry* starts a sentence and is a proper name. Both are reasons that it should begin with a capital letter. *Every day* and *daily* mean the same thing, and there is no reason to change these words.

---

2. Our Teacher dislikes students who speek out in class.

   (1) Change *Teacher* to *teacher* and *speek* to *speak.*
   (2) Change *students* to *student.*
   (3) Change *class* to *classes.*
   (4) Omit *out.*
   (5) No changes necessary.

The correct answer is **(1)**. *Teacher* does not fall into any of the groups of nouns that require capitals, and *speek* is spelled incorrectly. If you omitted *out,* you would change the meaning of the sentence. Most teachers prefer students who speak in class to those who just sit and silently stare.

---

3. Lets stop beating around the bush and hit him out of the ball park.

   (1) Change *beating* to *beeting.*
   (2) Change *ball park* to *ballparks.*
   (3) Capitalize *bush.*
   (4) Change *Lets* to *Let's* and *him* to *it.*
   (5) No changes necessary.

The correct answer is **(4)**. *Let's* stands for *let us,* and without the correction there is no subject for the sentence. Although you can use the phrase *hit it out of the ball park* without advocating violence, replacing *it* with *him* changes that completely. *Beat* and *beet* are homonyms—they sound the same. (If they were synonyms, they would *mean* the same thing.)

which is

4. My sister has a friend who comes from Oregon very far away from where she lives still they plan to meet at the corner store to drink coffee and eat a donut every year or so sometimes even sooner or later then they might be on a diet and have salad instead.

    (1) Insert a comma after *Oregon* and *which is* between *Oregon* and *very*.
    (2) Insert a period after *lives* and capitalize *still*.
    (3) Omit *sometimes even sooner or later*.
    (4) Replace *then* with *or*.
    (5) All of the above.

The correct answer is **(5)**. The original sentence is a mess. It is too long and has extra words in it. To correct it, you would have to make all the suggestions given. When you're writing your essay, avoid long, complicated sentences—they're hard to read and often lead to errors.

Directions: Correct the following passages to create correct, coherent passages.

Question 5 refers to the following paragraph.

(1) Unfortunately, her country was in financial trouble. (2) The Empress Dowager Cixi ruled China for 47 years. (3) She had spent money without thought for the future. (4) She was a very vain woman and always wanted to impress people with the wealth of her country. (5) When she was old and faced death, she decided that her tomb was not good enough for her and ordered it rebuilt.

5. To improve this paragraph, change the order of the sentences to:

    (1) 1, 2, 5, 4, 3
    (2) 2, 4, 1, 3, 5
    (3) 5, 3, 1, 2, 4
    (4) 3, 5, 2, 4, 1
    (5) 4, 5, 3, 1, 2

The correct answer is **(2)**. This order forms a coherent paragraph, which would read as follows:

The Empress Dowager Cixi ruled China for 47 years. She was a very vain woman and always wanted to impress people with the wealth of her country. Unfortunately, her country was in financial trouble. She had spent money without thought for the future. When she was old and faced death, she decided that her tomb was not good enough for her and ordered it rebuilt.

Question 6 refers to the following sentence.

This Saturday at the recreation center, there will be a world-class lawn-bowling tournament with people from all over the community who will arrive early in the morning and stay until late at night playing this great game for all to watch.

6. What corrections must be made to the sentence to make it easier to read?

   (1) Place a period after *tournament.*
   (2) Capitalize *people* and omit *with.*
   (3) Omit *who* from between *community* and *will.*
   (4) Place a comma after *night.*
   (5) All of the above.

The correct answer is **(5).** In order to make this very long, complex sentence readable, it should be broken into smaller sentences. Following the instructions indicated by (5) would produce a paragraph reading as follows:

> This Saturday at the recreation center, there will be a world-class lawn bowling tournament. People from all over the community will arrive early in the morning and stay until late at night, playing this great game for all to watch.

Question 7 refers to the following paragraph.

(1) My opponent, whom I have renamed Slowly Slowerton, does not believe in speed. (2) As your candidate for mayor, I would like to take the following position on this issue. (3) I, on the other hand, want to remove speed limits altogether. (4) I am opposed to lowering the speed limit on the roads in our community to 12 miles per hour. (5) He wants a city where it is faster to walk to work than to drive. (6) Of course, there may be a few accidents, but we will just have to be more careful. (7) In this community, we will have to find ways of looking after one another rather than have city hall rule our lives with silly rules. (8) He wants every person who cannot speed-walk to always be late. (9) He wants you to waste time and gas in getting where you want to go.

7. What would be the first and last sentence in a logically arranged speech?

   (1) first sentence, 3; last sentence, 9
   (2) first sentence, 5; last sentence, 7
   (3) first sentence, 7; last sentence, 8
   (4) first sentence, 2; last sentence, 7
   (5) first sentence, 5; last sentence, 7

The correct answer is **(4).** Making the changes suggested in (4) would produce a paragraph like this:

> As your candidate for mayor, I would like to take the following position on this issue. I am opposed to lowering the speed limit on the roads in our community to 12 miles per hour. My opponent, whom I have renamed Slowly Slowerton, does not believe in speed. He wants a city where it is faster to walk to work than to drive. He wants every person who cannot speed-walk to always be late. He wants you to waste time and gas in getting where you want to go. I, on the other hand, want to remove speed limits altogether. Of course, there may be a few accidents, but we will just have to be more careful. In this community, we will have to find ways of looking after one another rather than have city hall rule our lives with silly rules.

The other suggestions would produce a paragraph without a strong opening or closing. Remember when you're writing your essay that having good opening and closing sentences is important.

Question 8 refers to the following paragraph.

(1) The meeting opened at 7 p.m. with Harold in the chair? (2) The first order of business was the reading of the minutes! (3) Since there were no additions or corrections, they were passed on a motion by Judy, seconded by Vivienne? (4) There was no new business to report. (5) A motion for adjournment was passed at 7:20 p.m. on a motion by Sam and Elizabeth! (6) The next monthly meeting will be called at the discretion of the chair.

---

8. Correct the punctuation in the paragraph.

(1) In Sentence 2, change the exclamation point after *minutes* to a period.

(2) In Sentence 1, change the question mark after *chair* to a period.

(3) In Sentence 3, change the question mark after *Vivienne* to a period.

(4) In Sentence 5, change the exclamation point after *Elizabeth* to a period.

(5) All of the above.

The correct answer is **(5)**. Sentences 1 and 3 are not questions and do not need question marks. Sentences 2 and 5 are not exclamations and do not need exclamation points. Making these corrections would produce the following passage:

The meeting opened at 7 p.m. with Harold in the chair. The first order of business was the reading of the minutes. Since there were no additions or corrections, they were passed on a motion by Judy, seconded by Vivienne. There was no new business to report. A motion for adjournment was passed at 7:20 p.m. on a motion by Sam and Elizabeth. The next monthly meeting will be called at the discretion of the chair.

VIII. Social Studies

A. Test Format

The GED Social Studies Test is made up of 50 multiple-choice questions to be answered in 70 minutes (or 1½ minutes per question). These questions assess your knowledge in the following subject areas:

- **American history (12 or 13 questions, or 25 percent):** Passages may have to do with the American Revolution, the Civil War, colonization, Reconstruction, industrial development, the Great Depression, and so on. Sixty percent of these questions may be based on visual passages including illustrations, maps, and charts. To prepare for this section, read articles and books concerning historical material.

- **World history (7 or 8 questions, or 15 percent):** These questions may be similar to American history, except that they deal with history from around the world, some of which may predate U.S. history.

- **Civics and government (12 or 13 questions, or 25 percent):** These passages deal with civic life, government, politics (especially the U.S. system), America's relations with other countries, and the role of the United States in the world. Material about civics and government may be found in newspapers and news magazines. Older issues can be found in libraries.

- **Economics (10 questions, or 20 percent):** Economics is the study of how the Earth's resources are used to create wealth, which is then distributed and used to satisfy the needs of mankind. It involves the world of banking and finance in both small businesses and large corporations. It includes workers and owners who import and export manufactured goods, natural resources, and services. Economic articles may be found on the Internet and in newspapers, magazines, and books.

- **Geography (7 or 8 questions, or 15 percent):** Geography deals with the world including land masses and oceans. This also includes the impact of weather, environmental conditions, and the division and use of land. To prepare for geographic questions, you need to practice reading maps and answering questions about them. You also can read geography magazines, Web sites, and library books about topics of geographic interest.

The GED Social Studies Test assesses higher-level thinking skills. You are not required to try to remember facts, such as the year that the Declaration of Independence was signed. But you are expected to understand social studies principles, concepts, and events. The test questions can be divided into the following types:

- **Comprehension:** 10 questions, or 20 percent
- **Application:** 10 questions, or 20 percent
- **Analysis:** 20 questions, or 40 percent
- **Evaluation:** 10 questions, or 20 percent

B. Types of Questions—A Detailed Look

The GED Social Studies Test measures your ability to understand and interpret concepts and principles in history, geography, economics, and civics. You're required to draw upon your previous knowledge of events, ideas, terms, and situations that may be related to social studies.

The test is about **50 percent reading-oriented questions** and about **50 percent visual-materials questions;** some questions are a combination of the two. The GED Social Studies Test's questions involving visual materials rely on graphs, maps, tables, political cartoons, diagrams, photographs, and artistic works. Graphs and charts demonstrate trends and relationships between different sets of information.

Here's a closer look at each of the four question types, along with some example questions.

1. Comprehension Questions

Comprehension questions test your ability to identify information and ideas and interpret their meaning. You should be able to understand information presented in articles and excerpts, as well as in maps, charts, and graphs. This can involve determining the main point of the passage, restating the information, summarizing ideas, and identifying implications of this information.

EXAMPLES:

The comprehension example questions are based on the following passage.

Seventy-five percent of Americans are urban dwellers and, in spite of the booming economy, 30 percent of workers earn poverty or near-poverty wages. Low-wage workers are now the lowest paid in the industrialized world, with more than 20 percent of children in the United States living in poverty. The number of U.S. citizens who work in more than one job has increased 92 percent between 1973 and 1997, with 43 percent of workers putting in more than 50 hours per week. Young entry-level workers without a college education saw their real wages fall by 20 percent between 1979 and 1997. On the other hand, the CEOs (chief executive officers) of major corporations now earn 419 times more than the average salary of their employees. The richest 1 percent of the population now earns as much wealth as the bottom 95 percent.

> Which of the following statements best summarizes this passage's central theme?
>
> **(1)** Many Americans live in cities.
> **(2)** The income of entry-level workers has increased.
> **(3)** The income of CEOs has decreased.
> **(4)** There is a major disparity between income levels.
> **(5)** All of the above.

The correct answer is **(4).** The "central theme" of the passage is the inequity that exists between the incomes of the richest citizens and the lowest wage earners. Choice (1), while true, does not represent the theme of the passage. Choices (2) and (3) are incorrect according to the passage; therefore, choice (5) cannot be relevant.

According to the passage, what impact does a college education have on a worker's income level?

(1)   There is no difference.
(2)   The worker's income rises.
(3)   The worker's income declines.
(4)   The worker works more hours.
(5)   The worker has more jobs.

The correct answer is **(2).** The passage tells us that entry-level workers, without a college education, saw their income decrease by 20 percent. Therefore, by comparison, the college-educated workers must have seen a rise in income. The rest of the choices are either incorrect or not relevant.

Where do major CEOs fit among income earners?

(1)   Bottom 95 percent
(2)   Top 20 percent
(3)   About 43 percent
(4)   At 75 percent
(5)   Top 1 percent

The correct answer is **(5).** According to the passage, the CEOs would occupy the top 1 percent of income earners. While they would also be in the top 20 percent (2), this is not the best answer. Choices (1), (3), and (4) are incorrect.

2. Application Questions

Application questions assess your ability to use information and ideas in different ways to explore meanings or solve problems. You should be able to use the information from the passage to solve a problem in a different situation or context. You'll be asked to use the information and ideas in a different set of circumstances.

EXAMPLES:

The application example questions are based on the following passage.

According to the United States Constitution, the responsibility for public education is divested to the states. Each of the 50 states has its own department of education, which delegates the actual operation of schools, from kindergarten through grade 12, to a number of local public school districts. One approach to school reform has meant that virtually every state has set standards of accountability for curriculum content and academic performance for students at each grade level and for each subject area. These results are typically made public, with comparison data across districts, so that communities can assess their district's performance in relation to other districts.

> Who is directly responsible for the operation of public schools in the United States?
>
> **(1)** The United States Constitution
> **(2)** Departments of education
> **(3)** Local school districts
> **(4)** State governments
> **(5)** The House of Representatives

The correct answer is **(3).** Choice (3) is the best answer because local public school districts are directly responsible for the operation of public schools. Although the United States Constitution delegates responsibility to each of the 50 states, the actual operation of public schools is delegated to local school districts. Therefore, choices (1), (2), and (4), while relevant, are not the best answers. Choice (5), the House of Representatives, is incorrect.

> How is school reform promoted?
>
> **(1)** Standards of accountability
> **(2)** Curriculum content
> **(3)** Academic performance
> **(4)** Test scores
> **(5)** Teacher evaluation

The correct answer is **(1).** According to the passage, choice (1), "standards of accountability," is the best answer. While these standards may involve curriculum content (choice 2) and academic performance (choice 3), these are but parts of the overall standards. Choices (4) and (5), while relevant, are not mentioned in the passage.

> How do communities assess their school performance?
>
> **(1)** Public awareness
> **(2)** District's performances
> **(3)** Local accountability
> **(4)** Comparison of data
> **(5)** Media exposure

The correct answer is **(4).** The results of performance assessments are made public; therefore, choice (4) "comparison of data" is the best answer. While choices (1), (2), and (3) may be relevant factors, they are not the best answer to the question. Choice (5) is not mentioned in the passage, although "media exposure" may be a means to inform the community.

3. Analysis Questions

Analysis questions test your ability to break down information and understand how ideas relate to each other. This could involve comparing ideas and exploring their relationships. You need to know the difference between a fact, an opinion, and a hypothesis. You may be asked to find ideas not specifically stated or recognize a writer's historical point of view. What is the difference between a fact and an opinion? Why does an event happen and what are the results? What conclusion can you draw from the information presented?

EXAMPLES:

The analysis example questions are based on the following passage.

With a land area of almost 2 million square kilometers and a population of about 96 million, Mexico shares borders with the United States to the north and Guatemala and Belize to the southeast. It is a representative, democratic, and federal republic with a government composed of legislative, executive, and judicial branches. The country is divided into 31 sovereign states, as well as the federal district in which the capital, Mexico City, is located.

Approximately 80 percent of the population is of mixed European and North American Indian or African slave ancestry *(mestizo)*, while 10 percent is of purely indigenous descent *(indégena)*. Mexicans are predominantly Roman Catholic Spanish-speakers, but more than 50 distinct indigenous peoples maintain their own languages and cultural traditions. The indigenous population is over-represented in the poverty statistics, in which 28 million Mexicans are estimated to live in extreme poverty, with an additional 12 million classified as poor.

What makes Mexico a federal republic?

(1) It has a population of 96 million.
(2) It is divided into sovereign states.
(3) It has a land area of 2 million square kilometers.
(4) The government is composed of three branches.
(5) The capital is Mexico City.

The correct answer is **(2)**. A federal republic is made up of a number of sovereign states forming a decentralized form of government. A population of 96 million (choice 1) and a land area of 2 million square kilometers (choice 3) are not directly related to being a federal republic. The facts that the government has three branches (choice 4) and the capital is Mexico City (choice 5) also are not relevant to the question.

Which term does NOT describe Mexican society?

(1) Multicultural
(2) Multilingual
(3) Homogeneous
(4) Indigenous descent
(5) Slave ancestry

The correct answer is **(3)**. *Homogeneous* means "uniform in structure, essentially alike." All other answer choices are mentioned in the passages as descriptors of Mexican society. *Multicultural* (choice 1) means many cultures, while *multilingual* (choice 2) refers to multiple languages. *Indigenous descent* (choice 4) and *slave ancestry* (choice 5) are terms that may be used to describe the diversity of Mexico's population.

> Which segment of the population is the most impoverished?
>
> **(1)** North American Indians
> **(2)** African slaves
> **(3)** Spanish speakers
> **(4)** Roman Catholics
> **(5)** Indigenous peoples

The correct answer is **(5).** According to the passage, choice (5) "indigenous peoples" are a minority that is over-represented in the poverty statistics. Spanish speakers (choice 3) and Roman Catholics (choice 4) refer to the majority of citizens. North American Indians (choice 1) and African slaves (choice 2) are incorrect choices.

4. Evaluation Questions

Evaluation questions assess your ability to make judgments about the material's appropriateness, accuracy, and differences of opinion, as well as the role that information and ideas play in influencing current and future decision-making. You should be able to judge the accuracy of material presented in the passage. Does the information represent a particular point of view? What determines the reasons for the decision-making? How are trends used to predict an outcome? How do you assess the accuracy of facts presented?

EXAMPLES:

The evaluation example questions are based on the following passage.

During the last decades, Hungary has experienced a process of transition, which has had far-reaching consequences for the economy and society as a whole. But it is important to underline that this process was initiated much earlier than in the neighboring countries. In the 1980s, a gradual process of democratization and of decentralization was introduced, and the private sector became increasingly significant. Dynamic entrepreneurs began to appear, and intellectuals were quite aware of new ideas and developments on the international scene.

It is not so surprising, therefore, that when the change of regime took place around 1990, Hungary went through the transition process at a particularly rapid pace. Drastic measures of privatization and economic reform were undertaken, as well as far-reaching institutional changes involving a large degree of decentralization. During the early 1990s, economic restructuring and the loss of export markets (especially in the Soviet Union) had serious adverse effects on the standard of living. There was a deep economic recession, with unemployment, poverty, and inequalities between regions and social groups appearing for the first time.

> How did Hungary's economic changes compare to other Eastern European nations?
>
> **(1)** They were more far-reaching.
> **(2)** They were more important.
> **(3)** They were more gradual.
> **(4)** They were less significant.
> **(5)** They were much later.

The correct answer is **(1).** According to the passage, Hungary's economic and social changes were "far-reaching" as compared to neighboring countries. They may also have been "more important" (choice 2) but that is not the best answer. More gradual (choice 3), less significant (choice 4), and much later (choice 5) are incorrect choices.

> What factors were responsible for changes in Hungary's society in 1990?
>
> **(1)** Democratization
> **(2)** Decentralization
> **(3)** Entrepreneurs
> **(4)** Intellectuals
> **(5)** All of the above

The correct answer is **(5)**. According to the passage democratization, decentralization, entrepreneurs, and intellectuals all contributed to changes in the economic and social order in 1990.

> What was the chief reason for the decline in Hungary's standard of living in the early 1990s?
>
> **(1)** Privatization
> **(2)** Loss of export markets
> **(3)** Economic reform
> **(4)** Regional inequalities
> **(5)** The Hungarian revolution

The correct answer is **(2)**. The chief reason for decline in the standard of living was the loss of export markets. This resulted in a deep economic recession leading to unemployment and poverty. Privatization (choice 1), economic reform (choice 3), and regional inequalities (choice 4) may also have had some impact but they were not the chief reasons. The Hungarian revolution (choice 5) is an incorrect choice because it occurred many years before.

C. Test Strategies

To improve your skills and get better results, try the following strategies before taking the GED Social Studies Test:

- **Read, read, read!** The best way to prepare for the reading-based questions is to practice reading excerpts or passages from a variety of documents. Following is a list of suggested reading to help you prepare. The important thing is to gain experience reading this type of material. The more you read, the better prepared you'll be when you encounter this type of material on the test.

  On the test, you will be presented with at least one passage of each of the following types of documents. You don't have to know all the details of what's in them, but you do have to become a bit familiar with the language so that you can answer the questions. Look up these types of documents in the library or on the Internet to become familiar with the way they are written.
  - Declaration of Independence
  - U.S. Constitution
  - Landmark Supreme Court cases
  - Consumer information guides
  - Political speeches
  - Almanacs

- **Get visual.** To prepare for visual materials questions, study the maps you see on television, in newspapers, and in magazines. Familiarize yourself with U.S. and world geography by studying a globe or an atlas. Study examples of charts and graphs in newspapers, magazines, and other texts to learn to understand what information is being presented or compared.

- **Quiz yourself.** Ask yourself questions about what you've read. Try to understand the main ideas so as to explain them to others.

- **Review the example questions and work the practice questions:** There are example questions in Section B, earlier in this chapter. More questions for practice appear at the end of this chapter. Work through these questions and check your answers. If you answered a question correctly, read the explanation to reinforce the reasoning. If you answered incorrectly, read the explanation, and then reread the question to see where you went wrong. Additional sample questions can be found online on the GED Web site (www.acenet.edu/Content/NavigationMenu/ged/test/prep/sample_questions.htm).

- **Take the practice test.** Take the full-length Social Studies Practice Test (Chapter XIII). Do so under test conditions, setting a timer. Check your answers and review the explanations.

D. Practice

Remember that the Social Studies Test does not measure your ability to recall information. It requires you to read a passage, analyze the information, evaluate its accuracy, and draw conclusions according to the printed text or visual materials contained in the passage. You then must choose the best answer to each question.

1. Questions

Questions 1 through 4 are based on the following passage excerpted from U.S. History For Dummies, *2nd Edition, by Steve Wiegand, copyright 2009 by Wiley Publishing, Inc. Reprinted with permission of John Wiley & Sons, Inc.*

Taking It to the Bank

The first Bank of the United States, whose majority stockholder was the federal government and which had helped the nation get a grip on its finances, had been created at the urging of Alexander Hamilton in 1790. But it had been allowed to expire in 1811, and a horde of state-chartered banks swarmed to take its place. In 1811, there were 88 state banks; by 1813, the number was 208, and by 1819, 392. Most of them extended credit and printed currency far in excess of their reserves; when the war came, most of them couldn't redeem their paper for a tenth of its worth.

In 1816, Congress chartered a second Bank of the United States, with capital of $35 million. The idea was to provide stability to the economic system by having a large bank that would serve as the federal government's financial agent. But the new bank's managers were corrupt, stupid, or both, and they lent money like mad to land-crazed Americans flocking to the West.

In 1819, land prices dropped, manufacturing and crop prices collapsed, and scores of overextended banks failed. The yahoos who were first put in charge of the second Bank of the United States finally got the boot; new management stepped in, clamped down hard on credit, and foreclosed on virtually all its debtors.

But the Panic of 1819, the nation's first widespread financial crisis, triggered strong resentment toward the Bank, which was nicknamed "the Monster." The Bank was particularly hated in the credit-dependent West, which saw it as a creature of rich financiers and speculators in New York and New England. The West's antipathy toward the bank drove a wedge between the regions.

1. Which of the following sentences summarize the main point to be found in the first paragraph?

   (1) There were many state-chartered banks.
   (2) Alexander Hamilton helped the nation get a grip on its finances.
   (3) To protect the value of the currency, the country needed one federal bank.
   (4) Most banks extended credit and printed currency.
   (5) The War of 1812 was fought between the United States and Britain.

2. Which of the following sentences, adapted from the second paragraph, address the need for a stable financial system?

   (1) Congress chartered a second bank.
   (2) The new bank's managers were corrupt.
   (3) Land-crazed Americans flocked to the West.
   (4) They lent money like mad.
   (5) A large bank would serve as the federal government's financial agent.

3. Which of the following conclusions can be drawn from the third paragraph?

   (1) Prices collapsed.
   (2) New management saved the Bank of the United States.
   (3) Yahoos got the boot.
   (4) Scores of banks failed.
   (5) The weather was warm and sunny.

4. Which of the following accurately describes the reason for resentment toward the bank?

   (1) Panic of 1819
   (2) Widespread financial crisis
   (3) Credit-dependent West
   (4) Creature of rich financiers
   (5) All of the above

Questions 5 through 8 are based on the following passage excerpted from U.S. History For Dummies, *2nd Edition, by Steve Wiegand, copyright 2009 by Wiley Publishing, Inc. Reprinted with permission of John Wiley & Sons, Inc.*

Prohibition Begins

Even before the country's inception, Americans had been a hard-drinking bunch, and the social and private costs they paid for it had been high. But on January 16, 1920, the nation undertook a "noble experiment" to rid itself of the effects of Demon Rum. It was called *Prohibition,* and it was a spectacular failure.

There is some statistical evidence that Americans drank less after Prohibition began than they did before. But overall, the ban on booze was a bad idea. For one thing, it encouraged otherwise law-abiding citizens to visit *speak-easies* where alcohol was sold illegally. The number of "speaks" in New York City at the end of the decade, for example, was probably double the number of legal saloons at the beginning.

Gangsters like "Scarface" Al Capone and George "Bugs" Moran made fortunes selling bootleg booze, and they became celebrities doing it, despite the violence that was their normal business tool. Capone's Chicago mob took in $60 million a year at its peak—and murdered more than 300 people while doing it. But bullets weren't the gangsters' only tools. They also bought off or bullied scores of federal, state, and local officials to look the other way, which only added to public disrespect for law and government.

Part of the disrespect for government was well deserved. Even though Congress and a string of presidents paid lip service to the idea of Prohibition to make the anti-liquor lobby happy, many of the politicians were regular customers for the bootleggers. Congress provided only 1,550 federal agents to enforce the ban throughout the entire country, and criminal penalties for bootlegging were relatively light.

5. In the first paragraph, what is meant by "noble experiment"?

   (1) Hard-drinking bunch
   (2) Social and private costs
   (3) Demon Rum
   (4) Prohibition
   (5) The right to vote

6. What was the result of Prohibition?

   (1) Americans drank less.
   (2) Booze was banned.
   (3) Citizens visited "speak-easies."
   (4) Alcohol was illegal.
   (5) All of the above.

7. Why did the public lose respect for law and government during Prohibition?

   (1) Gangsters became celebrities.
   (2) Officials were corrupted.
   (3) People were murdered.
   (4) Fortunes were made selling booze.
   (5) Violence was a business tool.

8. Who were the strongest supporters of Prohibition?

    (1) Congress
    (2) A string of presidents
    (3) Politicians
    (4) The anti-liquor lobby
    (5) Bootleggers

Questions 9 through 12 refer to the following passage, which is excerpted from the Declaration of Independence.

The Declaration of Independence

In every stage of these Oppressions We have Petitioned for Redress in the most humble terms: Our repeated Petitions have been answered only by repeated injury. A Prince, whose character is thus marked by every act which may define a Tyrant, is unfit to be the ruler of a free people.

Nor have We been wanting in attentions to our British brethren. We have warned them from time to time of attempts by their legislature to extend an unwarrantable jurisdiction over us. We have reminded them of the circumstances of our emigration and settlement here. We have appealed to their native justice and magnanimity, and we have conjured them by the ties of our common kindred to disavow these usurpations, which would inevitably interrupt our connections and correspondence. They too have been deaf to the voice of justice and of consanguinity. We must, therefore, acquiesce in the necessity, which denounces our Separation, and hold them, as we hold the rest of mankind, Enemies in War, in Peace Friends.

We, therefore, the Representatives of the united States of America, in General Congress, Assembled, appealing to the Supreme Judge of the world for the rectitude of our intentions, do, in the Name, and by Authority of the good People of these Colonies, solemnly publish and declare, That these United Colonies are, and of Right ought to be Free and Independent States; that they are Absolved from all Allegiance to the British Crown, and that all political connection between them and the State of Great Britain, is and ought to be totally dissolved; and that as Free and Independent States; they have full Power to levy War; conclude Peace, contract Alliances, establish Commerce, and to do all other Acts and Things which Independent States may of right do. And for the support of this Declaration, with a firm reliance on the protection of divine Providence, we mutually pledge to each other our Lives, our Fortunes and our sacred Honor.

9. Who was "the Prince" referred to in the first paragraph?

    (1) A tyrant
    (2) King George III
    (3) A free people
    (4) The ruler
    (5) All of the above

10. What grievance was NOT directed at the British government in the Declaration?

    (1) Unwarrantable jurisdiction
    (2) Emigration and settlement issues
    (3) Lack of native justice
    (4) The right to keep slaves
    (5) Interruption of correspondence

11. What did the Colonies hope to gain from the Declaration?

   (1) To be free and independent states
   (2) To be absolved from allegiances to the Crown
   (3) To be able to dissolve all connections
   (4) To be able to wage war
   (5) All of the above

12. What does "divine Providence" refer to in the passage?

   (1) Our Fortunes
   (2) Our sacred Honor
   (3) The will of God
   (4) Acts and Things
   (5) Independent States

Questions 13 through 16 refer to the following passage excerpted from U.S. History For Dummies, *2nd Edition, by Steve Wiegand, copyright 2009 by Wiley Publishing, Inc. Reprinted with permission of John Wiley & Sons, Inc.*

World War II

One of the most immediate problems was dealing with the menace posed by German submarines, or *U-boats,* in the Atlantic. Traveling in packs, the subs sank three million tons of Allied shipping in the first half of 1942 alone. But the Allies worked out a system of convoys and developed better anti-sub tactics. Most importantly, they built far more cargo ships than the Germans could possibly sink.

In the summer of 1942, Allied planes began bombing targets inside Germany. Eventually, the bombing would take a terrible toll. In 1943, 60,000 people were killed in the city of Hamburg, and the city of Dresden was all but destroyed.

In the fall of 1942, Allied armies, under a relatively obscure American commander named Dwight D. Eisenhower, launched an attack in North Africa against Hitler's best general, Erwin Rommel. The green American troops were whipped soundly at the Kasserine Pass in Tunisia. But in a return match—while Rommel was in Germany—a combined U.S. and British force defeated the Germans at El Alamein and drove them out of Egypt.

From Africa, the Allies invaded Sicily, and then advanced into the Italian mainland. Mussolini was overthrown and eventually executed by his own people. But the German army poured troops into the country and it took until the end of 1944 for Italy to be completely controlled.

On the Eastern Front, meanwhile, the Russian army gradually had turned the tables on the invading Germans and begun pushing them back, despite staggering civilian and military losses. And in England, the Allies, under the leadership of Eisenhower, were preparing the greatest invasion force the world had ever seen.

13. What made the U-boats so effective in the Atlantic?

   (1) They had a system of convoys.
   (2) They had anti-sub tactics.
   (3) They built more ships.
   (4) They traveled in packs.
   (5) All of the above.

14. When did the Allies begin bombing inside Germany?

    (1) The first half of 1942
    (2) Summer of 1942
    (3) Fall of 1942
    (4) 1943
    (5) The end of 1944

15. Where was General Eisenhower's first victory?

    (1) Tunisia
    (2) Egypt
    (3) Kassarine Pass
    (4) El Alamein
    (5) Sicily

16. What happened on the Eastern Front?

    (1) Mussolini was overthrown.
    (2) The German Army poured into the country.
    (3) The Russian Army pushed back the Germans.
    (4) The Allies prepared for an invasion.
    (5) Japan bombed Pearl Harbor.

2. Answers

1. **(3)** This is an example of a comprehension question. To answer this question, you must understand the main idea of the paragraph. Be careful of answers such as (1), (2), and (4), which are mentioned in the paragraph but do not convey the main idea of the paragraph. Although they do provide information contained in the paragraph, they don't summarize the main idea. Choice (5) has nothing to do with the information contained in the paragraph.

2. **(5)** To answer this application question, you must understand the results of instability in the financial sector. Choices (1), (2), (3), and (4) provide some information concerning attempts to obtain stability, but they don't address the application of the federal government's intervention to stabilize the financial system.

3. **(2)** This is an example of an analysis question. Choices (1), (3), and (4) involve conditions—such as collapsing prices, incompetent managers, and failing banks—that demonstrated the need for new management to save the bank. Choice (5) has no relevance to the paragraph.

4. **(5)** This is an example of an evaluation question. Choices (1), (2), (3), and (4) describe points of resentment between the East and the West concerning the bank, which was nicknamed "the Monster" by its opponents. The Panic of 1819 resulted in a widespread financial crisis, which was blamed on the rich Eastern financiers by the credit-dependent West. Therefore, choice (5), which includes all these factors, is the correct choice.

5. **(4)** Choices (1), (2), and (3) may be reasons for imposition of Prohibition, but they are not the "noble experiment" referred to in the passage. Choice (5) is not mentioned anywhere in the passage.

6. **(5)** According to the second paragraph, choices (1), (2), (3), and (4) all were a result of Prohibition being proclaimed. According to statistics, Americans drank less after Prohibition. But many citizens also visited "speak-easies" to get illegal alcohol even though "booze was banned." Therefore, Choice (5) is correct.

7. **(2)** Gangsters paid off or bullied corrupt federal, state, and local officials, causing the public to lose respect for law and government. As a result, gangsters used violence as a business tool to murder people, make illegal fortunes, and become celebrities.

8. **(4)** According to the fourth paragraph, the strongest supporters of Prohibition were the anti-liquor lobby. Presidents and members of Congress supported Prohibition only to gain political points with the anti-liquor lobby. Many politicians were, in fact, customers of speak-easies. Bootleggers might also have supported Prohibition because it made them a lot of money.

9. **(2)** Although King George III also may have been referred to as "a Tyrant" or "the ruler," the formal title for the King remains the best answer. Choice (3) is incorrect.

10. **(4)** There was no mention in the passage of "the right to keep slaves." All the other choices—jurisdiction, emigration, justice, and correspondence—are grievances mentioned in the passage.

11. **(5)** According to the Declaration of Independence, the Colonies demanded to be free and independent, with no connection or allegiance to the Crown, and able to wage war and secure peace—all of which are covered in choices (1), (2), (3), and (4).

12. **(3)** "Providence" may be defined as God's will, while "divine" pertains to God. Sacred (or holy) Honor, Fortunes, Acts and Things, and Independence do not convey the correct meaning.

13. **(4)** According to the passage, the German U-boats sank three million tons of Allied shipping because they "traveled in packs." A system of convoys, anti-sub tactics, and building more ships all were ways that the Allies responded to the success of the U-boats.

14. **(2)** According to the passage, Allied bombing began inside Germany in the "summer of 1942." The other choices refer to different events during the war.

15. **(4)** General Eisenhower led the Allied Army to victory at El Alamein after being defeated at the Kassarine Pass in Tunisia. This victory allowed the Allies to invade Sicily after driving the Germans out of Egypt.

16. **(3)** The Russian Army was able to push back the Germans despite staggering civilian and military losses on the Eastern Front. The overthrow of Mussolini and the German invasion of Italy happened on the Western Front, as did planning for the Allied invasion of France. The Japanese attack on Pearl Harbor was not part of the war in Europe.

IX. Science

A. Test Format

The GED Science Test consists of 50 multiple-choice questions and allows you 80 minutes to answer them. The content of the questions is based on the following subject areas, which are usually covered in high school science courses:

- **Physical science:** 17 or 18 questions, or about 35 percent
  - Structure of atoms
  - Structure and properties of matter
  - Chemical reactions
  - Motions and forces
  - Conservation of energy and increase in disorder
  - Interactions of energy and matter
- **Life science:** 22 or 23 questions, about 45 percent
  - The cell
  - Molecular basis of heredity
  - Biological evolution
  - Interdependence of organisms
  - Matter, energy, and organization in living systems
  - Behavior of organisms
- **Earth and space science:** 10 questions, about 20 percent
  - Energy in the Earth system
  - Geochemical cycles
  - Origin and formation of the Earth
  - Origin and formation of the universe

The GED Science Test is essentially a test of reading comprehension. It evaluates your ability to assess and interpret information presented in provided text passages and visual materials. You need to have some basic science knowledge, but you are not expected to memorize specific scientific information.

B. Types of Questions—A Detailed Look

The questions on the GED Science Test are based on text or visual passages. Visual material may be graphs, tables, charts, or diagrams and may account for up to 60 percent of the questions.

Text passages will vary in length and may be followed by one or more questions. About 25 percent, or 12 or 13 questions, will be in sets of questions based on one passage. The rest will be questions based on individual short passages.

1. Questions Based on Text

On the GED Science Test, you'll be presented with questions based on text passages. You have two choices in answering these questions:

- You can skim or read the passage and then answer the question.
- You can read the question and skim the answers looking for keywords, and then read the passage to find out which answer is correct.

The way you proceed depends on the passage and the question. If the question asks specific information like a definition, you might want to skim the answers first and then go back to the passage to match an answer with the information presented.

EXAMPLE:

The following question refers to the following passage.

Detergents Better than Soap

If we wish to wash our clothes, we are faced with a chemical decision. Should we use a detergent or soap to clean the apparel? The actual answer is affected more by the water used in washing than in the chemical we add to clean the clothes. Soap will form a scum in hard water and detergent will not. The actual cleaning may not be that different in soft water, but in hard water we would see a difference.

In washing clothes, the main determinant of how clean they will be after washing is:

(1) The chemical added.
(2) The amount of soap used.
(3) The hardness of the water.
(4) The brand of detergent used.
(5) The mechanism used in the washing machine.

The correct answer is **(3)**. According to the passage, soap will form a scum in hard water that will make the clothes look dirty. The other answers may have a ring of truth to them but cannot be backed up by information in the passage, and your answers must be supported by the information in the passage.

2. Questions Based on Visual Materials

On the GED Science Test, you'll also be presented with questions based on visual materials. Tables, graphs, and diagrams are visual representations of data or information and can be "read" if you do so carefully. Most people are more used to reading words than visual material, but with practice you can do it.

a. Tables

A table presents data in a concise, organized manner. Tables have headings that tell you what the information in the table means. In the case of the following table, the right-hand column also indicates the units. In a table, the information that is horizontal is said to be in *rows,* and the information that is vertical is said to be in *columns.* If you wanted to find the relative weight on Earth, you would look down the left column until you found Earth and then across the row until you found 150, which would be the relative weight in pounds.

In answering questions based on tables, read the headings first and then the question to understand what information you're looking for.

EXAMPLES:

The example questions are based on the following table.

Relative Weights on Various Planets	
Planet	Relative Weight (in pounds)
Mercury	58
Venus	136.5
Earth	150
Mars	57
Jupiter	381
Saturn	162
Uranus	136.5
Neptune	178.5

On which planet would a person who weighs 127 pounds on Earth weigh the least?

(1) Mercury
(2) Mars
(3) Saturn
(4) Uranus
(5) Neptune

The correct answer is **(2)**. From the information in the table, a person would weigh the least on Mars. This would be independent of her actual weight on Earth.

If the force of gravity on a person determines her weight, which planet has the largest force of gravity?

(1) Mercury
(2) Mars
(3) Saturn
(4) Uranus
(5) Neptune

The correct answer is **(5)**. A person would weigh the most on Neptune because it has the greatest force of gravity value.

153

b. Graphs

A chart or graph is a visual representation of data presented. Charts and graphs show relative information most easily. If you wanted to represent the data in the earlier table in the form of a chart or graph, you could do so as in the following figure.

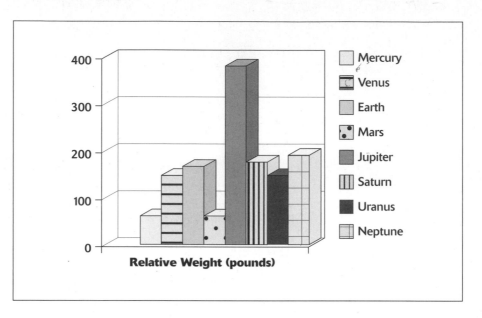

This type of graph is called a bar graph because the data is presented in the form of bars, each of which is proportional to the relative size of the data. Although the vertical axis is calibrated in the units given, it would be very difficult to give a definite answer to the size of any of the bars. Relative size is usually immediately apparent.

EXAMPLE:

On which planet would you weigh the most?

(1)   Mercury
(2)   Mars
(3)   Jupiter
(4)   Saturn
(5)   Neptune

The correct answer is **(3).** The bar representing the relative weight on Jupiter is the highest, which means that you would weigh the most on Jupiter.

If you wanted to represent the same data on a line graph, you would produce the following figure.

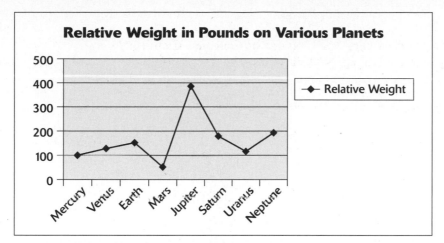

EXAMPLE:

On which planet would a car that weighs 2,000 pounds on Earth weigh the least?

(1) Mercury
(2) Venus
(3) Earth
(4) Mars
(5) Jupiter

The correct answer is **(4).** The point on the line graph representing the lowest relative weight is Mars. Line graphs give an easy-to-understand picture of relative amounts.

The information represented by a line graph is relative and the position of points on the line can give you an indication of the size of the data. Unless you have an amazingly accurate graph, you couldn't read absolute data from the graph, but reading relative information is usually possible.

c. Diagrams

Diagrams can be read in a similar way to charts, graphs, and passages. They contain information as visuals. The first thing you have to do when reading a diagram is to look for the title and then the labeling. In the following diagram, the title is "Lens," which indicates that the diagram will be about a lens or lenses. The labels indicate the type of lens that the information presented is about. In the first case, the information presented is about a convex lens. Looking at the diagram, you can see that this type of lens refracts rays of light in a specific manner. Combining this with the other information about the behavior of rays of light passing through a particular type of lens would allow you to answer the question.

EXAMPLE:

The example question is based on the following diagram.

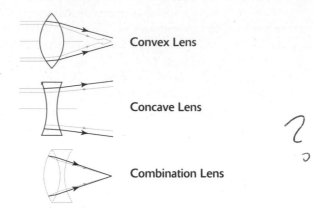

Convex Lens

Concave Lens

Combination Lens

Which lens or combination of lenses would you use to start a fire by concentrating the rays of the sun on a piece of paper?

(1) Convex lens
(2) Combination lens
(3) Concave lens
(4) Either a convex or a combination lens
(5) None of the above

The correct answer is **(4).** Either a convex lens or a combination lens would concentrate the rays of the sun on a spot, which would have the effect of concentrating the energy on that spot, raising the temperature, and increasing the possibility of setting fire to the paper. The concave lens would diverge the rays of light (spread them out).

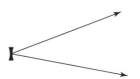

C. Test Strategies

Here are some strategies to help you succeed on the Science Test:

- **Brush up on your science knowledge and vocabulary.** The Science Test requires a basic knowledge of the subject matter and a familiarity with the vocabulary of science. Study Section D, at the end of this chapter; some vocabulary terms are included there for all three science subject areas.

- **Read, read, read!** We've tried to give you a short introduction to each content area that may be on the test (see Section D). If you're familiar with a topic, you may want to read a bit to see if there is any new information on the subject. If a topic is unfamiliar to you, read and research as much as you need to get a general understanding of it. You can do this on the Internet or at the library.

- **Review the example questions.** Example questions are sprinkled throughout this chapter. Use your hand or a piece of paper to cover the answer and explanation while you're answering the question. After you answer the question, check your answer and, if it's right, read the explanation to reinforce the reasoning. If you got it wrong, read the explanation, reread the question to see where you went wrong, and reread the science review material. If you're still struggling with the question, expand your reading until it all makes sense. Additional sample questions can be found online on the GED Web site (www.acenet.edu/Content/NavigationMenu/ged/test/prep/sample_questions.htm).

- **Use the scientific method.** One of the ways to handle science questions is to try to think like a scientist by using what is commonly called the scientific method. Read more on this method below and follow it to help you answer Science Test questions.

- **Take the practice test.** Take the Science Practice Test (Chapter XIV). Do so under test conditions, setting a timer. Check your answers and review the explanations.

The Scientific Method

The term *scientific method* is often used to describe how scientists go about investigating and experimenting. It is a method with several steps:

- The first step in investigating a phenomenon is formulating a question that you want to answer through research or experimentation.

- Second, you look at external research to formulate a hypothesis.

- Third, you test the hypothesis through experimentation and/or observation for the purpose of gathering evidence. To be scientifically valid, the evidence must be observable, measurable, and empirical. Sometimes evidence is gathered though a study of research done by others.

- Fourth, you analyze all the data gathered and, from that analysis, you can attempt to draw a conclusion.

Scientific Method Vocabulary

empirical: Developed through observation.

evidence: Material or data used to support or not support a theory.

experimentation: Carrying out experiments.

formulate a hypothesis: A prediction based on prior knowledge. In experimentation, hypotheses are supported or not based on the data obtained from the experiment.

investigating a phenomenon: Looking into something that has been observed.

measurable: Able to be measured in an accurate manner using a specific unit of measurement.

observable: Able to be observed (or perceived) by more than one person.

observation: Noticing or perceiving.

reproducible: Able to be reproduced more than once by more than one person.

scientifically valid: Scientifically authoritative.

EXAMPLE:

> Karen has been assigned a project by her science teacher with the advice that she should use the scientific method. What type of evidence should she gather?
>
> **(1)** Observable
> **(2)** Measurable
> **(3)** Empirical
> **(4)** Environmental
> **(5)** 1, 2, and 3

The correct answer is **(5).** Evidence should be observable, measurable, and empirical; its location doesn't make a difference.

D. Science Review

We've provided this basic science review to help you prepare for the Science Test. This is not a comprehensive review of each of the sciences. You should plan to do some reading on your own about the various subjects because the more reading you do, the more ideas and vocabulary you're exposed to.

For additional science review, you can visit CliffsNotes.com (http://www.cliffsnotes.com/sciences-study-guides.html) or reference these other great *CliffsNotes* titles:

CliffsQuick Review Biology

CliffsNotes Chemistry Quick Review

CliffsQuickReview Earth Science

CliffsQuickReview Astronomy

1. Physical Science

Physical science studies nonliving systems and includes chemistry and physics.

Chemistry—Chemistry is the branch of physical science concerned with the composition, behavior, structure, and properties of matter, as well as the changes matter undergoes during chemical reactions. *Matter* is a vague term for what things are made of, but in spite of the vagueness of the term, chemistry is an exact science with rules and theories.

EXAMPLES:

> José is conducting an experiment in his lab. He wants to see if he can create the three states of water. He could do that by:
>
> **(1)** Heating it to 212°F.
> **(2)** Heating it to 100°F.
> **(3)** Cooling it below 32°F.
> **(4)** Leaving it at room temperature.
> **(5)** 1, 3, and 4.

The correct answer is **(5)**. Heating water to 212°F will turn it into steam (gas); cooling it below 32°F will turn it to ice (solid); and leaving it at room temperature will allow it to stay as water (liquid). Heating it to 100°F will have no effect except creating hot water.

The next example question is based on the following passage.

Allergies

Have you ever wondered why some people sneeze during the spring and fall seasons? They may be suffering from allergies. An *allergic reaction* occurs when the person's body becomes *hypersensitive* to a substance that may normally be considered harmless, such as pollen or dust. These substances are called *allergens*. While people who do not suffer from allergies can tolerate these substances, allergic people have to try to avoid them or take some type of treatment to reduce their sensitivity.

> A person suffering from allergies may sneeze when exposed to:
>
> **(1)** Cold.
> **(2)** Bad jokes.
> **(3)** Allergens.
> **(4)** Soap and water.
> **(5)** Treatments.

The correct answer is **(3)**. Allergens are specifically referred to in the passage. In this question, skimming the passage after reading the question and answers might save you some time.

The next two example questions refer to the following diagram and text.

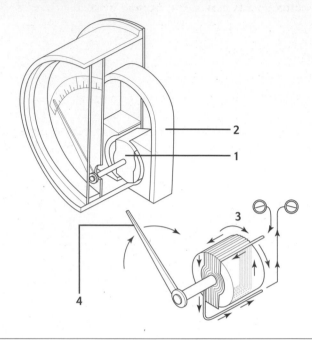

A galvanometer is an instrument for measuring extremely small currents. A coil is wound around an iron core **(1)** suspended between the poles of a horseshoe magnet **(2)**. When a current flows in the coil, it induces a magnetic field in the core that causes it to move **(3)** in the field of the horseshoe magnet, registering as a deflection of the attached pointer **(4)**.

A galvanometer is used for measuring:

(1) Water pressure.
(2) Wind velocity.
(3) Direction of travel.
(4) Extremely small currents.
(5) Magnetic fields.

The correct answer is **(4)**. The galvanometer was designed to measure extremely small currents; this is stated in the passage beside the diagram. Answer (5) is mentioned but in a different context.

The coil wound around the iron core is attached to the indicator needle and has a magnetic current induced in it when:

(1) The pointer is wound up.
(2) A small current is passed through it.
(3) Static electricity is detected.
(4) It is plugged into the household current.
(5) The case is shaken.

The correct answer is **(2)**. The material states that the galvanometer measures an extremely small current; household current is not extremely small, and it is alternating current.

Physics—Physics is the branch of physical science that deals with understanding how the world and universe behave. Among other concepts, it includes matter and its movement through space and time, energy, force, and work.

There are **three laws of physics** that you should be aware of:

- **Newton's First Law of Motion** states that a body at rest will remain at rest unless acted upon by an external force. Every body moving in a straight line at a uniform velocity will remain so unless acted upon by an external force.
- **Newton's Second Law of Motion** states that a force acting on a body produces an acceleration that is inversely proportional to the mass of the object and directly proportional to the magnitude of the force.
- **Newton's Third Law of Motion** states that for every action there is an equal and opposite reaction. If a boxer hits a wall with a certain force, then the wall exerts an equal and opposite force on the boxer.

EXAMPLE:

> Harvey is nailing together his deck. Every time he hits the nail with his hammer, he feels a shock in his wrist. What is the explanation based on a knowledge of physics?
>
> **(1)** Equal and opposite reaction
> **(2)** Rate of change of position
> **(3)** Body at rest remains at rest
> **(4)** Electrostatic forces
> **(5)** Every particle attracts every other particle

The correct answer is **(1)**. When Harvey hits the head of the nail with his hammer, according to Newton, the head of the nail is hitting back on the hammer and Harvey feels this force in his wrist. The other answers are associated with principles of physics, just not this one.

a. Structure of Atoms

Matter is composed of atoms, which can be visualized as a tiny solar system. At the center of this system is the nucleus, composed of protons (positively charged) and neutrons (electrically neutral) and responsible for most of the mass of the atom. Electrons (negatively charged), which travel at unbelievable speeds, exist outside the nucleus.

Atoms are electrically neutral, which means that they must have the same number of protons and electrons. *Nuclear force* holds the atom together in spite of the opposing charges. Electrons are thought to travel around the nucleus is a cloud-like atmosphere.

EXAMPLES:

> The number of protons and neutrons in the nucleus determine what the atom is. Different elements have different numbers of protons and neutrons in their nuclei.
>
> What determines the name of a substance?
>
> **(1)** Hardness
> **(2)** State
> **(3)** Number of electrons
> **(4)** Number of protons and neutrons
> **(5)** Density

The correct answer is **(4).** The passage states that different elements have different numbers of protons and neutrons in their nucleus.

The next two example questions refer to the following passage.

Nuclear Chain Reaction

The explosion of the atomic bomb is an example of a nuclear chain reaction. In this reaction, a neutron strikes the nucleus of a uranium-235. This neutron becomes part of the nucleus and forms uranium-236, which is very unstable and splits into two smaller nuclei. This splitting gives off a great deal of energy and releases several neutrons, which can continue the reaction. Under certain conditions, this can become a chain reaction, which can cause mass destruction if uncontrolled or, if properly controlled and monitored, power a nuclear generator.

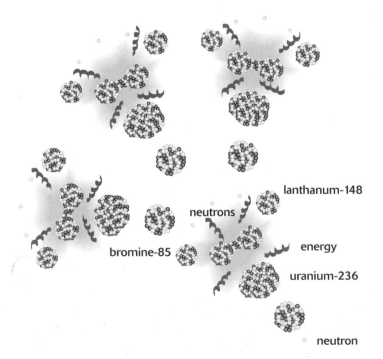

An atomic bomb is an example of:

(1) A chemical reaction.
(2) Formation of a solution.
(3) A chain reaction.
(4) Physical properties.
(5) The power of science.

The correct answer is **(3)**. According to the passage, the atomic bomb is an example of a chain reaction. The passage along with the diagram is provided to make a complex concept a little simpler so that the questions can be answered. On the test, make sure that you pay attention to diagrams because they can clarify some complex ideas.

Nuclear reactions can be used to:

(1) Make bombs.
(2) Power a nuclear generator.
(3) Become a source of tremendous amounts of electric power.
(4) Destroy cities.
(5) All of the above.

The correct answer is **(5)**. The power unleashed by a nuclear reaction can be used to aid civilization by providing a source of electricity and heat or destroy it in a nuclear firestorm.

b. Structure and Properties of Matter

Matter is composed of atoms. An *element* is made up of a single type of atom, and a *compound* is composed of two or more atoms that can interact with each other by transferring or sharing electrons, which creates *bonds*.

Solids, liquids, and gases may be composed of the same elements but differ in the distances between molecules and atoms. The energy that binds the atoms and molecules together is also different. A solid would have the least distance between atoms and molecules, and a gas would have the most; thus, a gas would have the least energy binding its atoms and a solid the most.

Example:

Matter is composed of:

(1) Forces.
(2) Chemicals.
(3) Molecules.
(4) Electrons, protons, and neutrons, all of which comprise an atom.
(5) Ions.

The correct answer is **(4)**. Matter is composed of atoms, which are composed of electrons, protons, and neutrons. The other answers sound like physics terms, but they don't answer the question.

c. Chemical Reactions

When one set of chemical substances is transformed into another, the substances are said to undergo a chemical reaction. Chemical reactions can be *spontaneous* (requiring no input of energy) or *nonspontaneous* (requiring an input of energy).

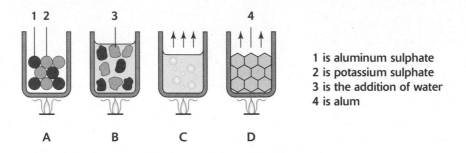

1 is aluminum sulphate
2 is potassium sulphate
3 is the addition of water
4 is alum

Heating aluminum sulphate and potassium sulphate produces no reaction (A).
If they are dissolved in water and heated until evaporation, alum is produced.

Alum is formed from aluminum sulphate and potassium sulphate. If the two chemicals are put together, nothing will happen (A). When water is added to *dissolve* the two chemicals (B), they form a *solution* (C), and with the addition of more heat until the liquid *evaporates,* alum is formed (D).

EXAMPLE:

> Donald wanted to create a reaction that would warm his small lab. What type of reaction would he want?
>
> **(1)** Atomic
> **(2)** Endothermic
> **(3)** Exothermic
> **(4)** Fusion
> **(5)** Spontaneous

The correct answer is **(3).** Exothermic reactions give off heat, which would warm his lab. Choices (1) and (4) would do more than warm his lab, and choice (5) is too general to be considered for a question looking for a specific answer.

d. Motions and Forces

When a force acts upon an object, motion is produced. If the force is positive and increasing, the object accelerates. If the force is constant, the object moves with constant velocity. If the force is negative and decreasing, the object decelerates.

Example:

> Lois is driving along the road when she sees a stop sign in the distance. In order to stop in time, what should she do?
>
> **(1)** Open the windows.
> **(2)** Put the transmission in neutral.
> **(3)** Apply a negative force using the brakes.
> **(4)** Downshift the transmission.
> **(5)** Open the door.

The correct answer is **(3)**. Applying a negative force to a moving object will result in deceleration, which is what she wanted. Choices (2) and (4) might eventually stop the car, but choice (3) is better.

e. Conservation of Energy and Increase in Disorder

The Law of Conservation of Energy states that *energy* can be neither created nor destroyed. It only can be transformed from one form to another. This means that the total energy of the universe is constant.

Energy can be *kinetic* (the energy of motion), *potential* (the energy of position), or *electromagnetic* (the energy contained by a field).

In a *thermodynamic system,* the universe tends to become less organized and less orderly over time. *Entropy* is the amount of disorder in the universe; the higher the entropy, the greater the disorder.

Example:

> Garry was making coffee by warming up his water in a microwave oven. His younger brother came in to watch and asked Garry how the water was being heated to a boil. What explanation should Garry have given his brother?
>
> **(1)** The oven is heating the water.
> **(2)** The turntable is heating the water.
> **(3)** The magnetron is transferring energy to the water.
> **(4)** There are heating elements in the microwave oven.
> **(5)** Heat is being drawn in by the fan and concentrated.

The correct answer is **(3)**. The energy from the magnetron (the part that produces the energy) transfers the energy to the water, causing it to heat up and boil. This question depends on some general knowledge both of energy transfer and microwaves. However, looking at the other answers, the best answer is (3) because the others refer to other means of heating water.

f. Interactions of Energy and Matter

Any wave, including water waves, can transfer energy when they interact with matter. When the waves hit the shore, there is a transfer of energy from the wave to the shore. There are different types of waves, such as sound waves, seismic waves, light waves, and electromagnetic waves. Types of electromagnetic waves are radio waves, microwaves, infrared radiation, visible light, ultraviolet light, X-rays, and gamma rays.

Materials often are divided into two groups, depending on the ability for electrons to flow in them. *Conductors,* such as metals, allow the electrons to flow easily. In *insulators,* the electrons cannot flow. If you look at a piece of commercial cable, the middle is copper, a metal that is a good conductor, surrounded by a plastic or rubber material, which is an insulator. This product allows electricity to flow easily through the copper while protecting people from the electricity by surrounding it with an insulator.

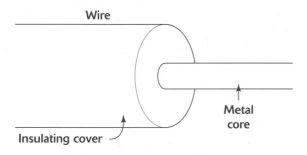

Example:

> Karen spent the day at the beach and got sunburned. She wondered how she could get a burn when it wasn't even hot outside. Her doctor prescribed a cream for the burn and explained that the burn was caused by:
>
> **(1)** Electromagnetic waves from space.
> **(2)** Infrared waves from the sun.
> **(3)** X-rays.
> **(4)** Ultraviolet light from the sun.
> **(5)** Gamma rays.

The correct answer is **(4)**. Sunburns are caused by ultraviolet rays from the sun. The other answers are wrong, but choice (2) is deceptive. If you didn't have some science background, you might associate *infrared* with heat, which would be technically correct but not in the context of sunburn.

g. Vocabulary

Following are some physical science terms that you'll want to familiarize yourself with in preparation for the Science Test. Some of the terms on the following list are included primarily because they appear in example questions in this chapter. As you do your reading in physical science, you may find terms that you do not understand. Look up the meanings and add them to your vocabulary list.

acceleration: The rate of change of velocity as a function of time.

allergen: Anything that causes an allergy.

allergic reaction: The body's reaction to an allergen.

atom: The smallest particle of an element that still retains the unique chemical properties of that specific element. It consists of a central nucleus surrounded by negatively charged electrons.

atomic number of an atom: Determined by the number of protons in the nucleus.

boiling point: The temperature point above which a substance exists as a gas and below which it exists as a liquid.

bonds: Force(s) holding together molecules.

center of gravity or a center of mass: An object behaves as if all its weight or mass were concentrated at that point.

chemical reaction: The creation of different chemical substances by breaking or forming chemical bonds.

compound: A substance composed of more than one element.

conservation of energy: Total energy remains constant, and energy cannot be created or destroyed.

covalent bonding: The stable balance of forces between atoms when they share electrons.

density of a substance: Mass per unit volume.

dissolve: Create a solution by mixing something with water.

electrical force: Interaction of charged particles.

electromagnetic energy: Energy in the form of electrical and/or magnetic waves.

electromagnetism: What happens when moving particles with an electric charge interact.

electrons: Subatomic particles having a negative electric charge.

electrostatic forces: Interaction of charged particles at rest.

element: Made up of one type of atom.

endothermic reaction: A reaction that absorbs energy in the form of heat.

energy: $e = mc^2$ (mass × speed of light squared). Energy is the ability to do work. $e = mc^2$ is a formula developed by Einstein to show that matter and energy are the same and are related by a constant squared.

entropy: The degree of orderliness to any system.

evaporate: To transition from a liquid to a gas.

exothermic reaction: A reaction in which energy is released, often in the form of heat.

force: A push or pull that can change the state of motion of an object. If no net force is applied to an object, there will be no change in motion.

freezing point: The temperature point above which a substance exists as a liquid and below which it exists as a solid.

gamma rays: Electromagnetic radiation with short wavelength.

gaseous state: A substance is in a gaseous state when it expands to fill whatever container it is in.

gravitational potential energy: Energy that two objects have because of their mass and separation.

gravity: Every particle of matter in the universe attracts every other particle with a force that can be calculated mathematically.

hypersensitive: Allergic to common substances.

infrared radiation: Invisible electromagnetic radiation; can produce heat.

ion: An atom that has lost or gained electrons.

ionic bonding: An ionic bond is the bond formed by electrostatic attraction between ions with opposite charges in a chemical compound.

light waves: Visible electromagnetic radiation.

liquid state: A substance is in a liquid state when it remains at a fixed volume but adapts to the shape of its container.

living system: A system that interacts with its environment and exhibits the characteristics normally associated with life.

kinetic energy: Energy of motion.

magnetic force: Interaction of charged particles in motion.

magnitude: Relative size or length of a vector quantity.

matter: Matter is composed of atoms; it occupies space and has mass. The properties of matter are weight, volume, mass, and density.

microwaves: High-frequency electromagnetic waves.

molecule: An electrically neutral group of at least two atoms held together by a very strong bond.

motion: Movement.

neutrons: Subatomic particles that have no net electric charge.

nonliving system: A system that does not interact with its environment or show any of the characteristics normally associated with life.

nonspontaneous reaction: A chemical reaction that requires input of external energy.

nuclear chain reaction: Neutrons that are released as a result of nuclear fission collide with neighboring atomic nuclei, releasing them. The reaction continues exponentially, creating tremendous heat.

nuclear force: The force holding the nucleus of an atom together.

nucleus: Consists of protons and neutrons in most atoms.

potential energy: Energy of position.

products: Matter produced by a chemical reaction and usually having different properties from the reactants.

protons: Subatomic particles that have an electrical charge of +1 and are part of each atom.

quarks: Elemental particles that are a constituent of matter and combine to form composite particles such as protons and neutrons.

radio waves: Electromagnetic waves of medium frequency.

reactants: Substances initially involved in a chemical reaction.

scalar: Mathematically has only magnitude.

seismic waves: Shock waves in solid rock (often caused by earthquakes).

sensitivity: The ability to react to a stimulus.

solar system: The sun and all the planets revolving about it. Also includes the objects revolving around the planets like moons.

solid state: A substance is in a solid state when it maintains a fixed volume and shape.

solution: Homogeneous dispersal of two or more substances.

sound waves: Waves that produce sound.

speed: Magnitude of velocity without respect to its vector qualities.

spontaneous reaction: A chemical reaction proceeding without external energy input.

subatomic particles: Particles that are smaller than atoms.

thermodynamic system: A system that uses or produces heat.

transfer of energy: Energy can be transferred by heat transfer and doing work.

triple point: The temperature point at which a substance can exist as a gas, a liquid, and a solid.

ultraviolet light: Light with a shorter wavelength than visible light. Ultraviolet light can cause burns to skin.

uranium-235: A radioactive isotope of uranium used in bombs and as a fuel in nuclear reactors.

uranium-236: An isotope of uranium; radioactive waste.

vector: Mathematically has both magnitude and direction.

velocity: The rate of change of position and direction of an object.

visible light: Light that can be seen by the naked eye.

wave: A disturbance that moves from point to point in a medium without moving the points of the medium.

work: Force times distance.

X-rays: Electromagnetic radiation capable of penetrating solids.

2. Life Science

Life science studies living organisms and includes biology, ecology, and botany.

a. The Cell

The functional basic unit of life is the cell. *Organisms* may range from *unicellular* (one cell) to *multicellular* (many cells). Most *bacteria* are unicellular and most animals are multicellular. Humans have about 60 trillion to 100 trillion cells.

EXAMPLE:

The basic unit of life is:

(1) A cell.
(2) A proton.
(3) DNA.
(4) An electron.
(5) Bacteria.

The correct answer is **(1)**. The cell is the basic unit of life, and that would be considered part of general knowledge.

b. Molecular Basis of Heredity

Children inherit traits from their parents; this is the example of genetics most familiar to all of us. A 19th-century scientist (and monk), Gregor Mendel, speculated that organisms inherit traits via unit factors. Today we know that unit factors correspond to regions within the DNA of the organism that code for specific proteins.

DNA is a molecule comprised of repeating subunits called nucleotides. Nucleotides have one of four specific nitrogenous bases abbreviated with the letters G, C, T, and A. DNA (shown below) has the shape of a long twisted ladder (double-helix), a result of repeating nucleotides and bonding characteristics. The sequence of the bases in the repeating nucleotides is the genetic code, which serves as the blueprint for all life forms.

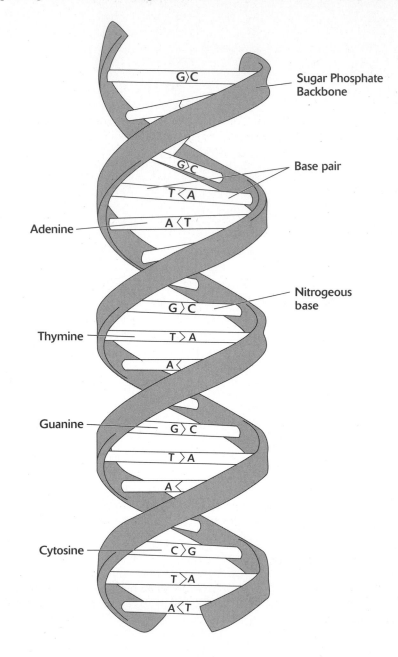

EXAMPLE:

Clara wants to grow the world's biggest cucumber. She has to decide where to put her money and efforts. What would stand the best chance of growing a huge cucumber?

(1) Special fertilizer
(2) Enriched soil
(3) Grow lights
(4) Seeds from huge cucumbers
(5) Constant attention

The correct answer is **(4)**. According to Mendel, offspring inherit their traits from their parents. The off-spring, huge cucumbers, would inherit the huge gene from their huge cucumber parents. The other answers might have a small effect on the size of the plants, but the seeds would carry the traits needed.

c. Biological Evolution

Any genetic change, small or large, in a population, inherited over several generations, is considered to be biological evolution. These changes have to be at the genetic level (the genes show evidence of change) and this change can be passed on from generation to generation.

EXAMPLE:

Sylvia was tracing her family tree and was able to go back six generations and get photographs and paintings of the male members of her family. She noticed that each one of them was substantially taller than his peers. What could this indicate as a possibility for her male children?

(1) They could speak English.
(2) They could have long hair.
(3) They could be taller than their peers.
(4) They could be smarter than their peers.
(5) They could prefer casual clothing.

The correct answer is **(3)**. If height is regarded as a genetic change and it is noticeable over several generations, it is a possibility that the next generation of males would be taller than their peers. In evolution, there is no certainty because, in this case, there was no genetic testing to determine if this was a change in the genes, but it is a very strong possibility based on the evidence.

d. Interdependence of Organisms

Living organisms depend on one another to remain alive, grow, and reproduce. Humans eat large fish, which consume smaller fish, which consume water plants and smaller fish, and so on. Small water plants and humans are interdependent.

EXAMPLE:

> Lyle was trying to explain to his little cousin, Rose, that she should not try to kill all the ladybugs she saw, even if she was afraid of them. He told her that ladybugs eat large numbers of insects that eat the leaves of plants, and some of these leafy plants are eaten by humans in salads. Lyle tried to explain how living organisms are interdependent and thought Rose understood when she said that we shouldn't kill worms and grubs. Rose said that we depended on worms and grubs because:
>
> **(1)** They are living creatures.
> **(2)** They provide food for chickens which we eat.
> **(3)** They can be used to aerate the soil.
> **(4)** They taste good fried for food.
> **(5)** Some wild birds eat them.

The correct answer is **(2)**. The other answers seem reasonable except they fail to show an interdependence between humans and worms and grubs.

e. Matter, Energy, and Organization in Living Systems

Living systems or self-organizing systems of varying sizes interact with their environment by exchanging information and material-energy.

EXAMPLE:

Living Systems Theory

Miller, a current scientist working in the field of living systems theory, suggests that systems have mutual interrelationships and that those interrelationships cross hierarchical levels. For example, the member countries of a supranational system such as the European Common Market benefits from the activities of each member nation. At the other end of the scale, cells in a living system live on the nutrients from its suprasystem or environment.

> A cell benefits from its environment because:
>
> **(1)** The environment protects the cell from predators.
> **(2)** The environment provides nutrients to the cell.
> **(3)** It is better to live in a group than alone.
> **(4)** The environment's activities help the cells.
> **(5)** Nations depend on each other.

The correct answer is **(2)**. The passage states that "cells in a living system live on the nutrients from its suprasystem or environment." This is an example of a type of question in which it would be beneficial to read the question and skim the passage. The word *environment* would then lead your eyes to the correct answer.

f. Behavior of Organisms

B. F. Skinner, an American psychologist, developed a theoretical basis for the behavior of organisms. He theorized that, through conditioning, an organism could be made to repeat an activity over and over again. He used rats in what was later to be called the "Skinner box" and was able to alter their behavior through a series of rewards or reinforcements for repeating the action. In this way, he was able to shape the organism's behavior.

We learn many behaviors in this way. If you go out in the rain wearing rubber boots, your feet don't get wet. Not getting your feet wet is a reward for wearing rubber boots. The next time it rains, you'll probably wear rubber boots because it's more comfortable than walking around with wet feet. However, being human, you may decide to go out in the rain wearing sandals and end up with wet feet. The reinforcement only increases the chance of something happening. It can't *guarantee* that it will happen.

EXAMPLE:

Amy was conducting an experiment to see if she could make a squirrel run around in circles through conditioning. Which of the following possible scenarios would likely prove successful?

(1) Put a harness and a leash on the squirrel and attach the end of the leash to a pole. When the squirrel is taken off the leash, it should run in circles.

(2) Wait until the squirrel runs in a circle and then give it a reward. After that, give the squirrel a reward each time it runs in a circle.

(3) Put the squirrel in a circular cage. When the squirrel is released from the cage, it will run in circles.

(4) Construct a model-train setup with a circular course. Put the squirrel on one car and leave the train running in circles for several hours. When the train stops, the squirrel will run in circles.

(5) Squirrels don't run in circles.

The correct answer is **(2)**. If you accept the theory of Skinner, then the reward should begin to shape the squirrel's behavior and repeated rewards would strengthen it. The other answers don't include any rewards, and, according to Skinner, some type of reward is necessary for conditioning to take place.

g. Vocabulary

Following are some life science terms that you'll want to familiarize yourself with in preparation for the Science Test. Some of the terms on the following list are included primarily because they appear in example questions in this chapter. As you do your reading in life science, you may find terms that you do not understand. Look up the meanings and add them to your vocabulary list.

bacteria: One-celled organisms, some of which are capable of causing disease.

behavior of organisms: The way in which organisms act.

cell: The basic structural unit of all life forms.

conditioning: To establish a particular repeated response in a subject.

diffraction: The slight bending of a ray of light as it passes over the edge of an object.

DNA: The molecule that transfers genetic traits in living creatures.

energy: The capacity or ability to do work.

environment: External physical conditions.

evolution: Changes from generation to generation in the gene pool through various genetic processes.

gene: Basic unit of heredity.

genetics: Science of heredity.

interdependent: Depend on each other.

lens: An optical device that allows light to pass through it and is capable of refracting or bending the light. A lens may be convex, concave, flat (plano), or a combination.

living systems: Self-organizing systems that can be referred to as alive and that interact with the environment.

matter: A physical substance.

molecular basis of heredity: The passage of characteristics from one generation to the next using DNA as the blueprint for life.

multicellular: An organism having many cells.

nucleotides: Groups of molecules linked together to form the building blocks of DNA.

organism: Individual life form composed of mutually interdependent parts consisting of one or more cells.

reinforcement: A reward that increases the likelihood that a certain behavior will be repeated.

refraction: The change in direction of a light wave when it passes from one medium to another—for example, from air to a glass lens.

reproduce: To bear offspring.

self-organizing system: Process whereby structure appears within a system without external forces or influences.

traits: Characteristics determined through genetics.

unicellular: An organism having one cell.

3. Earth and Space Science

Earth and space science studies includes geology, astrophysics, and geochemistry.

a. Energy in the Earth System

The Earth has sources of energy both internal and external. The largest source of external energy is the sun, which provides vast amounts of energy. The core of the Earth is molten rock, which has the potential to provide heat energy to the surface of the Earth.

EXAMPLE:

> Quincy was designing a new subdivision and was looking for a different way of heating the houses that would be more efficient than each house having a furnace burning gas to produce heat. Which of the following methods would stand a good chance of working?
>
> **(1)** Place solar panels on each roof with additional panels in the yards to create energy to heat water to circulate through the heating system of each house.
> **(2)** Build large windmills to use the electricity generated to charge storage batteries, which could provide electricity to heat the houses.
> **(3)** Drill deep enough into the Earth to reach a temperature that would heat circulating water, which could be used to heat the houses.
> **(4)** Build a glass wall around each house and use the heat generated by the sun to heat the houses.
> **(5)** All of the above.

The correct answer is **(5)**. Each of the systems would use energy that the Earth is exposed to and transfer it where it's needed (to heat the houses).

b. Geochemical Cycles

Geochemical cycles are the movement between living and nonliving forms in the environment. Of all the elements that are involved in geochemical cycles, four are most important to us: carbon, nitrogen, phosphorus, and sulfur. These are important to us because, among other things, they allow the oceans to absorb carbon dioxide to slow global warming.

EXAMPLE:

Human beings are involved in biochemical cycles through their use of chemicals in daily life. Fossil fuels are carbon-based fuels; we use them daily as we commute to work. Before becoming gasoline or other petrochemicals, these carbon compounds were stored in the Earth in relatively environmentally safe storage. By extracting the carbon-based oil, we move the carbon into a new pool. Here it is converted to gasoline and then, when burned, to carbon dioxide and carbon monoxide, which are released into the atmosphere. Once released into the atmosphere, they have the ability to raise the temperature of the Earth by several degrees, which may not seem like much but affects agriculture, living conditions, and availability of land for habitation and animals. One universal hope is that forests and oceans can absorb the extra carbon compounds. There is also great concern that our clear-cutting of forests will just speed up this process.

One significant cause of global warming is the fact that

(1) The sun is getting closer to the Earth.
(2) Cars are adding carbon compounds to the atmosphere.
(3) More heat is being reflected off the Earth.
(4) Summers are getting longer.
(5) There are more people who smoke today.

The correct answer is (2). The passage addresses the problems of converting carbon-based compounds in the Earth to gasoline to be used in cars. The other answers are not mentioned in the passage and may or may not be relevant in general conversation, but the only answer that is relevant on the test is the one mentioned in the passage. One of the problems of reading widely in science is that some of the material read is conjecture or part of general knowledge, which cannot be used to answer questions on this test.

c. Origin and Evolution of the Earth System

The Earth is said to be 4.6 billion years old. At this time, it is thought that part of the solar system spun off and, through gravitational forces, became larger and more compact. This produced a large mass that floated through space in an orbit around the sun. As it floated, the material that came together to form it cooled and solidified to form the crust of the Earth. It is thought that the moon was originally part of the mantle of the Earth, which spun off to orbit around the Earth.

Telling the age of the Earth is very difficult. We all know how old we are because people were present at our birth and records were kept. There were no people present to observe the birth of the Earth and, thus, no first-person records. We have to depend on other methods. One of these methods is carbon dating of rocks.

Carbon Dating

Carbon-14 dating helps us determine the age of any material that was once alive. Carbon-14 is a radioactive isotope, which decays from carbon-14 to nitrogen over the course of time. Decay is the spontaneous change from one nucleus to another through changes in number of atomic particles. The rate of decay is constant and can give us an indication of age.

While living organisms are alive, they consume carbon, some of which is carbon-14, either directly in the case of plants or indirectly though consuming plant food. Once an organism dies, it stops consuming carbon, and the process of radioactive decay of the carbon-14 becomes important because it is measurable.

EXAMPLE:

How does carbon dating help estimate the age of a fossil?

(1) The fossil gives off carbon.
(2) The amount of carbon a fossil consumes can be measured.
(3) The rate of radioactive decay of carbon-14 is constant and measurable.
(4) The carbon-14 tells the scientist how old it is.
(5) The amount of carbon in a fossil is measurable.

The correct answer is **(3)**. As stated in the passage, carbon-14 undergoes radioactive decay in a constant and measurable way. The other answers have no basis in the passage and some have no basis in fact, but you're looking for the best answer from the passage and that is choice (3).

d. Origin and Formation of the Universe

There are three main theories to explain the origin and evolution of the universe:

- **The Big Bang Theory:** In the beginning, all the matter in the universe was concentrated in an extremely dense, extremely hot ball until a huge explosion occurred, breaking the matter into pieces and expelling them in all directions. These pieces formed the stars and galaxies now known as the universe.
- **The Steady State Theory:** This theory states that the number of galaxies in the universe is a constant; as old galaxies disappear, new ones are formed.
- **The Pulsating Theory:** This theory states that the universe is constantly expanding and contracting, which means that it is pulsating.

EXAMPLE:

Our universe was formed by an explosion, which blew particles out from a central hot mass. As these particles became concentrated by gravity, they formed solid and gaseous masses which became the stars and planets.

Earth was originally formed by:

(1) Rocks.
(2) Gases.
(3) An explosion.
(4) Space.
(5) Gravity.

The correct answer is **(3)**. The question asks what originally formed the Earth, and the only specific choice that is in the passage is choice (3). Choice (5) might be a possible answer if the question did not specify "originally." Questions and answers must be read carefully. Gravity is mentioned in the passage but as something that acted upon the particles after the original explosion.

e. Vocabulary

Following are some earth and space science terms that you'll want to familiarize yourself with in preparation for the Science Test. Some of the terms on the following list are included primarily because they appear in example questions in this chapter. As you do your reading in earth and space science, you may find terms that you do not understand. Look up the meanings and add them to your vocabulary list.

agriculture: Food production.

biosphere: The basic parts of the planet Earth that all contain life—lithosphere (rock from the center to the surface), hydrosphere (water), and atmosphere (air).

carbon compounds: Compounds based on the carbon atom.

carbon dating: Determining the age of an object by the amount of carbon-14 within it.

carbon dioxide: Gas formed during breathing or by burning some substances.

carbon monoxide: Poisonous gas produced by burning with insufficient air.

core of the Earth: Molten center of the Earth.

decay: Spontaneous change from one nucleus to another through changes in number of atomic particles.

energy: The capacity or ability to do work.

external energy: Sources of energy outside the Earth.

formation of the Earth: A continuous change in the Earth system.

fossil fuels: Carbon-based fuels.

geochemical cycle: Changes in concentration of various elements and compounds in the chemistry of the Earth.

habitatation: Living space.

internal energy: Sources of energy within the Earth.

mantle of the Earth: The region between the Earth's surface and its core.

molten rock: Magma produced by active volcanoes.

orbit: Path.

origin of the universe: Theory of how the universe was created.

radioactive isotope: An unstable isotope that spontaneously emits radiation.

X. Language Arts, Reading

A. Test Format

The Language Arts, Reading test consists of 40 multiple-choice questions to be answered in 65 minutes (or 1½ minutes per question). The test is comprised of four types of questions:

- **Comprehension:** 8 questions, or 20 percent
- **Application:** 6 questions, or 15 percent
- **Analysis:** 12 to 13 questions, or 30 percent to 35 percent
- **Synthesis:** 12 to 13 questions, or 30 percent to 35 percent

The Language Arts, Reading test assesses how well you read and how well you understand what you've read. It consists of a mixture of literary passages (roughly 75 percent) and nonfiction passages (roughly 25 percent):

Literary passages—The test contains at least one passage from each of the following fictional literature genres:

- **Drama:** Drama passages—excerpts from plays—tell a story using the words and actions of the characters. The stage directions describe the place and costumes. Stage directions are usually printed in *italics* and can provide valuable information to assist in answering the questions that follow the passage.
- **Poetry:** Poetry is a form of literature in which ideas and emotions are often concentrated and require careful analysis. Poems should be read slowly and carefully to best understand the message that the poet is trying to deliver.
- **Prose fiction:** Prose fiction passages are excerpts from novels and short stories in which the author draws from his or her imagination.

Nonfiction passages—Nonfiction passages are drawn from the following sources:

- **Critical review of visual and performing arts:** Critical reviews of the visual and performing arts are often found in newspapers and magazines. These may include reviews of theatrical performances, novels, concerts, movies, television shows, gallery openings, restaurants, and so on.
- **Nonfiction prose:** Nonfiction is not material that the author creates in his or her own mind; instead, it is based on fact or reality. Prime examples of nonfiction prose are journalists' articles in newspapers or magazines. This book is also an example of nonfiction prose.
- **Workplace and community documents:** These documents relate to employment and community-focused areas such as
  - Mission statements that define an organization's role in the community
  - Employer-related statements that describe company policies
  - Goal or vision statements that detail what an organization hopes to accomplish through its activities
  - Legal documents such as leases, purchase orders, bank statements, letters, and so on
  - Manuals that accompany a purchase or are used to define a set of operating procedures

B. Types of Questions—A Detailed Look

As mentioned earlier, approximately 75 percent of the passages on the Language Arts, Reading test are literary, and the remaining 25 percent are nonfiction.

The four types of questions are described in detail in this section, along with examples of each question type.

1. Comprehension

Comprehension questions test your ability to read a source of information, understand it, and restate it in your own words. Comprehension questions might ask you to rephrase what you've read without losing the meaning of the passage. Ideas can be summarized to demonstrate the meaning and implications of what the passage suggests.

The comprehension example questions are based on the following passage, an excerpt from "Mandalay" by Rudyard Kipling (1892).

> By the old Moulmein Pagoda, lookin' lazy at the sea,
> There's a Burma girl a-settin', and I know she thinks o' me;
> For the wind is in the palm-trees, and the temple-bells they say:
> "Come you back, you British soldier; come you back to Mandalay!"
>   Come you back to Mandalay,
>   Where the old Flotilla lay:
>   Can't you 'ear their paddles chunkin' from Rangoon to Mandalay?
>   On the road to Mandalay,
>   Where the flyin'-fishes play,
>   An' the dawn comes up like thunder outer China 'crost the Bay!

Why do you think the speaker dreams of Mandalay?

(1) He is a British soldier.
(2) He misses his girlfriend.
(3) He enjoys the climate.
(4) He wants to worship at the Pagoda.
(5) He longs for riches.

The correct answer is **(2)**. In the passage, we learn that a Burmese girl may be waiting for his return to Mandalay. The fact that he is a British soldier (1) and may have visited the Pagoda (4) are not best answers. Neither the climate (3) nor riches (5) is mentioned in the passage.

> What is the "road to Mandalay"?
>
> **(1)** Wind in the palm-trees
> **(2)** The sound of temple-bells
> **(3)** Paddles chunkin'
> **(4)** A long sea voyage
> **(5)** Flyin'-fishes playing

The correct answer is **(4).** To travel from Britain to Burma requires "a long sea voyage." We learn that Mandalay must be a seaport because the passage mentions "paddles chunkin'" (3) and "flyin'-fishes" (5). However, these are not best answers to the passage. Palm trees (1) and temple-bells (2) are also incorrect choices.

2. Application

Application questions assess your ability to use the information in the passage in answering questions involving both stated and suggested information. Application questions often ask you to apply what you're learned in the passage to real-life situations.

The application example questions are based on the following passage from "Gold Seekers of '49" by Edwin D. Sabin (1915).

It has taken Americans to build the Panama Canal, and it took the Americans to build California. These are two great feats of which we Americans of the United States may well be proud: the building of that canal, in the strange tropics 2,000 miles away across the water, and the up-rearing of a mighty State, under equally strange conditions, 2,000 miles away across plains and mountains.

On the Isthmus men of many nationalities combined like a vast family; each man, from laborer to engineer, doing his stint, without favoritism and without graft, toward the big result. So in California likewise a people collected from practically all the world became Americans together under the Flag, and working shoulder to shoulder—rich and poor, old and young, educated and uneducated, no matter what their manner of life previously—they joined forces to make California worthy of being a State in the Union.

> What was one result from the building of the Panama Canal?
>
> **(1)** The gold rush began.
> **(2)** Plains and mountains were crossed.
> **(3)** The tropics were 2,000 miles away.
> **(4)** The state of California prospered.
> **(5)** The flag was raised.

The correct answer is **(4).** The Panama Canal helped California to prosper as a state. Plains and mountains (2) and the tropics (3), while mentioned in the passage, do not answer the question. The gold rush (1) and flag raising (5) are not referred to in the passage.

> Who built the Panama Canal?
>
> (1)   People of many nationalities
> (2)   The rich and the poor
> (3)   The young and the old
> (4)   The educated and the uneducated
> (5)   All of the above

The correct answer is **(5).** Per the passage, choices (1) through (4) all contributed to the successful completion of the Panama Canal.

3. Analysis

By examining the style and structure of the passage, you should be able to draw conclusions, determine the tone of the passage, understand consequences, and make inferences. You have to be sure that the consequences you identify are based on the content of the passage, not on your own previous knowledge. Analysis questions can include cause-and-effect relationships, the type of language used, and presentation of details.

The analysis example questions are based on the following passage, an excerpt from "All You Can Eat" by Murray Shukyn.

I thought of Sandy, who supervised a call center and wondered if it was a bank call center. Then I would understand why her job was so important. That was probably why she had to work so hard. I was beginning to appreciate Sandy's responsibilities.
    "Operator forty-eight, can I help you?" a voice said.
    "I lost my bank card," I said.
    "Where did you lose your card?" operator forty-eight asked.
    "If I knew that, I would go back and look for it," I replied.
    "In what city did the loss occur?" operator forty-eight asked.
    "The same city you're in," I immediately answered.
    "You lost your card in Manila," operator forty-eight said.
    "No, I'm in Toronto," I said with a question in my voice. "Where are you?"
    "In a call center in the Philippines. How can I help you?" operator forty-eight replied in a friendlier tone.

> What phrase best describes Sandy's performance?
>
> (1)   Hard worker
> (2)   Thoughtful person
> (3)   Dedicated employee
> (4)   Careless supervisor
> (5)   Helpful operator

The correct answer is **(1).** According to the excerpt, choice (1) "hard worker" best describes Sandy's performance. She also may have been thoughtful (2), dedicated (3), and helpful (5), but these qualities are not mentioned in the passage. We have no reason to believe that she was careless (4).

> What is the main conclusion to be drawn from this passage?
>
> **(1)** People lose their bank cards.
> **(2)** Operators can be friendly.
> **(3)** Call centers don't always provide local service.
> **(4)** Callers should be patient.
> **(5)** It pays to be inquisitive.

The correct answer is **(3)**. From the passage we learn that the operator is located thousands of miles away. The other choices, while relevant, do not represent the main idea that the author wishes to convey.

4. Synthesis

These questions require you to identify and compare and contrast information from different parts of the passage. You should be able to integrate information from multiple sources in the passage. The questions measure your ability to understand the overall tone, point of view, style, purpose, and organization of the passage.

The synthesis example questions are based on the following passage, an excerpt from "Time Management for Parents" by Achim Krull and Murray Shukyn.

Time management is a family affair. One approach is to have weekly family meetings when each member tells everyone what their goals and deadlines are for the week. These become the family goals. Then everyone can figure out their role in helping all members of the family to achieve the goals. Creating a written summary that can be posted somewhere allows everyone to keep track of what is supposed to happen.

The second form has two questions asking the student what steps were not achieved and how to change the process for the next set of steps or goal. These are a deliberately set open-ended opportunity to discuss everything from setting realistic goals to issues of procrastination. Both of these topics are discussed in the section addressed to the student because they are real issues. When faced with daunting tasks, we often procrastinate. It may be that extra trip for a coffee, or a quick game between working on something else on the computer. This is not something to give your students a hard time about, but it is something they need to recognize. After all, taking a break is good if it keeps one sharp while working toward a goal. Taking a break to avoid facing the work is another issue.

> How does time management benefit the family?
>
> **(1)** Family meetings are important.
> **(2)** Students learn to make lists.
> **(3)** Summaries can be posted.
> **(4)** It helps everyone to achieve their goals.
> **(5)** It keeps the family together.

The correct answer is **(4)**. According to the passage, time management helps all family members to achieve their goals. Other benefits of time management—family meetings (1), making lists (2), posting summaries (3), and working together (5)—are but parts of the overall process.

> What impact does procrastination have on the time-management process?
>
> **(1)** It helps to set goals.
> **(2)** It encourages problem-solving.
> **(3)** It can be a source of distraction.
> **(4)** It keeps one sharp.
> **(5)** It provides open-ended discussion.

The correct answer is **(3).** The passage tells us that procrastination may be a source of distraction whereby goals are not achieved. Procrastination does not support goal setting (1) or problem solving (2). While taking a break can help to keep one sharp (4) or provide opportunities for discussion (5), these are not the best answers.

C. Test Strategies

To prepare for the test, you need to work on your reading and comprehension skills. Each passage and question should be read carefully to find the right answer. Here are a few tips to assist in preparation:

- **Read, read, read!** Read carefully as much fictional and nonfictional material as possible, including novels, poems, plays, short stories, magazines, and newspapers. Even reading labels and cereal boxes can aid in your preparation. Remember that the GED includes passages written in three time periods: before 1920, between 1920 and 1960, and after 1960. Visit the library for books and stories written during these periods to better understand the situations described and differences in the choice of vocabulary used by the author. If you have trouble deciding which representative books and stories to read, ask the librarian to help you.

- **Quiz yourself.** Ask yourself questions about what you've read. Try to understand the main ideas so as to explain them to others.

- **Look it up!** Use a dictionary to discover the meaning of new words you find in your reading. To enrich your vocabulary, try to use these new words in a sentence or use them in conversation with family and friends.

- **Review the example questions and work the practice questions:** There are example questions in Section B, earlier in this chapter. More questions for practice appear at the end of this chapter. Work through these questions and check your answers. If you answered a question correctly, read the explanation to reinforce the reasoning. If you answered incorrectly, read the explanation, and then reread the question to see where you went wrong. Additional sample questions can be found online on the GED Web site (www.acenet.edu/Content/NavigationMenu/ged/test/prep/sample_questions.htm).

- **Take the practice test.** Take the full-length Language Arts, Reading Practice Test (Chapter XV). Do so under test conditions, setting a timer. Check your answers and review the explanations.

D. Practice

1. Questions

Questions 1 through 4 refer to the following poem, "In High Flight," by John Gillespie Magee, Jr. (1941).

Who Can Reach to the Heavens?

Oh, I have slipped the surly bonds of earth,
And danced the skies on laughter-silvered wings;
Sunward I've climbed and joined the tumbling mirth
Of sun-split clouds—and done a hundred things
You have not dreamed of—wheeled and soared and swung
High in the sunlit silence. Hov'ring there,
I've chased the shouting wind along and flung
My eager craft through footless halls of air.
I've topped the wind-swept heights with easy grace,
Where never lark, or even eagle, flew;
And, while with silent, lifting mind I've trod
The high untrespassed sanctity of space,
Put out my hand and touched the face of God

1. What is the occupation of the speaker in the poem?

    (1) Aviator
    (2) Mountain climber
    (3) Sailor
    (4) Clergyman
    (5) Biologist

2. What phrase tells us the poet is referring to the flight of an aircraft?

    (1) Laughter-silvered wings
    (2) Wheeled and soared
    (3) Eager craft
    (4) Hov'ring there
    (5) All of the above

3. What word best describes the poet's attitude as expressed in the poem?

    (1) Free
    (2) Fearful
    (3) Delirious
    (4) Silent
    (5) Surly

4. How do you know the poet is a religious person?

    (1) He slipped the surly bonds.
    (2) He danced the skies.
    (3) He touched the face of God.
    (4) He topped the wind-swept heights.
    (5) He joined the tumbling clouds.

Questions 5 through 9 refer to the following excerpt from Murray Shukyn's short story "Just Another Day" (2008).

Just Another Day

Sitting in his car on an empty street, alone, Irving knew that he had not handled that well. He had not handled many, many situations well. He was not a good father, even though he was a good provider. Out of the corner of his eye, he noticed a group of teenagers turning the corner. This group of boys and girls looked lively, speaking in loud voices. Automatically, he locked the doors of his car as they slowly approached. They seemed so happy, so carefree. Irving wished for the days he had been so happy, had so few responsibilities.

Irving Solnicki watched the group of teenagers approach him, walking, jostling each other, trading taunts and jokes. He watched them so intently, he did not notice the small, red, two-door car with the darkly tinted windows slowly cruise up behind him with headlights off and windows closed. Irving was watching the teenagers carefully. It was easier now; they were only about ten feet in front of his car. Suddenly, the group scattered and a few took refuge beside Irving's car door. The small, red, two-door car approached from the rear with the driver's window open. Irving noticed a glint of shiny metal protruding from the window of the car. He could not figure out what was happening. The teenagers scattering; the car with the metal pipe sticking out the window; and the dull thuds coming from the street were like a dream. Irving was not sure what to make of it until the red car pulled even with his, and he saw that the pipe looked like one of those automatic weapons he often saw on television. The passenger-side window of Irving's car shuddered, as a hole developed in it, with a rather loud bang. Irving Solnicki felt a sharp pain in his right temple and warmth oozing around it. He started to lift his hand to see what it was, but it just stopped as he slumped over the wheel, pressing on the horn button, creating a din in the quiet street with the scattering teenagers and the small, red, two-door car speeding away.

Suddenly, it was quiet except for a car horn loudly, soulfully lamenting in the night.

5. Why was Irving sitting alone in his car on an empty street?

    (1) He was resting his eyes.
    (2) He was waiting for someone.
    (3) He had not handled a family situation well.
    (4) He liked to watch teenagers.
    (5) He was lost.

6. Why would Irving lock his car doors as the teenagers approached?

    (1) He was afraid of teenagers.
    (2) It was an automatic reaction.
    (3) He was afraid of being happy.
    (4) He didn't want them to come into his car.
    (5) The teenagers had few responsibilities.

7. Why is it important to mention that Irving did not notice the small, red, two-door car approaching?

    (1) The red car will crash into Irving's car.
    (2) The red car is going to give the teenagers a lift.
    (3) A relative of Irving is driving the red car.
    (4) Red cars always mean trouble is coming.
    (5) The red car is about to play an important role in the development of the story.

8. What was the glint of shiny metal sticking out from the car window?

    (1) A piece of pipe
    (2) A golf club
    (3) A gun
    (4) A camera
    (5) Not enough information given

9. Why would the author describe the sound of the horn as a lament?

    (1) Irving died from the gunshot.
    (2) Horns always sound sad.
    (3) Irving was singing a sad song.
    (4) The teenagers were frightened by the horn.
    (5) The red car drove off leaving Irving alone.

Questions 10 through 13 refer to the following passage from a course manual.

Prior Learning Assessment and Recognition

This course is based on a Prior Learning Assessment and Recognition (PLAR) model, which utilizes preparation for a standardized challenge examination as a component of the PLAR. In addition, candidates are guided through the creation of a portfolio, which can be evaluated by the college for admission or advanced standing. This is an opportunity for adults who have learned in informal as well as formal venues, to document and assess their prior learning. The course is intense and concentrated and is not meant for every applicant. Candidates who score low in the pretest, and who indicate educational gaps in the counseling interview, should be directed to remedial programs before beginning such a rigorous course. Those who score extremely well in the pretest might be advised to apply directly to take challenge examinations, such as the GED examinations or other examinations as required by the college. This course is meant for candidates who will gain from review and remediation but do not require extensive teaching.

10. What does the course prepare candidates for?

    (1) A preparation program
    (2) The creation of a portfolio
    (3) GED tests
    (4) A challenge examination
    (5) College entrance

11. Who is eligible to enroll in the course as specifically mentioned in the passage?

    (1) Adult learners
    (2) High school students
    (3) College students
    (4) Recent immigrants
    (5) All of the above

12. Where should candidates with low pretest scores be directed?

    (1) A counseling interview
    (2) A rigorous course
    (3) Remedial programs
    (4) Educational gaps
    (5) GED examinations

13. What is the course not meant for?

    (1) Review
    (2) Remediation
    (3) Challenge examinations
    (4) Extensive teaching
    (5) All of the above

Questions 14 through 18 refer to the following excerpt from the play "Last Shrink Sitting" by Murray Shukyn (2005).

Last Shrink Sitting

HOMELESS MAN: Hello, how are you?

NORMAN: I'm fine thank you, and you?

HOMELESS MAN: I feel the need for culture.

NORMAN: That's nice. Excuse me.

HOMELESS MAN: If you could give me the cost of a single ticket to a play, I could absorb some of the culture.

NORMAN: I'm sorry. I don't have any change.

HOMELESS MAN: Change? I don't want to go to an amateur production where they take up a collection at the end. Culture, man, real actors performing real plays!

NORMAN: I really can't help you.

HOMELESS MAN: Did you eat yesterday?

NORMAN: Yes.

HOMELESS MAN: Did you eat today?

NORMAN: Yes.

HOMELESS MAN: Then you're better off than me. Give me some money.

NORMAN: No!

HOMELESS MAN: Give me some money, and I won't hit you in the face.

NORMAN steps back. HOMELESS MAN approaches.

HOMELESS MAN: Give me ten dollars, and I won't hit you in the stomach.

NORMAN continues backing away with the HOMELESS MAN approaching at the same rate.

HOMELESS MAN: Give me twenty dollars so I won't cut myself and bleed on you. I could have terrible diseases, you know.

NORMAN: *(turning)* You're nuts!

HOMELESS MAN: Do you think I would live in an alley if I were the poster boy for mental health? Of course, I'm nuts. Give me some money or I'll go berserker all over you.

NORMAN turns and sprints out of the alley. The HOMELESS MAN just stands, staring after him.

HOMELESS MAN: Have a nice day. It was nice almost doing business with you.

14. In the closing line of the scene, why does the homeless man say, "It was nice almost doing business with you"?

    (1) Norman didn't buy anything from him.
    (2) The homeless man ran out of stock.
    (3) Norman wouldn't give him any money.
    (4) Norman wasn't interesting in buying anything from the homeless man.
    (5) Norman was in too much of a hurry to buy anything.

15. How does the homeless man respond to Norman's refusal?

    (1) He walks away from Norman
    (2) He starts to cry.
    (3) He screams at Norman.
    (4) He begins to threaten Norman.
    (5) He jumps up and down.

16. Why does the homeless man ask whether Norman had eaten in the last couple days?

    (1) He was asking Norman for money and wanted to prove a point.
    (2) He was concerned that Norman was not eating well.
    (3) Norman looked very thin and pale.
    (4) Norman's stomach was making strange noises.
    (5) Norman had food stains on the front of his clothing.

17. Why does the homeless man infer that he will cut himself?

    (1) He is suicidal.
    (2) He has nothing else to do with his knife.
    (3) He wants to make a point and is sure that Norman will understand.
    (4) He says that he will bleed all over Norman and might have terrible diseases.
    (5) He wants to show Norman how serious he is about eating.

18. Why wouldn't the homeless man accept change if it were offered?

    (1) Change is much heavier than paper money, and he is tired.
    (2) He wants to buy a ticket for a cultural event, and that costs more money.
    (3) He prefers eating in upscale restaurants, and they're more expensive.
    (4) He has a hole in his pocket, and it would fall out.
    (5) He is allergic to certain metals and doesn't want a rash on his hands.

2. Answers

1. **(1)** The correct choice is *aviator,* which is a synonym for pilot. Although the poem speaks of wind-swept heights, the speaker in the poem certainly isn't a mountain climber. Sailor, clergyman, and biologist are not relevant to the poem.

2. **(5)** The first four choices have some reference to an aircraft or its flight pattern: wings, soared, craft, and hovering.

3. **(1)** The poet tells us that he is free of the earth. The other choices—fearful, delirious, silent, and surly—do not describe the poet's attitude.

4. **(3)** The fact that the poet reached out his hand to touch the face of God would indicate that he has religious beliefs. The other choices are descriptions of his flight path as the aircraft climbed higher in the sky.

5. **(3)** The first few sentences of the first paragraph tell you that there was a situation that he, as a father, had not handled well.

6. **(2)** Locking the doors was an automatic reaction according to the end of the first paragraph. Choices (1) and (4) may have been true, but they are not mentioned in the passage. Choices (3) and (5) have no connection to the passage.

7. **(5)** The red car plays an immediate role in the development of the story, and Irving's not noticing it makes it more powerful. Choices (1), (2), and (3) have nothing to do with the story, and (4) has nothing to do with anything.

8. **(3)** From the description in the passage and the subsequent events, the shiny metal object must have been a gun. The other choices are remotely possible but are not mentioned in the paragraph.

9. **(1)** Although the passage doesn't specifically state that Irving died, there are many clues to make that the best answer. The shot to the temple and the subsequent slumping over the wheel would indicate a fatal injury.

10. **(4)** The course prepares candidates for a standardized challenge examination as a component of the PLAR model. While it also is a preparation program, which includes a portfolio, these are not the best answers. Other possible outcomes—GED tests and college entrance—also are not best answers.

11. **(1)** The passage tells us that this is a preparation course for adult formal and informal learners. Therefore, choice (1) is the correct choice. It is not available for high school or college students. Recent immigrants might qualify, but they must be adults not currently attending college.

12. **(3)** Those with low pretest scores are referred to by choice (3), "remedial programs." A rigorous course, educational gaps, and GED examinations are incorrect choices. The candidates might also be directed to a counseling interview, but that is not the best choice.

13. **(4)** According to the passage, the course is not meant for choice (4), those requiring "extensive teaching." It does, however, offer review, remediation, and preparation for challenge exams.

14. **(3)** The homeless man was asking for money, and Norman didn't give him any. The rest of the choices refer to a traditional manner of doing business, which this was not.

15. **(4)** Norman's refusal meets with a series of escalating threats. The rest of the choices have no foundation in the passage.

16. **(1)** The homeless man wanted some money and wanted to demonstrate to Norman that he was in a worse condition than Norman and deserved money. The rest of the choices have no basis in the passage. Remember that you should select the best answer based on the material in the passage.

17. **(4)** The homeless man threatens Norman with giving him some unnamed terrible disease by bleeding on him. Choices (1), (3), and (5) may or may not be correct, but they are not the best answers according to the passage. Choice (2) is wrong because there has been no mention of a knife, and although we can assume that in order to cut himself, the homeless man would need some instrument, there is no mention of it in the passage.

18. **(2)** The homeless man says that he wants to buy a ticket to a professional cultural event, and they're expensive. Choices (1) and (4) might make sense if they were mentioned in the passage. Choice (3) has no basis in the passage, and choice (5) is wrong.

XI. Mathematics

A. Test Format

The GED Mathematics Test consists of two parts. Part I has 25 questions to be completed in 45 minutes; you are provided a calculator to answer the questions in Part I. Part II also has 25 questions to be completed in 45 minutes; however, you are not permitted to use a calculator to answer the questions in Part II. If you figure 1½ minutes per question on average, you'll leave yourself time to answer the questions and go over any difficult ones at the end. The calculator portion isn't necessarily any easier—in fact, the questions may be harder. *Remember:* A calculator can help you calculate, not think.

The test is comprised of three types of questions:

- **Multiple choice:** 40 questions, or 80 percent
- **Coordinate-plane grid:** 5 questions, or 10 percent
- **Standard grid:** 5 questions, or 10 percent

The topics tested on the GED Mathematics Test are listed below. You'll find approximately the same number of questions on each of these four topics:

- Number operations and number sense
- Measurement and geometry
- Data analysis, statistics, and probability
- Algebra, functions, and patterns

You can arrive at the correct answer by using a calculator (when allowed), by doing the calculation in your head or on paper, or just by seeing the answer. You will be provided with a Casio fx-260 calculator for use on Part I, as well as with instructions on how to use it. A list of common math formulas also will be provided to you for use on both parts of the Mathematics Test.

Often, several of the answer choices are obviously incorrect, which makes it easier to choose the correct answer from the choices given because these obviously wrong answers can be eliminated. If a question is too hard or if you can't seem to figure it out, try to eliminate incorrect answers to improve your chances of guessing correctly. You don't have time to ponder the answers, so don't waste time on questions you can't get. *Remember:* No points are deducted if you answer a question incorrectly, so it is to your advantage to guess, even if you're not sure.

B. Types of Questions—A Detailed Look

The three question types are described in detail below, along with examples of each. For more on the four main topics covered on the exam, see Section D, later in this chapter.

Note: Some questions are based on charts and graphs, which are like picture stories. Each chart or graph has a label or title, which tells you what the graph or chart is all about. On a graph, the horizontal axis is called the *x*-axis and the vertical axis is called the *y*-axis. On both graphs and charts, each axis will be labeled; the labels give you important information about the visual.

1. Multiple Choice

When you're given a multiple-choice question, you have five answers to choose from. You indicate the correct answer by filling in the corresponding circle on your answer sheet. Following is an example of a multiple-choice question:

This chapter is about:

(1) Science.
(2) Reading.
(3) Mathematics.
(4) Writing.
(5) Social studies.

Fill in the circle to indicate the correct answer.

Because all the questions in this chapter concern mathematics, the correct answer is (3). Your answer should look like this:

Here are some additional multiple-choice question examples:

EXAMPLES:

If a racing car could travel an average of 200 mph in a 500-mile race and there were no interruptions, how long would it take the car to complete the race?

(1) 12.5 hours
(2) 3.0 hours
(3) 1.75 hours
(4) 2.5 hours
(5) 5.3 hours

The correct answer is **(4)**. To calculate the time required, $500 \div 200 = 2.5$ hours.

If a farmer could grow 183 bushels of corn per acre of land, how many bushels of corn would the farmer be able to grow on a 27-acre farm?

(1) 4,491
(2) 4,941
(3) 4,839
(4) 3,962
(5) 4,962

The correct answer is **(2)**. To calculate how many bushels of corn the farmer would be able to grow, the number of bushels yielded by one acre (183 bushels) should be multiplied by the number of acres (27 acres). So, the yield is $183 \times 27 = 4,941$ bushels.

If the perimeter of a carpet is 234 feet, what would be the effect of reducing the size of one side by 6 feet? The perimeter of the carpet would become:

(1) Longer.
(2) 12 feet shorter.
(3) 6 feet shorter.
(4) Wider.
(5) Not enough information given.   *Study*

The correct answer is **(2)**. Perimeter is equal to $2(l + w)$, where l is the length and w is the width. Reducing the size of one side would also reduce the size of the opposite side by the same amount, which would reduce the perimeter by twice the reduction, or 12 feet.

Alan and Jamie are helping each other paint their living rooms. Alan's living room has a perimeter of 52 feet and a ceiling height of 9 feet. Jamie's living room has a perimeter of 48 feet and a ceiling height of 9 feet 6 inches. How many more square feet have to be painted in Alan's room than in Jamie's?

(1) 12
(2) 21
(3) 9
(4) 4,140   *Study*
(5) 14

The correct answer is **(1)**. Alan's living room has a paintable area of $52 \times 9 = 468$ square feet, while Jamie's living room has a paintable area of $48 \times 9.5 = 456$ square feet. (Remember to change 9 feet 6 inches to 9.5 feet.) The difference is $468 - 456 = 12$ square feet.

2. Coordinate-Plane Grid

For the coordinate-plane grid, you may mark only one circle; the circle must represent an x and a y value, neither of which can be a decimal or a fraction.

When you have to plot a point, you're given a grid on which to do so. (See www.acenet.edu/Content/NavigationMenu/ged/etp/math_poster_plane_grid.pdf for more information and tips.) Following is an example of a coordinate-plane-grid question:

Locate the point (–2, 3) on the coordinate-plane grid.

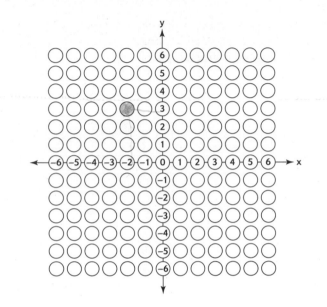

You would mark the grid as follows:

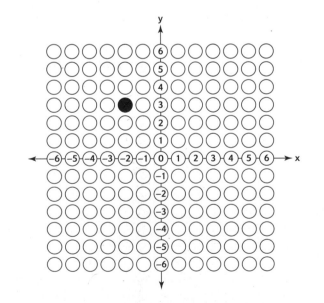

3. Standard Grid

For the standard grid, enter your answer in the columns in the top row (you can start in any column, provided that your entire answer can be entered), and completely fill in the bubble representing the character under each column. With this grid, no number can be negative, and fractions must be entered as decimals or improper fractions.

When you have to provide an answer that isn't multiple-choice or on a coordinate-plane grid, you enter the answer in the standard grid. (See www.acenet.edu/Content/NavigationMenu/ged/etp/math_poster_grid.pdf for more information and tips.) Following is an example of a standard-grid question:

An item cost $3.98 and the customer paid with a $5 bill. Indicate the amount of change the customer would receive on the standard grid.

The customer would receive $5.00 − $3.98 = $1.02 in change. You would mark the standard grid as follows:

C. Test Strategies

- **Answer the easy ones first.** The most efficient plan of action is to skim the questions as soon as you're told to begin the test and do the easy questions first. This will leave you a bit of extra time for the difficult questions. All the questions are worth the same amount—you get the same credit for an easy question as you do for a hard one.

- **Make an educated guess.** Educated guesses are a little different from ordinary guesses. For multiple-choice questions, you'll be given five possible choices. If one is obviously wrong, you have four left to consider. If three are possibly wrong, you have a 50-50 chance of getting the right answer. If you do a bit of mental math, you often can choose the right answer on the basis of the approximate answer you came up with. If you work backward from an answer to the question and it doesn't work, it can't be the right answer. Whatever you can do to increase your chances of getting the right answer will help you on the test.

- **Read carefully.** Math problems are little stories. Read them carefully. If you can visualize what's going on, you can probably solve the problem. Always be sure to answer the question from the information presented, not from what you may know or assume. For each question, there is a correct answer based on the information given, even if the correct answer is "not enough information given."

- **Pay attention to units of measurement.** Pay attention to units of measurement and note any changes in units. If you're asked for an answer in minutes, and the question gives times in hours, you need to do some converting.

- **Brush up on your math skills.** Study Section D, at the end of this chapter, in addition to any other math review resources you have available (we list a few suggestions at the beginning of Section D).

- **Review the example questions and work the practice questions.** There are example questions and practice questions sprinkled throughout this chapter. Work through these questions and check your answers. If you answer a question correctly, read the explanation to reinforce the reasoning. If you answer incorrectly, read the explanation, and then reread the question to see where you went wrong. Additional sample questions can be found online on the GED Web site (www.acenet.edu/Content/NavigationMenu/ged/test/prep/sample_questions.htm).

- **Take the practice test.** Take the full-length Mathematics Practice Test (Chapter XVI). Do so under test conditions, setting a timer. Check your answers and review the explanations.

D. Math Review

The purpose of this review is to familiarize you with the basic mathematic principles represented on the GED Mathematics Test and to give you practice in applying them so that you'll be able to work through the test.

For additional math review, you can visit CliffsNotes.com (http://www.cliffsnotes.com/math-study-guides.html) or reference these other great *CliffsNotes* titles:

CliffsNotes Math Review for Standardized Tests, 2nd Edition
CliffsNotes Basic Math and Pre-Algebra Quick Review
CliffsNotes Algebra I Quick Review
CliffsQuickReview Geometry

1. Number Operations and Number Sense

The GED Math test includes many questions concerning basic number operations and number sense. Here are some tips that you should remember when you take the test:

- Remember that if the answer choices are very close, estimation may not be accurate enough to get the correct answer.

- Round your answers to the nearest number you can handle in your head. If you were asked to multiply 33 by 48, you could think 30×50, which equals 1,500. The correct answer is 1,584 but the estimated answer would be close enough to make sure that the answer you chose was in the right range.

- Round to the nearest multiple of 10 and compensate for the rounding error if needed. For example, if the question is $140 - 39$, you can think of $140 - 40$, which is equal to 100; then you can use that as an approximate answer or add the one back to get 101, which is the correct answer.

- Sometimes you're faced with two or more numbers, each of which has a series of zeros at the end. If you had to add 4,000 and 3,800, you could think about temporarily ignoring the last two zeros in each number. Then you would be adding $40 + 38$, which equals 78. You can't really ignore zeros for very long and you have to put them back, which makes the answer 7,800.

- There are numbers that are just easier to work with for mental arithmetic. Say you were given the question, $15,270 \div 32$. If these numbers were $15,000 \div 30$, that would be a simple question. 15,270 and 15,000 are approximately equal, as are 32 and 30. You could try this approximation and see how it works in the question.

- If you are presented with a set of numbers to add, all of which are very close, such as in this example, you would add the approximate marks and divide the total by the number of subjects:

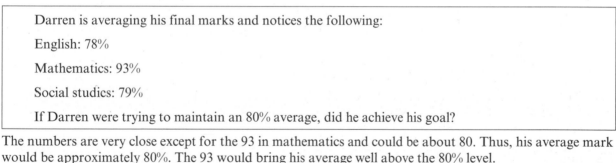

Darren is averaging his final marks and notices the following:

English: 78%

Mathematics: 93%

Social studies: 79%

If Darren were trying to maintain an 80% average, did he achieve his goal?

The numbers are very close except for the 93 in mathematics and could be about 80. Thus, his average mark would be approximately 80%. The 93 would bring his average well above the 80% level.

a. Whole Numbers

Our system of whole numbers is based on ten. The first ten whole numbers are, in order, 0, 1, 2, 3, 4, 5, 6, 7, 8, 9. After that, the first digit indicates the number that is multiplied by ten and the second digit indicates the number that is multiplied by 1. So, 64 is $(6 \times 10) + 4$, and it's also $60 + 4$. Because the units digit (the right-hand one, just before the decimal point, if one is present) is always in order, we know that 48 is one larger than 47 and one less than 49.

Whole numbers can be factored. They can be expressed as a series of numbers or factors, which multiply together to form the number, even if the factors are the number itself and 1. For example:

$$6 = 2 \times 3 \text{ or } 6 \times 1$$
$$18 = 9 \times 2 = 3 \times 3 \times 2 \text{ or } 18 \times 1$$
$$11 = 11 \times 1$$

Whole numbers such as 11 are prime numbers. A prime number is a number greater than 1 that has no factors except itself and 1. For example, 11 is a prime number because the only factors of 11 are 11 and 1.

You can factor any number by following some simple rules:

- A prime number can be divided only by itself and by 1.
- Any number ending in 0, 2, 4, 6, or 8 can be divided by 2.
- Any number ending in 0 or 5 can be divided by 5.
- Any number ending in 0 can be divided by 10.
- Any number whose digits add up to a multiple of 3 can be divided by 3. For example, with the number 66, if you add 6 + 6, you get 12, which is a multiple of 3, so you know that 66 can be divided by 3.
- Any number whose digits add up to a multiple of 9 can be divided by 9. For example, with the number 81, if you add 8 + 1, you get 9, which is a multiple of 9, so you know that 81 can be divided by 9.

These simple rules can make mental arithmetic a little easier on the GED Mathmatics Test. For example, if you wanted to multiply 63 by 25, you could easily figure out that 63 is $3 \times 3 \times 7$ and 25 is 5×5. This means that 63×25 is $3 \times 3 \times 7 \times 5 \times 5 = 15 \times 15 \times 7 = 225 \times 7 = 1,575$.

EXAMPLES:

Andy made a wager with his classmates that he could tell them the prime factors of any number under 200 within 1 minute. To test his skill, Gloria asked him for the prime factors of 174. Andy smiled and told her the prime factors. What were the prime factors that Andy told Gloria?

(1) 2, 2, 3, and 5
(2) 2, 3, and 29
(3) 3, 4, and 39
(4) 2 and 87
(5) 1 and 174

The correct answer is **(2)**. The prime factors of any number are the factors that can no longer be broken down into further factors. If you look at 174, you see that it ends in 4, so 2 is a factor. Then $174 \div 2 = 87$, and $8 + 7 = 15$, which is a multiple of 3. So, 87 is divisible by 3, and $87 \div 3 = 29$, which is a prime number. Andy was lucky that one of the factors was a large prime number, or he would've ended up with a much longer string of prime factors.

Jessie is playing a new game called "What's That Number?" The announcer asks for a number greater than 10 that is doubled and then the result multiplied by 5. Which answer would win the game for Jessie?

(1) 110
(2) 150
(3) 175
(4) 200
(5) Not enough information given

The correct answer is **(5)**. Whole numbers can be used in any operation to form other numbers, provided that enough information is given to determine the answer. Choice (3) is wrong because the operations of doubling a number (multiplying by 2) and then multiplying the product by 5 would be the same as multiplying by 10, and any number multiplied by 10 would end in 0. You often can eliminate an answer using mental arithmetic by looking at it. Number(s) multiplied by 2 always produce an even product, and numbers multiplied by 5 always produce a product ending in 5 or 0. Because division is the opposite operation of multiplication, numbers ending in 0 always have a factor of 5 and 10. Practicing these mental shortcuts can save you valuable time on the GED.

Donald was using a tape measure to measure the length of his room. The tape measure was 10 yards long, and his room was 21 feet long. How many feet longer was the tape measure than Donald's room?

(1) 3
(2) 7
(3) 9
(4) 11
(5) 12

The correct answer is **(3)**. Converting the length of the tape measure into feet, 10 yards = $10 \times 3 = 30$ feet. The length of Donald's room is 21 feet, so $30 - 21 = 9$ feet. The answer is yards (which you weren't asked for) is 3, and if you didn't pay attention to the units of measure, you might've just subtracted $21 - 10 = 11$. *Remember:* The numbers have to be in the same units *before* you can perform mathematical operations on them.

b. Integers

Integers are whole numbers—positive, negative, or zero—without decimal components. Integers can be added, subtracted, multiplied, and divided.

Study

There are two main subsets of integers. One subset is 1, 2, 3, and so on, where all the numbers are positive. The other main subset of integers is –1, –2, –3, and so on, where all the numbers are negative. Integers can be drawn on a number line, like this:

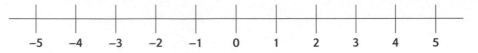

The positive integers are on the right side of the zero, and they increase in value, moving from the center to the right. The negative integers are on the left side of the zero, and they decrease in value moving from the center to the left.

One property of an integer is that it has an absolute value that is the size of the integer without the direction—in other words, it's always positive or zero. Absolute value is written as $|n|$. Thus, the absolute value of –4 is written as $|-4| = 4$.

Integers can be added, subtracted, multiplied, and divided as long as you watch the signs.

To add integers, the simplest way is to combine all the positive integers and all the negative integers and combine the result. For example,

$$-5 + 3 + 7 = -5 + 10 = 5$$

To subtract integers, if there are only two integers (for example, $8 - 2$), the difference between them is 6 and the larger number is positive, so the answer would be 6.

To multiply integers, you count the number of negative signs. If there is an even number of negative signs, the answer is positive. If there is an odd number of negative signs, the answer is negative. For example,

$$-3 \times -6 = 18$$
$$-3 \times 6 = -18$$

To divide integers, you have to keep track of the signs. If both the *divisor* (the integer dividing) and the *dividend* (the integer being divided) have the same sign, the *quotient* (answer) will be positive. If the divisor and the dividend have different signs, the quotient will be negative. For example,

$$36 \div 6 = 6$$
$$-36 \div -6 = 6$$
$$36 \div -6 = -6$$

Remember: You can't divide by 0.

Integers can be used in pairs to determine a location on a grid because a grid is just a series of perpendicular number lines. In this case, the first integer of the pair indicates the position on the x-axis or the horizontal position. The second integer of the pair indicates the position on the y-axis or the vertical position.

The point (5, –3) would appear as the following on the coordinate-plane grid:

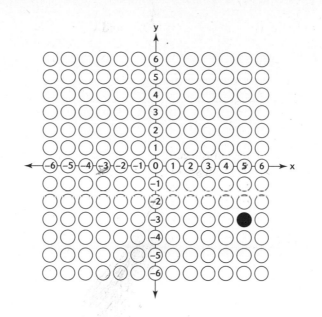

The simplest way to compare the size difference of two integers is to visualize them on a number line. This will give you clues about the relative size of the integers. The number to the right is always larger.

To subtract 8 from 5, start at 0 and count five spaces to the right and then count eight spaces to the left to arrive at −3.

$$5 - 8 = -3$$

EXAMPLES:

Robbie and Sandy are having a reading contest. Robbie has read 497 pages in a very long book, but Sandy has read 239 pages in one book and 261 pages in another book. Who is leading in the reading contest at the moment?

(1) It's a tie.
(2) Robbie.
(3) Sandy.
(4) The contest isn't yet over.
(5) Reading two books doesn't count.

The correct answer is **(3)**. Sandy has read 239 + 261 = 500 pages, and Robbie has read 497 pages. Choices (4) and (5) could be correct or incorrect, but there is no information about the contest to tell us the rules and besides, the question asks, "Who is leading in the reading contest at the moment?" You can eliminate choice (1) by completing the calculation. The number of pages read is so close that approximations wouldn't give you the correct answer.

> Two classmates are comparing their heights. Tom is 5 feet 11 inches tall, and Robert is 5 feet 9 inches tall. What is the height difference between Tom and Robert in inches?
>
> **(1)** 5
> **(2)** 4
> **(3)** 3
> **(4)** 2
> **(5)** 1

The correct answer is **(4)**. The difference between the two heights is the difference between the inches because the feet are the same. The height difference is $11 - 9 = 2$ inches.

c. Fractions

Fractions can be added, subtracted, multiplied, and divided.

In a fraction, the top number is called the *numerator* and the bottom number is called the *denominator*.

To add or subtract fractions, the denominators must be equal. You can make the denominators equal by multiplying each by a number that would produce denominators that are the same number. This number is called the *common denominator*. If you multiply the denominator by a number, you must multiply the numerator by the same number.

For example, to add $\frac{1}{2}$ and $\frac{2}{3}$, you need to get the denominators the same. Here's how:

$$\frac{1}{2} + \frac{2}{3} = \frac{1 \times 3}{2 \times 3} + \frac{2 \times 2}{3 \times 2} = \frac{3}{6} + \frac{4}{6} = \frac{7}{6} = 1\frac{1}{6}$$

To multiply fractions, multiply the numerators to get the product of the numerators, and multiply the denominators to get the product of the denominators. For example,

$$\frac{1}{2} \times \frac{2}{3} = \frac{1 \times 2}{2 \times 3} = \frac{2}{6} = \frac{1}{3}$$

To divide one fraction by another, *invert* (switch the numerator and denominator) the second fraction and multiply. For example,

$$\frac{1}{2} \div \frac{2}{3} = \frac{1}{2} \times \frac{3}{2} = \frac{3}{4}$$

Many fractions can be simplified—the numerator and the denominator can be divided by the same number until there is no number that will divide into each equally. Sometimes the only number that will divide evenly into the numerator and denominator is 1, and the fraction is called a reduced fraction. For example,

$$\frac{8}{16} = \frac{8 \div 8}{16 \div 8} = \frac{1}{2}$$

If the number is made up of a whole number and a fraction, it is called a *mixed number*. An example of a mixed number is $3\frac{1}{2}$.

If the numerator and denominator are both positive or both negative and the numerator is smaller than the denominator (for example, $\frac{1}{2}$), the fraction is proper and smaller than 1. If both the numerator and denominator are positive or negative and the numerator is larger than the denominator (for example, $\frac{5}{2}$), the fraction is improper and larger than 1. If either the numerator or denominator is negative, the fraction will be smaller than 1.

A mixed number (a number and a fraction—for example, $2\frac{1}{2}$) can always be expressed as an improper fraction by multiplying the denominator by the whole number and using the product plus the old numerator as the new numerator. For example,

$$2\frac{1}{2} = \frac{(2 \times 2) + 1}{2} = \frac{5}{2}$$

Any fraction has an endless number of equivalent fractions because multiplying the numerator and denominator of the fraction by the same (nonzero) number produces an equivalent fraction. Thus, $=\frac{1}{2} = \frac{4}{8} = \frac{8}{16}$.

When two fractions have equal denominators, the one with the larger numerator is the larger fraction. When two fractions have equal numerators, the one with the larger denominator is the smaller fraction.

EXAMPLES:

Alex and José are looking for an apartment to share and find two buildings in the same area. Alex loves to cook and wants to live close to the supermarket so that he can shop each day for his groceries. José spends all his time reading and wants to be close to the library. If the supermarket is three blocks from one apartment and five blocks from a second apartment, what fraction would indicate the relative distance of the closer supermarket to the further supermarket for each apartment?

(1) $\frac{5}{3}$

(2) $\frac{2}{5}$

(3) $\frac{5}{2}$

(4) $\frac{3}{5}$

(5) $\frac{1}{2}$

The correct answer is **(4)**. The closer apartment is three blocks away, the farther apartment is five blocks away, and the fraction would be the shorter distance over the farther distance or $\frac{3}{5}$. Choice (1) is the fraction upside down, and the other answers are wrong.

Glen and Dave were looking for a deal on school sweatshirts for their baseball team. After a lot of shopping around, they narrowed it down to three suppliers. Supplier A offered them $\frac{1}{3}$ off each sweatshirt. Supplier B offered them $\frac{8}{25}$ off each sweatshirt. Supplier C offered them $\frac{3}{9}$ off each sweatshirt. Which supplier offered them the best deal?

(1) Supplier A.
(2) Supplier B.
(3) Supplier C.
(4) Suppliers A and C offer the same discount.
(5) Suppliers A and B offer the same discount.

The correct answer is (4). Suppliers A and C offered them the same discount because $\frac{1}{3}$ and $\frac{3}{9}$ are equivalent fractions.

Sierra is entertaining three of her friends and they decide to order pizza. Unfortunately, it arrives unsliced and she has to divide the pie so that each of her friends gets an equal share. What fraction of the pizza would each piece be?

(1) $\frac{1}{3}$

(2) $\frac{1}{4}$

(3) $\frac{1}{5}$

(4) $\frac{1}{6}$

(5) $\frac{1}{7}$

The correct answer is (2). If Sierra has three friends over and wants all four people to share the pizza equally, then each person would get $\frac{1}{4}$ of the pizza. In working with fractions, the numerator of a fraction indicates the number of parts of a whole that are considered. In this case, each person was going to get one piece and the numerator would be 1. The denominator indicates the number the whole is divided into. In this case, the pizza was divided into four sections, one equal section for each person. Each person will get one of the four equal sections or $\frac{1}{4}$.

d. Decimals

Decimals or decimal fractions are fractions based on a denominator of ten. If we were to look at a number such as 23.345, we would know that the whole number is 23, which is 20 + 3 and the value of the digit gets bigger as you go from the decimal point to the left.

Then, there is the decimal point, which says that, from that point on, the value of the numbers gets smaller as you go from the decimal point to the right.

Decimal	Equivalent Fraction
0.3	$\frac{3}{10} = \frac{300}{1,000}$
0.04	$\frac{4}{100} = \frac{40}{1,000}$
0.005	$\frac{5}{1,000}$
0.345	$\frac{345}{1,000}$

To the right of the decimal point the number gets smaller

Decimals can be added, subtracted, multiplied, and divided just like whole numbers. To add or subtract decimal fractions, you must always keep the decimal points in line, which ensures that the place values of the numbers you're adding or subtracting are equal. Here's an example of aligning the decimals and adding:

$$34.782$$
$$+ \ 7.309$$
$$42.091$$

To multiply decimal fractions, you have to remember that these are fractions and multiply using the rules of multiplication of integers. Here's an example:

$$3.7$$
$$\times \ 2.4$$
$$148$$
$$\underline{74}$$
$$888$$

But where do you put the decimal point? The simple answer is that you add the number of decimal places in the two multiples—in this case, two—and count off that number from the right. That would produce a product of 8.88. The reason for this is that $3.7 = 3\frac{7}{10} = \frac{37}{10}$ and $2.4 = 2\frac{4}{10} = \frac{24}{10}$. Multiplying the fractions, $\frac{37}{10} \times \frac{24}{10} = \frac{888}{100} = 8.88$.

To divide decimals, there is another approach. If you wanted to divide 36.6 by 2.4, you would write it as $36.6 \div 2.4$, which would become $366 \div 24$ (because you move all decimal points the same number of spaces to the right and then you divide). The quotient is 15.25.

EXAMPLES:

> Max is shopping for clothes and sees a jacket he really likes. Store A has the jacket on sale for 40% off the regular price, and Store B is offering it for 0.6 of its regular price. If the jacket originally cost $49.99 in both stores, how much would Max have to pay for the jacket on sale at the lower price?
>
> **(1)** $49.99
> **(2)** $39.99
> **(3)** $29.99
> **(4)** $19.99
> **(5)** $9.99

The correct answer is **(3)**. Looking at the two discounts, you'll notice that they're the same. If an item is discounted 40%, then the price is 60% of the original (100% − 40% = 60%). Max would then pay 60%, or 0.6, of the original price for the jacket on sale: 0.6 × $49.99 = $29.99. The other answers are wrong, although choice (4) is close to the *discount* Max would've received, which means that this problem requires you to pay close attention. You could estimate the answer by using 60% of $50, which is $30 and choice (3) is just a penny away.

> José was shopping for school supplies and needed two binders. Looking at the binder display, he saw just the type of binder he needed. It cost $4.95, but the sign said that there was a $1.50 discount for buying two. If José bought two binders, how much would he pay for each binder after applying the discount?
>
> **(1)** $4.95
> **(2)** $3.45
> **(3)** $4.20
> **(4)** $3.20
> **(5)** -$4.45

The correct answer is **(3)**. If José received a discount of $1.50 for buying two binders, he would get a discount of $1.50 ÷ 2 = $0.75 per binder. This would reduce the price to $4.95 − $0.75 = $4.20. Our money system is basically a decimal system that we're all familiar with, and you can use this to your advantage.

> Sally has finished 0.6 of her reading course. If the total course is ten months long, how many months does Sally have left?
>
> **(1)** 2
> **(2)** 3
> **(3)** 4
> **(4)** 5
> **(5)** 6

The correct answer is **(3)**. Start by calculating 0.6 of 10, which is 0.6 × 10 = 6. But don't forget: This is how much Sally has *completed,* and you were asked how much time *remains* in the course, which is 10 − 6 = 4 months. You have to read even the simplest questions carefully to make sure that you're answering the question.

e. Percentages

When you're working with percentages, you're really working with fractions whose denominators are always 100. To calculate a percentage, you can use the percentage as the numerator and 100 as the denominator, and use any of the common operations. Once you have the fraction, it can easily be turned into a decimal by dividing the denominator into the numerator.

If, for example, you are offered a discount of 40% at a store, they are saying that they will take $\frac{40}{100}$ or $\frac{4}{10}$ or $\frac{2}{5}$ of the price off the original price. Remember that fractions can be reduced by dividing the top number (called the numerator) and the bottom number (called the denominator) by the same number. In this case, we divide $\frac{40}{100}$ by 10 to get $\frac{4}{10}$ and then divide again by 2 to get $\frac{2}{5}$. Because 40% can be expressed as a fraction, it can also be expressed as a decimal fraction. For example, $40\% = \frac{40}{100} = 0.4$. This allows us to use percentages in different ways.

If the original price of the item was $100 and the discount was 40%, you could calculate the discount by multiplying $100 by $\frac{40}{100}$ or 0.4. In each case the answer would be $40, which would be the discount.

i. Practice

Practice converting percentages to fractions to decimals by completing this table:

Percentage	Decimal	Fraction
34%	0.34	
		$\frac{3}{5}$
100%		
		$\frac{24}{25}$
	0.98	
75%		

ii. Answers

The correct answers to this table would be:

Percentage	Decimal	Fraction
34%	0.34	$\frac{17}{50}$
60%	0.6	$\frac{3}{5}$
100%	1	1
96%	0.96	$\frac{24}{25}$
98%	0.98	$\frac{49}{50}$
75%	0.75	$\frac{3}{4}$

EXAMPLES:

> Jeff is shopping for new shirts and notices a special sale. If he buys one shirt, there is a discount of 10% on it. If he buys two shirts, there is a discount of 30% off the second shirt. If he buys three shirts, there is a discount of 40% off the third shirt purchased, and the discount for four shirts or more is 50% off the most expensive shirt. Jeff sees five shirts he really likes but wants to save the most money he can.
>
> Shirt 1 costs $29.95.
>
> Shirt 2 costs $59.95.
>
> Shirt 3 costs $39.95.
>
> Shirt 4 costs $29.95.
>
> Shirt 5 costs $49.95.
>
> Which shirt should Jeff buy fifth to save the most money?
>
> **(1)** Shirt 1
> **(2)** Shirt 2
> **(3)** Shirt 3
> **(4)** Shirt 4
> **(5)** Shirt 5

The correct answer is **(2)**. The shirt bought last would create the biggest discount on that shirt and sensible Jeff would want to save by getting the biggest discount on his shirts. Because Shirt 2 is the most expensive, it would create the biggest savings if he bought it as the fourth or fifth shirt.

> Carol is investing $200 she got for her birthday. Bank A offers her 3% simple interest for a year, but Bank B says that it will invest her money in a certificate that will pay her no interest but a bonus of $5.75 after one year. Bank C offers Carol 2% simple interest for a year with a bonus of $2.50 after one year. Which bank will return the most money to Carol after one year?
>
> **(1)** Bank A
> **(2)** Bank B
> **(3)** Bank C
> **(4)** None of the banks
> **(5)** Not enough information given

The correct answer is **(3)**. Bank A is offering her $200 \times 0.03 = $6. Bank B is offering her $5.75. Bank C is offering her $200 \times 0.02 = $4, plus a bonus of $2.50, for a total of $6.50, which is the greatest return on her money. Choices (4) and (5) can be eliminated quickly because there is enough information to get an answer and one of the banks must be best unless they were all offering her the same return.

f. Relationship of Basic Arithmetic Operations

Arithmetic operations are related to one another. Subtraction is the opposite of addition. Addition of positive numbers creates a sum larger than either of the numbers added. For example, if $5 + 1 = 6$, then $6 - 1 = 5$ and $6 - 5 = 1$.

Here's another example: If you were adding the total bill for your grocery shopping, the sum would be larger than the price for each item. If you bought more than you could afford, subtracting items would make the sum of the items smaller. If Dave bought $20.04 worth of groceries but only had a $20 bill in his pocket, he would have to leave behind one or more items to reduce his total to $20 or less.

Addition and multiplication are related because multiplication is repeated additions of the same number (for example, $3 \times 4 = 4 + 4 + 4 = 12$).

Memorizing the multiplication tables is a far more efficient way of multiplying in your head, but if you get stuck, remembering that multiplication is repetitive addition of the same number can help. If you want to multiply 6×7 and you remember only that $5 \times 7 = 35$, you can figure out 6×7 by adding 7 to 35 to get 42.

Subtraction and division are related because division is repetitive subtractions of the same number. Again, memorizing the division tables is a more efficient way to divide, so keep this in mind if you're stuck on the test.

Multiplication and division are related and are opposite operations:

$$3 \times 4 = 12$$
$$12 \div 3 = 4$$

EXAMPLES:

Fernando was given a skill-testing question to answer in order to claim a prize at the local radio station. He was asked to calculate $23 + 45 - 59 - 45 + 59$. What should his answer be?

(1) 21
(2) 23
(3) 25
(4) 45
(5) 59

The correct answer is **(2)**. Because addition and subtraction are opposite operations, adding and then subtracting 45 and 59 has no effect on the 23. The other answers are the numbers that were added and subtracted and a few wrong answers. The important thing to remember is that, in any questions with numbers, you need to read the question carefully. In this case, if you read carefully, you noticed that 45 and 59 are both added and subtracted, leaving you with 23.

Josie was doing the mechanical arithmetic portion of her test and came across the following question: $46 \div 23 \times 54 \div 92 \div 54 \times 92 \times 23$. What should her answer be?

(1) 2
(2) 23
(3) 46
(4) 54
(5) 92

The correct answer is **(3)**. Multiplication and division are opposite operations. In this case, the numbers 23, 54, and 92 are both multiplied and divided, which cancels them out, leaving 46 as the answer. *Remember:* If addition/subtraction is mixed with multiplication/division, then the order of operations is used.

g. Exponents

It's a good idea to have a general idea of the rules of exponents:

- The exponent tells you the number of times the number or base is to be multiplied by itself. For example, $6^3 = 6 \times 6 \times 6 = 216$.
- Any negative exponent means to divide by the number to that power. For example, $n^{-e} = \dfrac{1}{n^e}$.
- Any number to the power of 0 equals 1. For example, $2,948^0 = 1$. Note 0^0 is not defined.
- Any number to the power of 1 equals the number. For example, $345^1 = 345$.
- To multiply two or more numbers involving exponents, if the base is the same, add the exponents to get the product. For example, $8^3 \times 8^7 = 8^{3+7} = 8^{10}$.
- To divide two numbers involving exponents with a common base, subtract the exponents to get the answer. For example, $5^8 \div 5^3 = 5^{8-3} = 5^5$.
- To raise an exponent to an exponent, multiply the exponents. For example, $(4^3)^2 = 4^{3 \times 2} = 4^6$.
- To raise two or more numbers in a product to a common exponent, raise each one to the exponent. For example, $(2 \times 3)^4 = 2^4 \times 3^4$ or 6^4.
- To raise a fraction to a power, raise the numerator and the denominator to the power. For example, $\left(\dfrac{3}{4}\right)^8 = \dfrac{3^8}{4^8}$.

There are a few other rules or laws of exponents, but these should take you through the GED test.

EXAMPLES:

Solve the following equation for e: $2^e = 256$.

(1) 5
(2) 6
(3) 7
(4) 8
(5) 9

The correct answer is **(4)**. In this equation, you're dealing with exponents. An exponent may be called a power, but no matter what it's called, it has a definite meaning and follows certain rules. N^e means a number N multiplied by itself e times and is usually read "N to the eth." In this case, you're looking for a power of 2 that would equal 256. If the problem is on the section of the test where calculators are allowed, you can use a calculator to find the answer. But if the problem appears on the section where you have to use your brain and paper and pencil, you can do it this way:

$2^1 = 2$
$2^2 = 4$
$2^3 = 8$
$2^4 = 16$

$2^5 = 32$
$2^6 = 64$
$2^7 = 128$
$2^8 = 256$

which is the answer to the problem. In this case, the number 256 is an exact power of 2. If the number given were 257, the problem would have been extremely difficult and probably wouldn't appear on the GED test. Problems on the GED test are all possible within the time frame given for answering them. If you find a problem that's so complex that you need many minutes to try to figure it out, leave it. You're better off not answering one very difficult question than not finishing the test because you spent all your time on that one question.

Carlos is a whiz at math but a little lazy about helping around the house. His father offers to pay him $15 a week to rake the leaves each day. Carlos says that he won't work weekends but will take 2¢ for the first day and the square of yesterday's amount each day and would only accept the last day's pay. How much more than his father was offering would Carlos get on the last day for the first week's work?

(1) $27
(2) $168
(3) $640.36
(4) $655.36
(5) $672.36

The correct answer is **(3)**. This is a good question to use a calculator to find the answer. Exponential functions like this get large very quickly. In this case, you could sketch out a table:

Day	Amount (cents)
1	2
2	4
3	16
4	256
5	65,536

On the fifth day, Carlos would be owed 65,536 pennies or $655.36. But, his father had offered him $15 a week, so he would get $655.36 – $15.00 = $640.36 more than his father's original offer. Choice (5) is the amount Carlos would get, but it doesn't answer the question. The other answers are wrong. If you converted to dollars before the calculation, you would have gotten a different answer because the powers of a decimal get smaller and the units given were cents, not dollars. Always read carefully to ensure that you convert, if necessary, but at the right time.

h. Scientific Notation

Scientists often work in very large or very small numbers. They would waste a lot of time writing all those numbers each time they needed them, so they developed a system called scientific notation. Instead of writing 700,000,000, they could write 7.0×10^8 or $7.0 \times 100,000,000$. In scientific notation, all the significant digits are always shown with the decimal point after the first digit multiplied by a power of 10 to keep the structured numbers equivalent.

If the number is greater than 1, the power of ten is positive; if the number is less than 1, the power of ten is negative. 1,234,567 could be written in scientific notation as 1.234567×10^6.

EXAMPLES:

Jason was working in a physics lab for the summer, but he could never figure out how big or small numbers written in scientific notation really were. In the last report he read, two items were 1.493×10^{-4} feet. apart. If Jason just wanted to know how far apart they were using regular notation, what distance would he use in feet?

(1) 1.493
(2) 0.0001493
(3) 0.01493
(4) 0.001493
(5) 149,300

The correct answer is **(2)**. In order to switch scientific notation to regular notation, you multiply 1.493×10^{-4}, which would be 0.0001493. A quick way to do this on a test is to move the decimal point four spaces to the right, from 0.0001493 to 1.493 for a negative power (or do the opposite for a positive power).

$$0.0001493 \longrightarrow 1.493$$
$$1 \; 2 \; 3 \; 4$$

Ahmed was researching the distance to the moon from the Earth and found the figure: 238,857 miles from the center of the Earth to the center of the moon. His teacher asked him to write this in scientific notation. What number should Ahmed write?

(1) 238,857
(2) 238,000
(3) 2.38857×10^5
(4) 23.8×10^5
(5) 2.3×10^5

The correct answer is **(3)**. Scientific notation means writing the number with the decimal after the first number and multiplying by a power of ten. The simple way to do this is to count from right to left and increase the power by 1 for each digit. In this example, you would move the decimal point five places to the left and that would make 5 the power of ten. If you had only an approximate number, choice (5) might have been acceptable, but Ahmed was writing what he believed to be an accurate number.

i. Ratios

A ratio is a fraction-like number that compares two quantities. In comparing ratios, the units must be the same. Like fractions, the numbers in a ratio always can be divided evenly by the same number to produce a simplified ratio (unless the ratio is already reduced).

The ratio of 5 to 8 may be written in different ways, such as 5 to 8, or 5:8, or $5 \div 8$, or $\frac{5}{8}$. The numbers 5 and 8 are the terms of the ratio.

Because ratios are fractions, the denominator can never be 0.

EXAMPLES:

Abdul really likes soda. One day when it was on sale, he bought 25 cases of soda (20 cases of ginger ale and 5 cases of cola). What ratio of cola to ginger ale did Abdul buy?

(1) 20:25

(2) 1:4

(3) 4:1

(4) 25:5

(5) 5:4

The correct answer is **(2)**. Abdul bought 5 cases of cola and 20 cases of ginger ale. A ratio compares numbers measured in the same units—in this instance, the unit is a case. When you compare the number of cases of cola bought to the number of cases of ginger ale bought, it's 5 to 20, usually written 5:20. Ratios usually are written in the lowest terms—that is, by dividing the numbers by any number or numbers that would divide equally into both. You'll notice that both 5 and 20 can be divided by 5 evenly. The ratio would then become 1:4.

If you divide one integer by another, you get a rational number or a ratio. If, for example, you divided 3 by 4, the result would be $\frac{3}{4}$ or 3:4.

Kelly and Gloria were having a contest to see who could read the most books in a month. In one month, Kelly read three books, one with 325 pages, one with 242 pages, and 115 pages of a third book. Gloria read two books, one with 505 pages and the other with 268 pages. What is the ratio of pages read by Kelly to pages read by Gloria?

(1) 628:773

(2) 682:773

(3) 773:682

(4) 773:628

(5) 628:682

The correct answer is **(2)**. Kelly read a total number of pages of: 325 + 242 + 115 = 682. Gloria read a total number of pages of: 505 + 268 = 773. The ratio of pages read by Kelly to that read by Gloria is 682:773.

j. Proportions

An equation expressing the equality of two ratios is called a proportion and may be written in different ways: $\frac{a}{b} = \frac{c}{d}$ may be written $a:b = c:d$, or $a:b::c:d$ (read as "a is to b as c is to d"), where a and d are called the *extremes* and b and c are called the *means*. The product of the extremes equals the product of the means (that is, $ad = bc$) and is called cross-multiplication.

If one of the terms is unknown—for example, a, which could be represented by x—then $xd = bc$ and $x = \frac{bc}{d}$.

EXAMPLES:

> Alice just got a part-time job at a local restaurant, which prepares its sodas by mixing a concentrate with soda water. If the ratio of concentrate to soda water is 1 gallon of concentrate to 15 gallons of soda water, how many ounces of concentrate would Alice need to produce the Belly-Buster Special Soda, which is 32 ounces of pure delight?
>
> **(1)** 1
> **(2)** 15
> **(3)** 2
> **(4)** 4
> **(5)** 3

The correct answer is **(3).** The ratio of concentrate to soda water is 1:15. In order to solve this problem, we need to use a proportion. Adding 1 gallon of concentrate to 15 gallons of soda water would produce 16 gallons of Special Soda. In this case, Alice doesn't need 16 gallons of soda but 32 ounces; 32 is double 16, so she can maintain the consistent units in the ratio. Then she can produce a proportion by multiplying the original ratio by 2 to produce 2:32. This means Alice needs 2 ounces of concentrate to produce 32 ounces of Special Soda.

> Danny is tending bar at a local restaurant and the manager has a new idea. He has put a tip container on the bar and has told Danny that he will divide tips this way: Seven parts go to the waiter, two parts go to the bartender, and one part goes to the manager. If the tip container contains $320 at the end of the night, what portion would go to Danny?
>
> **(1)** $32
> **(2)** $46
> **(3)** $23
> **(4)** $64
> **(5)** $224

The correct answer is **(4).** Each of the following gets a proportion of the tips. If you add up all the proportions, you would get 10, which makes for easy calculation. The waiter would get $\frac{7}{10}$ of the tips. The owner would get $\frac{1}{10}$ of the tips and Danny would get $\frac{2}{10}$ of the tips, or $\frac{1}{5}$. Multiplying $320 by $\frac{1}{5}$ would produce $64.

k. Roots

If we consider the exponential equation, $\sqrt[e]{N} = R$, where N is a number or the base, e is the index of the root, and R is the root, we could read the equation as the eth root of N is R. A root of such an equation is one of a predetermined number of factors that produce the product required. All this is good mathematics, but on the GED test, you'll likely be asked to calculate nothing more than a square root or even a cube root.

If the question is on the part of the test on which you can use a calculator, the work is done for you. If the concept of roots is still confusing, first try to remember that roots and powers are opposites. If you multiply 3×3, you get 9 or, to put it another way, $3^2 = 9$. If you're asked for the square root of 9, or which two equal factors multiply together to form a product of 9, you could either know or calculate the factors to be 3 and 3. The usual place to calculate roots is in problems about rectangles. If you're given the area of a square, the length or width is the square root. If you're given the volume of a cube, each dimension is the cube root.

EXAMPLES:

Elana has always wanted a hot tub in the shape of a cube. Finally, after getting her first bonus on the job, she can afford it. She wants her hot tub to be able to hold 125 cubic feet of water, but she doesn't know how wide a tub that would produce. After some research, she figures it out. How wide will her hot tub be in feet?

(1) 1
(2) 2
(3) 3
(4) 4
(5) 5

The correct answer is **(5)**. Because Elana wants the hot tub to be a cube, each dimension will be the cube root of the volume, which is 125 cubic feet. Mentally, you would know that $5 \times 5 \times 5 = 125$. This means that each dimension, including the width, would be 5 feet.

Alvin was shopping for new carpet. He needed a square carpet to cover a space about 9 feet by 8 feet. The store with the best prices sold square carpets by the square foot. The pattern Alvin preferred was marked at 81 square feet. If he chooses to buy this carpet, how much smaller or larger will it be than the space he had planned for the carpet?

(1) 72 square feet smaller
(2) 9 square feet smaller
(3) 72 square feet larger
(4) 9 square feet larger
(5) 23 square feet larger

The correct answer is **(4)**. To calculate the dimensions of a square carpet, you would have to find the square root of the area. Remember that area equals length times width, and both the length and the width are equal in a square. The square root of 81 is 9, which means that the carpet would measure 9 feet on each side. The space that Alvin wanted to cover was 9 feet by 8 feet. The area of this space is $9 \times 8 = 72$ square feet. Subtracting the area Alvin wanted to cover from the total area of the carpet , $81 - 72 = 9$ square feet. It is important to know the dimensions of the carpet to see if it would approximately fit the space.

l. Selecting the Appropriate Operations

You may see a few questions on the GED test asking you what operations you would use to solve a problem but not actually asking you to solve the problem. Some of these questions are simple. If you wanted to calculate the area of a surface, you would multiply; if you wanted to calculate the perimeter you would add and then multiply. Knowing what operations to perform and the order in which to perform them in is an important skill for the test.

EXAMPLES:

Donna bought a car that uses, on average, a gallon of gas for each 23 miles traveled in the city. If gas costs $3.07 a gallon, what operations would you use to calculate how far Donna could travel, on average, for $20 of gas?

(1)   Multiply then divide.
(2)   Divide then multiply.
(3)   Add then multiply.
(4)   Divide then add.
(5)   Subtract then add.

The correct answer is **(2)**. To calculate how far Donna could travel for $20 of gas, we would first divide $20 by $3.07 to see how many gallons of gas she would use. Because she can travel 23 miles for each gallon, we would multiply the number of gallons by 23. The correct operations would be to divide and then multiply.

Doreen got a summer job on a farm gathering eggs. She was paid 2 cents an egg for her work. At the end of the day, she knew how many eggs she had gathered and her per-egg pay. How could she calculate her daily income?

(1)   Add.
(2)   Subtract.
(3)   Multiply.
(4)   Divide.
(5)   Add then multiply.

The correct answer is **(3)**. Doreen would calculate her daily income by multiplying the amount she was paid per egg by the number of eggs she gathered.

m. Methods for Calculating Your Answers

On the GED test, you'll have to answer a series of questions requiring you to perform calculations with your brain, pencil and paper, and a scientific calculator. These calculations will involve whole numbers, fractions, decimals, and integers. The only way to become proficient in these calculations is to practice. Here are some questions to practice on. They're not anything like what you'll find on the test—they're just practice in different ways of calculating an answer.

First, look at the question, and then use your brain to estimate an answer. Next, calculate the answer using a pencil and paper. Finally, use a calculator to calculate the same question to two decimal places. Your first answer should be close to the second and third. If not, you might want to spend extra time on the next section of this review.

Remember: If more than one operation is present in a question, the order of operations is **b**rackets, **e**xponents, **d**ivide or **m**ultiply (work left to right), and **a**dd or **s**ubtract (work left to right). The memory device for this is *BEDMAS*.

study

i. Questions

Question	Calculate Mentally	Calculate with Pen and Paper	Calculate with Calculator
$2(15 - 6) + 23$			
$348 \div 29$			
$248 + 197 - 199$			
$21 + 24 \div 3 + (7 \times 16) - 3$			
$\sqrt{4^2 - 3(7 + 6)}$			
$6abc + d$ where $a = 4$, $b = 0.4$, $c = \frac{21}{5}$, and $d = 23$			
The length in inches of a wall, 18 feet 7 inches long			
The amount of water a pool 24 feet long, 18 feet wide, and 5 feet 6 inches deep would hold when filled to the brim			
The length of the hypotenuse of a right triangle whose other two sides are 1 yard and 4 feet			
The square of the number of days in March			
$|-243| + 375$			
The square root of 20,736			
The average of 25, 18, 37, and 19			
What is the difference between the mean and the median of 19, 33, 9, and 24?			
What is the perimeter of a rectangle whose sides are 2 yards and 4 feet 6 inches?			
What is the area of a circle with radius 7 inches? ($\pi = 3.14$)			
$23 + (-48) \times 14 \div 7$			
The distance between the tip of George's thumb and his little finger when fully extended is about 8 inches. If he were trying to estimate the length of a board 4 feet 8 inches long, how many times would George have to span along the length?			

continued

Question	Calculate Mentally	Calculate with Pen and Paper	Calculate with Calculator
The average length of a song on Felix's iPod is 3 minutes 30 seconds. How many songs would he have to store to play for 1 hour and 15 minutes?			
$\dfrac{-27+\sqrt{8^2-6(3-8)}}{27}$			
$\sqrt{9^2+6^2}$			
$38 + 6^3 - 25 - (17 + 26)$			
What time is 7 hours and 18 minutes after 1:24 a.m.?			
$256.46 \div 0.04$			
$2{,}494 \times 2.397$			
What is the perimeter in inches of a circular garden with a diameter of 2.5 yards?			
If a car travels an average of 35 mph and leaves at 1 p.m., when would it arrive after a 49-mile trip?			
Write the prime factorization of 256.			

ii. Answers

After you complete the table with all your computations in the preceding section, check your answers.

Question	Answer
$2(15 - 6) + 23$	41
$348 \div 29$	12
$248 + 197 - 199$	246
$21 + 24 \div 3 + (7 \times 16) - 3$	138
$\sqrt{4^2-3(7+6)}$	No answer. You cannot find the square root of a negative number.
$6abc + d$ where $a = 4$, $b = 0.4$, $c = \dfrac{21}{5}$, and $d = 23$	63.32
The length in inches of a wall, 18 feet 7 inches long	223
The amount of water a pool 24 feet long, 18 feet wide, and 5 feet 6 inches deep would hold when filled to the brim	2,376 cubic feet
The length of the hypotenuse of a right triangle whose other two sides are 1 yard and 4 feet	5 feet
The square of the number of days in March	961
$|-243| + 375$	618
The square root of 20,736	144
The average of 25, 18, 37, and 19	24.75

Question	Answer
What is the difference between the mean and the median of 19, 33, 9, and 24?	0.25
What is the perimeter of a rectangle whose sides are 2 yards and 4 feet 6 inches?	21 feet or 7 yards
What is the area of a circle with radius 7 inches? ($\pi = 3.14$)	153.86 square inches
$23 + (-48) \times 14 \div 7$	-73
The distance between the tip of George's thumb and his little finger when fully extended is about 8 inches. If he were trying to estimate the length of a board 4 feet 8 inches long, how many times would George have to span along the length?	7 times
The average length of a song on Felix's iPod is 3 minutes 30 seconds. How many songs would he have to store to play for 1 hour and 15 minutes?	21 songs. The mathematical answer is 21.43, but you cannot record 0.43 of a song if asked for the number of songs.
$\dfrac{-27 + \sqrt{8^2 - 6(3-8)}}{27}$	$-0,64$
$\sqrt{9^2 + 6^2}$	10.82
$38 + 6^3 - 25 - (17 + 26)$	186
What time is 7 hours and 18 minutes after 1:24 a.m.?	8:42 a.m.
$256.46 \div 0.04$	6,411.5
$2,494 \times 2.397$	5,978.12
What is the perimeter in inches of a circular garden with a diameter of 2.5 yards?	7.85 yards
If a car travels an average of 35 mph and leaves at 1 p.m., when would it arrive after a 49-mile trip?	2:24 p.m.
Write the prime factorization of 256.	2^8

2. Measurement and Geometry

a. Perpendicular Lines

Two lines that intersect forming a right angle at the point of intersection are considered perpendicular. We make some assumptions in everyday life pertaining to perpendicular lines:

- We assume that walls are perpendicular to the floor.
- We assume that the corners of a regular sheet of paper are formed by two perpendicular lines.
- We know that the corners of squares and rectangles are perpendicular.

In a triangle, if one of the angles is a right angle, the two sides forming the right angle are perpendicular and the triangle is called a right triangle. The side opposite the right angle is called the hypotenuse.

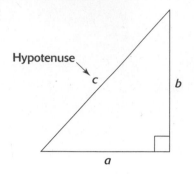

Use the Pythagorean theorem ($a^2 + b^2 = c^2$; a and b are legs and c the hypotenuse of a right triangle) to solve the following problem.

> A right triangle has a hypotenuse of length 12 inches and one side of length 4 inches. What is the length in inches of the third side to two decimal places?
>
> **(1)** 12.48
> **(2)** 11.31
> **(3)** 13.13
> **(4)** 144
> **(5)** 16

The correct answer is **(2)**. The equation to calculate the sides of a right triangle is $c = \sqrt{a^2 + b^2}$, where c = the length of the hypotenuse and a and b are the lengths of the other two sides. Substituting the known quantities in the equation would produce $12 = \sqrt{4^2 + b^2}$ or $144 = 16 + b^2$. Then $b^2 = 144 - 16 = 128$, and $b = 11.31$ inches, correct to two decimal places.

b. Equations of Lines

Parallel lines are lines that never meet and are always the same distance apart and have the same slopes.

EXAMPLE:

> If the equation of a line is $y = mx + 3$, where 3 is the y-intercept and m is the slope, what would be the effect of using different values for m?
>
> **(1)** No effect
> **(2)** A series of parallel lines
> **(3)** A series of spoke-like lines passing through (3, 0)
> **(4)** A series of spoke-like lines passing through (0, 3)
> **(5)** A series of perpendicular lines

The correct answer is **(4)**. Because the y-intercept is constant but the slope is variable, all lines would pass through the y-intercept (0, 3) and look like the spokes of a wheel.

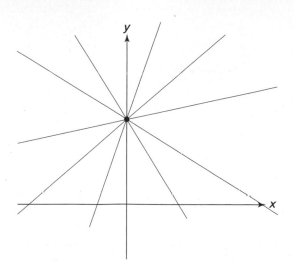

c. Geometric Figures

Two figures are **congruent** if one can be exactly slipped over the other. This can be accomplished by moving, flipping, or rotating one to exactly fit over the other.

Two figures are congruent when one can be exactly superimposed over another. If the two figures were triangles, when one triangle is superimposed on the other, each side would exactly fit over the corresponding side and each angle would fit exactly over the corresponding angle. If you did this with real triangles, you could not see the bottom triangle because it would be exactly and completely covered by the top triangle.

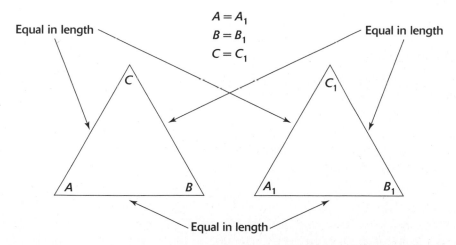

If the figures were rectangles, one would fit exactly over the other and each side would be exactly the same size as the corresponding side on the other. Because they are rectangles, the angles would all be right angles and would fit exactly.

EXAMPLE:

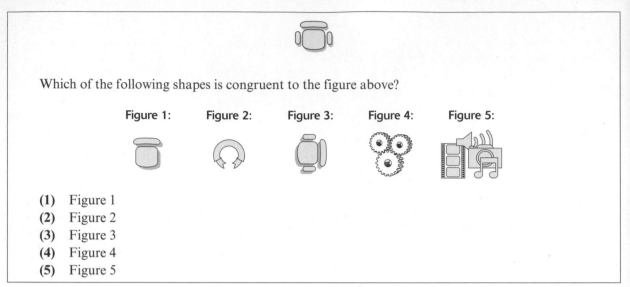

Which of the following shapes is congruent to the figure above?

Figure 1:   Figure 2:   Figure 3:   Figure 4:   Figure 5:

(1)   Figure 1
(2)   Figure 2
(3)   Figure 3
(4)   Figure 4
(5)   Figure 5

The correct answer is **(3).** If you were to rotate the sample figure 90 degrees, it would fit over Figure 3.

If two geometrical shapes differ only in size they are said to be **similar.** Corresponding sides of similar figures are all in the same ratio. Corresponding angles are congruent. For example:

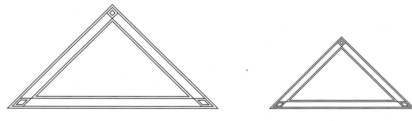

Triangle A   Triangle B

Above, Triangle A is similar to Triangle B because it has the same shape, with corresponding angles equal in size.

Here's another example:

Parallelogram A   Parallelogram B

The two parallelograms above are similar because they are identical in every aspect but size.

Some questions may ask you to describe or analyze a geometric figure.

EXAMPLES:

How would you describe the following figure?

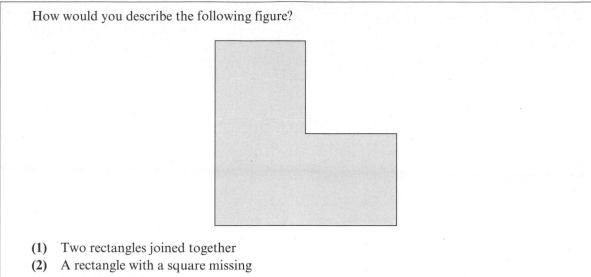

(1) Two rectangles joined together
(2) A rectangle with a square missing
(3) An L-shaped figure
(4) A rectangle and a square joined together
(5) All of the above

The correct answer is **(5).** If you take a closer look at the given figure, you can see the following, which is a rectangle joined to a square. Because a square is technically a rectangle, (1) is correct; (2) is correct; (3) is a description of the shape; and (4) is correct. This means that (5) is correct.

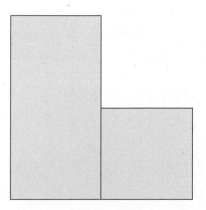

Describe the rotation of the following figure:

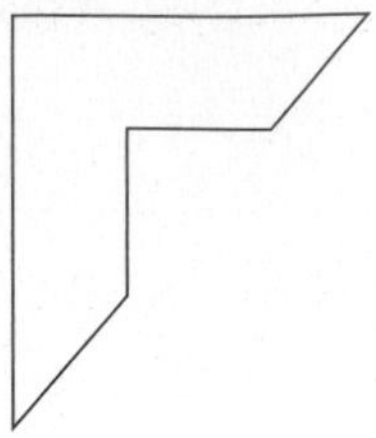

to

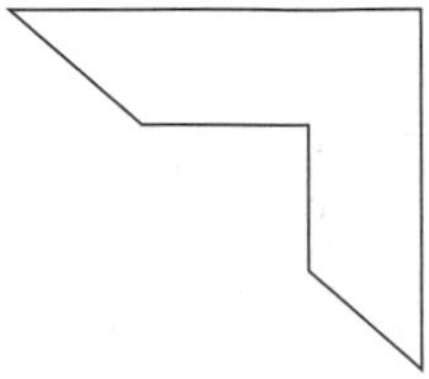

(1) 45 degrees
(2) 90 degrees
(3) 135 degrees
(4) 180 degrees
(5) 360 degrees

The correct answer is **(2).** If you have trouble visualizing this rotation, cut an approximate shape out of paper and try rotating around a point, using a protractor to measure angles.

d. Slope and *y*-Intercept of a Line

The **slope of a line** is defined as the rise divided by the run, where the rise is the vertical distance and the run is the horizontal distance. The slope of a line joining two known points (x_1, y_1) and (x_2, y_2) can be calculated using the following equation:

$$\text{slope of a line} = \frac{y_2 - y_1}{x_2 - x_1}$$

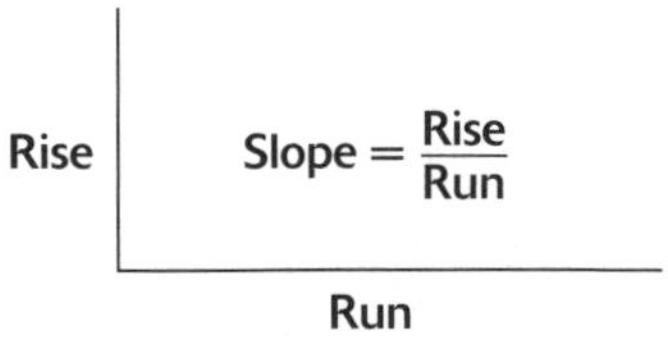

Rise $\text{Slope} = \dfrac{\text{Rise}}{\text{Run}}$

Run

The **y-intercept of a line** is the point on the graph where the line intersects the y-axis or where the coordinate x is 0. A very useful equation relating y-intercept and slope is $y = mx + b$, where x and y are coordinates on the line, m is the slope, and b is the y-coordinate of the y-intercept of the line.

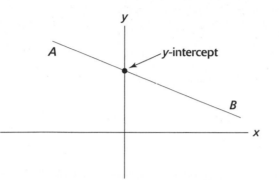

e. The Intersection of Two Lines

The point of intersection of two lines is the common point of the two lines, where they cross one another. At this point, both lines have a common point with the same coordinates.

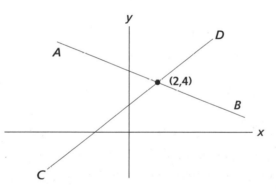

For example, line segment AB intersects line segment CD at point (2, 4). This point would satisfy the equations of both lines.

Coordinates indicate points on a graph. By joining these points, shapes can be drawn.

EXAMPLE:

Describe the geometric figure that would be formed by joining $A(-3, 3)$, $B(3, 3)$, $C(1, -3)$ and $D(-5, -3)$.

(1) Rectangle
(2) Square
(3) Parallelogram
(4) Rhombus
(5) Trapezoid

The correct answer is **(3)**. A quadrilateral with opposite sides parallel and opposite angles equal but not equal to 90 degrees is called a parallelogram. If the opposite angles were right angles, the figure would be a rectangle, which is a special quadrilateral. The completed figure would look like this:

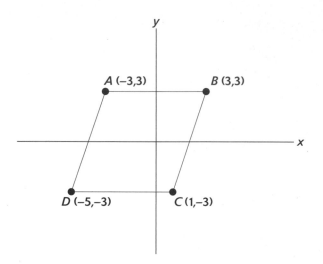

f. Methods for Calculating Your Answers

i. Questions

Estimate and calculate solutions to the following problems.

Note: Although the questions on the test will be multiple choice, these questions require answers to give you practice in computation and estimation. Complete each of the blank columns.

As you fill in the blank cells, think about which method of finding the answer would be simplest, easiest, and fastest. Not all questions require exact calculation and not all estimates are close enough to be used in finding the answer. Decide which method to use by looking at the question and the possible answers. If the answers are very different, usually an approximation will tell you which one is correct. If the answers are close together in value, a calculation is probably better.

	Problem	Information	What Is Asked?	Estimation	Calculation
Length	What would be the inner dimensions of a frame made to fit an 8-x-10-inch picture with a 1-inch border around it?				
Perimeter	What is the perimeter of a 3-x-2-yard carpet in feet?				
Area	What is the area of a 9-x-12-foot rectangle in square yards?				
Surface area	What is the surface area of a 50-foot-long circular pipe with a circumference of 36 inches?				
Volume	How many cubic feet of water will an aquarium measuring 2 feet in length, 1 foot 9 inches in depth, and 1 foot 6 inches in height hold?				
Angle measurement	On a compass, what direction is 90 degrees clockwise from north?				
Capacity	If regular gasoline weighs 6.2 pounds per gallon, how much additional weight would filling a 21-gallon gasoline tank add to the overall weight of a car?				
Weight	If someone lost an average of 4.5 pounds per month, what would be his total weight loss from September 1 through June 30?				

ii. Answers

	Problem	Information	What Is Asked?	Estimation	Calculation
Length	What would be the inner dimensions of a frame made to fit an 8-×-10-inch picture with a 1-inch border around it?	Picture: Length = 8 inches Width = 10 inches Border = 1 inch on each side	Find inner dimensions of frame.	Length of picture + 2 inches (border top and bottom) by width of picture + 2 inches (border left and right side) is 10 inches by 12 inches.	8 + 2 = 10 10 + 2 = 12 Outside dimensions of frame are 10 inches by 12 inches.
Perimeter	What is the perimeter of a 3-×-2-yard carpet in feet?	Length = 3 yards = 9 feet Width = 2 yards = 6 feet	Find perimeter Formula: $P = 2(l + w)$ P is the perimeter, l is the length, and w is the width.	Perimeter is 18 feet + 12 feet = 30 feet	$P = 2(l + w)$ $P = 2(9 + 6)$ $P = 30$
Area	What is the area of a 9-×-12-foot rectangle in square yards?	Length = 12 feet = 4 yards Width = 9 feet = 3 yards	Find area Formula: $A = lw$, where A is the area, l is the length, and w is the width.	Area is $4 \times 3 =$ 12 square yards	$A = lw$ $A = 4 \times 3$ $A = 12$
Surface area	What is the surface area of a 50-foot-long circular pipe with a circumference of 36 inches?	Surface area of pipe (cylinder) Length = 50 feet Perimeter = 36 inches = 3 feet	Find surface area Formula: $S = Pl$, where S is the surface area, P is the perimeter, and l is the length.	Surface area is $50 \times 3 = 150$ square feet	$S = Pl$ $S = 50 \times 3 = 150$
Volume	How many cubic feet of water will an aquarium measuring 2 feet in length, 1 foot 9 inches in depth, and 1 foot 6 inches in height hold?	Length = 2 feet Width = 1 foot 9 inches = 1.75 feet. Height = 1 foot 6 inches = 1.5 feet	Find volume Formula: $V = lwh$, where V is the volume, l is the length, w is the width, and h is the height.	Volume: $V = 2 \times 1\frac{3}{4} \times 1\frac{1}{2}$ $= 2 \times \frac{7}{4} \times \frac{3}{2}$ $= \frac{42}{8}$ ≈ 5	Volume: $V = lwh$ $V = 2 \times 1.75 \times 1.5$ $V = 5.25$
Angle measurement	On a compass, what direction is 90 degrees clockwise from north?			One-quarter turn from north is east.	One-quarter turn from north is east.

	Problem	Information	What Is Asked?	Estimation	Calculation
Capacity	If regular gasoline weighs 6.2 pounds per gallon, how much additional weight would filling a 21-gallon gasoline tank add to the overall weight of a car?	Weight of 1 gallon of gasoline = 6.2 pounds Capacity of tank = 21 gallons	Additional weight = capacity of tank multiplied by the weight of a gallon of gasoline	Additional weight = 21 × 6 ≈ 126 pounds	Additional weight = 21 × 6.2 = 130.2 pounds
Weight	If someone lost an average of 4.5 pounds per month, what would be his total weight loss from September 1 through June 30?	Weight loss September through June = 10 months	Total weight loss = average monthly weight loss multiplied by the number of months	Total weight loss is 4.5 pounds × 10 = 45 pounds	Total weight loss is 4.5 pounds × 10 = 45 pounds

3. Data Analysis, Statistics, and Probability

a. Data Analysis

Tables, charts, and graphs are methods of displaying information in an easy-to-see form. Displaying data in these formats makes trends and growth patterns more visible, allowing you to make inferences from the collected information.

The following example question asks you to interpret the data in the bar graph and make an inference.

EXAMPLE:

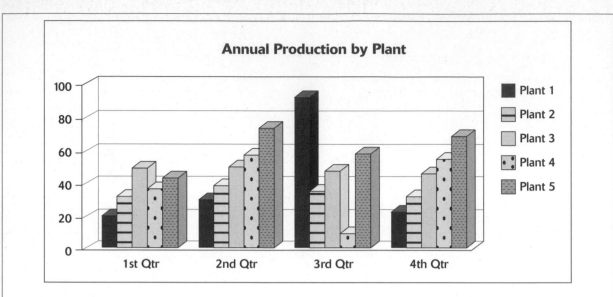

Annual Production by Plant

This bar graph indicates annual production by plant. One of the plants had a strike lasting two weeks. From the graph, which plant had the strike?

(1) Plant 1
(2) Plant 2
(3) Plant 3
(4) Plant 4
(5) Plant 5

The correct answer is **(4).** The bar graph for Plant 4 in the third quarter shows a dramatic drop in production compared to production in the other quarters. It is assumed that, during a strike, production would decrease and that's indicated by choice (4).

The next three example questions are based on the data in the "Median Price of Houses in Florida" table.

EXAMPLES:

Median Price of Houses in Florida				
Year	**Q1**	**Q2**	**Q3**	**Q4**
2000	$126,015	$130,765	$133,991	$135,970
2001	$137,696	$142,006	$145,547	$146,467
2002	$148,697	$154,040	$158,942	$162,030
2003	$164,424	$169,112	$174,417	$179,306
2004	$184,309	$192,702	$199,771	$205,480
2005	$213,204	$222,668	$230,708	$235,610
2006	$237,739	$239,340	$237,046	$234,942
2007	$232,913	$230,821	$226,839	$215,170
2008	$200,817	$196,520	$189,640	$175,702
2009	$162,861	$167,915	$173,472	$171,657
2010	$166,100			

The following example question asks you to interpret the data in the table and draw a conclusion.

> These figures represent median house prices in Florida over the last ten years. Considering the numbers presented, what conclusion could you reach?
>
> **(1)** In general, median prices have risen over the last ten years.
> **(2)** Median prices have stabilized over the last few years.
> **(3)** Median prices are the lowest they have been in the last ten years.
> **(4)** Housing in Florida is a bargain.
> **(5)** Not many people in Florida can afford housing at these prices.

The correct answer is **(1).** The median price for a house in Florida in the first quarter of 2010 was $166,100. In the first quarter of 2000, the median price was $126,015, which is lower than the 2010 price. Although you may have read about housing problems in Florida or noticed that there was a price bubble from 2003 to 2008, none of this was asked for in the question. You must answer the question based on only the information provided in the question.

The following example question asks you to interpret the data in the table and evaluate an argument.

> Consider the table of median house prices in Florida. In 2006, the Supreme Court ruled in favor of military recruiting on college campuses. Explain how this might have affected house prices.
>
> Median house prices reached their peak in 2006 because:
>
> **(1)** More young people joined the army.
> **(2)** Contractors were building fewer houses.
> **(3)** More people were looking for houses as an investment.
> **(4)** There had been distress sales the years before.
> **(5)** Not enough information given.

The correct answer is **(5).** Any or all of the answers might be right, but none of them can be argued based on the data presented. You can use only the information presented to answer the question.

233

The following example question asks you to interpret the data in the table and determine how best this data could be represented graphically, a bar graph in this case.

Using the previous table of median house prices for the first quarter of the years 2000 to 2010, consider which of the following bar graphs would accurately represent the data.

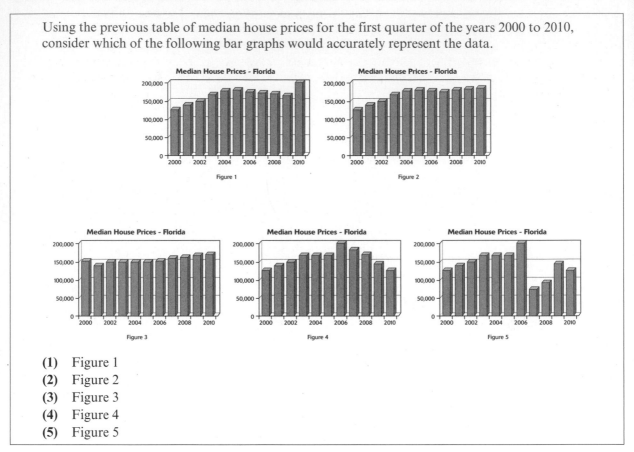

(1) Figure 1
(2) Figure 2
(3) Figure 3
(4) Figure 4
(5) Figure 5

The correct answer is **(4).** The most accurate representation is Graph 4. The other graphs show trends that are not apparent in the table figures.

b. Statistics and Probability

Statistics are numerical data that describe a fact or an event. You are exposed to statistics in your everyday life—political polls, surveys, baseball batting averages, and so on. Statistics is also a process—making educated guesses about outcomes involving numbers.

One of the most familiar uses of statistics is to determine **probability**—the chance of some occurrence. Probability is expressed as a ratio (the number of favorable outcomes to the total number of possible outcomes). For example, the probability of drawing an ace from a well-shuffled standard deck of cards is $\frac{4}{52}$, because there are 4 aces in a 52-card deck.

i. Mean, Median, and Mode

Mean, median, and mode are common statistics. The **mean** is the arithmetic average of a set of numbers and is calculated by adding the numbers and dividing by the number of numbers. The **median** is the middle number of an ordered list of numbers. To find the median number of a set of different numbers, put the numbers in ascending (smallest to largest) order. If the number of numbers in the set is odd, the middle number of the set is the median. If the number of numbers is even, average the two middle numbers to get the median. The **mode** is the number that appears most often in a set of numbers. There can be more than one mode or none at all.

Consider the following set of numbers:

$$90, 4, 30, 96, 25, 13$$

To find the mean, add the numbers:

$$90 + 4 + 30 + 96 + 25 + 13 = 258$$

And divide by 6 (the number of numbers):

$$258 \div 6 = 43$$

To find the median, first place the numbers in ascending order:

$$4, 13, 25, 30, 90, 96$$

Because there are six numbers, an even number, the two middle numbers are 25 and 30. Calculate the average of these two numbers:

$$(25 + 30) \div 2 = 27.5$$

Because no number occurs more than once, there is no mode in this set of numbers.

4. Algebra, Functions, and Patterns

a. Multiple-Use Equations

Recognize that a variety of problem situations may be modeled by the same function or type of function. An equation may have a specific meaning or use and it is also an equation. For example, the equation of a straight line with slope = m and y-intercept = b is $y = mx + b$. It is also a linear equation, meaning that no power is greater than 1.

EXAMPLE:

> What is the equation representing a straight line with slope = −4 and y-intercept = 5?
>
> **(1)** $-4x + y = 5$
> **(2)** $4x - y = 5$
> **(3)** $4x + y = 5$
> **(4)** $-4x - y = 5$
> **(5)** $4x + y = -5$

The correct answer is **(3)**. Using the equation $y = mx + b$ and substituting $m = -4$ and $b = 5$ produces $y = -4x + 5$ or $4x + y = 5$.

Here's another scenario. The equation for a parabola with vertex $(0, 0)$ is $y = ax^2$, which is a quadratic equation because there is a square of a variable.

EXAMPLE:

> Solve the equation $y = ax^2$ for a, if $x = 4$ and $y = 8$.
>
> **(1)** $\dfrac{1}{4}$
>
> **(2)** $\dfrac{8}{4}$
>
> **(3)** $\dfrac{2}{8}$
>
> **(4)** $\dfrac{1}{2}$
>
> **(5)** $\dfrac{1}{16}$

The correct answer is **(4)**. If the equation is rewritten so that the variable is on the left side, it becomes $a = \dfrac{8}{4^2} = \dfrac{8}{16} = \dfrac{1}{2}$.

b. Different Representations of Data

A question may ask you to choose the graph that best corresponds to a given table or may ask you which graph or chart corresponds to a given graph or chart.

i. Tables and Graphs

Tables such as the following can be drawn as graphs.

	1st Quarter	2nd Quarter	3rd Quarter	4th Quarter
East	20.4	27.4	90	20.4
West	30.6	38.6	34.6	31.6
North	45.9	46.9	45	43.9

This table would look like this, when drawn as a graph:

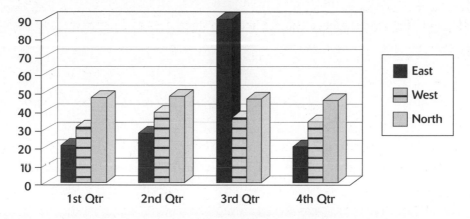

EXAMPLE:

Which bar graph represents the information in the following table?

1st Quarter	2nd Quarter	3rd Quarter	4th Quarter
25	75	50	20

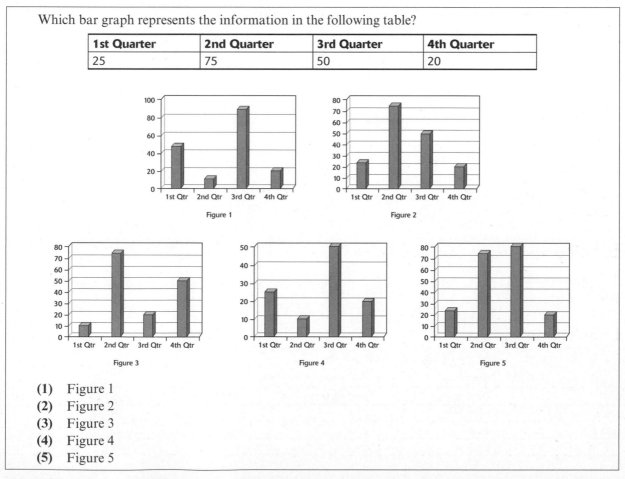

(1) Figure 1
(2) Figure 2
(3) Figure 3
(4) Figure 4
(5) Figure 5

The correct answer is **(2).** Because the y-axis is labeled in quantities, by comparing the heights of the bars, the one graph that represents the data in the table will become obvious.

ii. Different Types of Graphs

There are different types of graphs:

- Line graphs

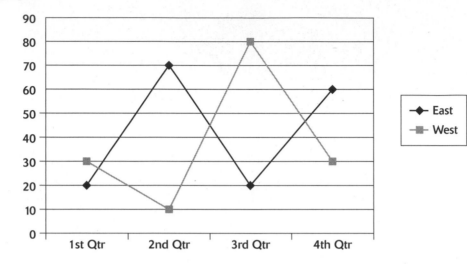

- Pie graphs

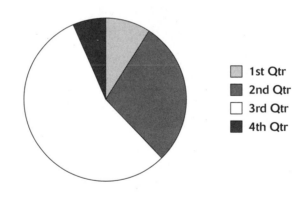

- Bar graphs

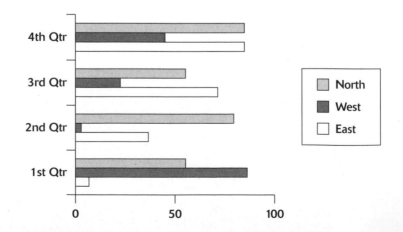

- Area graphs

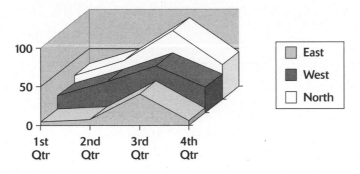

If the same data is used, different graphs can be drawn to show the same result.

For example, using the following table:

	1st Quarter	2nd Quarter	3rd Quarter	4th Quarter
East	4	7	40	5
West	20	38.6	60	31.6
North	30	50	90	43.9

A bar graph could be drawn:

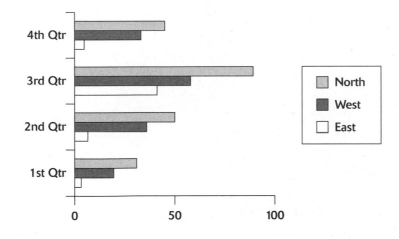

Or a line graph:

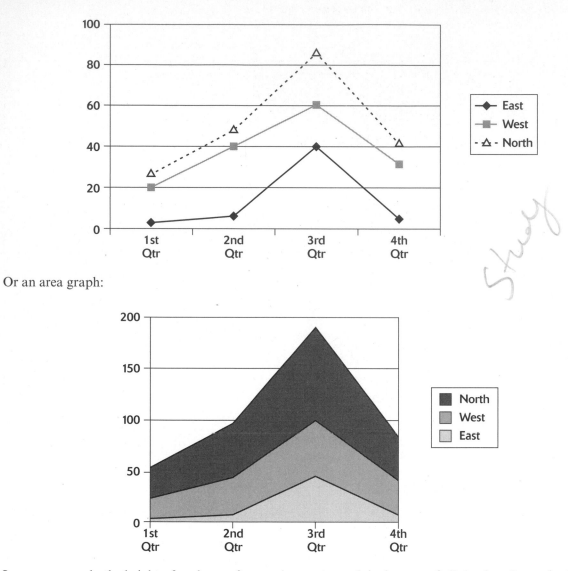

Or an area graph:

In an area graph, the height of each area for east, west, or north is the sum of all the data for each of east, west, and north (40 + 60 + 90 = 190 for the third quarter).

All these graphs present the same information and show the same trends because they were created from the same set of data. Any of them could form the basis for a question.

EXAMPLE:

From the following graph, who has the highest average on his or her final exams?

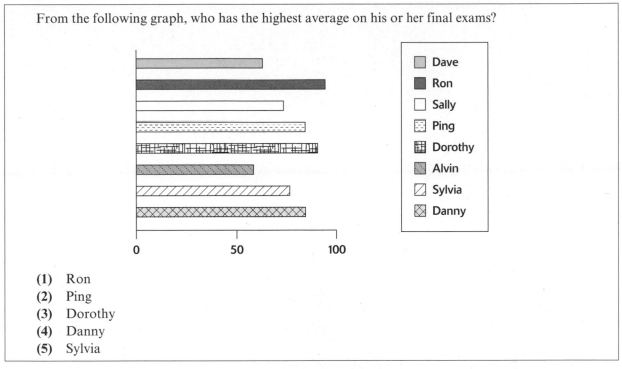

(1) Ron
(2) Ping
(3) Dorothy
(4) Danny
(5) Sylvia

The correct answer is **(1)**. Examining the graph, the bar representing Ron's average is the longest and that means that Ron would have had the highest average.

iii. Verbal Descriptions

A question may ask you to choose an answer from five verbal descriptions of a graph or may ask you which graph corresponds to a verbal description.

EXAMPLE:

If the following graph represents the number of pies eaten by each contestant in a pie-eating contest, which contestant won?

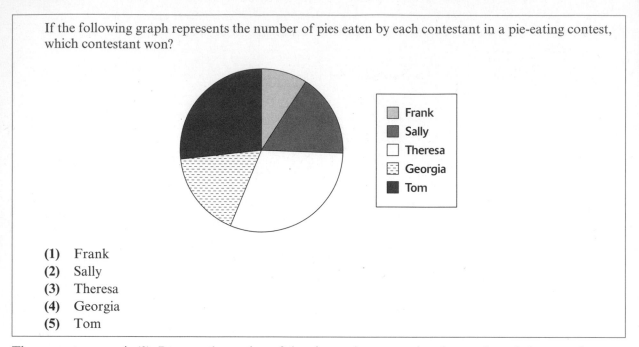

Frank
Sally
Theresa
Georgia
Tom

(1) Frank
(2) Sally
(3) Theresa
(4) Georgia
(5) Tom

The correct answer is **(3).** Because the section of the pie graph representing the number of pies eaten by Theresa is the largest, she would have consumed the most pies and been the winner.

To convert a pie graph into a table of values, the angular measure of each segment would have to be measured and converted to percentages by comparing it with the number of degrees in a circle. Then the percentages would be used to calculate the individual numbers from the total number, if known. If the total number were not known, the specific data could not be found. All of this is beyond the scope of the GED test.

Which of the following graphs best represents the following information:

The highest temperature reached in classroom 247 during the month of June was 78 degrees Fahrenheit.

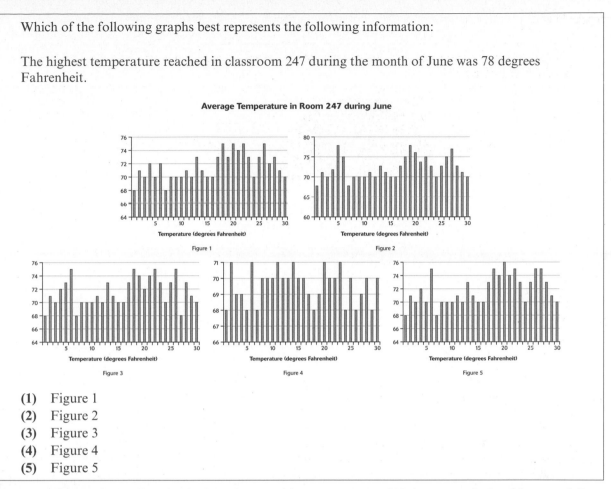

The correct answer is **(2)**. Graph 2 is the only one with temperatures of 78 degrees on it. Looking carefully at the other graphs, the *y*-axis does not go as high as 78 degrees; therefore, the temperature could not have reached 78 degrees.

iv. Creating Equations

An equation can be created from a verbal statement or an equation can be read as a verbal statement. For example:

A merchant determines that the price that must be charged for an article in the store must equal the sum of the cost of the article, the markup in dollars required to show a reasonable return on investment, the total overhead costs for the store divided by the number of articles sold per month, and the bank charges incurred by the merchant for all the dealings with the bank including interest charges divided by the number of items. Translate the information given into an equation, indicating what each variable stands for.

$P = C + M + O + B$, where P = the selling price of an article, C = the cost of an article, M = the markup in dollars, O = the overhead costs divided by the number of articles sold in an average month, and B = the bank charges for running a business and including the interest on articles in stock but unsold divided by the number of items.

EXAMPLE:

Explain the following equation: $E = \frac{M}{G}$, where E is the average fuel consumption of a car, M is the number of miles traveled, and G is the fuel used to travel M miles.

(1) The average fuel consumption equals the number of gallons of gas used divided by the distance traveled.
(2) The average fuel consumption equals the distance traveled in a week divided by the fuel used.
(3) The average fuel consumption equals the distance traveled divided by the fuel used in a week.
(4) The average fuel consumption equals the number of miles traveled divided by the fuel used to travel that distance.
(5) The average fuel consumption equals the number of gallons of fuel used divided by the days between fill-ups.

The correct answer is **(4)**. Reading the equation in English would be, "The average fuel economy equals the number of miles traveled divided by the fuel used to travel that distance." The other answers do not reflect the information as presented in the equation.

c. Algebraic Expressions and Equations

You need to be able to create and use algebraic expressions and equations to model situations and solve problems. For example, you can use the following expression to find the area of two rooms with the same width: $A = (l_1 + l_2) \times w$, where A is the combined area of the two rooms, l_1 is the length of the first room, l_2 is the length of the second room, and w is the common width.

EXAMPLE:

A company is quoting a price for carpeting two rooms in a house. The first room is 18 feet by 12 feet, and the second room is 12 feet by 12 feet. How many square feet of carpeting would be required for these two rooms?

(1) 630
(2) 480
(3) 360
(4) 380
(5) 400

The correct answer is **(3)**. Using the equation $A = (l_1 + l_2) \times w$ and substituting, $A = (18 + 12) \times 12 = 360$ square feet. Be careful of answers that are close to the correct answer, especially if you're using mental math to approximate answers.

d. Applying Formulas

For some questions, you need to be able to apply formulas (know how to use a formula to find the answer to a problem) in order to answer a question. The formula to calculate the surface area of a cylinder (including the two caps) is $2\pi r^2 + 2\pi rh$, where r is the radius of the cylinder and h is the height.

EXAMPLE:

> If the outside of a cylindrical fuel tank measuring 8 feet long and 4 feet across had to be painted with two coats of paint, and 1 gallon of paint will cover 360 square feet, how much paint, calculated to one decimal point, will be required to finish the job?
>
> **(1)** 1 gallon
> **(2)** 0.7 gallon
> **(3)** 7 gallons
> **(4)** 0.5 gallon
> **(5)** 0.9 gallon

The correct answer is **(2)**. Using the formula $2\pi r^2 + 2\pi rh$ and substituting, the surface area to be painted would be $(2 \times 3.14 \times 2 \times 2) + (2 \times 3.14 \times 2 \times 8) = 25.12 + 100.48 = 125.6$ square feet. Because two coats are needed, the area to be covered is $125.6 \times 2 = 251.2$ square feet. One gallon of paint will cover 360 square feet. The amount of paint needed is $251.2 \div 360 = 0.7$ gallon, to one decimal point.

e. Solving Equations

You need to be able to solve three types of equations: first-degree, quadratic, and exponential. Let's take these one at a time.

i. First-Degree Equations

A first-degree equation can be solved by gathering all the variables on the left side and all the constants on the right and then simplifying.

EXAMPLE:

> Solve the following equation for g.
>
> $$3g + 7 = 22$$
>
> **(1)** 3
> **(2)** 4
> **(3)** 5
> **(4)** 6
> **(5)** 7

The correct answer is **(3)**. To solve the equation, gather the variable, g, on the left side and the constants on the right. This produces $3g = 22 - 7 = 15$ or $g = 5$.

ii. Quadratic Equations

A quadratic equation has two roots or two number or expressions that satisfy the equation. A quadratic equation can have two equal roots or no root at all.

If a number or expression satisfies an equation, when it is substituted in the equation, both sides have the same value. A quadratic equation, $ax^2 + bx + c = 0$, can be solved using the formula $x = \dfrac{-b \pm \sqrt{b^2 - 4ac}}{2a}$, where x represents one root, a is the coefficient of x^2, b is the coefficient of x, and c is the constant term.

EXAMPLE:

> Solve the equation $4x^2 + x = 2$ for x to two decimal places.
>
> **(1)** 84 and 59
> **(2)** 0.84 and −0.59
> **(3)** 2 and 3
> **(4)** $-\dfrac{1}{4}$ and 1
> **(5)** −0.84 and 0.59

The correct answer is **(5)**. Use the formula $x = \dfrac{-b \pm \sqrt{b^2 - 4ac}}{2a}$ to find the values for x. Substituting,

$$x = \frac{-1 \pm \sqrt{1 - (4)(4)(-2)}}{2(4)}$$
$$= \frac{-1 \pm 5.74}{8}$$
$$= -\frac{6.74}{8} \text{ or } \frac{4.74}{8}$$
$$= -0.84 \text{ or } 0.59$$

iii. Radical Equations

$l = \sqrt{a^2 + b^2}$ is an equation containing a radical. It also contains a square-root instruction, which is the opposite of squaring. In this equation, the unknown is not a power, so all you have to do is solve the expression inside the square-root sign and then find the square root of that result.

EXAMPLE:

> If $a = 3$ and $b = 4$, solve the equation $l = \sqrt{a^2 + b^2}$ for l. The value of l is:
>
> **(1)** 1
> **(2)** 2
> **(3)** 3
> **(4)** 4
> **(5)** 5

The correct answer is **(5).** Substitute the values for a and b in the equation:

$$l = \sqrt{a^2 + b^2}$$
$$= \sqrt{3^2 + 4^2}$$
$$= \sqrt{9 + 16}$$
$$= \sqrt{25}$$
$$= 5$$

If the equation had been $l^2 = \sqrt{a^2 + b^2}$, then it would be:

$$l^2 = \sqrt{3^2 + 4^2}$$
$$= \sqrt{25}$$
$$= 5$$
$$l = \pm\sqrt{5}$$
$$= \pm 2.24$$

rounded to two decimal places. Remember that when you solve the equation, the answer could be either positive or negative, because squaring a negative number produces a positive number as a product.

EXAMPLE:

Solve the equation $y^2 = 16$ for y. The value(s) of y would be:

(1) 4
(2) ±4
(3) 5
(4) ±5
(5) 16

The correct answer is **(2).** If $y^2 = 16$, then $y = \pm\sqrt{16} = \pm 4$.

f. Solving Systems of Linear Equations

To solve a system of linear equations, find a number to multiply the equations by that will make the coefficients of one of the variables equal or opposites.

For example, consider the system of linear equations:

$$4x - 6y = 28$$
$$2x + 5y = 18$$

If the first equation were multiplied by 1 and the second by 2, the equations would become

$$4x - 6y = 28$$
$$4x + 10y = 36$$

and subtracting the first from the second would produce

$$16y = 8 \text{ or } y = \frac{1}{2}$$

To find the value of x, substitute the value of y in either equation (let's use the first equation):

$$4x - 6\left(\frac{1}{2}\right) = 28$$
$$4x = 28 + 3$$
$$4x = 31$$
$$x = \frac{31}{4}$$

g. Direct and Indirect Variation

When the ratio of the values of two related variables always remains the same, the variables vary directly with each other. When the ratio of the values of two related variables vary inversely, the variables vary indirectly with each other.

Here's a simple example: If you arrive earlier by driving faster, your travel time and your speed vary indirectly. If you use more fuel by increasing your speed, then your speed and your fuel consumption vary directly.

If x varies directly as y, then $x = ky$ for some constant k.

EXAMPLE:

A machine has been manufactured with a control mechanism to set the speed of the machine. If the control mechanism is moved one step from 1 to 2, the speed doubles. If the control were moved from 1 to 3, what effect would that setting have on the machine?

(1) The speed would double.
(2) The speed would stay the same.
(3) The speed would be four times faster.
(4) The speed would be six times faster.
(5) Not enough information is given.

The correct answer is **(3)**. If the speed doubles for each one-step increment, the speed doubles. A change from 1 to 3 would produce an increase in speed of $2 \times 2 = 4$.

A politician notices that as the number of cars increases, the number of accidents increases, until a critical point where every square inch of road has cars on it and none of them can move. Then the number of accidents decreases substantially.

The first half of this statement is a direct variation. As the number of cars increases, the number of accidents increases. The second half of the statement is that, after a critical point, the number of accidents decreases because the cars cannot move. This is an indirect variation because the number of cars is increasing approaching the critical point, but the number of accidents is decreasing because of the extreme congestion.

You could represent an indirect variation by the equation $y = \frac{C}{x}$, where x and y represent the frequency of events and C is a constant.

EXAMPLE:

> The speed of a car determines the distance traveled in a specific time. If some event happened that slowed a car's speed to half on Wednesday from that on Tuesday, what effect would that have on the time required to make the trip?
>
> **(1)** It would remain the same.
> **(2)** The trip would take twice as long on Wednesday.
> **(3)** The trip would take half as long on Wednesday.
> **(4)** The trip would take one-and-a-half times as long on Wednesday.
> **(5)** The trip would take two-thirds as long on Wednesday.

The correct answer is **(2)**. Using the equation $y = \frac{C}{x}$ and substituting Tuesday's speed for x and Wednesday's speed for y, you would obtain $y = \frac{C}{\frac{1}{2}x} = \frac{2C}{x} = 2\left(\frac{c}{x}\right)$, where s is the speed on Wednesday and C is the time required for the trip. C would then equal 2, or twice as long.

XII. Language Arts, Writing Full-Length Practice Test with Answer Explanations

Answer Sheet

Part I

1 ① ② ③ ④ ⑤	26 ① ② ③ ④ ⑤
2 ① ② ③ ④ ⑤	27 ① ② ③ ④ ⑤
3 ① ② ③ ④ ⑤	28 ① ② ③ ④ ⑤
4 ① ② ③ ④ ⑤	29 ① ② ③ ④ ⑤
5 ① ② ③ ④ ⑤	30 ① ② ③ ④ ⑤
6 ① ② ③ ④ ⑤	31 ① ② ③ ④ ⑤
7 ① ② ③ ④ ⑤	32 ① ② ③ ④ ⑤
8 ① ② ③ ④ ⑤	33 ① ② ③ ④ ⑤
9 ① ② ③ ④ ⑤	34 ① ② ③ ④ ⑤
10 ① ② ③ ④ ⑤	35 ① ② ③ ④ ⑤
11 ① ② ③ ④ ⑤	36 ① ② ③ ④ ⑤
12 ① ② ③ ④ ⑤	37 ① ② ③ ④ ⑤
13 ① ② ③ ④ ⑤	38 ① ② ③ ④ ⑤
14 ① ② ③ ④ ⑤	39 ① ② ③ ④ ⑤
15 ① ② ③ ④ ⑤	40 ① ② ③ ④ ⑤
16 ① ② ③ ④ ⑤	41 ① ② ③ ④ ⑤
17 ① ② ③ ④ ⑤	42 ① ② ③ ④ ⑤
18 ① ② ③ ④ ⑤	43 ① ② ③ ④ ⑤
19 ① ② ③ ④ ⑤	44 ① ② ③ ④ ⑤
20 ① ② ③ ④ ⑤	45 ① ② ③ ④ ⑤
21 ① ② ③ ④ ⑤	46 ① ② ③ ④ ⑤
22 ① ② ③ ④ ⑤	47 ① ② ③ ④ ⑤
23 ① ② ③ ④ ⑤	48 ① ② ③ ④ ⑤
24 ① ② ③ ④ ⑤	49 ① ② ③ ④ ⑤
25 ① ② ③ ④ ⑤	50 ① ② ③ ④ ⑤

CUT HERE

CUT HERE

Part II

CUT HERE

Part I

Time: 75 minutes

50 questions

Directions: Choose the best answer to each question.

Questions 1 through 11 refer to the following business letter.

THE TRAINING RENEWAL FOUNDATION
750 Millway Ave., Unit 6
Concord, MA 12345

The Michael Di Base Charitable Foundation, Inc.
70 Tigi Court, Suite 102
Vaughan, NY 54321

Dear Sir or Madam:

(1) Thank you for your invitation to submit an initial letter of enquiry. (2) The Training Renewal Foundation (TRF) is a nonprofit charitable organization located in the City of Vaughan. (3) Since its incorporation in 1996 TRF's mandate has been to serve disadvantaged youth and other displaced workers seeking skills, qualifications, and employment opportunities.

(4) During 2006, TRF has joined with the Region of York Social Services & Housing department to create the Employment Assistance and Retention Network (EARN) pilot project.

(5) Foreign-trained professionals, trades people, entrepreneurs, and managers are assisted in finding employment through the Region's Community Development Investment Fund. (6) Pre-employment training include confidence building, interpersonal skills, goal-setting, problem-solving, résumé preparation, computer literacy, educational upgrading, and parenting skills. (7) Transferable skills are assessed and acreditation secured to achieve employment. (8) To assist participants and their families, home computers, internet connections, and telephone access are provided.

(9) To date 50 participants and their families have been assisted by EARN. (10) A number of social assistance recipients already have been able to secure employment. (11) Others are pursuing the following new certification; further education; training to resume their former careers; or alternate employment opportunities.

Thank you for considering the Training Renewal Foundation in your inaugural grant-making process.

Yours sincerely,

Dale E. Shuttleworth, Ph.D.
Executive Director

1. Sentence 1: Thank you for your invitation to submit an initial letter of enquiry.

   Which change should be made to Sentence 1?

   (1) Change <u>Thank you</u> to <u>Thanking you</u>.
   (2) Change <u>enquiry</u> to <u>inquiry</u>.
   (3) Change <u>an</u> to <u>a</u>.
   (4) Change <u>your</u> to <u>you're</u>.
   (5) No change required.

2. Sentence 2: The Training Renewal Foundation (TRF) is a nonprofit charitable organization located in the City of Vaughan.

   Which correction should be made to Sentence 2?

   (1) Change <u>nonprofit</u> to <u>non profit</u>.
   (2) Change <u>is</u> to <u>was</u>.
   (3) Change <u>Foundation</u> to <u>foundation</u>.
   (4) Change <u>TRF</u> to <u>TFR</u>.
   (5) No change required.

3. Sentence 3: Since its incorporation in 1996 TRF's mandate has been to serve disadvantaged youth and other displaced workers seeking skills, qualifications, and employment opportunities.

   Which punctuation should be added to Sentence 3?

   (1) Place a comma after <u>youth</u>.
   (2) Place a colon after <u>seeking</u>.
   (3) Change <u>workers</u> to <u>worker's</u>.
   (4) Change <u>TRF's</u> to <u>TRFs</u>.
   (5) Place a comma after <u>1996</u>.

4. Sentence 4: During 2006, TRF has joined with the Region of York Social Services & Housing department to create the Employment Assistance and Retention Network (EARN) pilot project.

   Which correction should be made to Sentence 4?

   (1) Change <u>(EARN)</u> to <u>(earn)</u>.
   (2) Change <u>department</u> to <u>Department</u>.
   (3) Remove the comma after <u>2006</u>.
   (4) Change <u>has joined</u> to <u>have joined</u>.
   (5) No correction required.

5. Sentence 5: Foreign-trained professionals, trades people, entrepreneurs, and managers are assisted in finding employment through the Region's Community Development Investment Fund.

   Which change should be made to Sentence 5?

   (1) Change <u>through</u> to <u>threw</u>.
   (2) Change <u>Region's</u> to <u>Regions'</u>.
   (3) Change <u>are assisted</u> to <u>are assisting</u>.
   (4) Change <u>Foreign-trained</u> to <u>Foreign trained</u>.
   (5) No change required.

6. Sentence 6: Pre-employment training include confidence building, interpersonal skills, goal-setting, problem-solving, résumé preparation, computer literacy, educational upgrading, and parenting skills.

   Which correction should be made to Sentence 6?

   (1) Change <u>include</u> to <u>includes</u>.
   (2) Change <u>résumé</u> to <u>resume</u>.
   (3) Change <u>goal-setting</u> to <u>goal setting</u>.
   (4) Change <u>problem-solving</u> to <u>problem solving</u>.
   (5) Change <u>Pre-employment</u> to <u>Preemployment</u>.

7. Sentence 7: Transferable skills are assessed and acreditation secured to achieve employment.

   Which change should be made to Sentence 7?

   (1) Change <u>transferable</u> to <u>transfirable</u>.
   (2) Change <u>acreditation</u> to <u>accreditation</u>.
   (3) Change <u>assessed</u> to <u>asessed</u>.
   (4) Change <u>achieve</u> to <u>acheive</u>.
   (5) No change required.

8. Sentence 8: To assist participants and their families, home computers, internet connections, and telephone access are provided.

   Which correction should be made to Sentence 8?

   (1) Change <u>their</u> to <u>they're</u>.
   (2) Replace the comma after <u>families</u> with a colon.
   (3) Change <u>access</u> to <u>excess</u>.
   (4) Change <u>internet</u> to <u>Internet</u>.
   (5) Change <u>are provided</u> to <u>is provided</u>.

9. Sentence 9: To date 50 participants and their families have been assisted by EARN.

How should Sentence 9 be improved?

(1) Change 50 to fifty.
(2) Place a comma after date.
(3) Change their to there.
(4) Change have been to is being.
(5) No improvement required.

10. Sentence 10: A number of social assistance recipients already have been able to secure employment.

Which is the best way to improve the underlined portion of Sentence 10?

(1) have already been able
(2) have been already able
(3) have been able already
(4) have been able
(5) No improvement required.

11. Sentence 11: Others are pursuing the following new certification; further education; training to resume their former careers; or alternate employment opportunities.

Which punctuation change should be made to Sentence 11?

(1) Change the semicolon after certification to a comma.
(2) Change the semicolon after careers to a comma.
(3) Place a colon after following and replace the semicolons with commas.
(4) Change the semicolon after education to a comma.
(5) Place a dash after following.

Questions 12 through 19 refer to the following passage.

Training Interns in Education

(1) T.I.E. participants are educators from a variety of cultural backgrounds. (2) They are selected through consideration of a wide range of criterion. (3) This includes the following examination of their academic documents; relevant experience in teaching or working with children and adolescents; and any references that they can provide.

(4) Intensive individual interviews were conducted with each potential participants to determine both their psychological suitability for working in schools, and the level of their determination to succeed in the course. (5) Also they were questioned at length about their training and experience.

(6) The T.I.E. investigation of the successful participant's varied backgrounds found that, while academic training and teaching experiences differed in a variety of ways, the substance was very similar in terms of rigorously high expectations.

(7) The curriculum for the T.I.E. programme has been designed and modified to meet the unique needs of the participants. (8) The guiding aim was to give the participants a full understanding of the educational system and the proficiency to function in a culturally diverse schooling climate.

12. Sentence 1: T.I.E. participants are educators from a variety of cultural backgrounds.

Which change should be made to Sentence 1?

(1) Change <u>T.I.E.</u> to <u>TIE</u>.
(2) Change <u>are</u> to <u>were</u>.
(3) Change <u>cultural</u> to <u>cultured</u>.
(4) Change <u>backgrounds</u> to <u>background</u>.
(5) No correction required.

13. Sentence 2: They are selected through consideration of a wide range of criterion.

Which correction should be made to Sentence 2?

(1) Change <u>through</u> to <u>threw</u>.
(2) Change <u>consideration</u> to <u>considerations</u>.
(3) Change <u>They are</u> to <u>Their</u>.
(4) Change <u>criterion</u> to <u>criteria</u>.
(5) No correction required.

14. Sentence 3: This includes the following examination of their academic documents; relevant experience in teaching or working with children and adolescents; and any references that they can provide.

Which punctuation should be added to Sentence 3?

(1) Change the semicolon after <u>documents</u> to a comma.
(2) Place a colon after <u>following</u> and replace the semicolons with commas.
(3) Change the semicolon after <u>adolescents</u> to a comma.
(4) Place a comma after <u>teaching</u>.
(5) Place a comma after <u>references</u>.

15. Sentence 4: Intensive individual interviews were conducted with each potential participants to determine both their psychological suitability for working in schools, and the level of their determination to succeed in the course.

Which change should be made to Sentence 4?

(1) Change <u>were</u> to <u>was</u>.
(2) Change the first <u>their</u> to <u>they're</u>.
(3) Change <u>participants</u> to <u>participant</u> and change <u>their</u> to <u>her</u> in both places.
(4) Change <u>course</u> to <u>coarse</u>.
(5) Change the second <u>their</u> to <u>there</u>.

16. Sentence 5: <u>Also they were questioned</u> at length about their training and experience.

    Which is the best way to write the underlined portion of Sentence 5?

    (1) <u>They also were questioned</u>.
    (2) <u>They were also questioned</u>.
    (3) <u>They were questioned also</u>.
    (4) <u>Also were they questioned</u>.
    (5) No change required.

17. Sentence 6: The T.I.E. investigation of the successful participant's varied backgrounds found that, while academic training and teaching experiences differed in a variety of ways, the substance was very similar in terms of rigorously high expectations.

    Which correction should be made to Sentence 6?

    (1) Change <u>participant's</u> to <u>participants'</u>.
    (2) Remove the comma after <u>that</u>.
    (3) Remove the comma after <u>ways</u>.
    (4) Change <u>similar</u> to <u>similiar</u>.
    (5) Change <u>rigorously</u> to <u>rigourously</u>.

18. Sentence 7: The curriculum for the T.I.E. programme has been designed and modified to meet the unique needs of the participants.

    Which correction should be made to Sentence 7?

    (1) Change <u>curriculum</u> to <u>curricula</u>.
    (2) Change <u>has been</u> to <u>had been</u>.
    (3) Change <u>programme</u> to <u>program</u>.
    (4) Change <u>needs</u> to <u>need</u>.
    (5) No correction required.

19. Sentence 8: The guiding aim was to give the participants a full understanding of the educational system and the proficiency to function in a culturally diverse schooling climate.

    What changes should be made to Sentence 8?

    (1) Change <u>a full</u> to <u>awful</u>.
    (2) Change <u>system</u> to <u>sistem</u>.
    (3) Change <u>to function</u> to <u>functioning</u>.
    (4) Change <u>was</u> to <u>is</u>.
    (5) Change <u>diverse</u> to <u>diverts</u>.

Questions 20 through 29 refer to an adaptation of an excerpt from Green Business Practices For Dummies *by Lisa Swallow, copyright 2009 by Wiley Publishing, Inc. Reprinted with permission of John Wiley & Sons, Inc.*

Revitalizing Your Local Economy

(1) In response to the forest of chain stores peppering the landscape of any U.S. town in which people outnumber livestock an exploding number of self-described independent businesses are popping up. (2) Those who have weathered chain-store mania are banding together to crate their own retail force to be reckoned with. (3) From community groups to whole regional areas, hometown teams are committed to revitalizing their local economies. (4) In fact, independent business alliances across the U.S. are predicting that buy-local movements will make as big of an impact as buy-organic movements has in recent years. (5) Buying local can seem like a rather quaint idea, much like typewriters and poodle skirts. (6) Au contraire it's more than a movement; it's a revolution—an opportunity that's loaded with potential and serves as a key component of a sustainable business model.

(7) By infusing they're local economies with a surge of enthusiasm and committing to using one another as resources, hometown businesses are bringing the focus back to Main Street. (8) You can harness the same local enthusiasm by offering a wide variety of products and services that are produced and/or distributed by independent entreprenors. (9) After you have an idea of what relocalization means to you and your community, you can employ education and outreach efforts such as community-based social marketing campaigns oriented toward changing behaviors to help get consumers on board. (10) In this chapter, I show you how to make your business part of the buy-local movement and how to encourage you're stakeholders to jump on board.

20. Sentence 1: In response to the forest of chain stores peppering the landscape of any U.S. town in which people outnumber livestock an exploding number of self-described independent businesses are popping up.

    Which punctuation should be added to Sentence 1?

    (1) Add a comma after <u>response</u>.
    (2) Add a comma after <u>livestock</u>.
    (3) Remove the periods after <u>U</u> and <u>S</u>.
    (4) Place a comma after <u>self-described</u>.
    (5) Place a semicolon after <u>town</u>.

21. Sentence 2: Those who have weathered chain-store mania are banding together to crate their own retail force to be reckoned with.

    Which correction is required in Sentence 2?

    (1) Change <u>weathered</u> to <u>whethered</u>.
    (2) Change <u>chain-store</u> to <u>chainstore</u>.
    (3) Change <u>retail</u> to <u>retale</u>.
    (4) Change <u>crate</u> to <u>create</u>.
    (5) No correction required.

22. Sentence 3: From community groups to whole regional areas, hometown teams are committed to revitalizing their local economies.

Which change is required in Sentence 3?

(1) Change <u>economies</u> to <u>economy's</u>.
(2) Change <u>are</u> to <u>were</u>.
(3) Change <u>revitalizing</u> to <u>revitalising</u>.
(4) Change <u>hometown</u> to <u>home-town</u>.
(5) No change required.

23. Sentence 4: In fact, independent business alliances across the U.S. are predicting that buy-local movements will make as big of an impact as buy-organic movements has in recent years.

Which change should be made to Sentence 4?

(1) Remove the comma after <u>fact</u>.
(2) Change <u>alliances</u> to <u>alliants</u>.
(3) Change <u>has</u> to <u>have</u>.
(4) Remove the hyphen between <u>buy</u> and <u>local</u>.
(5) Remove the hyphen between <u>buy</u> and <u>organic</u>.

24. Sentence 5: Buying local can seem like a rather quaint idea, much like typewriters and poodle skirts.

Which improvement should be made to Sentence 5?

(1) Remove the comma after <u>idea</u>.
(2) Change <u>can</u> to <u>may</u>.
(3) Change <u>typewriters</u> to <u>typeriters</u>.
(4) Change <u>skirts</u> to <u>shirts</u>.
(5) No improvement required.

25. Sentence 6: Au contraire it's more than a movement; it's a revolution—an opportunity that's loaded with potential and serves as a key component of a sustainable business model.

How can Sentence 6 be improved?

(1) Place an exclamation point after <u>contraire</u> and capitalize the first <u>it's</u>.
(2) Change the semicolon after <u>movement</u> to a comma.
(3) Remove the apostrophe from the second <u>it's</u>.
(4) Change <u>that's</u> to <u>thats</u>.
(5) Change <u>serves</u> to <u>served</u>.

26. Sentence 7: By infusing they're local economies with a surge of enthusiasm and committing to using one another as resources, hometown businesses are bringing the focus back to Main Street.

Which change is required to Sentence 7?

(1) Place a comma after <u>enthusiasm</u>.
(2) Change <u>Main</u> to <u>main</u>.
(3) Change <u>they're</u> to <u>their</u>.
(4) Change <u>are bringing</u> to <u>is bringing</u>.
(5) Change <u>resources</u> to <u>resoarces</u>.

27. Sentence 8: You can harness the same local enthusiasm by offering a wide variety of products and services that are produced and/or distributed by independent entreprenors.

Which correction is required to Sentence 8?

(1) Change <u>can</u> to <u>could</u>.
(2) Change <u>are produced</u> to <u>is produced</u>.
(3) Place a comma after <u>services</u>.
(4) Change <u>entreprenors</u> to <u>entrepreneurs</u>.
(5) Change <u>and/or</u> to <u>and-or</u>.

28. Sentence 9: After you have an idea of what relocalization means to you and your community, you can employ education and outreach efforts such as community-based social marketing campaigns oriented toward changing behaviors to help get customers on board.

Which improvement should be made to Sentence 9?

(1) Place parentheses before <u>such</u> and after <u>behaviors</u>.
(2) Remove the comma after <u>community</u>.
(3) Remove the hyphen between <u>community</u> and <u>based</u>.
(4) Place a hyphen between <u>social</u> and <u>marketing</u>.
(5) Change <u>behaviors</u> to <u>behaviours</u>.

29. Sentence 10: In this chapter, I show you how to make your business part of the buy-local movement and how to encourage you're stakeholders to jump on board.

Which correction should be made to Sentence 10?

(1) Change the comma after <u>chapter</u> to a colon.
(2) Remove the hyphen between <u>buy</u> and <u>local</u>.
(3) Place a semicolon after <u>movement</u>.
(4) Change <u>on board</u> to <u>onboard</u>.
(5) Change <u>you're</u> to <u>your</u>.

Questions 30 through 40 refer to the following presentation.

School-Community Partnerships

1. In the 1960s, school boards in the nation sought ways to assist schools in impoverished neighbourhoods.

2. The Ford foundation sponsored a field visit by educational administrators to study school-related programs funded by President Johnson's War on Poverty.

3. Whit Morris, Principal of Flemington Road Junior Public School in North York's Lawrence Heights public-housing project was one of the participants.

4. When he returned, he proposed to the school board a compensatory education program that included additional resource personel for the school.

5. One of the positions were the creation of the role of school-community worker to serve both a school of 1,200 students and the impoverished public-housing community that surrounded it.

6. Lawrence Heights, with a population of 6,000, consisted of the working poor and welfare recipients including immigrants and migrants.

7. A third of the families was single parent mother led.

8. The focus of Flemington's social services project was the community school concept whereby more than 55 programs were offered during the day and in the evening to meet the needs of parents, teachers, students, and other citizens of the community.

9. The community school concept sees the school as a focus for community living—the school as an extension of the community it serves.

10. The driving force behind the Flemington Community School was the Community School Advisory council—a partnership of community service agencies, local residents, and school personnel.

11. Parents with preschool children had to leave often the community for medical or social service appointments, or to attend family court several miles from Lawrence Heights.

30. Sentence 1: In the 1960s, school boards in the nation sought ways to assist schools in impoverished neighbourhoods.

Which correction is needed in Sentence 1?

(1) Remove the comma after <u>1960s</u>.
(2) Change <u>1960s</u> to <u>1960's</u>.
(3) Change <u>boards</u> to <u>board's</u>.
(4) Change <u>neighbourhoods</u> to <u>neighborhoods</u>.
(5) Change <u>ways</u> to <u>weights</u>.

31. Sentence 2: The Ford foundation sponsored a field visit by educational administrators to study school-related programs funded by President Johnson's War on Poverty.

Which change should be made to Sentence 2?

(1) Change <u>school-related</u> to <u>school related</u>.
(2) Change <u>foundation</u> to <u>Foundation</u>.
(3) Change <u>Johnson's</u> to <u>Johnsons</u>.
(4) Change <u>Poverty</u> to <u>poverty</u>.
(5) No change required.

32. Sentence 3: Whit Morris, Principal of Flemington Road Junior Public School in North York's Lawrence Heights public-housing project was one of the participants.

Which punctuation should be added to Sentence 3?

(1) Change <u>York's</u> to <u>Yorks</u>.
(2) Place a comma after <u>School</u>.
(3) Add a comma after <u>project</u>.
(4) Place a period after <u>Whit</u>.
(5) Change <u>York's</u> to <u>Yorks'</u>.

33. Sentence 4: When he returned, he proposed to the school board a compensatory education program that included additional resource personel for the school.

Which correction should be made to Sentence 4?

(1) Change <u>program</u> to <u>programs</u>.
(2) Change <u>compensatory</u> to <u>compenstory</u>.
(3) Change <u>resource</u> to <u>resources</u>.
(4) Change <u>personel</u> to <u>personnel</u>.
(5) No correction required.

34. Sentence 5: One of the positions were the creation of the role of school-community worker to serve both a school of 1,200 students and the impoverished public-housing community that surrounded it.

Which change should be made to Sentence 5?

(1) Change <u>role</u> to <u>roll</u>.
(2) Change <u>were</u> to <u>was</u>.
(3) Remove the hyphen between <u>school</u> and <u>community</u>.
(4) Change <u>1,200</u> to <u>1200</u>.
(5) Change <u>surrounded</u> to <u>surround</u>.

35. Sentence 6: Lawrence Heights, with a population of 6,000, consisted of the working poor and welfare recipients including immigrants and migrants.

Which change in punctuation should be made to Sentence 6?

(1) Place a dash after <u>recipients</u>.
(2) Remove the comma after <u>Heights</u>.
(3) Remove the comma after <u>6,000</u>.
(4) Place a comma after <u>poor</u>.
(5) No change required.

36. Sentence 7: A third of the families <u>was single parent mother led</u>.

Which is the best way to improve the underlined portion of Sentence 7?

    (1) <u>were single parent, mother-led</u>
    (2) <u>were single parent, mother-lead</u>
    (3) <u>was single parent, mother led</u>
    (4) <u>was single parent, mother-led</u>
    (5) <u>were single parent mother-lead</u>

37. Sentence 8: The focus of Flemington's social services project was the community school concept whereby more than 55 programs were offered during the day and in the evening to meet the needs of parents, teachers, students, and other citizens of the community.

How may Sentence 8 be improved?

    (1) Change <u>Flemington's</u> to <u>Flemingtons'</u>.
    (2) Place a period after <u>concept</u>, omit <u>whereby</u>, and begin a new sentence with <u>More</u>.
    (3) Place a comma after <u>day</u>.
    (4) Change <u>were</u> to <u>was</u>.
    (5) No improvement required.

38. Sentence 9: The community school concept sees the school as a focus for community living—the school as an extension of the community it serves.

How should Sentence 9 be corrected?

    (1) Change <u>community school</u> to <u>community-school</u>.
    (2) Change <u>community living</u> to <u>community-living</u>.
    (3) Change <u>extension</u> to <u>extention</u>.
    (4) Change <u>it</u> to <u>it's</u>.
    (5) No correction required.

39. Sentence 10: The driving force behind the Flemington Community School was the Community School Advisory council—a partnership of community service agencies, local residents, and school personnel.

Which change should be made to Sentence 10?

    (1) Change <u>Advisory</u> to <u>advisory</u>.
    (2) Change <u>council</u> to <u>Council</u>.
    (3) Change <u>behind</u> to <u>between</u>.
    (4) Place capitals on <u>community service</u> and <u>agencies</u>.
    (5) Change <u>personnel</u> to <u>personel</u>.

40. Sentence 11: Parents with preschool children <u>had to leave often</u> the community for medical or social service appointments, or to attend family court several miles from Lawrence Heights.

How may the underlined portion of Sentence 11 be improved?

(1) <u>often had to leave</u>
(2) <u>had often to leave</u>
(3) <u>had to often leave</u>
(4) <u>often have to leave</u>
(5) No improvement required

Questions 41 through 45 refer to the following passage.

What Are the GED Tests?

(1) The General Educational Development (GED) is an International testing program for adults who have been unable to complete high school. (2) The GED is based on the same principals as the PLA Portfolio Development (i.e., that adults acquire knowledge, skills, and concepts through working, training, traveling, reading, and other informal learning). (3) The GED Tests are designed to measure this level of "educational maturity" gained through experience, which is often equal to, or above, the level of a high school graduate. (4) The GED is actually a battery of five tests in the core high school curricula areas of writing, social studies, science, literature and the arts, and mathematics. (5) The tests measure important knowledge and skills usually acquired during a regular high school program of study such as the ability to understand and apply information; evaluate, analyze, and draw conclusions; and express ideas and opinions in writing.

41. Sentence 1: The General Educational Development (GED) is an International testing program for adults who have been unable to complete high school.

Which change should be made to Sentence 1?

(1) Change <u>International</u> to <u>international</u>.
(2) Place a comma after <u>adults</u>.
(3) Change <u>unable</u> to <u>notable</u>.
(4) Change <u>have been</u> to <u>had been</u>.
(5) No change required.

42. Sentence 2: The GED is based on the same principals as the PLA Portfolio Development (i.e., that adults acquire knowledge, skills, and concepts through working, training, traveling, reading, and other informal learning).

Which correction should be made to Sentence 2?

(1) Change <u>is</u> to <u>will be</u>.
(2) Add a colon after <u>Development</u>.
(3) Change <u>acquire</u> to <u>akwire</u>.
(4) Change <u>principals</u> to <u>principles</u>.
(5) No correction required.

43. Sentence 3: The GED Tests are designed to measure this level of "educational maturity" gained through experience, which is often equal to, or above, the level of a high school graduate.

    Which punctuation change is required in Sentence 3?

    (1) Omit quotation marks around <u>educational maturity</u>.
    (2) Remove the comma after <u>experience</u>.
    (3) Place a comma after <u>maturity</u>.
    (4) Remove commas after <u>to</u> and <u>above</u>.
    (5) No change required.

44. Sentence 4: The GED is actually a battery of five tests in the core high school curricula areas of writing, social studies, science, literature and the arts, and mathematics.

    Which correction should be made to Sentence 4?

    (1) Change <u>actually</u> to <u>actionally</u>.
    (2) Change <u>core</u> to <u>corps</u>.
    (3) Change <u>curricula</u> to <u>curriculum</u>.
    (4) Change <u>is</u> to <u>was</u>.
    (5) Change <u>battery</u> to <u>batterie</u>.

45. Sentence 5: The tests measure important knowledge and skills usually acquired during a regular high school program of study such as the ability to understand and apply information; evaluate, analyze, and draw conclusions; and express ideas and opinions in writing.

    How may Sentence 5 be improved?

    (1) Change <u>measure</u> to <u>measured</u>.
    (2) Place a period after <u>study</u> and then begin a new sentence <u>They include the ability. . . .</u>
    (3) Remove the semicolon after <u>information</u>.
    (4) Remove the semicolon after <u>conclusions</u>.
    (5) No improvement required.

Questions 46 through 50 refer to the following excerpt from a literary proposal.

Re: Community Education and Economic Renewal for a Multicultural Society

Rationale: (1) The process of community education was first espoused in the 20th century by the American philosopher John Dewey 1907, and further refined by Edward Olsen in the U.S. and Henry Morris in the U.K. (2) Community education may be defined as "an approach to education that advocates the identification and utilization of human, physical, and organizational resources in the community to enhance the learning process and more affectively to respond to human needs so as to improve the quality of both personal and community life."

(3) One outgrowth of the community education process had been "community economic development," which might be defined as "a plan of action to build new resources that will strengthen the local community internally, as well as its relations with the larger world."

(4) The community education process has influenced the development of a series of policys, projects, and innovations in public education and economic development, beginning in the 1960s. (5) These have included: the community school concept, community-resource learning, the education foundation, alternatives in education, co-operative education, school-based childcare, multicultural education, adult basic literacy, the adult day school, the small business incubator, business/education partnerships, and skill training for the unemployed—including immigrants and refugees.

46. Sentence 1: The process of community education was first espoused in the 20th century by the American philosopher John Dewey 1907, and further refined by Edward Olsen in the U.S. and Henry Morris in the U.K.

    Which change should be made to Sentence 1?

    (1) Change philosopher to Philosopher.
    (2) Change first to underline{1st}.
    (3) Change further to farther.
    (4) Place parentheses around 1907 and remove the comma following it.
    (5) Change refined to refind.

47. Sentence 2: Community education may be defined as "an approach to education that advocates the identification and utilization of human, physical, and organizational resources in the community to enhance the learning process and more affectively to respond to human needs so as to improve the quality of both personal and community life."

    Which correction should be made to Sentence 2?

    (1) Change utilization to utilisation.
    (2) Change organizational to organisational.
    (3) Change affectively to effectively.
    (4) Change personal to personnel.
    (5) No correction required.

48. Sentence 3: One outgrowth of the community education process had been "community economic development," which might be defined as "a plan of action to build new resources that will strengthen the local community internally, as well as its relations with the larger world."

    How would you change Sentence 3?

    (1) Change <u>had been</u> to <u>has been</u>.
    (2) Remove quotation marks around <u>community economic development</u>.
    (3) Remove the comma after <u>internally</u>.
    (4) Change <u>its</u> to <u>it's</u>.
    (5) Change <u>resources</u> to <u>resource</u>.

49. Sentence 4: The community education process has influenced the development of a series of policys, projects, and innovations in public education and economic development, beginning in the 1960s.

    Which correction should be made to Sentence 4?

    (1) Remove the comma between <u>development</u> and <u>beginning</u>.
    (2) Change <u>policys</u> to <u>policies</u>.
    (3) Change <u>has influenced</u> to <u>have influenced</u>.
    (4) Change <u>economic</u> to <u>economical</u>.
    (5) Change <u>1960s</u> to <u>1960's</u>.

50. Sentence 5: These have included: the community school concept, community-resource learning, the education foundation, alternatives in education, co-operative education, school-based childcare, multicultural education, adult basic literacy, the adult day school, the small business incubator, business/education partnerships, and skill training for the unemployed—including immigrants and refugees.

    Which improvement should be made to Sentence 5?

    (1) Remove the colon after <u>included</u>.
    (2) Change <u>education foundation</u> to <u>education-foundation</u>.
    (3) Change <u>community-resource</u> to <u>community resource</u>.
    (4) Change <u>school-based</u> to <u>school based</u>.
    (5) No improvement required.

IF YOU FINISH BEFORE TIME IS CALLED, CHECK YOUR WORK ON THIS SECTION ONLY. DO NOT WORK ON ANY OTHER SECTION IN THE TEST.

Part II

Time: 45 minutes

1 essay question

Look at the box on the following page. In the box, you find your assigned topic and the letter of that topic.

You must write only on the assigned topic.

You have 45 minutes to write on your assigned essay topic. If you have time remaining in this test period after you complete your essay, you may return to the multiple-choice section. Do not return the Language Arts, Writing test booklet until you finish both Parts I and II of the Language Arts, Writing Test.

On the GED, two evaluators will score your essay according to its overall effectiveness. Their evaluation will be based on the following features:

- Well-focused main points
- Clear organization
- Specific development of your ideas
- Control of sentence structure, punctuation, grammar, word choice, and spelling

Remember: You must complete both the multiple-choice questions (Part I) and the essay (Part II) to receive a score on the Language Arts, Writing Test.

To avoid having to repeat both parts of the test, be sure to observe the following rules:

- Before you begin writing, jot notes or outline your essay on the sheets provided.
- For your final copy, write legibly in ink so that the evaluators will be able to read your writing.
- Write on the assigned topic. If you write on a topic other than the one assigned, you won't receive a score for the Language Arts, Writing Test.
- Write your essay on the lined pages of the separate answer sheet booklet. Only the writing on these pages will be scored.

Note that if you do not pass one portion of the test, you must take both parts over again.

Topic A

Cellphones have certainly made a difference in our lives. You may own and use one or have put up with other people who use them while driving or at the movies. Cellphones have made our lives better, more difficult, or both.

Write an essay explaining the positive or negative effects—or both—of this innovation in communication. Use examples to support your point of view and be as specific as possible.

IF YOU FINISH BEFORE TIME IS CALLED, CHECK YOUR WORK ON THIS SECTION ONLY. DO NOT WORK ON ANY OTHER SECTION IN THE TEST.

Answer Key

Part I

1. (2)	14. (2)	27. (4)	40. (1)
2. (5)	15. (3)	28. (1)	41. (1)
3. (5)	16. (2)	29. (5)	42. (4)
4. (2)	17. (1)	30. (4)	43. (5)
5. (5)	18. (3)	31. (2)	44. (3)
6. (1)	19. (4)	32. (3)	45. (2)
7. (2)	20. (2)	33. (4)	46. (4)
8. (4)	21. (4)	34. (2)	47. (3)
9. (2)	22. (5)	35. (5)	48. (1)
10. (1)	23. (3)	36. (1)	49. (2)
11. (3)	24. (2)	37. (2)	50. (5)
12. (5)	25. (1)	38. (5)	
13. (4)	26. (3)	39. (2)	

Answer Explanations

Part I

1. **(2)** We're speaking of a letter of <u>inquiry</u>—meaning to question or investigate. Its homonym, <u>enquiry</u>, is more often used in Britain.

2. **(5)** No change is required in this sentence.

3. **(5)** A comma is needed after <u>1996</u> to separate the introductory section from the main body of the sentence.

4. **(2)** A capital is required on <u>Department</u>, which refers to that formal section of the Region of York.

5. **(5)** No change is required.

6. **(1)** The singular subject <u>training</u> requires the singular form of the verb <u>includes</u>.

7. **(2)** This is a spelling error. The correct spelling is <u>accreditation</u>.

8. **(4)** The proper noun <u>Internet</u> requires a capital.

9. **(2)** A comma is needed after <u>date</u> to separate the introductory phrase from the rest of the sentence.

10. **(1)** Changing the phrase to <u>have already been able</u> places the adverb as close as possible to the verb it modifies.

11. **(3)** To improve the punctuation in this sentence, a colon is required after <u>following</u> and the semicolons should be replaced with commas.

12. **(5)** No correction is required.

13. **(4)** A plural noun <u>criteria</u> is required, not the singular noun <u>criterion</u>.

14. **(2)** A colon should be added after <u>following</u> to correct the punctuation.

15. **(3)** The singular form <u>participant</u> is required to agree with the adjective <u>each</u>.

16. **(2)** Changing the word order to <u>they were also questioned</u> is required to place the adverb close to the verb it modifies.

17. **(1)** The possessive plural <u>participants'</u> refers to the number of trainees involved in the program.

18. **(3)** This is another spelling error. <u>Program</u> is the American spelling, as opposed to <u>programme</u>, which is used in Britain.

19. **(4)** The present tense of the verb <u>to be</u> or <u>is</u> is required to agree with the verb tense used in the rest of the passage.

20. **(2)** A comma after <u>livestock</u> is needed to separate the introductory section from the rest of the sentence.

21. **(4)** This is a spelling error. The verb <u>create</u> is required, not the noun <u>crate</u>.

22. **(5)** No change is required.

23. **(3)** Another change in verb number. The plural <u>have</u> agrees with the plural subject <u>movements</u>.

24. **(2)** <u>May</u> is a less restrictive verb form than <u>can</u>, which means "to be able."

25. **(1)** The French term <u>au contraire</u> is an exclamation requiring an exclamation point. A new sentence should begin with a capital on <u>It's</u>.

26. **(3)** The adjective <u>their</u> is required—not its homonym <u>they're</u>, which means "they are."

27. **(4)** Another spelling error: The word is <u>entrepreneurs</u> not <u>entreprenors</u>.

28. **(1)** Placing the phrase "<u>such as community-based social marketing campaigns oriented toward changing behaviors</u>" in parentheses helps to simplify the complexity of the sentence.

29. **(5)** The possessive adjective <u>your</u> is needed rather than the contraction <u>you're</u>.

30. **(4)** Another American versus British difference in spelling. It's <u>neighborhoods</u> not <u>neighbourhoods.</u>

31. **(2)** The word <u>Foundation</u> requires a capital as a proper noun.

32. **(3)** An improvement in punctuation is required by placing a comma after <u>project</u>.

33. **(4)** Another error in spelling—change <u>personel</u> to <u>personnel</u>.

34. **(2)** A singular form of the predicate <u>was</u> is required to agree with the singular subject <u>one</u>.

35. **(5)** No change in punctuation is required.

36. **(1)** The rule with fractions is that the object of the preposition usually determines singularity or plurality. In this case, <u>families</u> would indicate that <u>were single parent, mother-led</u> is the best choice.

37. **(2)** To improve the sentence and make it easier to read, create a new sentence by placing a period after <u>concept</u> and beginning the new sentence with <u>More than 55 programs. . . .</u>

38. **(5)** No correction is required.

39. **(2)** A capital is required on <u>Council</u> to formally recognize this organization.

40. **(1)** The adverb <u>often</u> should be placed before the verb <u>had to leave</u>, which it modifies.

41. **(1)** A capital is not required on the adjective <u>international</u>.

42. **(4)** <u>Principals</u> are found in schools. <u>Principles</u> refer to factors.

43. **(5)** No correction is needed.

44. **(3)** <u>Curriculum</u> is the required singular form; <u>curricula</u> is the plural form.

45. **(2)** The sentence is improved by breaking it up into two sentences because it has a modification error. The skills (<u>the ability to understand . . .</u>) are placed too far away from the word <u>skills</u>.

46. **(4)** Parentheses should be placed around 1907 to separate the date from the rest of the sentence.

47. **(3)** The adverb <u>affectively</u> refers to causing emotion, but it's the homonym <u>effectively</u>, meaning "change or result," that is required.

48. **(1)** The present perfect tense <u>has been</u> is required to match the other verb tenses in the passage.

49. **(2)** To correct the spelling error, change <u>policys</u> to <u>policies</u>.

50. **(5)** Although this is a very long sentence, full of detail, no need for improvement is warranted.

Part II

As the test-graders read and evaluate your essay, they look for the following:

- Well-focused main points
- Evidence of clear organization
- Specific development of your ideas
- Proper sentence structure
- Correct grammar
- Necessary punctuation
- Appropriate use of words
- Correct spelling

Although every essay will be unique, we provide a sample here to give you a better idea of what the test-graders expect to see in your essay. Compare the structure of this sample essay to yours.

Sample Essay

My children and I recently signed up for a family-rate calling plan—complete with four separate phones and phone numbers—so that we could communicate more easily. Although I put off the purchase for several years, thinking that having a cellphone would make me so accessible to others that I would never get any time to myself, the truth is the phones have made all our lives easier.

My three children attend three different schools. The youngest, Doug, is in the fourth grade and takes a free acting class year-round at the local playhouse. His lessons run from 4 to 5 p.m. three days per week, but he can sometimes catch rides home with children in the class. Because I work until 5:30 p.m., my oldest daughter, Sydney, who is a junior in high school, waits for him to call to tell her whether he needs a ride. Before we had cellphones, Doug always had to find a working pay phone, and Sydney had to wait by the phone at home.

The middle child, Maggie, is in eighth grade and plays three sports: basketball, soccer, and track. I can usually pick her up from practice on my way home from work, but her practices end at different times each day. While she, too, used to have to hunt down a pay phone and call me at work, now she just calls and lets me know where she'll be waiting. I can run errands while I wait for her call instead of waiting at work or by the curb at her school.

The best part of the phones, though, is that whenever people want to reach any of the four of us, they call the number for the individual, not the entire family. I no longer answer the phone for all of Doug's, Maggie's, and Sydney's friends, and people trying to reach me no longer get a busy signal.

For us, cellphones are the ultimate convenience. In fact, we like our cellphones so much that we no longer have regular phone service in our home.

XIII. Social Studies Full-Length Practice Test with Answer Explanations

Answer Sheet

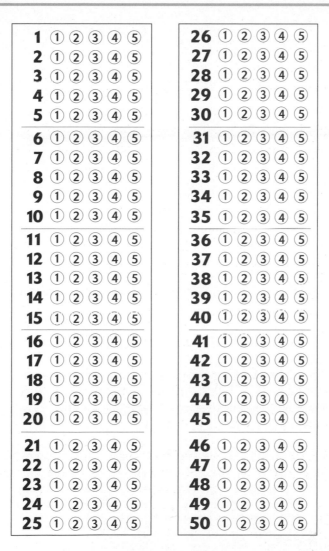

1 ① ② ③ ④ ⑤
2 ① ② ③ ④ ⑤
3 ① ② ③ ④ ⑤
4 ① ② ③ ④ ⑤
5 ① ② ③ ④ ⑤

6 ① ② ③ ④ ⑤
7 ① ② ③ ④ ⑤
8 ① ② ③ ④ ⑤
9 ① ② ③ ④ ⑤
10 ① ② ③ ④ ⑤

11 ① ② ③ ④ ⑤
12 ① ② ③ ④ ⑤
13 ① ② ③ ④ ⑤
14 ① ② ③ ④ ⑤
15 ① ② ③ ④ ⑤

16 ① ② ③ ④ ⑤
17 ① ② ③ ④ ⑤
18 ① ② ③ ④ ⑤
19 ① ② ③ ④ ⑤
20 ① ② ③ ④ ⑤

21 ① ② ③ ④ ⑤
22 ① ② ③ ④ ⑤
23 ① ② ③ ④ ⑤
24 ① ② ③ ④ ⑤
25 ① ② ③ ④ ⑤

26 ① ② ③ ④ ⑤
27 ① ② ③ ④ ⑤
28 ① ② ③ ④ ⑤
29 ① ② ③ ④ ⑤
30 ① ② ③ ④ ⑤

31 ① ② ③ ④ ⑤
32 ① ② ③ ④ ⑤
33 ① ② ③ ④ ⑤
34 ① ② ③ ④ ⑤
35 ① ② ③ ④ ⑤

36 ① ② ③ ④ ⑤
37 ① ② ③ ④ ⑤
38 ① ② ③ ④ ⑤
39 ① ② ③ ④ ⑤
40 ① ② ③ ④ ⑤

41 ① ② ③ ④ ⑤
42 ① ② ③ ④ ⑤
43 ① ② ③ ④ ⑤
44 ① ② ③ ④ ⑤
45 ① ② ③ ④ ⑤

46 ① ② ③ ④ ⑤
47 ① ② ③ ④ ⑤
48 ① ② ③ ④ ⑤
49 ① ② ③ ④ ⑤
50 ① ② ③ ④ ⑤

CUT HERE

CUT HERE

Time: 70 minutes

50 questions

Directions: Choose the best answer to each question.

Questions 1 through 7 refer to the following excerpt from U.S. History For Dummies, *2nd Edition, by Steve Wiegand, copyright 2009 by Wiley Publishing, Inc. Reprinted with permission of John Wiley & Sons, Inc.*

The Mayflower Compact

The Pilgrims (actually, they called themselves "the Saints" and everyone else "the Strangers," and weren't dubbed Pilgrims until much later by one of their Leaders) were mostly lower-class farmers and craftsmen who had decided the Church of England was still too Catholic for their tastes. So they separated themselves from the Church, thus resulting in everyone else calling them "Separatists." This did not please King James I, who suggested rather forcefully that they rejoin or separate themselves from England.

The Separatists we're concerned with did just that, settling in Holland in 1608. But after a decade of watching their children become "Dutchified," the English expatriates longed for someplace they could live as English subjects and still worship the way they wanted. The answer was America.

After going back to England and negotiating a charter to establish a colony, taking out a few loans, and forming a company, a group of 102 men, women, and children left England on September 16, 1620, on a ship called the *Mayflower.* (A second ship, the *Speedwell,* also started out, but sprang a leak and had to turn back.) The Mayflower was usually used for shipping wine between France and England. Its cargo for this trip was decidedly more varied than usual. Although the Pilgrims didn't really pack any smarter than had the Jamestown colonists, they did show some imagination. Among the things they took to the wilderness of North America were musical instruments, all kinds of furniture, and even books on the history of Turkey (the country, not the bird). One guy even brought 139 pairs of shoes and boots.

Despite a rough crossing that took 65 days, only one passenger and four crewmen died, and one child was born. After some preliminary scouting, they dropped anchor in a broad, shallow bay we know as Plymouth. (No evidence exists to indicate they landed on any kind of rock.)

1. Who were the Pilgrims in the passage?

    (1) Strangers
    (2) Lower-class farmers
    (3) Church leaders
    (4) King James I
    (5) The Dutch

2. Why did they want to separate from the Church of England?

    (1) It was too strange.
    (2) It was too forceful.
    (3) It was too saintly.
    (4) It was too Catholic.
    (5) It was too pleasing.

3. Where did the Separatists settle at first?

   (1) Holland
   (2) England
   (3) America
   (4) France
   (5) The New World

4. What did they require to establish a colony?

   (1) A crew
   (2) Passengers
   (3) Permission
   (4) The King's blessing
   (5) A charter

5. What had the Mayflower been previously used for?

   (1) Springing a leak
   (2) Shipping wine
   (3) Forming a company
   (4) Negotiating a charter
   (5) Going back to England

6. What did the Pilgrims bring with them on the voyage?

   (1) Musical instruments
   (2) Furniture
   (3) Books
   (4) Shoes and boots
   (5) All of the above

7. Where did the Mayflower actually land?

   (1) France
   (2) England
   (3) Plymouth
   (4) North America
   (5) Turkey

Questions 8 through 10 refer to the following political cartoon from GED For Dummies, *1st Edition, by Murray Shukyn and Dale E. Shuttleworth, Ph.D., copyright 2003 by Wiley Publishing, Inc. Reprinted with permission of John Wiley & Sons, Inc.*

8. What does the cartoon have to say about cellphones?

   (1) They're a wonderful invention.
   (2) They're an aid to communication.
   (3) They're a medical breakthrough.
   (4) They're a useful appliance.
   (5) They're injurious to health.

9. What is the best way to describe the cellphone user in the cartoon?

   (1) Foolhardy
   (2) Talkative
   (3) Considerate
   (4) Courageous
   (5) Cowardly

10. What tells us that cellphones represent a risk to health?

    (1) Going to the movies
    (2) Scientific research
    (3) Urban legends
    (4) Popular opinion
    (5) Crime reports

Questions 11 through 14 refer to the following excerpt from U.S. History For Dummies, *2nd Edition, by Steve Wiegand, copyright 2009 by Wiley Publishing, Inc. Reprinted with permission of John Wiley & Sons, Inc.*

The Boston Tea Party (1773)

Despite the widespread publicity surrounding the tragedy in Boston, cooler heads prevailed for the next year or two. Moderates on both sides of the Atlantic argued that compromises could still be reached.

Then the powerful but poorly run British East India Company found it had 17 million pounds of surplus tea on its hands. So the British government gave the company a monopoly on the American tea business. With a monopoly, the company could lower its prices enough to undercut the smuggled tea the colonists drank instead of paying the British tax. But even with lower prices, the colonists still didn't like the arrangement. It was the principle of the tax itself, not the cost of the tea. Shipments of English tea were destroyed or prevented from being unloaded or sold.

On December 16, 1773, colonists poorly disguised as Native Americans boarded three ships in Boston Harbor, smashed in 342 chests of tea, and dumped the whole mess into the harbor, where, according to one eyewitness, "it piled up in the low tide like haystacks." No one was seriously hurt, although one colonist was reportedly roughed up a bit for trying to stuff some of the tea in his coat instead of throwing it overboard.

King George III wasn't amused by the colonists' lack of respect. "The die is now cast," he wrote to his latest prime minister, Lord North, who had succeeded Townshend upon his sudden death. "The colonies must either submit or triumph."

11. How does the passage describe the British East India Company?

    (1) Powerful
    (2) Poorly run
    (3) A monopoly
    (4) Lowering prices
    (5) All of the above

12. How did the colonists avoid the tax on tea?

    (1) They gained a monopoly.
    (2) They had surplus tea.
    (3) They smuggled tea.
    (4) They undercut prices.
    (5) They destroyed the cargo.

13. What DIDN'T the colonists do in 1773?

    (1) Disguise themselves as Native Americans
    (2) Amuse King George
    (3) Smash chests
    (4) Board ships
    (5) Dump tea into the harbor

14. What was the most important outcome of the Boston Tea Party?

    (1) The Americans showed a lack of respect.
    (2) The die was cast.
    (3) People met with sudden death.
    (4) The American Revolution began.
    (5) The colonists were roughed up.

Questions 15 to 19 refer to the following excerpt from U.S. History For Dummies, *2nd Edition, by Steve Wiegand, copyright 2009 by Wiley Publishing, Inc. Reprinted with permission of John Wiley & Sons, Inc.*

Creating the Declaration

Jefferson set to work at a portable desk he had designed himself, and a few weeks later produced a document that has come to be regarded as one of the most eloquent political statements in human history. True, he exaggerated some of the grievances the colonists had against the king. True, he rather hypocritically declared that "all men are created equal," ignoring the fact that he and hundreds of other Americans owned slaves, whom they certainly didn't regard as having been created equal.

Overall though, it was a magnificent document that set forth all the reasons America wanted to go its own way—and why all people who wanted to do the same thing should be allowed to do so. After a bit of tinkering by Franklin, the document was presented to Congress on June 28.

At the demand of some Southern representatives, a section blaming the king for American slavery was taken out. Then, on July 2, Congress adopted the resolution submitted by Lee. "The second day of July, 1776, will be the most memorable epoch [instant of time] in the history of America," predicted John Adams. He missed it by two days, because America chose to remember July 4 instead—the day Congress formally adopted the Declaration of Independence, or as one member put it, "Mr. Jefferson's explanation of Mr. Lee's resolution."

15. What did Jefferson produce at his desk?

    (1) A document
    (2) Political statements
    (3) Human history
    (4) A list of grievances
    (5) An exaggeration

16. What did Jefferson ignore in his writing?

    (1) All the reasons America had for going its own way
    (2) The fact that all men are created equal
    (3) The fact that some Americans owned slaves
    (4) The Americans' grievances against the king
    (5) The fact that all people wanted to do the same thing

17. What section had to be taken out?

    (1) The tinkering done by Franklin
    (2) The section blaming the king for slavery
    (3) The resolution from Lee
    (4) The section referring to the most memorable epoch
    (5) All of the above

18. When was the document presented to Congress?

    (1) July 2, 1776
    (2) July 4, 1776
    (3) July 3, 1776
    (4) July 1, 1776
    (5) June 28, 1776

19. Who submitted the final resolution?

    (1) Adams
    (2) Jefferson
    (3) Lee
    (4) Franklin
    (5) Washington

Questions 20 through 24 refer to the following excerpt from the Declaration of Independence (1776).

Accusations against the King

For cutting off our trade with all parts of the world:

For imposing taxes on us without our consent:

For depriving us, in many cases, of the benefits of trial by jury:

For transporting us beyond seas to be tried for pretended offenses:

For abolishing the free system of English laws in a neighboring province, establishing therein an arbitrary government, and enlarging its boundaries, so as to render it at once an example and fit instrument for introducing the same absolute rule into these colonies:

For taking away our charters, abolishing our most valuable laws, and altering, fundamentally, the forms of our governments:

For suspending our own legislatures, and declaring themselves invested with power to legislate for us in all cases whatsoever:

He has abdicated governments here, by declaring us out of his protection and waging war against us.

He has plundered our seas, ravaged our coasts, burnt our towns and destroyed the lives of our people.

He is at this time transporting large armies of foreign mercenaries to complete the works of death, desolation, and tyranny, already begun with circumstances of cruelty and perfidy scarcely paralleled in the most barbarous ages, and totally unworthy the head of a civilized nation.

He has constrained our fellow-citizens, taken captive on the high seas, to bear arms against their country, to become the executioners of their friends and brethren, or to fall themselves by their hands.

He has excited domestic insurrections among us, and has endeavored to bring on the inhabitants of our frontiers the merciless Indian savages, whose known rule of warfare is an undistinguished destruction of all ages, sexes, and conditions.

20. According to the document, what was the king accused of?

    (1) Cutting off trade
    (2) Imposing taxes
    (3) Limiting trial by jury
    (4) Transporting Americans overseas for trial
    (5) All of the above

21. Where did the king abolish the free system of English laws?

    (1) In the Thirteen Colonies
    (2) In Great Britain
    (3) In a neighboring province
    (4) In foreign lands
    (5) In upper Canada

22. According to the passage, what was the king NOT guilty of?

    (1) Taking away charters
    (2) Waging war
    (3) Abdicating government
    (4) Encouraging freedom of speech
    (5) Destroying lives

23. What did the king use to force his will upon the colonies?

    (1) Foreign mercenaries
    (2) The British Army
    (3) Merciless savages
    (4) Fellow citizens
    (5) Executioners

24. What had the king encouraged among the colonists?

    (1) Death and desolation
    (2) Domestic insurrections
    (3) Barbarous ages
    (4) Undistinguished destruction
    (5) Execution of brethren

Questions 25 through 29 refer to the following passage.

A Country Profile

From the 1960s, Japan has made massive economic progress based largely on manufacturing industries with a move toward tertiary industry. By 1997, only 5.5 percent of the working population was employed in primary industry, with 31.9 percent in secondary industry and 61.8 percent in tertiary industry. A period of continuous economic growth came to an end in 1997, leading to calls for industrial and commercial restructuring. This coincided with increasing attention being paid to globalization, particularly to the impact of new information and communication technologies, which brought reforms in education.

Demographically, Japan has witnessed intensive urbanization and consequent rural depopulation. The government is concerned with the implications of a falling birth rate, the trend toward nuclear families and an aging population. Across the country, educational expectations have been heightened, with parents wishing to see their children attend prestigious schools followed by prestigious universities and, hopefully, attain high-status jobs. Increasingly, expectations have been high for both males and females. Social mobility, maintaining high living standards, and education have been seen to be closely linked.

Traditionally, the centralized administration has been strong in Japan, but in recent years important steps have been taken to deregulate and decentralize many areas of the public sector, including education. A package of laws designed to promote decentralization was passed in July 1999, with implementation beginning April 2000.

Such broad trends are reflected in national, regional, and local policies for educational reform. In 1996, the second Hashimoto Cabinet designated educational reform, alongside governmental administration, the economic structure, the financial system, the social welfare system, and the fiscal structure, as one of the government's major areas for reform. More recently, the Obuchi Cabinet took up education as a major agenda item and, in March 2000, established the National Commission on Educational Reform, a private discussion group of eminent citizens advising the prime minister.

25. What has been a major factor in Japan's economic growth since the 1960s?

   (1) Agriculture
   (2) Manufacturing
   (3) Forestry
   (4) Globalization
   (5) Commercial restructuring

26. What has most affected the demography of Japan since 1997?

   (1) Urbanization
   (2) Rural depopulation
   (3) Falling birth rate
   (4) Aging population
   (5) All of the above

27. What do Japanese parents most want their children to achieve?

   (1) Education
   (2) Nuclear families
   (3) High-status jobs
   (4) Increased living standards
   (5) Increased expectations

28. What has the Japanese government traditionally been known for?

   (1) Deregulation
   (2) Social mobility
   (3) Prestigious schools
   (4) Centralization
   (5) Decentralization

29. What was NOT a major area of reform for the government in 1996?

   (1) Educational policies
   (2) Government administration
   (3) Economic structure
   (4) Financial system
   (5) Sports and recreation

Questions 30 through 32 refer to the following graph from the U.S. Bureau of Justice Statistics.

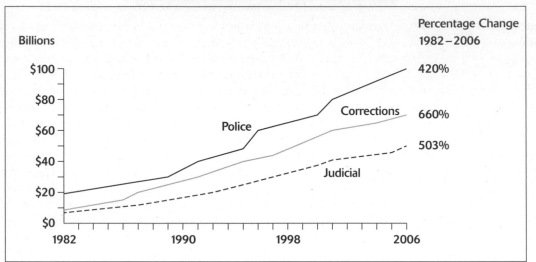

U.S. Criminal Justice Costs from 1982 to 2006

30. According to the graph, which service sector experienced the largest percentage of growth from 1982 to 2006?

   (1) Health and welfare
   (2) Police
   (3) Judicial
   (4) Corrections
   (5) Military

31. What was the cost of the judicial system in 2006?

   (1) About $40 billion
   (2) About $50 billion
   (3) About $60 billion
   (4) About $80 billion
   (5) About $70 billion

32. How have cost patterns changed for U.S. criminal justice from 1982 to 2006?

   (1) There has been a slight increase.
   (2) There has been a slight decrease.
   (3) There has been a significant increase.
   (4) There has been a significant decrease.
   (5) No change has been noted.

Questions 33 through 36 refer to the following excerpt from U.S. History For Dummies, *2nd Edition, by Steve Wiegand, copyright 2009 by Wiley Publishing, Inc. Reprinted with permission of John Wiley & Sons, Inc.*

Getting Industry and the Economy in Shape for World War II

Gearing up of the industry needed to wage a global war on two fronts was handicapped by a lack of manpower. More than 15 million Americans eventually served in the military. Training and supplying them was a staggering challenge. It took more than 6,000 people to provide food, equipment, medical services, and transportation to 8,000 soldiers. In addition, many raw materials, such as rubber, manila fiber, and oil, were in short supply. And to top it off, President Roosevelt was a great leader, but not a great administrator.

Nevertheless, Americans rose to the occasion. When FDR called for the production of 50,000 planes in a year, it was thought to be ridiculous. By 1944, the country was producing 96,000 a year. Technology blossomed. When metals became scarce, plastics were developed to take their place. Copper was taken out of pennies and replaced with steel; nickel was removed from nickels. War-inspired pragmatism even affected fashions: To save material, men's suits lost their pant cuffs and vests, and women painted their legs to take the place of nylons.

Other sacrifices were made as well. Gasoline and tires were rationed, as were coffee, sugar, canned goods, butter, and shoes. But the war proved to be more of an economic inconvenience than a real trial for most people.

Of course, all that military hardware had a hefty price tag. The federal government spent about $350 billion during World War II—or twice as much as it had spent *in total* for the entire history of the U.S. government up to that point. About 40 percent of that came from taxes; the rest came through government borrowing, much of that through the sale of bonds.

33. Which shortage most impacted America's ability to wage a global war?

   (1) Shortage of manpower
   (2) Shortage of training
   (3) Shortage of troops
   (4) Shortage of food
   (5) Shortage of medical service

34. How many planes were produced each year?

   (1) 46,000
   (2) 50,000
   (3) 76,000
   (4) 96,000
   (5) 100,000

35. What was used to solve the metals shortage?

   (1) Copper
   (2) Plastic
   (3) Steel
   (4) Nickel
   (5) Aluminum

36. How did rationing affect most people?

    (1) It was a sacrifice.
    (2) It was a hardship.
    (3) It was a real trial.
    (4) It had no effect.
    (5) It was an inconvenience.

Questions 37 through 40 refer to the following hypothetical newspaper column.

U.S. "Invades" Canada

Hillary Clinton, U.S. Secretary of State, arrived in Canada for the G8 Summit yesterday with her verbal guns blazing. She does not agree with Prime Minister Harper on several issues and used her style of gunboat diplomacy to tell him publicly.

Canada has advised NATO that it will withdraw troops from Afghanistan. This goes against American policy and Clinton told Harper so in public. Most disagreements of this type are sorted out behind closed doors. Clinton chose the public arena to try to whip Canada into American shape. The war has been unpopular in both countries, but that did not stop the U.S. from advocating more troops.

Although the Americans are embroiled in their own healthcare problems, Clinton gave Harper her views on abortion and maternal health and tried arm-twisting to solve their differences.

Harper is also in trouble with Clinton's America for convening a meeting on the Arctic Oceans. It seems our sovereignty has its limits with our neighbors.

Canadians are now wondering if this was the opening salvo in an invasion by coercion or just a misstep in what has been peaceful coexistence. Only time will tell.

37. How did Hillary Clinton arrive at the G8 Summit?

    (1) By Air Force One
    (2) With verbal guns blazing
    (3) With gunboat diplomacy
    (4) By special limousine
    (5) From Afghanistan

38. How are disagreements usually settled?

    (1) At NATO
    (2) In public
    (3) Through peaceful coexistence
    (4) By going to war
    (5) Behind closed doors

39. What is Harper's policy on Afghanistan?

    (1) Withdraw troops
    (2) Advocate more troops
    (3) Offer healthcare assistance
    (4) Support abortion and maternal health
    (5) Support Arctic sovereignty

40. What did the disagreement between Clinton and Harper concern?

    (1) Troop withdrawal
    (2) Views on abortion
    (3) Maternal health
    (4) Arctic sovereignty
    (5) All of the above

Questions 41 through 44 refer to the following chart excerpted from Green Business Practices For Dummies, *by Lisa Swallow, copyright 2009 by Wiley Publishing, Inc. Reprinted with permission of John Wiley & Sons, Inc.*

Greening of Existing Industries	
Traditional Industry Sector	**Niche Marketing Riding the Green Tidal Wave**
Accounting, business consulting, and legal services	Sustainability reporting, environmental management systems, and green business design and support
Appliances	Energy Star certification
Automobiles	Hybrids, electrics, scooters
Clothing	Ecofashion (hemp and organic textiles, recycled clothing)
Financial products	Socially responsible investment, microfinance
Grocery	Organics and naturals
Housing	Green buildings
Lawn and garden	Nontoxic and bio-based products
Medical care	Naturopathy, acupuncture
Travel and tourism	Ecotourism
Wood products	Sustainably harvested forestry, reclaimed wood products

41. How is the Green Tidal Wave different from traditional industry?

    (1) More oil and gas exploration
    (2) More energy conservation
    (3) More off-shore earthquakes
    (4) More nuclear power
    (5) More environmental pollution

42. How is clothing impacted by the greening of its industry?

    (1) Ecofashion
    (2) Hemp fabric
    (3) Organic textiles
    (4) Recycled material
    (5) All of the above

43. How should financial products reflect green business practices?

    (1) Organics and naturals
    (2) Travel and tourism
    (3) Social responsibility
    (4) Sustainable reporting
    (5) Bio-based products

44. Which industry can be affected by naturopathy?

    (1) Appliances
    (2) Medical care
    (3) Lawn and garden
    (4) Wood products
    (5) Housing

Questions 45 through 47 refer to the following political cartoon from GED *for Dummies,* 1st Edition, *by Murray Shukyn and Dale E. Shuttleworth, Ph.D., copyright 2003 by Wiley Publishing, Inc. Reprinted with permission of John Wiley & Sons, Inc.*

45. Which is the location for the cartoon?

  (1) Office suite
  (2) Laboratory
  (3) Playroom
  (4) Library
  (5) Kitchen

46. Which problem has the researcher been studying?

  (1) The common cold
  (2) A rare lung disease
  (3) Vision
  (4) Hearing
  (5) Limited patents for medicines

47. How does the cartoonist depict drug companies?

  (1) Dangerous
  (2) Religious
  (3) Greedy
  (4) Scary
  (5) Curious

Questions 48 through 50 refer to the following excerpt from U.S. History For Dummies, *2nd Edition, by Steve Wiegand, copyright 2009 by Wiley Publishing, Inc. Reprinted with permission of John Wiley & Sons, Inc.*

Obama's Historic Victory

Obama held a narrow lead through most of the summer. But as Election Day grew closer, the country's staggering economy came to dominate the campaign, and voters decided Obama was better equipped to deal with it.

It was a convincing victory, Obama won the popular vote in every section of the country but the South. He carried states no Democratic candidate had carried in 30 or 40 years. Obama's campaign leaned heavily on 21st-century technology and techniques, from sending Election Day voting reminders to cellphones to using Web sites to raise money and organize grassroots efforts. Obama also galvanized young voters and minorities to vote in record numbers.

"If there is anyone out there who still doubts that America is a place where all things are possible, who still wonders if the dream of our founders is alive in our time, who still questions the power of our democracy, tonight is your answer," Obama said in his Election Night victory speech in Chicago's Grant Park.

In 1858, the buying and selling of human beings was legal in America. In 1958, segregation and discrimination based on race was widespread. In 2008, an African American was elected 44th president of the United States.

The country had come a long way.

48. What had the most impact on the campaign?

    (1) The lack of leadership
    (2) The Iraq War
    (3) The heat of summer
    (4) The economy
    (5) The recent polls

49. What assured Obama's convincing victory?

    (1) Popular vote
    (2) Technology and techniques
    (3) Voting reminders
    (4) Grassroots efforts
    (5) All of the above

50. Why had the country come a long way?

    (1) Because of the dream of its founders
    (2) Because of the power of democracy
    (3) Because of the election of the first African-American president
    (4) Because of the selling of human beings
    (5) Because of racial discrimination

IF YOU FINISH BEFORE TIME IS CALLED, CHECK YOUR WORK ON THIS SECTION ONLY. DO NOT WORK ON ANY OTHER SECTION IN THE TEST.

Answer Key

1. (2)	14. (4)	27. (3)	40. (5)
2. (4)	15. (1)	28. (4)	41. (2)
3. (1)	16. (3)	29. (5)	42. (5)
4. (5)	17. (2)	30. (4)	43. (3)
5. (2)	18. (5)	31. (2)	44. (2)
6. (5)	19. (3)	32. (3)	45. (2)
7. (3)	20. (5)	33. (1)	46. (5)
8. (5)	21. (3)	34. (4)	47. (3)
9. (1)	22. (4)	35. (2)	48. (4)
10. (2)	23. (1)	36. (5)	49. (5)
11. (5)	24. (2)	37. (2)	50. (3)
12. (3)	25. (2)	38. (5)	
13. (2)	26. (5)	39. (1)	

Answer Explanations

1. **(2)** According to the passage, the Pilgrims were lower-class farmers and craftsmen. The other choices—strangers, church leaders, and the Dutch—are incorrect. King James I certainly wasn't a Pilgrim.

2. **(4)** The Pilgrims wanted to separate because they found the Church of England to be "too Catholic." The other choices—strange, forceful, saintly, and pleasing—were not reasons for separation.

3. **(1)** When the Separatists left England, they first settled in Holland. It was only later that they went to America in the New World. England and France are incorrect choices.

4. **(5)** To establish a new colony, a charter had to be negotiated with England. The other choices—crew, passengers, permission, and the King's blessing—although factors, are not the best answer.

5. **(2)** Before it was used to carry Pilgrims, the *Mayflower* had carried wine between France and England. The other choices are not relevant to the question.

6. **(5)** All the choices mentioned—musical instruments, furniture, books, and shoes and boots—were taken by the Pilgrims on the voyage.

7. **(3)** The Pilgrims first landed at a broad, shallow bay now known as Plymouth. North America is too general a destination. France, England, and Turkey are obviously incorrect choices.

8. **(5)** The cartoon depicts the cellphone as being a risk to one's health due to brain tumors, radiation, and careless driving. The other choices are not mentioned in the cartoon.

9. **(1)** The cellphone user is foolhardy in that he is operating dangerously. Other choices—considerate and courageous—are not shown in the cartoon. Neither talkative nor cowardly is the best answer.

10. **(2)** Scientific research indicates that cellphones may represent a risk to one's health. Movies, urban legends, popular opinion, and crime reports are incorrect choices.

11. **(5)** The author uses choices (1) through (4) to describe the British East India Company.

12. **(3)** The colonists engaged in tea smuggling to avoid the tax. The other choices do not relate to the question.

13. **(2)** The actions of the colonists in 1773 certainly wouldn't have amused King George, as he was losing control of the colonies.

14. **(4)** The most important outcome of the Boston Tea Party was undoubtedly the beginning of the American Revolution. The other choices, while also outcomes, were not the most important.

15. **(1)** Jefferson produced a document at his desk. The other choices may have been part of that document, but they were not the end product.

16. **(3)** In writing the document, Jefferson failed to acknowledge that some Americans owned slaves. The other choices were all related to the theme of the document and, therefore, were not ignored by Jefferson.

17. **(2)** To satisfy Southern delegates, the section "blaming the king for slavery" was removed from the document. Contributions by Franklin and Lee remained. It was John Adams who recognized that the document would be a "memorable epoch."

18. **(5)** It was on June 28, 1776, that the document was actually presented to Congress. Although they formally adopted the Declaration of Independence on July 4, 1776, this does not answer the question posed.

19. **(3)** According to the passage, the final resolution was submitted by Lee. The other names—Adams, Jefferson, and Franklin—are incorrect choices. Washington wasn't a representative to the Congress.

20. **(5)** According to the document, all the choices were accusations against the king.

21. **(3)** The passage states that the king abolished the free system of English law "in a neighboring province." The other choices are incorrect.

22. **(4)** The king certainly could not be accused of encouraging freedom of speech among the colonists. The other choices were all accusations.

23. **(1)** According to the document, the king hired foreign mercenaries to wage war on the colonists. Of course, the British Army was also involved, but that is not the best answer. Neither are the other choices—merciless savages, fellow citizens, or executioners.

24. **(2)** The passage states that the king encouraged "domestic insurrections" in efforts to put down the rebellion. The other choices are not the best answer.

25. **(2)** Japan's economic growth since the 1960s is as a result of its strength in manufacturing. Globalization and commercial restructuring are incorrect choices. Agriculture and forestry are not mentioned in the passage.

26. **(5)** Choices (1) through (4) all describe Japan's demography since 1997.

27. **(3)** According to the passage, Japanese parents most want their children to achieve "high-status jobs." Education would be just a contributing factor to attaining a high status.

28. **(4)** Traditionally, Japan has been known for its centralized form of governance. The other choices are incorrect.

29. **(5)** The passage does not mention sports and recreation as being a major area of reform. The other choices—educational policies, government administration, economic structure, and financial system—are all listed as areas to be reformed.

30. **(4)** According to the graph, Corrections (at 660 percent) shows the largest percentage of growth. This compares to the judicial at 503 percent and police at 420 percent. Military is not part of the graph.

31. **(2)** The graph tells us that about $50 billion was spent on the judicial system in 2006. The other choices are incorrect.

32. **(3)** Cost patterns have shown a significant increase from 1982 to 2006. All the other choices are incorrect.

33. **(1)** The passage states that a "shortage of manpower" most affected America's ability to wage a global war. Although training, food, and medical services are mentioned, they are not the best answer. Troops are not mentioned in the passage.

34. **(4)** According to the passage, 96,000 planes were built each year. The other choices are incorrect.

35. **(2)** Because there was a shortage of metal, plastics were used as a replacement. Copper, steel, nickel, and aluminum are all metals.

36. **(5)** Most people found rationing to be an inconvenience. Sacrifice, hardship, trial, and no effect might also have applied, but they aren't the best answer.

37. **(2)** According to the passage, Hillary Clinton arrived at the G8 Summit "with verbal guns blazing." The other choices—Air Force One and gunboat diplomacy—while mentioned, are not the best answer. By special limousine and from Afghanistan are incorrect answers.

38. **(5)** The passage states that disagreements are usually settled "behind closed doors." At NATO, in public, peaceful coexistence, and going to war are not correct answers.

39. **(1)** The passage states that Harper, as prime minister of Canada, intends to withdraw troops from Afghanistan. He certainly is not advocating more troops. The other choices don't relate to Afghanistan.

40. **(5)** All the choices mentioned in (1) through (4) were issues of disagreement between Clinton and Harper.

41. **(2)** The chart depicts the Green Tidal Wave's efforts to conserve energy. The other choices don't relate to energy conservation.

42. **(5)** Choices (1) through (4) all relate to the greening of the clothing industry.

43. **(3)** According to the table, green financial products should demonstrate social responsibility. The other choices are not reflective of green financial products.

44. **(2)** Because naturopathy is one of the health services, medical care is the correct answer. The other choices are not health-related services.

45. **(2)** The setting depicted in the political cartoon is obviously a laboratory, judging by the equipment being used. A microscope, test tubes, and so on would not normally be found in an office, playroom, library, or kitchen.

46. **(5)** According to the cartoon, the researcher has been studying ways to limit patent competition for medicines. The other choices are not referred to in the cartoon.

47. **(3)** The cartoonist presents drug companies as being greedy. The ability to control patents would obviously lead to increased profitability for the companies. The other choices do not reflect the theme of the cartoon.

48. **(4)** According to the passage, it was the economy that most influenced the outcome of the campaign. Leadership, summer heat, and poll results also may have had an impact, but they are not the best answer. The War in Iraq was not mentioned in the passage.

49. **(5)** Obama's victory was assured by all the choices—popular vote, technology and techniques, voting reminders, and grassroots efforts.

50. **(3)** For the first time in U.S. history, an African American had been elected president. The country had, indeed, come a long way. Although demonstrating democratic power and the founders' dreams were also signs of progress, they are not the best answer. Slavery and racial discrimination wouldn't be seen as examples of progress.

XIV. Science Full-Length Practice Test with Answer Explanations

Answer Sheet

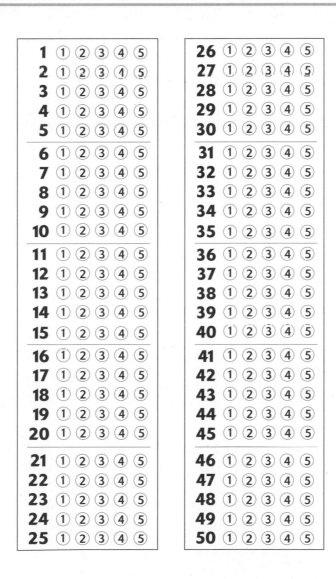

1 ① ② ③ ④ ⑤	26 ① ② ③ ④ ⑤
2 ① ② ③ ④ ⑤	27 ① ② ③ ④ ⑤
3 ① ② ③ ④ ⑤	28 ① ② ③ ④ ⑤
4 ① ② ③ ④ ⑤	29 ① ② ③ ④ ⑤
5 ① ② ③ ④ ⑤	30 ① ② ③ ④ ⑤
6 ① ② ③ ④ ⑤	31 ① ② ③ ④ ⑤
7 ① ② ③ ④ ⑤	32 ① ② ③ ④ ⑤
8 ① ② ③ ④ ⑤	33 ① ② ③ ④ ⑤
9 ① ② ③ ④ ⑤	34 ① ② ③ ④ ⑤
10 ① ② ③ ④ ⑤	35 ① ② ③ ④ ⑤
11 ① ② ③ ④ ⑤	36 ① ② ③ ④ ⑤
12 ① ② ③ ④ ⑤	37 ① ② ③ ④ ⑤
13 ① ② ③ ④ ⑤	38 ① ② ③ ④ ⑤
14 ① ② ③ ④ ⑤	39 ① ② ③ ④ ⑤
15 ① ② ③ ④ ⑤	40 ① ② ③ ④ ⑤
16 ① ② ③ ④ ⑤	41 ① ② ③ ④ ⑤
17 ① ② ③ ④ ⑤	42 ① ② ③ ④ ⑤
18 ① ② ③ ④ ⑤	43 ① ② ③ ④ ⑤
19 ① ② ③ ④ ⑤	44 ① ② ③ ④ ⑤
20 ① ② ③ ④ ⑤	45 ① ② ③ ④ ⑤
21 ① ② ③ ④ ⑤	46 ① ② ③ ④ ⑤
22 ① ② ③ ④ ⑤	47 ① ② ③ ④ ⑤
23 ① ② ③ ④ ⑤	48 ① ② ③ ④ ⑤
24 ① ② ③ ④ ⑤	49 ① ② ③ ④ ⑤
25 ① ② ③ ④ ⑤	50 ① ② ③ ④ ⑤

Time: 80 minutes

50 questions

Directions: Choose the best answer to each question.

Questions 1 through 3 refer to the following passage.

Structure of Atoms

Everything about us, including us, is composed of atoms. Atoms are the basic building block of matter and consist of parts (protons, neutrons, and electrons) but cannot be divided using chemicals. Electrons are negatively charged and move around the nucleus and account for most of the volume of the atom. Electrons are much smaller than protons or neutrons. Although electrons are bound to the nucleus, it is still possible to remove one or more electrons, resulting in ions of the original atom.

The nucleus is made up of protons and neutrons, which together create most of the mass of an atom. Protons are positively charged and bear a charge equal to an electron and, thus, are attracted to each other. Neutrons have no charge; consequently, the net charge of the nucleus is positive. If the number of neutrons in an atom is changed, an isotope of the atom is formed.

Atoms, isotopes, and ions are all related if they are formed from the same atom. If an electron has been removed from an atom to form an ion, that ion will have a negative charge. If an isotope of an atom is formed, it will still be electrically neutral but differ in mass since the atom is defined by the number of protons.

1. The nucleus of an atom is made up of

   (1) Electrons and neutrons.
   (2) Protons and neutrons.
   (3) Electrons and protons.
   (4) Neutrons.
   (5) Protons.

2. An isotope of an atom is formed by a

   (1) Change in the number of protons.
   (2) Change in the number of electrons.
   (3) Change in the charge of the atom.
   (4) Chemical reaction.
   (5) Change in the number of neutrons.

3. An ion of an atom would be formed by

   (1) Chemical reaction.
   (2) Varying the number of electrons.
   (3) Varying the number of protons.
   (4) Varying the number of neutrons.
   (5) Mechanical forces.

Questions 4 through 6 are based on the following information.

Everything around us—whether it is living or not—is composed of matter, which is defined as anything that has mass and takes up space. Matter may belong to one of two classifications: one is based on physical state and the other is based on composition.

- **Classification based on physical state:** Matter exists in four states:
  - **Solid:** Matter existing in a solid state is rigid and almost totally incompressible.
  - **Liquid:** Matter existing in a liquid state is fluid and has very low compressibility.
  - **Gas:** Matter existing in a gaseous state is fluid and highly compressible.
  - **Plasma:** Matter that is partly ionized is called plasma. It does not have a definite shape or volume (like a gas), but under the influence of a magnetic field, structures may be formed.

Water can exist as a solid called ice, where it is rigid and almost impossible to compress without breaking it into finer and finer particles, which is not compressing but subdividing. If you apply heat to ice, it becomes water—a fluid that has very low compressibility. Apply more heat, and the water becomes steam, which is a gas and is highly compressible. Water is one form of matter that can exist in three states depending on pressure and temperature.

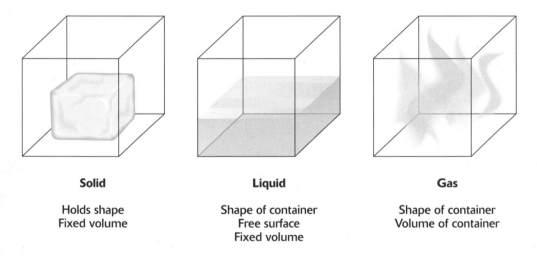

Solid	Liquid	Gas
Holds shape	Shape of container	Shape of container
Fixed volume	Free surface	Volume of container
	Fixed volume	

- **Classification based on composition of matter:** Matter also may be classified based on its compositions. An element is a substance that has atoms of all the same chemical nature. Examples of elements are oxygen and hydrogen.

  Matter that is a homogeneous mixture throughout is called a solution. An example of a solution is salt added to water.

  Matter that is formed by a mixture of two substances that remain the same but are mixed with one another is called a heterogeneous mixture. An example of a heterogeneous mixture is a combination of salt and pepper.

4. Matter can exist in four states, which are

   (1) Solid, mixture, plasma, and gas.
   (2) Liquid, solid, plasma, and solution.
   (3) Solid, liquid, gas, and plasma.
   (4) Liquid, solution, gas, and mixture.
   (5) Liquid, solution, plasma, and gas.

5. The state in which matter exists that is highly compressible is

   (1) Liquid.
   (2) Solution.
   (3) Mixture.
   (4) Gas.
   (5) Solid.

6. Water can exist in three states as

   (1) Liquid water, ice, and steam.
   (2) Liquid water, solutions, and steam.
   (3) Ice, mixtures, and solids.
   (4) Steam, gas, and solids.
   (5) Liquid water, solutions, and ice.

Question 7 refers to the following figure.

7. If the cyclist in the diagram wants to move forward, what must he do?

   (1) Lean forward in the seat.
   (2) Push down on the higher pedal.
   (3) Push down on the lower pedal.
   (4) Squeeze the handlebars.
   (5) Release the brakes.

Questions 8 and 9 refer to the following figure.

8. Two boys are standing facing each other wearing inline skates. If Boy X pushes as hard as he can and Boy Y does nothing, what will be the result?

   (1) Both boys will remain in the same position.
   (2) Boy X will move backward.
   (3) Boy Y will move backward.
   (4) Both boys will move backward.
   (5) Nothing will happen.

9. Boy X has a strange sense of humor. When Boy Y wants a turn pushing, Boy X turns his left foot 45 degrees, effectively creating a brake with his skates. What will happen if Boy Y pushes as hard as he can?

   (1) Both boys will move backward.
   (2) Boy X will move backward.
   (3) Boy Y will move backward.
   (4) Neither boy will move backward.
   (5) Boy X will move slowly.

Question 10 refers to the following passage.

Energy

   The ability to cause change or do work is defined as energy. The two main forms of energy are potential (stored energy) and kinetic (energy due to motion). If you carried a 1-pound weight to the roof of a tall building and held it on the edge, it would possess potential energy because you carried it to the top of the building. If it accidentally fell, it would possess kinetic energy.

10. A basketball player is waiting for her teammates while holding a basketball in her hands. What type of energy does the basketball possess as she holds it?

    (1) Nuclear
    (2) Kinetic
    (3) Stationary
    (4) Potential
    (5) Positional

Question 11 refers to the following passage.

Pure Substances and Mixtures

Most of the matter we're exposed to is really mixtures of substances and not pure ones. Pure substances have the same properties in any sample we find. It doesn't matter where the substance came from, it will always have the same chemical properties. Mixtures are composed of two or more substances, and a mixture's properties can vary from sample to sample depending on how much of each contributing substance it contains. Each sample, with varying ratios of components, will have differing properties.

11. The properties of a mixture can

    (1) Always be the same.
    (2) Vary from sample to sample.
    (3) Make them interesting to observe.
    (4) Be the same as pure substances.
    (5) Become the topic of popular discussion.

Question 12 refers to the following passage.

Differences in Chemical Reactions

Different classes of elements behave differently in chemical reactions but show group relationships. Metals tend to lose electrons when becoming involved in chemical reactions. Nonmetals gain or share electrons in chemical reactions.

Every atom has a valence or outer shell; the electrons in this shell have the weakest bond to the nucleus and, thus, are ripe for being taken by another atom. Electrons closer to the nucleus have the strongest attraction and are very difficult for another atom to attract or contribute. Shells, other than the valence shell are usually complete and stable. Atoms usually react in a way that produces a complete valence shell; in the case of metals, this means contributing electrons from the valence shell to create a complete and stable new valence shell.

12. Metals usually react in similar manners in chemical reaction by losing electrons. This occurs because

    (1) Metals no longer need the electrons.
    (2) The electrons are not connected to the atom.
    (3) The reaction is easier.
    (4) The atom prefers a complete valence shell.
    (5) Nonmetals are stronger than metals.

Question 13 refers to the following passage.

Structure of Atoms

When we think of atoms, we visualize something like our solar system with particles orbiting around a central core. This may or may not be accurate, but it's the simplest way of thinking about atoms.

At the center of this system is the nucleus, where our sun would be in a diagram of the solar system. The nucleus is made up of protons and neutrons and makes up almost all the mass of the atom. Spinning around the nucleus are the electrons, which are much smaller and have little mass compared to the nucleus.

Protons bear a positive charge, electrons bear a negative charge and neutrons are neutral. Atoms have an equal number of electrons and protons and are, thus, electrically neutral. Normally, like charges repel each other, but in the nucleus is a very powerful nuclear force that maintains stability in the nucleus.

13. The nucleus is composed of protons and neutrons held together by

   (1) Gravitational force.
   (2) Centrifugal force.
   (3) Nuclear force.
   (4) Centripetal force.
   (5) Magnetic force.

14. A car is traveling along a level road at a speed of 30 mph. Seeing a stop sign ahead, the driver decides to bring the car to a stop. What provides the force necessary to bring the car to a stop?

   (1) The driver's foot on the brake
   (2) The force of gravity
   (3) Wind resistance
   (4) Friction when the brakes are applied
   (5) Inertia

15. The basic functional unit of life is the

   (1) Neutron.
   (2) Proton.
   (3) Molecule.
   (4) DNA.
   (5) Cell.

Question 16 refers to the following passage.

Organisms and Viruses

An organism is comprised of one or more cells functioning as a stable unit and possessing all the characteristics of life. This definition excludes viruses because, in order to reproduce, viruses are dependent on the biochemical machinery of a host cell. Viruses have no metabolism of their own and, consequently, can neither synthesize nor organize the organic compound from which they are formed. Autonomous reproduction is, therefore, not possible, and viruses passively replicate using the machinery of the host cell. Viruses do have their own genes and can change just as organisms do.

16. Viruses are not considered the same as living organisms because

    (1) They make people sick.

    (2) They are not composed of molecules.

    (3) They depend on the host cell to reproduce.

    (4) They can replicate all by themselves.

    (5) They possess genes.

Questions 17 and 18 refer to the following passage.

Matter in the Living System

    Amino acids are involved in metabolism and are important to life. Amino acids join together to form proteins. The amino acids are linked in various configurations to form different proteins, and every protein can be identified chemically by the amino acids and their structure. Amino acids are very important for nutrition and human life. Without them, we would not have proteins.

    Each amino acid can exist in two forms: left-handed (levo- or L) and right-handed (dextro- or D) versions. The following figure represents the two versions of alanine.

L-alanine

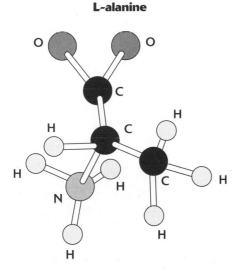

D-alanine

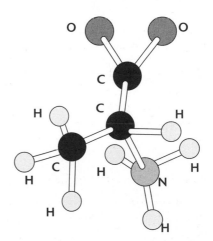

17. Proteins are formed by

    (1) Amino acid atoms.

    (2) Cows.

    (3) Linked amino acids.

    (4) Chemical reactions of amino acids.

    (5) An L and a D amino acid.

18. What is the difference between a levo- and a dextro- amino acid?

   (1) The chemical bonds

   (2) The composition of the molecule

   (3) The way they're used in metabolism

   (4) The configuration of the atoms in space

   (5) The manner in which they interact

Question 19 and 20 refer to the following figure and passage.

Resulting Offspring from Breeding Tall and Short Plants

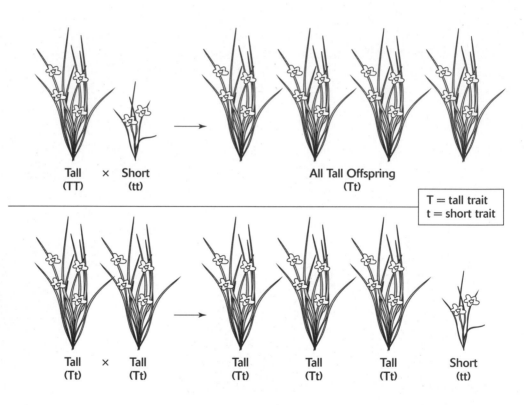

| Tall | × | Short | | All Tall Offspring |
| (TT) | | (tt) | | (Tt) |

T = tall trait
t = short trait

| Tall | × | Tall | | Tall | Tall | Tall | Short |
| (Tt) | | (Tt) | | (Tt) | (Tt) | (Tt) | (tt) |

Mendel and Evolution

    Mendel was a scientist who was interested in how future generations of plants would carry traits of the first generation. He hypothesized that there were two types of traits: recessive and dominant. To test his hypothesis, Mendel cross-bred pea plants, mating two tall plants and then mating a tall plant with a short plant.

    The two tall plants produced tall plants in the first generation of offspring but produced three tall and one short offspring in the second generation. The tall and the short produced all tall plants. He concluded that tall must be a dominant trait and short a recessive one and that each plant contained both. The third generation produced a plant with the recessive trait—a short plant.

19. Mendel hypothesized that there were two types of traits involved in heredity:

    (1) Tall and short
    (2) Dominant and short
    (3) Recessive and tall
    (4) Dominant and recessive
    (5) Male and female

20. Referring the diagram, why would breeding a tall plant and a short plant produce all tall plants?

    (1) Short plants cannot survive.
    (2) Tall plants get more sun.
    (3) The tall trait is dominant.
    (4) The tall trait is recessive.
    (5) These plants are always tall.

Question 21 refers to the following figure.

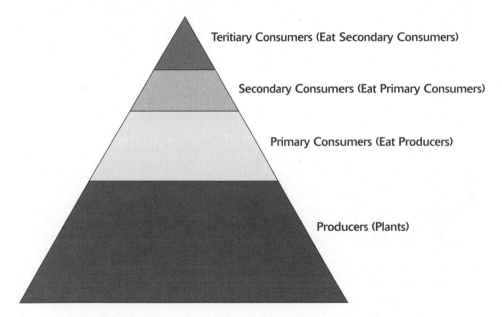

21. If lettuce were to become contaminated with salmonella, what effect would this likely have on salad-eating tertiary consumers?

    (1) They would likely eat fewer salads.
    (2) They would likely become ill.
    (3) They would likely become herbivores.
    (4) They would likely wash their lettuce.
    (5) It would likely have no effect.

Question 22 refers to the following diagram.

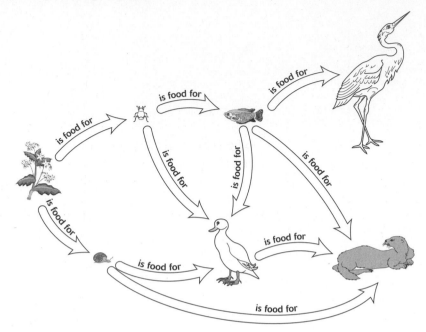

22. If snails suddenly disappeared, according to the diagram, what effect would this have?

    (1) It would have no effect.
    (2) Otters would grow thinner.
    (3) Insects would increase in number.
    (4) Otters would have to look for other food sources.
    (5) Otters would eat fewer fish.

23. If the hereditary traits of an organism are contained in the organism's DNA and if we could find a sample of DNA from a dinosaur, could the dinosaur be reproduced?

    (1) Yes.
    (2) Yes, but you would need two dinosaurs from the same species.
    (3) Yes, but the infant dinosaur would be too large for a laboratory.
    (4) No, because DNA does not survive that long.
    (5) The experiment would have to be attempted to find out.

Question 24 refers to the following passage.

Reproductive Cloning

If a scientist wanted to produce an animal with the same nuclear DNA as another animal, she might use a process called reproductive cloning, also known as somatic cell nuclear transfer (SCNT). During this process, genetic material from the nucleus of the donor animal is transferred to an egg that has had its nucleus removed. This removes the genetic material from the egg and allows the introduced genetic material to exist. In order to stimulate cell division, the egg is subjected to electric current. When the egg matures slightly, it is implanted in a female host where it develops until it is ready to be born.

24. If a scientist wanted to clone an animal, she would start with

   (1) SCNT.
   (2) An egg.
   (3) A somatic cell.
   (4) Genetic material from the donor.
   (5) Electric current.

Question 25 refers to the following passage.

Cells, Tissues, and Organs

Every living thing is made of at least one cell. Human beings are made of many cells. These cells group together to form tissue and then eventually organs, which do something specific in the human body.

When two or more tissues work together, they form an organ, such as the stomach, heart, or skin. Each of these organs performs a specific task, which is dependent on all the other tasks performed by the organs.

25. In the human body, cells group together to next form

   (1) Atoms.
   (2) Legs and arms.
   (3) Organs.
   (4) Tasks.
   (5) Work groups.

Questions 26 through 28 are based on the following figure and passage.

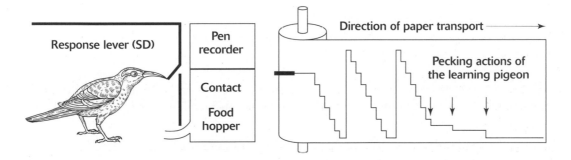

Animal Behavior

B. F. Skinner, a scientist, hypothesized that if an organism were given a reward for performing an action, that action would probably be repeated. In the diagram, the bird is rewarded with food for pecking at a lever. According to Skinner, that would increase the likelihood of the bird pecking at the lever.

This theory can be useful in real life. If you're trying to teach your dog to heel and you give him a reward each time he heels after you give him a vocal instruction to do so, there is a greater likelihood that the dog will follow the instruction. After many attempts, the dog will have learned to heel at your command.

26. If you want to teach your pet dog to come when you call, one way of training the dog would be to

    (1) Yell at the dog whenever he fails to come.
    (2) Reward the dog for coming to you when you call him.
    (3) Call the dog until he comes to you.
    (4) Leave the dog outside until he learns to come when called.
    (5) Do not feed the dog until he obeys.

27. In the diagram, the recorder shows that

    (1) The paper travels from right to left.
    (2) The bird will peck at the lever.
    (3) The pecking behavior increases with rewards.
    (4) The bird is hungry.
    (5) The bird is pecking at the lever to make the paper move.

28. Joan and Henry have a young son who sucks his thumb. In order to teach him not to suck his thumb, what might they do?

    (1) Put heavy gloves on their son.
    (2) Feed him only on days when he doesn't suck his thumb.
    (3) Scowl whenever he sucks his thumb.
    (4) Give him a meaningful reward whenever he doesn't suck his thumb.
    (5) Realize that it is very difficult to teach someone *not* to do something.

Question 29 is based on the following figure.

The Skinner Box

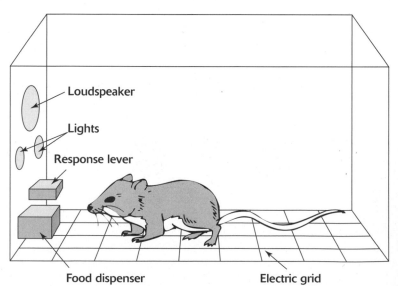

29. The Skinner box is used to condition small animals like rats. When the green light flashes and the rat hits the response lever, food is dispensed from the food dispenser. If the rat hits the response lever when the red light flashes, a mild shock is administered through the wire grid on the floor. Which is the best explanation of why the rat would learn to press the response lever when the green light goes on?

(1)   The green light is more pleasant than the red one.

(2)   The green light means go.

(3)   The food is used as a reward for pressing the lever when the green light comes on.

(4)   The mild shock is a reward for obeying instructions.

(5)   Rats like green lights.

Question 30 is based on the following diagram.

Biological Evolution

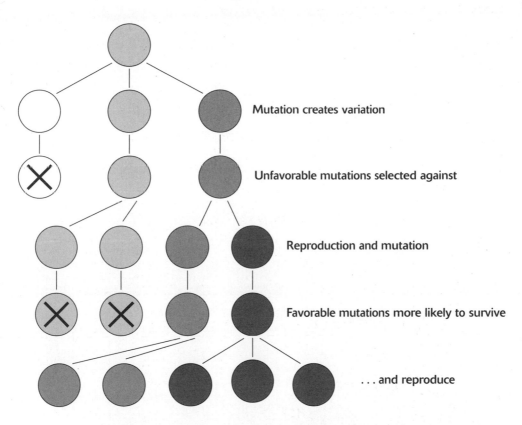

Mutation creates variation

Unfavorable mutations selected against

Reproduction and mutation

Favorable mutations more likely to survive

. . . and reproduce

30. In the preceding diagram, evolution says that favorable mutations are more likely to survive. If corn requires sunlight to thrive but tall plants are harder to harvest than short plants, which height of plants is more likely to survive?

   (1) Short plants
   (2) Both short and tall plants
   (3) Whatever the farmer plants
   (4) Tall plants
   (5) Not enough information provided

Question 31 is based on the following passage.

Endergonic and Exergonic Reactions

All the chemical reactions that take place in the body are collectively called metabolism. The reactions may be endergonic or exergonic. Endergonic reactions need a net input of energy to start the reaction. Exergonic reactions release energy. An example of an endergonic reaction is photosynthesis; the net input of energy is supplied by the sun. An example of an exergonic reaction is cell respiration, which burns food to release energy.

31. Metabolism is a collection of

   (1) Endergonic reactions.
   (2) Exergonic reactions.
   (3) Photosynthesis.
   (4) Cell respiration.
   (5) All the chemical reactions taking place in the body.

Questions 32 and 33 refer to the following passage.

Enzymes

Enzymes are catalysts, substances that start or speed up a chemical reaction without itself being changed, and speed up reactions by providing an alternate path requiring lower activation energy for the reaction. These catalysts are very choosy, only catalyzing certain reactions.

Enzyme catalytic activity is affected by the following factors: temperature, pH, and concentration of catalyst and substrate. Some substances have the ability to slow down or stop the activity of the enzyme and are called inhibitors.

32. Enzymes are considered catalysts because they

   (1) Help reactions to occur.
   (2) Make reactions easier to control.
   (3) Take part in chemical reactions and emerge as different substances.
   (4) Lower the energy required for the reaction to occur.
   (5) Join with substrates.

33. Enzyme activity is NOT affected by

    (1) Temperature.
    (2) pH.
    (3) Concentration of catalyst.
    (4) Concentration of substrate.
    (5) None of the above.

Questions 34 through 36 refer to the following passage.

Cell Theory

    Cell theory states that all living organisms are made up of one or more cells, which are the basic unit of life and have the same basic chemical composition. They may be unicellular or multicellular. Cell theory goes on to state that cells come from preexisting cells and that they are the basic unit of structure and function. In each cell is DNA, which passes on hereditary information from cell to cell.

34. All living organisms are composed of

    (1) One or more cells.
    (2) Life.
    (3) Chemicals.
    (4) Energy.
    (5) Enzymes.

35. The purpose of the DNA is to

    (1) Help the cell grow.
    (2) Provide the cell with energy.
    (3) Help the cell multiply.
    (4) Pass on hereditary information.
    (5) Change the color of the cell.

36. An organism that is unicellular would

    (1) Be nonliving.
    (2) Have difficulty reproducing.
    (3) Have only one cell.
    (4) Be small.
    (5) Have no DNA.

Question 37 refers to the following figure and passage.

DNA

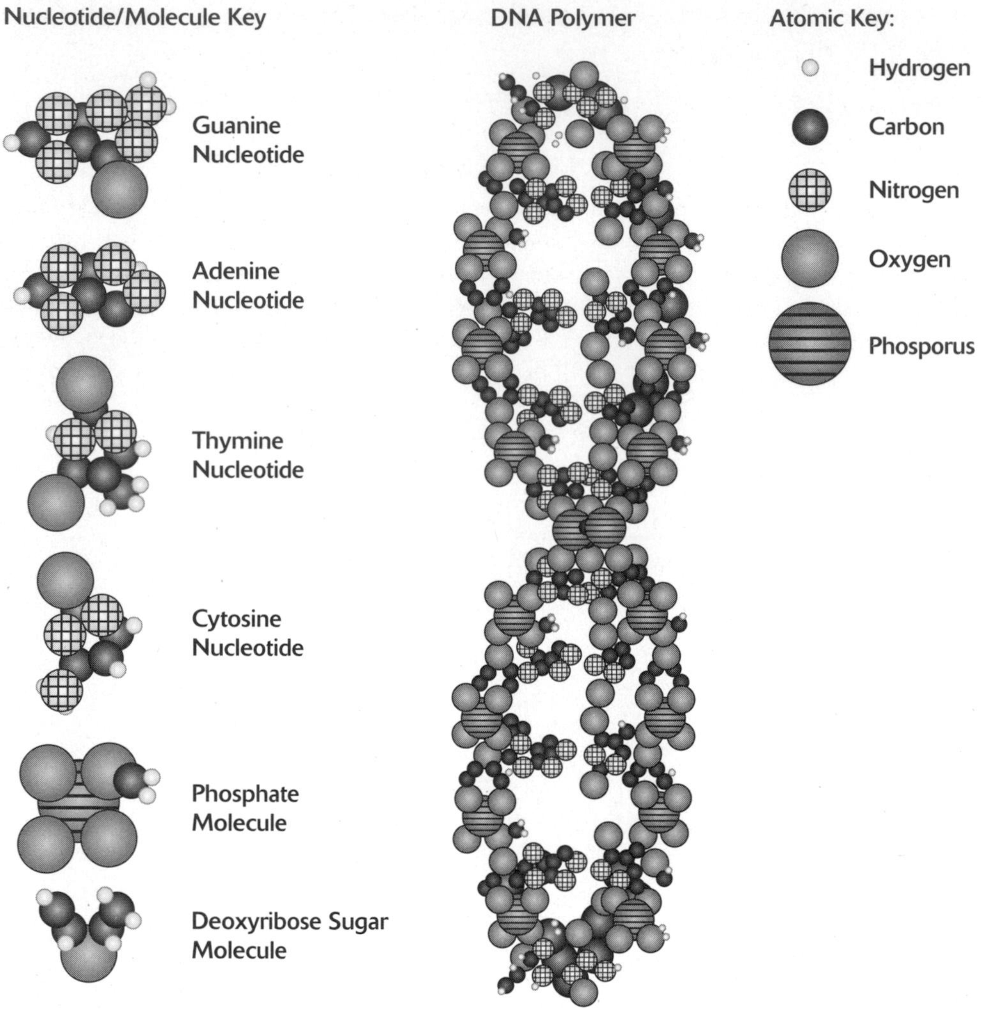

Nucleotide/Molecule Key

Guanine
Nucleotide

Adenine
Nucleotide

Thymine
Nucleotide

Cytosine
Nucleotide

Phosphate
Molecule

Deoxyribose Sugar
Molecule

DNA Polymer

Atomic Key:

Hydrogen

Carbon

Nitrogen

Oxygen

Phosporus

Molecular Basis of Heredity

We all carry the instructions for the characteristics of the next generation in our DNA. This is a large molecule forming a single chromosome in a cell. In humans, most cells have two copies of each of 23 different chromosomes. One of these copies comes from the father, and the other comes from the mother. The sex of the offspring is determined by a specific pair of chromosomes. Sometimes mutations occur in the DNA, but most of the mutations are insignificant.

37. Why do children often resemble both parents?

  (1) Cells determine characteristics.
  (2) They live with their parents.
  (3) Both parents are involved in producing offspring.
  (4) Both parents contribute characteristics through their DNA.
  (5) Some children are adopted.

Question 38 refers to the following passage.

Living on the Shark

Sharks are considered dangerous fish, and most other fish prefer to stay out of their way. Not so the Remora, which is a suckerfish. They're called suckerfish because their dorsal fins have modified to form a sucker or suction-cup-like appendage, which they can use to attach themselves to larger fish such as the shark. The Remora attaches itself to the shark and, because it's small and doesn't injure the shark with its sucker, neither benefits nor hurts the shark. The Remora does benefit from this action because the shark provides protection to the Remora (other fish seldom attack the shark) and the remnants of the shark's meals provide food for the Remora.

38. The Remora derives benefit from its association with the shark because

  (1) The Remora does not have to learn to swim.
  (2) The shark provides food and protection for the Remora.
  (3) Large fish are afraid of the Remora.
  (4) The shark feeds the Remora.
  (5) The Remora's sucker helps the shark attract food.

Questions 39 refers to the following passage and diagram.

Fission

When a heavier, unstable nucleus splits into two or more lighter nuclei releasing vast amounts of energy and two or three free neutrons, the process is known as nuclear fission.

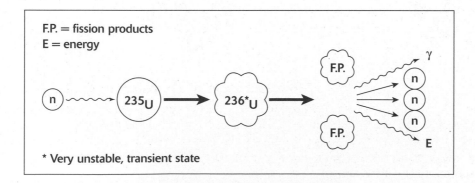

The free neutron can go on to produce other fissions producing free neutrons, which can produce many more fissions. This is known as a chain reaction and may or may not continue depending on a series of external conditions.

39. According to the diagram, what happens when a free neutron collides with an atom of U235?

    (1) It changes to U236.

    (2) It releases energy.

    (3) It releases free neutrons.

    (4) It assists in the creation of fission products.

    (5) All of the above.

Questions 40 through 42 refer to the following diagram and passage.

Car Strut

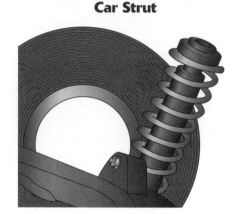

Springs

    Springs are made of elastic materials, which are materials that can change in shape and then restore themselves. When you push down on a spring, the shape of the spring changes—it gets shorter. When you release the force that you've been applying, the spring restores itself to its former shape and size. This property is most useful in designing a car strut.

    Roads are full of bumps and potholes. Bumps create a force upward on the tire and the potholes create a condition where the force exerted upward by the road is suddenly released. Without something between you and the road, every bump and pothole would be reflected by a corresponding bump inside the car.

    The spring in the strut acts as an intermediary and absorbs the forces of the bumps and potholes and returns to its former shape ready to begin work again.

40. How does the strut act to produce a smooth ride in the car?

    (1) It acts on the shock absorber to smooth out the movements of the shock absorber.

    (2) It absorbs the forces from irregularities in the road.

    (3) It creates forces that make the road smoother.

    (4) It bounces back and forth.

    (5) It is an elastic material.

41. Why is a car spring considered an elastic material?

(1) It can bounce.
(2) It can stretch and then restore itself.
(3) It is made of rubber.
(4) It can change its shape and then restore itself.
(5) It is all coiled up.

42. Why do cars require springs?

(1) To help the motor work efficiently
(2) To help the driver keep his attention on the road
(3) To smooth out the ride
(4) To make sure that the brakes stop the car
(5) To help the driver navigate around bumps

Questions 43 and 44 refer to the following diagram and passage.

Producing Electricity from the Sun's Energy

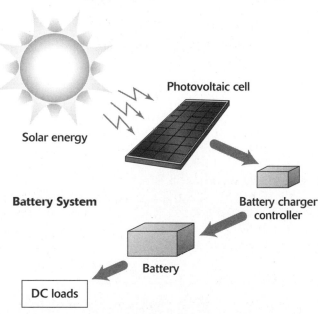

Solar Energy

A great deal of energy is delivered by the sun to the Earth every sunny day. For millennia, people just enjoyed the heat and light and didn't think about harnessing that energy. With the reducing supplies of oil and the environmental impact of combustion on the Earth, people are turning to the sun for answers.

Energy from the sun has the ability to create electricity through the use of photovoltaic cells. These cells can be mounted on rooftops or set up in fields. In any case, they'll produce electrical power—but the next question is what to do with that electrical power.

Rooftop photovoltaic cells can produce electricity for the use of the building every day when the sun is shining, but during the dark hours of the day, no electricity is produced. The simplest solution is to feed the electricity into the electric grid during the day and extract electricity from the grid during the dark hours of the day. Many local governments are promoting this system through subsidies for solar producers.

43. How can we use the free energy from the sun to run our appliances now?

    (1) Plug them into wall sockets.

    (2) Insist that our local electric authority investigate solar power.

    (3) Convert the energy with photovoltaic cells.

    (4) Put our appliances outside in the sun.

    (5) Attach the appliances to batteries that are left outside.

44. How is government trying to promote the increased use of solar energy?

    (1) By advertising the advantages of solar power

    (2) By building huge solar generation plants

    (3) By passing laws to require people to use solar energy

    (4) By paying people and companies to produce solar electricity

    (5) By making the use of solar power an election platform

Question 45 refers to the following diagram and passage.

Oxygen Cycle Reservoirs and Flux

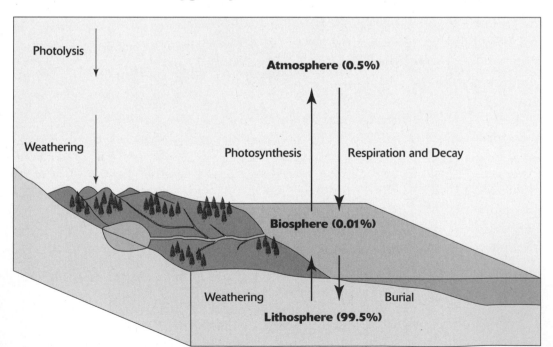

The Oxygen Cycle

The largest oxygen reservoir is within the Earth's crust and mantle. The largest oxygen source is photosynthesis. Oxygen is lost to the atmosphere through respiration and decay where oxygen is consumed and carbon dioxide is released.

45. What are opposite processes in the oxygen cycle according to the diagram and passage?

    (1) Respiration and decay
    (2) Photosynthesis and weathering
    (3) Photolysis and burial
    (4) Photosynthesis and respiration and decay
    (5) Decay and burial

Question 46 is based on the following passage.

The Origin of the Earth

The planet we now know as Earth was originally a massive object that attracted more matter by gravitational force. As the inner part of this mass became hotter and hotter, the metals began to melt and sink to the middle of this mass, creating a metallic core. It is thought that another planet crashed into the forming Earth and the collision released a hunk of mass that became the moon.

46. How do scientists think that the moon was formed?

    (1) A gigantic space rock was attracted to the Earth's gravitational field.
    (2) The mass of the moon attracted material to form a ball.
    (3) The moon formed at the same time as the Earth.
    (4) A mass of molten material spun around the Earth until it became solid.
    (5) A planet struck the molten surface of the Earth, releasing material.

Question 47 refers to the following passage.

Plate Tectonics

The Earth's lithosphere, which is part of the hard outer layer of the Earth, moves. To understand this movement, it is necessary to realize that the lithosphere is made up of seven or eight major tectonic plates and a lot of minor ones. The only time we're aware of the movement is during an earthquake, when the movement is sudden and violent.

47. One cause of earthquakes is

    (1) Underground vibrations
    (2) Volcanic eruptions under the Earth's surface
    (3) Collapse of an underground cave
    (4) Sudden movement of one of the tectonic plates
    (5) None of the above

Question 48 refers to the following passage.

The Big Bang Theory

One of the most accepted theories of how the universe was formed is called the Big Bang Theory. According to the Big Bang Theory, something happened billions of years ago. In essence, from nothing came all of the universe's matter and time began. All of the matter in the universe, which comprises stars, planets, moons, and so on, is explained by the theory.

48. Originally, the universe came from

   (1) Planets.
   (2) Rocks.
   (3) Nothing.
   (4) Space junk.
   (5) Carbon.

Question 49 refers to the following passage.

Volcanoes

Under the Earth's crust is a hot molten layer and if an opening develops, the hot magma escapes along with ash and gases. Volcanoes can be classified as active or dormant. Some volcanoes have not erupted in historical times and are called extinct. An active volcano may be erupting or likely to erupt in the near future and poses the greatest danger to people and animals in the area. Scientifically speaking, any volcano that has erupted in the last 10,000 years is considered active; using this definition, there are around 500 active volcanoes on Earth. There are around 50 active volcanoes in the United States, but few of these erupt in any one year. It is estimated that around 500 million people on Earth live close to active volcanoes.

49. What is an active volcano, from a scientific point of view?

   (1) One that has never erupted
   (2) One that is currently erupting
   (3) One that is releasing hot gases
   (4) One that has erupted in the last 10,000 years
   (5) One that has erupted in the last 500 years

Question 50 refers to the following figure.

The Carbon Cycle

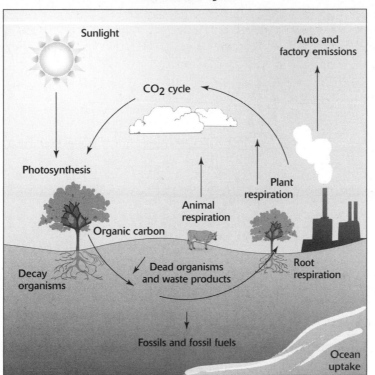

50. Looking at the illustration above, how would reducing emissions from cars and factories affect the overall amount of carbon dioxide in the atmosphere?

(1) It would reduce the amount of carbon dioxide in the atmosphere.

(2) It would increase the amount of carbon dioxide in the atmosphere.

(3) It would leave the amount of carbon dioxide in the atmosphere unchanged.

(4) It would interfere with photosynthesis.

(5) It would decrease the amount of fossil fuel.

IF YOU FINISH BEFORE TIME IS CALLED, CHECK YOUR WORK ON THIS SECTION ONLY. DO NOT WORK ON ANY OTHER SECTION IN THE TEST.

Answer Key

1. (2)	**14.** (4)	**27.** (3)	**40.** (2)
2. (5)	**15.** (5)	**28.** (5)	**41.** (4)
3. (2)	**16.** (3)	**29.** (3)	**42.** (3)
4. (3)	**17.** (3)	**30.** (4)	**43.** (3)
5. (4)	**18.** (4)	**31.** (5)	**44.** (4)
6. (1)	**19.** (4)	**32.** (4)	**45.** (4)
7. (2)	**20.** (3)	**33.** (5)	**46.** (5)
8. (4)	**21.** (2)	**34.** (1)	**47.** (4)
9. (3)	**22.** (4)	**35.** (4)	**48.** (3)
10. (4)	**23.** (5)	**36.** (3)	**49.** (4)
11. (2)	**24.** (4)	**37.** (4)	**50.** (1)
12. (4)	**25.** (3)	**38.** (2)	
13. (3)	**26.** (2)	**39.** (4)	

Answer Explanations

1. **(2)** The nucleus of the atom is made up of protons and neutrons according to the passage. The other choices are impossible combinations of the possible parts in the atom.

2. **(5)** Altering the number of neutrons creates an isotope, which will have a different mass. If it were possible to change the number of protons, a different element would be formed.

3. **(2)** An ion of an atom would be formed by varying the number of electrons. Varying the number of protons would form another element. Varying the number of neutrons would form an isotope. Chemical reaction and mechanical forces would have little effect on the electrons.

4. **(3)** The four states of matter are solid, liquid, gas, and plasma. Solutions and mixtures are not states but part of a classification system.

5. **(4)** Gas exists in a state that is highly compressible. Liquids and solids are not compressible, and solutions and mixtures are not states.

6. **(1)** Steam is the gas, ice is the solid, and water is the liquid. Solutions and mixtures are not states.

7. **(2)** Pushing down on the higher pedal creates a downward force that is translated by the chain and the transmission in the rear wheel to a forward motion. Pushing down on the lower pedal would have little effect because it is at a point where there will be no rotation of the pedals. The other choices are incorrect.

8. **(4)** Assuming that neither skate will stick on the floor as it rolls, the force applied by Boy X should cause both boys to move; because they are facing each other, they will each move backward.

9. **(3)** If Boy X locks his skates by turning his foot, all the force applied by Boy Y will move him backward.

10. **(4)** The basketball would possess potential energy because of its position above the floor. If she dropped it or threw it, it would possess kinetic energy, but she didn't. Choices (3) and (4) are not types of energy and choice (1) would create a very dangerous game.

11. **(2)** Because a mixture is made of two or more substances, each of which can be added in differing amounts, the properties of a mixture can vary from sample to sample. Choice (1) refers to pure substances and is a reminder to read passages carefully. The other choices are incorrect.

12. **(4)** The atom prefers a complete valence shell and, because metals usually have fewer electrons in that shell than nonmetals do, they lose them in an attempt to complete the valence or outer shell of electrons.

13. **(3)** The force holding the nucleus together is a nuclear force. The other choices are examples of forces but have nothing to do with the nucleus. This is one example when skimming the passage after reading the question might prove beneficial. The only force mentioned in the passage is nuclear force, which is the correct answer.

14. **(4)** Applying the brakes in a car creates a frictional force, which brings the car to a halt. Choice (1) seems possible, but it doesn't describe a force—it describes a position.

15. **(5)** The cell is the basic functional unit of life. This would be common knowledge from your basic science knowledge and reading.

16. **(3)** The passage states that viruses depend on the host cell to reproduce. Choice (1) may be correct but doesn't answer the question; choices (2) and (4) are wrong, and (5) does not answer the question. Always read the question carefully to make sure that the information given in the answer you choose answers the question. The information may be correct, but if it doesn't answer the question, it isn't the correct answer.

17. **(3)** Proteins are formed by amino acids linking together. The other choices are wrong, although some of them contain the words *amino acid.* Always read the choices carefully. Some may contain familiar words and still not answer the question or be wrong.

18. **(4)** Looking carefully at the diagram, you'll notice that the two forms differ in their configuration in space.

19. **(4)** Mendel hypothesized that there were two types of traits—dominant and recessive—which answers the question. The other choices are incorrect because both traits are not mentioned.

20. **(3)** Mendel said that the tall trait was dominant and, thus, would produce tall plants when bred with a short plant. This is a question that depends on your understanding of scientific vocabulary. If you understand the difference between *dominant* and *recessive,* the question is easy to answer; if you don't, it becomes very difficult. If you look carefully at the diagram, you'll see that all offspring plants contain both traits, but because the tall trait is dominant, they're all tall.

21. **(2)** Salmonella is an organism that can cause illness in humans, who are tertiary consumers. Washing the lettuce doesn't always destroy the salmonella, and herbivores eat lettuce.

22. **(4)** Otters depend on snails as part of their diet. If there were no more snails, the otters would have to look for other sources of food.

23. **(5)** The best answer is that the experiment would have to be attempted. What is presented is a question that might lead to a hypothesis. The hypothesis could lead to a series of investigations that might lead to an experimental design. Choices (2) and (4) are two of the questions that would have to be investigated but are not yet answers. Choice (3) is wrong because labs can be built in any size and choice (1) is too optimistic to be a real answer.

24. **(4)** According to the passage, the scientist would start with genetic material from the donor. Choice (1) is the process used, and choice (5) is what is used later to stimulate cell division in the egg. Choice (3) is the first two words in SCNT and is incorrect as well as incomplete.

25. **(3)** The cells group together to form tissues and then organs.

26. **(2)** According to Skinner, rewarding the dog will increase the chances of the dog coming when called. Choices (1), (4), and (5) are cruel and wouldn't work. Choice (3) will just wear out the owner and probably amuse the dog.

27. **(3)** The graph shows an increase in pecking behavior with the passage of time as the bird is rewarded for pecking. Choices (1) and (5) are wrong. There is nothing to suggest whether the bird is hungry.

28. **(5)** It is difficult to teach someone *not* to do something—according to Skinner, the reward increases the likelihood of the organism repeating an action. Joan and Henry are trying to get their son not to do something, which is decreasing the likelihood of an event. They have to find another way. Choice (1) might work but is unlikely and doesn't follow from any of the material presented. Choices (2) and (3) are cruel, and choice (4) is almost impossible because you would have to spend most of the day watching the child and giving him rewards for doing other things, which would probably just confuse the child.

29. **(3)** Pushing the lever when the green light comes on produces food for the rat, which is a reward for pushing the lever at the appropriate time and would increase the frequency of doing so at the right time.

30. **(4)** Tall plants are more likely to thrive and reproduce than short plants are.

31. **(5)** According to the passage, metabolism is collectively all the chemical reactions taking place in the body. Choices (1) and (2) are types of reactions, and choices (3) and (4) are examples of reactions that take place in the body. You often can understand scientific vocabulary by looking for clues in the sentence or passage. In this case, metabolism is defined in the passage.

32. (4) This answer is a summary of the first part of the passage.

33. (5) This question is a negative one (it asks for what enzyme activity is NOT affected by). The first four choices are factors that do affect enzyme activity. The correct answer is none of the above.

34. (1) The passage states that all living organisms are composed of cells. Choices (2), (3), and (4) are incorrect but may sound plausible if you just skimmed the passage.

35. (4) DNA passes on hereditary information from cell to cell. The other choices, except for choice (5), might make sense except that they are wrong. Choice (5) is just wrong.

36. (3) Sometimes a scientific word can be understood if you look at the parts of it. *Uni* means one; thus, *unicellular* means having one cell. When you meet an unfamiliar word on the science test, try to see if you understand any part of the word and make an educated guess from that.

37. (4) According to the passage, the instructions for the characteristics of the offspring are contained in the DNA of both parents. Choices (1) and (3) are partially correct, but choice (4) is more accurate and complete. Always look for a complete answer supported by the passage. Choice (2) is an interesting opening for an argument about environment but has nothing to do with the passage. Choice (5) may be interesting, but it has nothing to do with the passage or the question.

38. (2) The Remora's food and protection are provided by the shark. Choice (4) is wrong because the Remora feeds off the remnants of the shark's meals. If the Remora were not there, the excess food would just remain in the ocean for other organisms to eat, but the shark does not directly feed the Remora. Choices (1), (3), and (5) are wrong and have no basis in the passage or in fact.

39. (4) A fission reaction can continue without outside help because it produces the free neutrons needed to continue by the reaction itself.

40. (2) The shock absorber absorbs the forces created by the irregularities in the road. Choice (1) is partially correct, but nothing is mentioned about shock absorbers. A spring does not create forces (choice 3), and bouncing back and forth (choice 4) would make the ride of the car worse. Choice (5), while true, does not answer the question about how the strut works. Always read the question and choices carefully to make sure that you're answering the question correctly.

41. (4) A spring can change its shape and then restore itself. The car spring absorbs irregularities in the road by compressing and changing its shape, but then the energy present through the change in shape acts upon the spring to restore it to its original shape.

42. (3) The springs in the car smooth out the ride by absorbing the forces presented by the road.

43. (3) Photovoltaic cells have the ability to convert the energy from the sun into electricity. One hint, aside from the context of the passage, is that *photo* refers to light and *voltaic* refers to electricity. Choice (2) is a good idea, but it would take time to implement and the question refers to *now*.

44. (4) Offering subsidies to people usually increases the number of people who buy into a particular project. Photovoltaic cells are expensive; subsidies help defray the cost. Choices (1) and (5) would make sense in the long run but don't answer the question. Choices (2) and (3) are impractical in this economic climate.

45. (4) According to the diagram, photosynthesis is the production of oxygen from energy and carbon dioxide, and respiration and decay lead to carbon dioxide.

46. **(5)** According to the passage, a planet struck the surface of the Earth releasing a hunk of the surface, which flew into space to form the moon. The other choices may sound plausible if you haven't read the passage. The answer to the question is always included in the passage and other illustrative material if present.

47. **(4)** The closest answer to the question is choice (4). The others may sound reasonable or semi-reasonable, but the only one mentioned in the passage is choice (4), and the answer must be based on the passage.

48. **(3)** Because none of us was present at the beginning, we have to go by the theories of scientists who agree that the universe was formed from nothing initially.

49. **(4)** A volcano that has erupted in the last 10,000 years is considered active by scientists. Choices (2) and (3) might be correct from a layperson's point of view, but the scientific view supports choice (4).

50. **(1)** The diagram shows carbon dioxide being emitted into the atmosphere by automobiles and factories. If this amount were to be reduced, it would reduce the amount of carbon dioxide in the atmosphere. It would take a dramatic reduction of all forms of carbon dioxide emissions to interfere with photosynthesis (4).

Answer Sheet

1 ① ② ③ ④ ⑤
2 ① ② ③ ④ ⑤
3 ① ② ③ ④ ⑤
4 ① ② ③ ④ ⑤
5 ① ② ③ ④ ⑤
6 ① ② ③ ④ ⑤
7 ① ② ③ ④ ⑤
8 ① ② ③ ④ ⑤
9 ① ② ③ ④ ⑤
10 ① ② ③ ④ ⑤
11 ① ② ③ ④ ⑤
12 ① ② ③ ④ ⑤
13 ① ② ③ ④ ⑤
14 ① ② ③ ④ ⑤
15 ① ② ③ ④ ⑤
16 ① ② ③ ④ ⑤
17 ① ② ③ ④ ⑤
18 ① ② ③ ④ ⑤
19 ① ② ③ ④ ⑤
20 ① ② ③ ④ ⑤

21 ① ② ③ ④ ⑤
22 ① ② ③ ④ ⑤
23 ① ② ③ ④ ⑤
24 ① ② ③ ④ ⑤
25 ① ② ③ ④ ⑤
26 ① ② ③ ④ ⑤
27 ① ② ③ ④ ⑤
28 ① ② ③ ④ ⑤
29 ① ② ③ ④ ⑤
30 ① ② ③ ④ ⑤
31 ① ② ③ ④ ⑤
32 ① ② ③ ④ ⑤
33 ① ② ③ ④ ⑤
34 ① ② ③ ④ ⑤
35 ① ② ③ ④ ⑤
36 ① ② ③ ④ ⑤
37 ① ② ③ ④ ⑤
38 ① ② ③ ④ ⑤
39 ① ② ③ ④ ⑤
40 ① ② ③ ④ ⑤

Time: 65 minutes

40 questions

Directions: Choose the best answer to each question.

Questions 1 through 6 refer to Walt Whitman's poem "O Captain! My Captain" (1918).

What Happens to the Captain?

O Captain! my Captain! Our fearful trip is done,
The ship has weather'd every rack, the prize we sought is won,
The port is near, the bells I hear, the people all exulting,
While follow eyes the steady keel, the vessel grim and daring;
But O heart! Heart! Heart!
O the bleeding drops of red.
Where on the deck my Captain lies,
Fallen cold and dead.
O Captain! My Captain! Rise up and hear the bells,
Rise up—for you the flag is flung—for you the bugle trills,
For you bouquets and ribbon'd wreaths—for you the shores a-crowding
For you they call, the swaying mass, their eager faces turning;
Here Captain! dear father!
This arm beneath your head!
It is some dream that on the deck,
You've fallen cold and dead.
My Captain does not answer, his lips are pale and still,
My father does not feel my arm, he has no pulse nor will,
My ship is anchor'd safe and sound, its voyage closed and done,
From fearful trip the victor ship comes in with object won;
Exult O shores, and ring O bells!
But I with mournful tread,
Walk the deck my Captain lies,
Fallen cold and dead.

1. How do we know the trip was successful?

   (1) Our fearful trip is done.
   (2) The ship has weathered every rack.
   (3) The port is near.
   (4) The vessel is grim and daring.
   (5) The prize we sought is won.

2. What has the captain done in the poem?

   (1) He has exulted.
   (2) He has waved the flags.
   (3) He has rung the bells.
   (4) He has fallen to the deck.
   (5) He has risen up.

331

3. How do the people celebrate the ship's arrival?

   (1) With bouquets and wreaths
   (2) With crowded shores
   (3) With trilling bugles
   (4) With eager faces
   (5) All of the above

4. How does the speaker primarily relate himself to the captain?

   (1) As the captain's brother.
   (2) As the captain's friend.
   (3) As the captain's son.
   (4) As the captain's crewmate.
   (5) As the captain's sponsor.

5. What phrase does NOT refer to the captain's condition?

   (1) Bleeding drops of red
   (2) Anchor'd safe and sound
   (3) Lips are pale and still
   (4) No pulse nor will
   (5) Doesn't feel my arm

6. Which adjective best describes the tone of the poem?

   (1) Exalted
   (2) Fearful
   (3) Mournful
   (4) Victorious
   (5) Swaying

Questions 7 through 11 refer to the following excerpt from George Bernard Shaw's play "Major Barbara" (1905).

Why Is Undershaft Interested in the Salvation Army?

UNDERSHAFT: One moment, Mr. Lomax. I am rather interested in the Salvation Army. Its motto might be my own. Blood and Fire.

LOMAX: *(shocked)* But not your sort of blood and fire, you know.

UNDERSHAFT: My sort of blood cleanses: my sort of fire purifies.

BARBARA: So does ours. Come down tomorrow to my shelter—the West Ham Shelter—and see what we are doing. We're going to march to a great meeting in the Assembly at Mile End. Come and see the shelter and then march with us. It will do you a lot of good. Can you play anything?

UNDERSHAFT: In my youth I earned pennies, and even shillings occasionally, in the streets and in public house parlors by my natural talent for step dancing. Later on, I became a member of the Undershaft Orchestra Society, and performed passably on the tenor trombone.

LOMAX: *(scandalized, putting down the concertina)* Oh I say!

BARBARA: Many a sinner has played himself into heaven on the trombone, thanks to the Army.

LOMAX: *(to Barbara, still rather shocked)* Yes; but what about the cannon business, don't you know? *(to Undershaft)* Getting into heaven is not exactly in your line, is it?

LADY BRITOMART: Charles!!!

LOMAX: Well; but it stands to reason, don't it? The cannon business may be necessary and all that; we can't get along without cannons; but it isn't right, you know. On the other hand, there may be a certain amount of tosh about the Salvation Army—I belong to the Established Church myself—but still you can't deny that it's religion, and you can't go against religion, can you? At least unless you're downright immoral, don't you know?

7. Why did Barbara invite Undershaft to the shelter?

    (1) To earn pennies
    (2) To attend a great meeting
    (3) To march in the band
    (4) To step-dance
    (5) To be with them in the Assembly

8. What does step-dancing for pennies tell you about Undershaft?

    (1) He has natural talent.
    (2) He frequented public houses.
    (3) He was a skilled musician.
    (4) He performed passably.
    (5) He had an impoverished youth.

9. What can Undershaft contribute to the march?

    (1) Trombone playing
    (2) Pennies
    (3) Shillings
    (4) Step dancing
    (5) Natural talent

10. How would you describe Lomax's treatment of Undershaft?

  (1) Friendly
  (2) Critical
  (3) Encouraging
  (4) Philosophical
  (5) Bitter

11. Why might Undershaft's motto be "Blood and Fire"?

  (1) He doesn't belong to the Established Church.
  (2) He plays the trombone.
  (3) He is a sinner.
  (4) He makes cannons.
  (5) He marches for the Salvation Army.

Questions 12 through 15 refer to the following excerpt from Jack London's short story "In a Far Country" (1899).

Who Were the Complainers?

The two shirks and chronic grumblers were Carter Weatherbee and Percy Cuthfert. The whole party complained less of its aches and pains than did either of them. Not once did they volunteer for the thousand and one petty duties of the camp. A bucket of water to be brought, an extra armful of wood to be chopped, the dishes to be washed and wiped, a search to be made through the outfit for some suddenly indispensable article—and these two effete scions of civilization discovered sprains or blisters requiring instant attention. They were the first to turn in at night, with scores of tasks yet undone; the last to turn out in the morning, when the start should be in readiness before the breakfast was begun. They were the first to fall to at meal-time, the last to have a hand in the cooking; the first to dive for a slim delicacy, the last to discover they had added to their own another man's share. If they toiled at the oars, they slyly cut the water at each stroke and allowed the boat's momentum to float up the blade. They thought nobody noticed; but their comrades swore under their breaths and grew to hate them, while Jacques Baptiste sneered openly and damned them from morning till night. But Jacques Baptiste was no gentleman.

12. How does this author describe Weatherbee and Cuthfert?

  (1) Eager volunteers
  (2) Drawers of water
  (3) Choppers of wood
  (4) Shirks and grumblers
  (5) Washers of dishes

13. How did Weatherbee and Cuthfert avoid work?

  (1) By developing sprains or blisters
  (2) By being the first to turn in
  (3) By being the last to turn out
  (4) By being the last to have a hand
  (5) All of the above

14. How did the rest of the party feel about the two men?

   (1) They admired them.
   (2) They hated them.
   (3) They encouraged them.
   (4) They laughed at them.
   (5) They enjoyed their company.

15. Which adjective best describes Weatherbee and Cuthfert?

   (1) Dishonest
   (2) Helpful
   (3) Lazy
   (4) Weak
   (5) Strong

Questions 16 through 20 refer to the following policy document.

What Is Our Health and Safety Policy?

The management of Can-Learn International is vitally interested in the health and safety of its employees. Protection of employees from injury or occupational disease is a major continuing objective. Can-Learn International will make every effort to provide a safe, healthy work environment. All supervisors and workers must be dedicated to the continuing objective of reducing risk of injury.

Can-Learn International, as an employer, is ultimately responsible for worker health and safety. As President of Can-Learn International, I give you my personal promise that every reasonable precaution will be taken for the protection of workers.

The Occupational Health and Safety Act, which sets the standards for safe workplaces, is based on the internal responsibility system. This is a system of overlapping and concurrent duties of the employer, officers, directors, supervisors, and workers of Can-Learn International.

Supervisors will be held accountable for the health and safety of workers under their supervision. Supervisors are responsible for ensuring that machinery and equipment are safe and that workers work in compliance with established safe work practices and procedures. Workers must receive adequate training in their specific work tasks to protect their health and safety.

Every worker must protect his or her own health and safety by working in compliance with the law and with safe work practices and procedures established by Can-Learn International.

It is in the best interest of all parties to consider health and safety in every activity. Commitment to health and safety must form an integral part of this organization, from the president to the workers.

16. Who, within the company, is most interested in the health and safety of employees?

   (1) The workers
   (2) The union
   (3) The executive
   (4) The management
   (5) The company

17. What is the objective of the policy?

    (1) To increase profitability
    (2) To increase productivity
    (3) To have a safe and healthy workplace
    (4) To foster better labor relations
    (5) All of the above

18. Who is responsible for the safe operation of machinery?

    (1) The president
    (2) The supervisors
    (3) The directors
    (4) The officers
    (5) The workers

19. How can worker health and safety be protected?

    (1) By being trained adequately
    (2) By engaging in a responsibility system
    (3) By having concurrent duties
    (4) By complying with the law
    (5) By being held accountable

20. What sets the standards for a safe workplace?

    (1) The Internal Responsibility System
    (2) Can-Learn International
    (3) The federal government
    (4) The Occupational Health and Safety Act
    (5) The Workers Compensation Act

Questions 21 through 26 refer to an excerpt from John Masefield's military history The Old Front Line *(1917).*

What Was the View from the Trenches?

All that can be seen of it from the English line is a disarrangement of the enemy wire and parapet. It is a hole in the ground which cannot be seen except from quite close at hand. At first sight, on looking into it, it is difficult to believe that it was the work of man; it looks so like nature in her evil mood. It is hard to imagine that only three years ago that hill was cornfield, and the site of the chasm grew bread. After that happy time, the enemy bent his line there and made the salient a stronghold, and dug deep shelters for his men in the walls of his trenches; the marks of the dugouts are still plain in the sides of the pit. Then, on the 1st of July, when the explosion was to be a signal for the attack, and our men waited in the trenches for the spring, the belly of the chalk was heaved, and chalk, clay, dugouts, gear, and enemy, went up in a dome of blackness full of pieces, and spread aloft like a toadstool, and floated, and fell down.

From the top of the Hawthorn Ridge, our soldiers could see a great expanse of chalk downland, though the falling of the hill kept them from seeing the enemy's position. That lay on the slope of the ridge, somewhere behind the wire, quite out of sight from our lines. Looking out from our front line at this salient, our men saw the enemy wire almost as a skyline. Beyond this line, the ground dipped towards Beaumont Hamel (which was quite out of sight in the valley) and rose again sharply in the steep bulk of Beaucourt spur. Beyond this lonely spur, the hills ranked and ran, like the masses of a moor, first the high ground above Miraumont, and beyond that the high ground of the Loupart Wood, and away to the east the bulk that makes the left bank of the Ancre River Valley made all that marshy meadow like a forest. Looking out on all this, the first thought of the soldier was that here he could really see something of the enemy's ground.

It is true, that from this hill-top much land, then held by the enemy, could be seen, but very little that was vital to the enemy could be observed. His lines of supply and support ran in ravines which we could not see; his batteries lay beyond crests, his men were in hiding places. Just below us on the lower slopes of this Hawthorn Ridge he had one vast hiding place which gave us a great deal of trouble. This was a gully or ravine, about five hundred yards long, well within his position, running (roughly speaking) at right angles with his front line. Probably it was a steep and deep natural fold made steeper and deeper by years of cultivation. It is from thirty to forty feet deep, and about as much across at the top; it has abrupt sides, and thrusts out two forks to its southern side. These forks give it the look of a letter *Y* upon the maps, for which reason both the French and ourselves called the place the "Ravin en Y" or "Y Ravine." Part of the southernmost fork was slightly open to observation from our lines; the main bulk of the gully was invisible to us, except from the air.

21. What is all that can be seen from the English line?

   (1) A cornfield
   (2) An abandoned mine shaft
   (3) A dome of blackness
   (4) A disarrangement of the enemy wire and parapet
   (5) Enemy weapons

22. Why could the soldiers not see the enemy's position?

    (1) The enemy had retreated.
    (2) The falling of the hill obstructed their vision.
    (3) Trees were in the way.
    (4) The enemy was too far away.
    (5) It was too dark.

23. Why would it be important to be able to observe the enemy's supply and support routes?

    (1) The soldiers were curious.
    (2) It was important to be able to see what activities the enemy was carrying on.
    (3) Knowledge about the enemy's personal habits is important to a soldier.
    (4) The commanding officer might want to report the activities to headquarters.
    (5) Cutting off the enemy's supplies and support would weaken them.

24. Why would the gully be called Y Ravine by the soldiers?

    (1) The gully looked like a *Y* on a map.
    (2) The gully before it had been named X Ravine.
    (3) Soldiers like to give geographical features familiar names.
    (4) The enemy commander's name started with *Y*.
    (5) It was a private joke among the soldiers.

25. From this passage, how would you describe the conditions on the battlefield?

    (1) Placid
    (2) Interesting
    (3) Difficult
    (4) Messy
    (5) Quiet

Questions 26 through 31 refer to an excerpt from Criminology For Dummies, *by Steven Briggs, copyright 2009 by Wiley Publishing, Inc. Reprinted with permission of John Wiley & Sons, Inc.*

How Do You Make Punishments Fit the Crime?

In 2006, former Enron CEO Jeffrey Skilling was convicted of securities fraud and conspiracy, among other charges, and was sentenced to over 24 years in prison. (You didn't think I could talk about white-collar crime without mentioning Enron, did you?) For many people in the corporate world, this case was a signal event, marking a change in historic sentencing practices for white-collar criminals.

Previously, most people probably believed that the more common treatment of white-collar criminals resembled what Martha Stewart received for her convictions in 2004: five months in a federal "country club" and five months of home detention.

This common viewpoint is important because one significant reason why society imprisons criminals is to deter other people from committing similar crimes. If the risk of serious punishment isn't real, people may be more likely to run the risk of conviction, especially when the payoff is millions of dollars in profit.

But there are legitimate reasons why white-collar criminals have received relatively light sentences in the past. Perhaps most importantly, such cases are often very difficult to prove. Sometimes law enforcement agencies make plea agreements to resolve cases instead of committing massive resources to lengthy and costly trials that may have uncertain outcomes. In addition, white-collar crimes often involve significant financial harm to victims, so prosecutors may be willing to negotiate away jail time in exchange for making the defendant pay money back to victims.

Sometimes the prosecutor doesn't agree to a short jail sentence, but the judge imposes the sentence on her own. One significant theory of punishment holds that jail or prison should be reserved only for people too dangerous to remain in society. The argument goes that, because white-collar criminals usually commit financial crimes, society shouldn't spend a lot of money incarcerating them. Instead, jails should house people who are violent risks to society. Judges who subscribe to this theory may also believe that the damage to the professional reputation of a white-collar criminal is sufficient punishment in itself, without sentencing the criminal to a lengthy prison sentence.

26. What was Jeff Skilling convicted of in 2006?

    (1) Impersonation
    (2) Securities fraud
    (3) Blue-collar crime
    (4) False pretenses
    (5) All of the above

27. Which sentence did Skilling receive?

    (1) More than 10 months
    (2) More than 25 years
    (3) More than 5 months
    (4) More than 24 years
    (5) More than 24 months

28. Where did Martha Stewart NOT serve her sentence?

(1) In a penitentiary
(2) In a federal "country club"
(3) In home detention
(4) In a correctional facility
(5) In a rehab center

29. According to the passage, what is one reason society imprisons criminals?

(1) To fight crime
(2) To punish criminals
(3) To deter others
(4) To gain a payoff
(5) All of the above

30. Why have white-collar criminals received light sentences?

(1) Because their crimes are difficult to prove
(2) Because they make plea bargains
(3) To avoid costly trials
(4) To seek restitution
(5) All of the above

31. Whom should lengthy sentences be reserved for?

(1) Financial criminals
(2) Violent risks
(3) Those with professional reputations
(4) Those who receive sufficient punishment
(5) Repeat offenders

Questions 32 through 36 refer to the following excerpt from the short story "Patricia" by Murray Shukyn (2010).

What Was Patricia's Defense?

Patricia walks into the room. Furtively, she looks around, goes to the window and peers into the darkness. Relieved at what she doesn't see, she quickly leaves the room. Returning with a bright object in her hand, she places the nickel-plated revolver on the table, carefully inserts six bullets into the cylinder, clicks it shut, and nervously replaces it on the table at the ready.

Never again will she be a victim. Never again will that drunken lout strike her. Never again will she have to plaster makeup on herself to hide the bruises and welts resulting from a "discussion" with her live-in boyfriend.

Before he left, he gave her a preview of what was to come, and the stinging pain was all too fresh in her mind. She stared at her solution glistening in the light of the lamp, enticing her to pick it up just to feel the justice in the metal.

As she reached for it, she saw the headlights in the driveway. Her finger closed on the trigger as the door opened.

Never, ever again, she promised herself.

32. How would you characterize Patricia's state of mind as she waits?

    (1) Tranquil
    (2) Impatient
    (3) Determined
    (4) Curious
    (5) Stubborn

33. Why is the word *discussion* in quotation marks?

    (1) Patricia's boyfriend said, "discussion."
    (2) The author wants to emphasize the talks Patricia and her boyfriend had.
    (3) A discussion would not produce bruises and welts.
    (4) It describes the exchange of words between them.
    (5) No indication in the passage.

34. What effect did the preview referred to in paragraph 3 have on Patricia?

    (1) It made her look forward to the continuation of the discussion.
    (2) It made her want to go shopping for new shoes.
    (3) It had no effect. She just patiently waited for his return.
    (4) It gave her time to polish her revolver.
    (5) It made her determined to stop the cycle of abuse.

35. When did she reach for the revolver?

    (1) Just before she saw the car approaching the house
    (2) When the door opened
    (3) When she entered the room the first time
    (4) Immediately when she entered the room the second time.
    (5) When her boyfriend approached her

36. Why did Patricia promise herself, "Never, ever again"?

    (1) She was uncomfortable when her boyfriend went out alone.
    (2) The headlights coming up the driveway disturbed her sleep.
    (3) She didn't like to interrupt conversations.
    (4) She had had enough abuse and wanted it stopped.
    (5) She wanted her boyfriend to be nice to her.

Questions 37 through 40 refer to an excerpt from the novel "All You Can Eat" by Murray Shukyn (2008).

What Are Banks For?

This time I had to enter the bank and wait in line. The line was not too long, and I relaxed, looking at the poster decorating the wall. The interior of the bank was stark. There was one poster on every wall that didn't have an opening in it. Walls with doors or windows were bare. The tellers hid behind this huge counter with computers at each location. In front of the counter was a serpentine lineup device that made you cross parallel to the counter several times before arriving at the opening when you came face to face with a teller. It looked so sturdy that I just walked back and forth in front of the counter like a demented wanderer until I came to the end of the line. Within minutes, a young teller said, "Next," and it was my turn to do business with the bank.

"What can I do for you today," teller Jon inquired.

"I lost my bank card," I said.

"I'm sorry to hear that," Jon chirped in.

"I need a new one," I answered.

"That makes sense," Jon added.

"What do I have to do to get one?" I asked.

"Let's see if you're known to this branch," he said, going over to one of the side offices and returning with a frown on his face. "Sorry, no one at the branch knows you."

"I've been dealing here for years," I said, getting slightly annoyed.

"But how often do you come inside the branch?" Jon asked.

"Oh, this is the first time," I said. "I use the ATM and the Internet."

"But those don't require real people. If everyone did that, I would be out of a job. Do you want me to be unemployed?" Jon asked.

"No, of course not. I just want a replacement bank card," I said. "The person at the call center said that you would give me one."

"Of course, they would. Do you know where this bank's call center is located? What do they know about what happens in a branch halfway around the world?" Jon said, slightly peeved.

"I just want to get a new bank card so that I can take money out of my account and take my girlfriend for coffee," I said.

"Some big spender. Why don't you take her out to dinner? There's this fabulous restaurant right around the corner. They do all their banking here. Come right up to the counter, call me by name, and carry on their business. Everyone knows them," Jon said.

37. Why would the narrator wander back and forth in front of the counter before speaking to a teller?

   (1) He was nervous.
   (2) He was waiting for his favorite teller.
   (3) All the tellers were busy.
   (4) The lineup was controlled by a serpentine device.
   (5) He liked to pace about.

38. Why did the narrator have to go to the bank?

    (1) To get a new passbook
    (2) To make a deposit
    (3) To make a withdrawal
    (4) To cash a check
    (5) To get a new bank card

39. Why did Jon like the people from the restaurant right around the corner?

    (1) They come into the bank and call Jon by his name.
    (2) They serve good food.
    (3) Their prices are reasonable.
    (4) They bring Jon lunch when it's very busy.
    (5) They're Jon's relatives.

40. Why would Jon be peeved about the location of the call center?

    (1) Jon applied for a job at the call center.
    (2) The call center is understaffed because of where it's located.
    (3) It's located halfway around the world.
    (4) Jon's manager likes call centers.
    (5) Jon is jealous of people who work in distant places.

IF YOU FINISH BEFORE TIME IS CALLED, CHECK YOUR WORK ON THIS SECTION ONLY. DO NOT WORK ON ANY OTHER SECTION IN THE TEST.

Answer Key

1. (5)	11. (4)	21. (4)	31. (2)
2. (4)	12. (4)	22. (2)	32. (3)
3. (5)	13. (5)	23. (5)	33. (3)
4. (3)	14. (2)	24. (1)	34. (5)
5. (2)	15. (3)	25. (3)	35. (1)
6. (3)	16. (4)	26. (2)	36. (4)
7. (3)	17. (3)	27. (4)	37. (4)
8. (5)	18. (2)	28. (5)	38. (5)
9. (1)	19. (1)	29. (3)	39. (1)
10. (2)	20. (4)	30. (5)	40. (3)

Answer Explanations

1. **(5)** *The prize we sought is won* is the best answer to the question. *Weathered every rack* and *grim and daring* refer to the ship. *Fearful trip* and *port is near* don't answer the question.

2. **(4)** The poem tells us that the captain has fallen to the deck. He certainly isn't exulting, waving flags, ringing bells, or rising up.

3. **(5)** Choices (1) through (4) all refer to the celebration of the ship's arrival.

4. **(3)** According to the poem, the captain is the speaker's father. The other choices are incorrect.

5. **(2)** The phrase *anchor'd safe and sound* refers to the ship, not the captain.

6. **(3)** The adjective that best describes the tone of the poem is *mournful* because, although the voyage has been successful, the captain has lost his life.

7. **(3)** Barbara was recruiting players for her marching band and saw Undershaft as a candidate. The other answer choices (attending a meeting, earning pennies, step-dancing, and being in the Assembly) don't express her interest in Undershaft.

8. **(5)** You know Undershaft had an impoverished youth because he had to step-dance for pennies to survive. During this time, poor children danced as entertainment for people who might throw them pennies. This way of living was a bit above begging in that the children provided some entertainment for the money donated.

9. **(1)** Undershaft was a trombone player who could contribute his musical talents to the marching band. Step-dancing, pennies, or shillings aren't contributions to the band. Natural musical talent could be a correct answer, but because a more specific answer exists, you need to rule out this one.

10. **(2)** Lomax criticizes Undershaft's work as a cannon manufacturer, implying that Undershaft won't get to heaven because of his work with cannons. Lomax may be bitter and he may be philosophical, but those words don't describe his treatment of Undershaft. *Friendly* and *encouraging* certainly don't describe Lomax's demeanor, either.

11. **(4)** Undershaft's motto could be "Blood and Fire" because he manufactures cannons used to kill people in war. Playing the trombone, being a sinner, belonging to the church, and marching aren't related to blood and fire.

12. **(4)** The author describes Weatherbee and Cuthfert as "shirks and chronic grumblers" in the very first sentence of the passage and then supports this description throughout the passages with examples. All the other choices are not used to describe the men.

13. **(5)** The author uses choices (1) through (4) to describe Weatherbee and Cuthfert's behavior to avoid work.

14. **(2)** Because of their behavior, the author tells us that the party hated the two men.

15. **(3)** According to the passage, the best adjective to describe the two men would be *lazy*. They also may have been dishonest and weak. Helpful and strong are incorrect choices.

16. **(4)** The document states that it's "the management" who is interested in the health and safety of employees. The other choices mentioned may feel the same way, but they aren't the best answers.

17. **(3)** The objective of the policy is to ensure a "safe, healthy work environment." Other choices are not relevant.

18. **(2)** The passage tells us that the supervisors have the major responsibility for the safe operation of machinery. The other choices—president, directors, officers, and workers—don't have direct responsibility.

19. **(1)** According to the passage, health and safety can be protected if the workers receive "adequate training." The other choices are not best answers.

20. **(4)** The standards are set by the Occupation and Health Safety Act. The other choices are incorrect.

21. **(4)** The first line states this answer. Although (1) and (3) are mentioned, neither is the best answer to the question.

22. **(2)** The first sentence of the second paragraph outlines the answer. The other choices are not mentioned in the passage.

23. **(5)** In a battle, each side would want to prevent the other side from replenishing supplies and getting reinforcements. The other choices might be interesting, but none is the best answer to the question.

24. **(1)** The passage states that the ravine or gully looked like a *Y* on the map. The other choices are incorrect.

25. **(3)** According to the passage, battlefield conditions must have been difficult. Choices (1), (2), and (5) are wrong, and (4) is not the best answer.

26. **(2)** The passage states that Skilling was convicted of "securities fraud." The other choices are not found in the passage.

27. **(4)** According to the passage, Skilling received a sentence of more than 24 years.

28. **(5)** Martha Stewart did not serve her sentence in a rehab center. The other choices might be used to identify where she did serve her time.

29. **(3)** The passage states that society imprisons criminals to deter crime. Society may imprison criminals to fight crime and to punish, but these aren't best answers.

30. **(5)** In the passage, choices (1) through (4) are given as reasons for light sentences.

31. **(2)** Lengthy sentences should be reserved for people who are "violent risks" to society. Repeat offenders might also be considered, but these criminals aren't mentioned.

32. **(3)** From the description of her feelings in the passage, especially in the last line, it is clear that Patricia was determined. Choices (2) and (5) may have been part of her state of mind at one time or another, but there is no indication of that in the passage. Choices (1) and (4) are incorrect.

33. **(3)** The interaction between Patricia and her boyfriend must have been violent to produce bruises and welts.

34. **(5)** The preview made her determined to stop it in any way that she could. The other four choices might have been acceptable in another passage, but they have little relationship to this one.

35. **(1)** Patricia reached for the revolver before she saw the headlights. The other situations may be part of the passage but are not the best answer to the question.

36. **(4)** Patricia had had enough of the abuse, as is indicated in the passage, and she wanted to end it forever.

37. **(4)** The lineup was controlled by a serpentine device according to the first paragraph in the passage. The other choices are not mentioned in the passage, although they might or might not be true. You must answer the questions using only the information in the passage.

38. **(5)** He had to go into the bank to replace his lost bank card. The other activities might take place in a bank but are not mentioned in the passage.

39. **(1)** In the passage, Jon, the teller, makes a point of saying that the people from the restaurant come into the branch and call him by name when they get to the counter.

40. **(3)** The call center is located halfway around the world and that peeves Jon, although the exact reason for this is not given in the passage. The remaining choices cannot be used for this question.

XVI. Mathematics Full-Length Practice Test with Answer Explanations

Answer Sheet

Part I

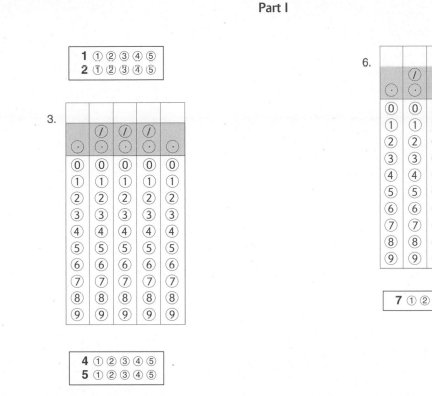

8.

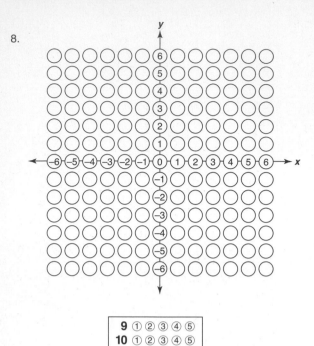

12.

	$\oslash$	$\oslash$	$\oslash$	
$\odot$	$\odot$	$\odot$	$\odot$	$\odot$
⓪	⓪	⓪	⓪	⓪
①	①	①	①	①
②	②	②	②	②
③	③	③	③	③
④	④	④	④	④
⑤	⑤	⑤	⑤	⑤
⑥	⑥	⑥	⑥	⑥
⑦	⑦	⑦	⑦	⑦
⑧	⑧	⑧	⑧	⑧
⑨	⑨	⑨	⑨	⑨

9 ① ② ③ ④ ⑤
10 ① ② ③ ④ ⑤
11 ① ② ③ ④ ⑤

13 ① ② ③ ④ ⑤
14 ① ② ③ ④ ⑤
15 ① ② ③ ④ ⑤
16 ① ② ③ ④ ⑤
17 ① ② ③ ④ ⑤
18 ① ② ③ ④ ⑤
19 ① ② ③ ④ ⑤
20 ① ② ③ ④ ⑤
21 ① ② ③ ④ ⑤
22 ① ② ③ ④ ⑤
23 ① ② ③ ④ ⑤
24 ① ② ③ ④ ⑤
25 ① ② ③ ④ ⑤

Part II

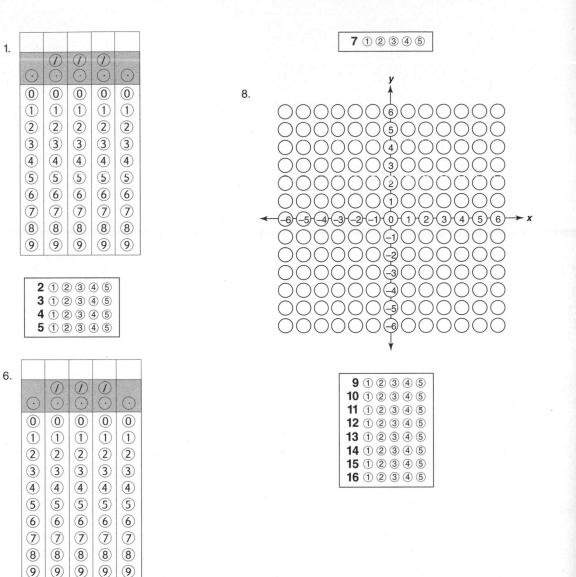

1.

2. ① ② ③ ④ ⑤
3. ① ② ③ ④ ⑤
4. ① ② ③ ④ ⑤
5. ① ② ③ ④ ⑤

6.

7. ① ② ③ ④ ⑤

8.

9. ① ② ③ ④ ⑤
10. ① ② ③ ④ ⑤
11. ① ② ③ ④ ⑤
12. ① ② ③ ④ ⑤
13. ① ② ③ ④ ⑤
14. ① ② ③ ④ ⑤
15. ① ② ③ ④ ⑤
16. ① ② ③ ④ ⑤

CUT HERE

17.

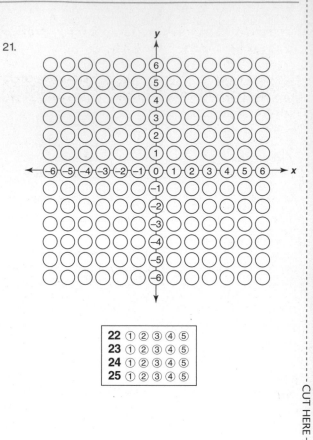

18 ① ② ③ ④ ⑤
19 ① ② ③ ④ ⑤
20 ① ② ③ ④ ⑤

21.

22 ① ② ③ ④ ⑤
23 ① ② ③ ④ ⑤
24 ① ② ③ ④ ⑤
25 ① ② ③ ④ ⑤

CUT HERE

For the GED Mathematics Test, you will be provided with a list of mathematical formulas for your reference, like the one provided here.

Formulas	
AREA of a: square rectangle parallelogram triangle trapezoid circle	Area = side^2 Area = length × width Area = base × height Area $=\frac{1}{2}\times$ base × height Area $=\frac{1}{2}\times\left(\text{base}_1+\text{base}_2\right)\times$ height Area $=\pi\times$ radius^2; π is approximately equal to 3.14
PERIMETER of a: square rectangle triangle	Perimeter = 4 × side Perimeter = (2 × length) + (2 × width) Perimeter = side$_1$ + side$_2$ + side$_3$
CIRCUMFERENCE of a circle	Circumference = π × diameter; π is approximately equal to 3.14
VOLUME of a: cube rectangular solid square pyramid cylinder cone	Volume = edge^3 Volume = length × width × height Volume $=\frac{1}{3}\times\left(\text{base edge}\right)^2\times$ height Volume $=\pi\times$ radius^2 × height; π is approximately equal to 3.14 Volume $=\frac{1}{3}\times\pi\times$ radius$^2\times$ height; π is approximately equal to 3.14
COORDINATE GEOMETRY	distance between points $=\sqrt{\left(x_2-x_1\right)^2+\left(y_2-y_1\right)^2}$; $\left(x_1,y_1\right)$ and $\left(x_2,y_2\right)$ are two points on a plane slope of a line $=\dfrac{y_2-y_1}{x_2-x_1}$; $\left(x_1,y_1\right)$ and $\left(x_2,y_2\right)$ are two points on the line
PYTHAGOREAN RELATIONSHIP	$a^2+b^2=c^2$; a and b are sides, and c is the hypotenuse of a right triangle
MEASURES OF CENTRAL TENDENCY	**mean** $=\dfrac{x_1+x_2+...+x_n}{n}$; where the xs are the values for which a mean is desired, and n is the total number of values for x **median** = the middle value of an odd number of ordered scores, and halfway between the two middle values of an even number of ordered scores
SIMPLE INTEREST	interest = principal × rate × time
DISTANCE	distance = rate × time
TOTAL COST	total cost = (number of units) × (price per unit)

For the GED Mathematics Test, you will be provided with a calculator to be used on Part I only of the GED Mathematics Test. The test site will also provide general calculator instructions, like the ones below.

Calculator Instructions

To prepare the calculator for use the first time, press the ON (upper-rightmost) key. "DEG" will appear at the top-center of the screen and "0" at the right. This indicates the calculator is in the proper format for all your calculations.

To prepare the calculator for another question, press the ON or the red AC key. This clears any entries made previously.

To do any arithmetic, enter the expression as it is written. Press = (equals sign) when finished.

EXAMPLE A: 8 – 3 + 9

First press ON or AC

Enter the following: 8 , – , 3 , + , 9 , =

The correct answer is 14.

If the expression in parentheses is to be multiplied by a number, press × (multiplication sign) between the number and the parenthesis sign.

EXAMPLE B: 6 (8 + 5)

First press ON or AC

Enter the following: 6 , × , (, 8 , + , 5 ,) , =

The correct answer is 78.

To find the square root of a number

* First enter the number.

* Next press the SHIFT (upper-leftmost) key ("SHIFT" appears at the top-left of the screen).

* Then press x^2 (third from the left on top row) to access its second function: square root.

DO NOT press SHIFT and x^2 at the same time.

EXAMPLE C: $\sqrt{64}$

First press ON or AC

Enter the following: 6 , 4 , SHIFT , x^2 , =

The correct answer is 8.

To enter a negative number, such as –8

* Enter the number without the negative sign (enter 8).

* Press the "change sign" (+/–) key, which is directly above the 7 key.

All arithmetic can be done with positive and/or negative numbers.

EXAMPLE D: –8 – (–5)

First press ON or AC

Enter the following: 8 , +/– , – 5 , +/– , =

The correct answer is –3.

Part I

Time: 45 minutes

25 questions

Directions: You may use a calculator on this part of the test. Choose one answer for each question. Mark your answers on the answer sheet provided. Completely fill in the bubble corresponding to the correct answer.

For the coordinate-plane grid, you may mark only one circle; the circle must represent an x and a y value, neither of which can be a decimal or a fraction.

For the standard grid, enter your answer in the columns in the top row (you can start in any column, provided that your entire answer can be entered), and completely fill in the bubble representing the character under each column. With this grid, no number can be negative, and fractions must be entered as decimals or improper fractions.

1. Sally was shopping for a flat-screen TV. She had set a budget of $900 for the set, delivery, and installation. As she shopped, she kept track of the prices in a table:

	Store A	Store B	Store C	Store D
Price	$1,200	$1,250	$1,500	$1,100
Discount	20%	30%	50%	10%
Delivery	$35	$0	$95	$0
Installation	$112.50	$0	$125	$0

Which store is offering Sally the best deal?

(1) Store A.
(2) Store B.
(3) Store C.
(4) Store D.
(5) All prices are the same.

2. Jan and Jean were very competitive friends. Jan announced that she was reading 398 pages of fiction each week. Jean said she could easily read $1\frac{1}{4}$ as many pages each week. Jan immediately challenged Jean to a battle of the books. How many pages per week would Jean have to read to win the challenge?
(1) 483
(2) 399
(3) 498
(4) 427
(5) 497

3. In a track-and-field event, the runners finished a race with the following times:

Runner	Time (seconds)
1	4.574
2	5.429
3	4.803
4	4.583
5	4.961

Enter the runner's winning time on the standard grid.

4. Herbert was concerned about the cost of operating his car. Because it was fairly new, his main concern was the cost of gasoline. He could document the distance he traveled each week and the number of gallons of gasoline he used for this distance, and he knew the cost of gasoline per gallon that week, but he couldn't figure out how to calculate his cost of fuel per week. What operations and in what order should Herbert use to estimate the cost of fuel per year for his car?

   (1) Multiply the cost of gasoline per gallon by the number of weeks in a year.
   (2) Divide the number of miles driven by 12 and multiply by the cost per gallon.
   (3) Add the number of miles driven to the cost of gasoline and divide by the number of gallons used.
   (4) Multiply the number of gallons per week used by the cost per gallon and then by 52.
   (5) Divide the miles traveled by the cost of a gallon of gasoline and multiply by the number of gallons used.

5. Don's son had problems learning to multiply. He tried memorizing the multiplication tables but still was frustrated. Don tried to help by explaining that multiplying was just an efficient way of performing another operation. Which operation did Don mean?

   (1) Addition
   (2) Subtraction
   (3) Division
   (4) Squaring
   (5) None of the above

6. Georgia won a contest in which she had to answer a skill-testing question before she was awarded the prize. The skill-testing question was

$$123 + 49 - 21 \times 8 \div 4 + 23 \times 2 =$$

Indicate the correct answer on the standard grid.

7. Herbert was trying to figure out how much carpeting he would need to cover the floor of the square living room of his small apartment. He estimated that he would need 156 square feet of carpet to cover the floor. If his room was 12.5 feet long, how many square feet would Herbert have needed if he had calculated the amount using a calculator?

   (1) 15.625
   (2) 156.25
   (3) 1,562.50
   (4) 15,625
   (5) 156,250

8. In the following diagram, where would side AC cross the x-axis if it were extended? Mark your answer on the coordinate plane grid.

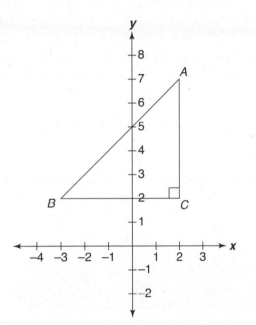

9. Find the length of the hypotenuse of the right-angled triangle ABC, where $\angle C = 90°$ and each side has an edge length as indicated in the diagram.

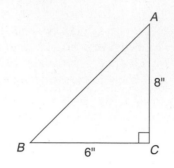

The length of AB, in inches, is:

(1) 36
(2) 64
(3) 10
(4) 12
(5) 100

10. Find the point where a line with slope 1 and y-intercept $(0, 4)$ intercepts a line through $P(4, 8)$ and $Q(-2, -1)$. What is the point of intersection?

(1) $(8, 4)$
(2) $(4, 8)$
(3) $(1, 4)$
(4) $(4, 1)$
(5) $(-4, -8)$

11. Ken wanted to carpet his apartment, except for the kitchen and bathroom. He summarized the size of the rooms in a table:

Room	Size (in feet)
Living room	20 × 18
Dining room	12 × 14
Bedroom	18 × 24
Hallways	10 × 3

The flooring store was having a sale, but only 115 square yards of the carpet Ken really wanted were left at the sale price. If Ken buys the 115 square yards of carpet, how many square yards of carpet will be left over when he is done?

(1) 10
(2) 5
(3) 7
(4) 15
(5) 2

12. If a plane could maintain an average speed of 575 miles per hour, how long would it take to fly the 2,444 miles between New York City and Los Angeles? Enter your answer correct to two decimal points on the standard grid.

13. The Smith family was considering buying a backyard swimming pool. The dimensions they settled on were 30 feet by 18 feet with an average depth of 3 feet. The salesperson told them that they would get substantially more room to swim by increasing the width by 12 feet. How much more surface area in square feet would they get by following the salesperson's suggestion?

    (1) 540
    (2) 900
    (3) 360
    (4) 450
    (5) 630

Questions 14–17 refer to the following table.

Percentage of 15+ Population Smoking Compared to Lung Cancer Death Rates (LCDR)				
Country	Males		Females	
	Smoker Prevalence (% Age 15+)	LCDR per 100,000 Smokers	Smoker Prevalence (% Age 15+)	LCDR per 100,000 Smokers
Austria	42	157.6	27	50.7
Finland	27	258.1	19	54.7
France	40	171.5	27	28.5
Germany	36.8	193.8	21.5	56.7
Israel	45	84.7	30	40.3
Japan	59	81.2	14.8	85.1
Norway	36.3	127.5	35.5	43.4
Portugal	38	107.1	15	45.3
Spain	48	143.8	25	21.6
Sweden	22	161.4	24	63.8
United States	28.1	305.7	23.5	157
Average	**38.4**	**162.9**	**23.8**	**58.8**

14. Looking at the table, which of the following are possible conclusions:

    (1) More smokers die of lung cancer in Finland than in any other country.
    (2) The fewest deaths among smokers are in Portugal.
    (3) The lowest percentage of 15+ female smokers is in Japan.
    (4) Over half the population 15+ in the United States smokes.
    (5) On average, 129.6 smokers per 100,000 die of lung cancer.

15. Which of the following graphs indicates that the lung cancer death rates for the selected countries are nearly equal?

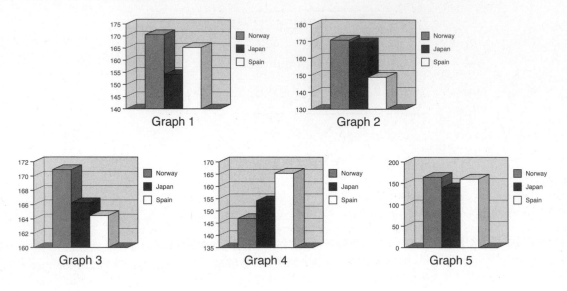

Graph 1

Graph 2

Graph 3

Graph 4

Graph 5

(1) Graph 1
(2) Graph 2
(3) Graph 3
(4) Graph 4
(5) Graph 5

16. If everyone in Austria quit smoking, how would that affect the average percentage of people over the age of 15 who smoked in France?

The average smoker prevalence of persons 15+ who smoked in France would

(1) Increase by 63.42%.
(2) Decrease by 4.78%.
(3) Remain the same.
(4) Decrease by 1.22%.
(5) Increase by 4.78%.

17. If the population of the United States age 15+ were 217,148,103, how many people age 15+ in the United States smoked? (Assume that the population is 50% female.)

(1) 14,028,419.75
(2) 56,024,210.57
(3) 62,418,092.36
(4) 10,857,405
(5) 42,412,078.75

18. Claudia's class of 34 students took a survey on likes and dislikes of dishes. The results produced the following table:

Type of Dish	Number of Positive Responses
Meat	25
Fish	12
Vegetarian	2
Stew	18
Pasta	12

What conclusion could be reached from these answers?

(1) People in Claudia's class were hungry.
(2) Most people surveyed preferred easy-to-prepare dishes.
(3) Pasta dishes received the most votes.
(4) Meat dishes were a favorite.
(5) Most people preferred dishes with meat or fish.

19. Donald surveyed the students in his high school on the recording artist they enjoyed listening to and came up with the following results:

Artist	Genre	Total Number of Votes
ABBA	Pop	68
The Beatles	Rock, pop	137
Elvis Presley	Rock, pop, country	119
Madonna	Pop	103
Michael Jackson	Pop, R&B, soul	146
Pink Floyd	Rock	87
Queen	Rock	74

Based on this limited survey, who are the most and least popular artists, respectively?

(1) Michael Jackson and the Beatles
(2) Elvis Presley and Pink Floyd
(3) ABBA and Queen
(4) ABBA and Michael Jackson
(5) Elvis Presley and the Beatles

20. Consider the equation, $y = mx + b$, where m is the slope and b is the y-intercept. What would be the result of substituting various values for b while keeping everything else the same?

    (1)   A sequence of lines all going through the same point

    (2)   A sequence of lines randomly scattered

    (3)   A sequence of parallel lines

    (4)   A sequence of perpendicular lines

    (5)   A sequence of lines intersecting in a point on the x-axis

21. If an algebraic expression for the Pythagorean theorem is $l = \sqrt{a^2 + b^2}$, where l is the length of the hypotenuse, and a and b are the lengths of the other two sides, what would be the length, to one decimal point, of a side of a right triangle with a hypotenuse of 23 and a second side of 16?

    (1)   529.5

    (2)   256.0

    (3)   165.9

    (4)   15.6

    (5)   16.5

22. In the formula $d = \dfrac{-b \pm \sqrt{b^2 - 4ac}}{2a}$, solve for d to one decimal place if $a = 4$, $b = 11$, and $c = 3$.

    (1)   25 or 195

    (2)   2.6 or 0.5

    (3)   −2.4 or −0.3

    (4)   4.2 or 0.3

    (5)   1.3 or 0.4

23. A technician setting up a rock concert sound system was told that the volume level decreases in inverse proportion to the distance from the stage according to the following equation $I = k\dfrac{1}{r}$, where I is the volume, k is a constant, and r is the distance from the source, $r > 0$. If the sound level at the stage was 100, what would it be 10 feet from the stage?

    (1)   10

    (2)   100

    (3)   0.1

    (4)   110

    (5)   Not enough information given

24. In the following graph, what general trend can you discern?

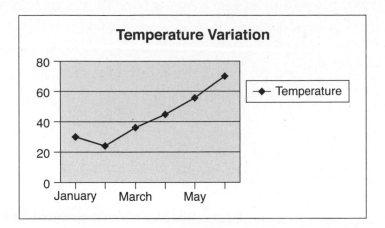

(1) The weather is nice in June.
(2) In general, the temperature rises toward summer.
(3) January is the coldest month.
(4) The least rainfall is in March.
(5) Not enough information given.

25. In the following equation, what would be the result of an increase in the value of F?

$$v - \frac{a}{ta} = F - \frac{v}{tv}$$

(1) The value of v would increase.
(2) The value of v would decrease.
(3) The value of v would remain the same.
(4) The value of v would be squared.
(5) The value of v would be one-half of t.

IF YOU FINISH BEFORE TIME IS CALLED, CHECK YOUR WORK ON THIS
SECTION ONLY. DO NOT WORK ON ANY OTHER SECTION IN THE TEST.

Part II

Time: 45 minutes

25 questions

Directions: You may NOT use a calculator for this part of the test. Choose one answer for each question. Mark your answers on the answer sheet provided. Completely fill in the bubble corresponding to the correct answer.

For the coordinate-plane grid, you may mark only one circle; the circle must represent an *x* and a *y* value, neither of which can be a decimal or a fraction.

For the standard grid, enter your answer in the columns in the top row (you can start in any column, provided that your entire answer can be entered), and completely fill in the bubble representing the character under each column. With this grid, no number can be negative, and fractions must be entered as decimals or improper fractions.

---

1. Enter the decimal equivalent of $\frac{1}{8}$ on the standard grid.

2. Alan was looking for a bargain in MP3 players. He passed by a store offering a 28% discount on an MP3 player priced at $49.99. How much would he save by buying the MP3 player at this store?

   (1) $12
   (2) $13
   (3) $14
   (4) $15
   (5) $16

3. If you put the following fractions in order from smallest to largest, which one would be in third place in order of increasing size?

$$\frac{1}{2}, \frac{1}{6}, \frac{1}{7}, \frac{1}{4}, \frac{1}{9}, \frac{1}{8}, \frac{1}{3}, \text{ and } \frac{1}{5}$$

   (1) $\frac{1}{2}$

   (2) $\frac{1}{4}$

   (3) $\frac{1}{7}$

   (4) $\frac{1}{8}$

   (5) $\frac{1}{6}$

4. If you wanted to calculate the volume of a rectangular fish tank to find out the maximum amount of water it would hold, what operation would you use?

   (1) Addition
   (2) Squaring
   (3) Subtraction
   (4) Exponents
   (5) Multiplication

5. If you calculated a result by multiplying a number by something and then adding to the product, what operations and in what order would you use to arrive back at the original number?

   (1) Divide and then subtract.
   (2) Subtract and then divide.
   (3) Subtract and then multiply.
   (4) Add and then subtract.
   (5) Add and then divide.

6. Calculate the value of $25 + 36 \times 11 + 243 - 199$. Enter your answer on the standard grid.

7. Tom needed to buy six new shirts, each of which cost $24.99. Approximately how much would he spend for the shirts?

   (1) $175
   (2) $200
   (3) $150
   (4) $120
   (5) $100

Question 8 refers to the following graph.

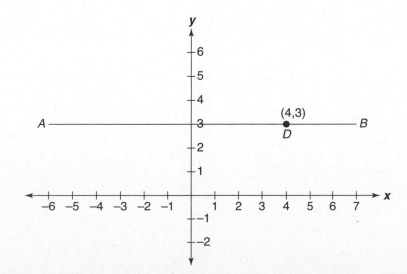

8. Mark the point where a line perpendicular to *AB* and passing through *D*(4, 3) would intersect the *x*-axis on a coordinate-plane grid.

9. How many faces does a standard die have?

   (1) 3
   (2) 4
   (3) 5
   (4) 6
   (5) 7

10. Write an equation for the line *AB* with a slope of $\frac{3}{5}$ and *y*-intercept (0, 8). The equation needed is $y = mx + b$, where *m* is the slope and *b* is the *y*-intercept, in the form $ax + by + c = 0$.

    (1) $5x + 3y - 40 = 0$

    (2) $3x - 5y + 40 = 0$

    (3) $3x + 5y + 8 = 0$

    (4) $5x - 3y + 40 = 0$

    (5) $5x - 3y - 8 = 0$

11. Sally has a contract to tile around a swimming pool 75 feet long and 28.5 feet wide. If each tile is 9 inches square, how many tiles will it take to go around the entire edge of the pool?

    (1) 276
    (2) 267
    (3) 280
    (4) 820
    (5) 290

12. Read the meter below. (Always round back to the lower number.)

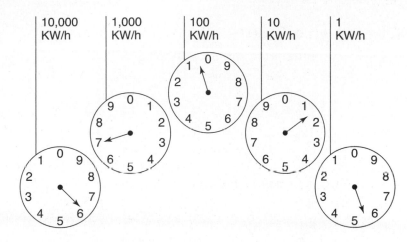

From the meter reading, calculate the total cost of electricity since the meter was installed and read all zeros, if electricity has cost 16¢ per kilowatt hour since the meter was installed.

(1) $67,016.08
(2) $10,722.40
(3) $17,072.26
(4) $10,272.56
(5) $12,756.26

13. Dawn has a large living room and can use either a 9-x-12-foot rug or a 10-x-14-foot rug. How much more floor, in square feet, will be covered by the larger rug?

(1) 140
(2) 32
(3) 108
(4) 23
(5) 36

14. The mathematics teacher made a graph to show the final averages in mathematics for the top seven students.

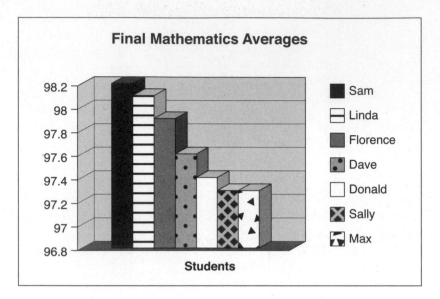

From the graph, what is the difference in average mark between the student who stood first and the one who stood fourth?

(1) 0.3
(2) 0.4
(3) 0.5
(4) 0.6
(5) 0.7

15. The following table details the dropout rate in the United States for the years from 2004 to 2009.

U.S. Dropout Rate, 2004–2009	
Year	Total (%)
2003	10.9
2004	9.8
2005	10.7
2006	9.4
2007	8.7
2008	8.6
2009	8.4

How would you describe the general trend shown in the table?

(1) A lot of students dropped out of school.
(2) School dropout rates have been increasing.
(3) School dropout rates have been steady.
(4) More students are staying in school each year.
(5) More students are looking for part-time work to stay in school.

Question 16 refers to the following table.

U.S. Unemployment Status (Ages 16 and Over)	
Year	Total (%)
2003	6.0
2004	5.5
2005	5.1
2006	4.6
2007	4.6
2008	5.8
2009	9.3

16. Considering the answer and information in question 15, what might be a conclusion about the relationship between unemployment rates and high school dropouts?

(1) As unemployment rises, dropout rates decrease.
(2) As unemployment falls, dropout rates decrease.
(3) As unemployment rises, dropout rates increase.
(4) As unemployment falls, dropout rates decrease.
(5) Not enough information given.

17. At a sales meeting, the monthly average salaries were posted for the top three salespeople. The summary is shown in the following table.

Monthly Average Salaries			
	Salesperson 1	**Salesperson 2**	**Salesperson 3**
January	$4,569	$5,082	$3,997
February	$4,802	$5,385	$4,001
March	$4,207	$5,293	$4,099
April	$4,978	$5,583	$4,378
May	$5,049	$5,997	$4,997
June	$6,003	$6,104	$5,006

By how many dollars would the lowest salesperson have had to increase his total monthly sales from July to September to exceed the top-selling salesperson's January-to-June sales by at least $1? Record your answer on the standard grid.

18. The ad for Car A claims that its highway mileage is 18.8 miles per gallon with diesel fuel. The ad for Car B claims that its highway mileage is 18.1 miles per gallon with regular gas; the ad claims that Car B is more economical. What conclusion would you reach?

(1) Car B is more economical.
(2) Car A is more economical.
(3) Both cars are equally efficient.
(4) Car B is a better car.
(5) Not enough information given.

Question 19 refers to the following table.

Name	Average Number of Pages Read Monthly
Loren	483
Frank	398
Saul	501
Rachel	529
Noah	473
Arden	388

19. How many more pages did the person who read the greatest average number of pages read than the average of all the people in the table?

(1) 76
(2) 62
(3) 64
(4) 67
(5) 66

20. Don drove 36 more miles than twice the number of miles that George drove. If you represented the number of miles driven by Don as D and the number of miles driven by George as G, what would the equation representing the statement be?

    (1) $D + 36 = G$

    (2) $G = 2D + 36$

    (3) $D = 2G + 36$

    (4) $D + G = 36$

    (5) $D + 2G = 36$

21. The formula of a line is $y = mx + b$. On the coordinate-plane grid, draw the point with the y-coordinate equal to 3 on the line having m equal to $\frac{5}{2}$ and b equal to 8.

22. Harry is eating from a giant ice cream cone and wonders how much his cone would hold if it were filled with ice cream to the brim. He measures the cone and finds it to be 3 inches across the top and 5 inches high. How many cubic inches of ice cream, to one decimal place, would the cone hold?

    (1) 11.6
    (2) 16.7
    (3) 18.1
    (4) 7.6
    (5) 11.8

23. Evaluate for K if $K = \dfrac{n}{r(n-r)}$, where $n = 12$ and $r = 8$.

    (1) $\dfrac{1}{2}$

    (2) $\dfrac{3}{8}$

    (3) $\dfrac{1}{4}$

    (4) $\dfrac{1}{12}$

    (5) $\dfrac{5}{8}$

24. Solve the following set of equations for y.

$$7x + 4y = 8$$
$$3x + 4y = 6$$

The value of y is:

(1) $\frac{8}{9}$

(2) $\frac{7}{8}$

(3) $\frac{9}{8}$

(4) $\frac{9}{6}$

(5) $\frac{5}{8}$

25. How would doubling a affect the value of N in the equation $N = \sqrt{b^2 - 4ac}$ if initially $b = 5$, $c = 4$, and $a = 3$? (Consider only real values.)

(1) N would be twice as large.
(2) N would be half as large.
(3) N would stay the same.
(4) N would equal 3.
(5) N would have no value.

IF YOU FINISH BEFORE TIME IS CALLED, CHECK YOUR WORK ON THIS
SECTION ONLY. DO NOT WORK ON ANY OTHER SECTION IN THE TEST.

Answer Key

Part I

1. (2)	**8.** (2, 0)	**15.** (3)	**22.** (3)
2. (3)	**9.** (3)	**16.** (3)	**23.** (5)
3. 4.574	**10.** (2)	**17.** (2)	**24.** (2)
4. (4)	**11.** (2)	**18.** (5)	**25.** (1)
5. (1)	**12.** 4.25	**19.** (4)	
6. 176	**13.** (3)	**20.** (3)	
7. (2)	**14.** (3)	**21.** (5)	

Part II

1. 0.125	**8.** (4, 0)	**15.** (4)	**22.** (5)
2. (3)	**9.** (4)	**16.** (5)	**23.** (2)
3. (3)	**10.** (2)	**17.** $6,967	**24.** (3)
4. (5)	**11.** (3)	**18.** (5)	**25.** (5)
5. (2)	**12.** (2)	**19.** (4)	
6. 465	**13.** (2)	**20.** (3)	
7. (3)	**14.** (4)	**21.** (−2, 3)	

Answer Explanations

Part I

1. **(2)** In order to work out the best price, you need to work out the part answers. For Store A, the price after the discount is $960; this is above her budget, so no further calculations are needed. For Store B, the price after the discount is $875; there are no delivery and installation charges, so the total price is $875. For Store C, the price after the discount is $750; the delivery charge is $95 and the installation charge is $125, so the total price is $750 + $95 + $125 = $970, which is above her budget. For Store D, the price after the discount is $990; this is above her budget, so no further calculations are needed.

2. **(3)** If Jan read 398 pages, Jean would have to read 497.5 pages for a draw (rounds up to 498 pages). By reading 498 pages, Jean would've won the challenge. There are two ways of calculating this:

$$398 \cdot 1\frac{1}{4} = 398 \cdot \frac{5}{4} = \frac{398 \cdot 5}{4} = \frac{1,990}{4} = 497\frac{1}{2}$$

Or you can use the decimal equivalent of $1\frac{1}{4}$, which is 1.25:

$$398 \times 1.25 = 497.5$$

3. **4.574** The answer on the standard grid would look like this:

4. **(4)** Multiply the gallons used per week by the cost per gallon to get the cost per week. Because there are 52 weeks per year, multiply by 52 to estimate the cost per year.

5. **(1)** Multiplication is an efficient way of performing repetitive additions.

6. **176** Remember the order of operations, BEDMAS (brackets, exponents, division, multiplication, addition, and subtraction). Look at the question:

$$123 + 49 - 21 \times 8 \div 4 + 23 \times 2$$

And organize it according to the order of operations:

$$123 + 49 - ([21 \times 8] \div 4) + (23 \times 2) = 123 + 49 - 42 + 46 = 176$$

The answer would look like this on the standard grid:

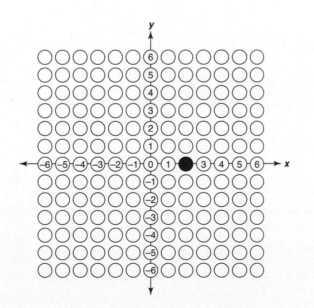

7. **(2)** If the room were 12.5 feet long, the actual area to be covered would be 156.25 square feet. Herbert's estimate ignored the decimal point between the 2 and the 5.

8. **(2, 0)** If AC were extended down to the x-axis, it would cross at (2,0). The answer on the coordinate-plane grid would look like this:

9. **(3)** To find the length of the hypotenuse, you use the equation $l = \sqrt{a^2 + b^2}$, where l is the length of the hypotenuse, a is the length of BC or 6 inches, and b is the length of AC or 8 inches. Substituting, $l = \sqrt{6^2 + 8^2} = \sqrt{36 + 64} = \sqrt{100} = 10$ inches.

10. **(2)** Any values of x and y that satisfy the equations of both lines give the point of intersection.

    The equation of a line with slope 1 and y-intercept of (0, 4) is $y = mx + b$. Substituting, $y = x + 4$ or $x - y = -4$.

    The equation of a line through (4, 8) and (−2, −1) is $y = y_1 + \dfrac{(y_2 - y_1)}{(x_2 - x_1)}(x - x_1)$. Substituting, $y = 8 + \dfrac{(-1-8)}{(-2-4)}(x - 4) = \dfrac{3x + 4}{2}$; or cross-multiplying, $2y = 3x + 4$ or $3x - 2y = -4$.

    The equations are $x - y = -4$ and $3x - 2y = -4$.

    Multiply the first equation by −2 to get $-2x + 2y = 8$. Then add the equations to get $x = 4$ and substitute in the first equation to get $y = 8$.

    The point of intersection would be (4, 8).

11. **(2)** To calculate the amount of carpeting required for the apartment, you need to calculate the area of each room and add the areas together.

    Living room: $20 \times 18 = 360$ square feet

    Dining room: $12 \times 14 = 168$ square feet

    Bedroom: $18 \times 24 = 432$ square feet

    Hallways: $10 \times 3 = 30$ square feet

    Total area = 360 + 168 + 432 + 30 = 990 square feet

    To convert square feet into square yards, you have to divide by 9. So, $990 \div 9 = 110$ square yards.

    Because he needed 110 square yards but bought 115 square yards, he would have an extra $115 - 110 = 5$ square yards of carpet.

12. **4.25** To calculate the time required for the flight, divide the distance by the average speed: $2,444 \div 575 = 4.25$ hours (rounded to two decimal places), which would be entered on a standard grid as follows:

13. **(3)** To calculate the difference in surface area, you first need to calculate each surface area and subtract.

    Suggested pool: $30 \times 30 = 900$ square feet

    Original pool: $30 \times 18 = 540$ square feet

    Difference = 360 square feet

    Or you could multiply the additional width by the length: $12 \times 30 = 360$ square feet.

14. **(3)** From the table, you can see that the lowest percentage of 15+ female smokers is in Japan. The rest of the conclusions cannot be supported from data in the table.

15. **(3)** In order to compare the graphs, you must first make note of the y-axis and the difference between the largest number and the smallest number, and the number of people represented by each division. For example, Graph 3 has a difference of 12, which means that each division on the y-axis represents two people. On the other hand, the divisions in Graph 5 go from 0 to 200 and each division represents 50 people.

16. **(3)** The number of smokers in each country is independent of the number of smokers in another country. Changing the percentage of smokers in Austria would not change the percentage of people in France who smoked.

17. **(2)** You can calculate the number of smokers in the United States as of the time this data was gathered by adding the number of male and female smokers 15+. To arrive at this number, using the assumption that males and females are equally represented in the population, divide the population by two to arrive at 108,574,051.5. Then the number of male smokers is $0.281 \times 108{,}574{,}051.5 = 30{,}509{,}308.47$ and the number of female smokers is $0.235 \times 108{,}574{,}051.5 = 25{,}514{,}902.1$. Adding the two numbers together would produce a sum of 56,024,210.57.

18. **(5)** If you add the number of responses for meat and fish dishes, you arrive at 37, which exceeds the other responses.

19. **(4)** Michael Jackson had the highest number of votes recorded, and ABBA had the least.

20. **(3)** If the slope remains the same and the y-intercept changes, the lines would be parallel but with different points of intersection with the y-axis.

21. **(5)** Using the equation $l = \sqrt{a^2 + b^2}$, you would substitute $l = 23$ and $a = 16$ to give you $23 = \sqrt{16^2 + b^2}$ or $529 = 256 + b^2$ (square both sides of the equation) or $b^2 = 529 - 256 = 273$. It follows that $b = 16.5$.

22. **(3)** If you substitute $a = 4$, $b = 11$, and $c = 3$ in the equation, you get
    $$d = \frac{-11 \pm \sqrt{11^2 - 4 \cdot 4 \cdot 3}}{2 \cdot 4} = \frac{-11 \pm \sqrt{121 - 48}}{8} = -2.4 \text{ or } -0.3.$$

23. (5) Because no value is given for *k*, you have no way of calculating the volume.

24. (2) The value of temperature rises as the months pass from February to June on the graph.

25. (1) In this linear equation, increasing the value of one side increases the value of the other side.

Part II

1. **0.125** To convert a fraction into a decimal, you divide the top number (the numerator) by the bottom number (the denominator). So, $\frac{1}{8} = 1 \div 8 = 0.125$. The answer on a standard grid would look like this:

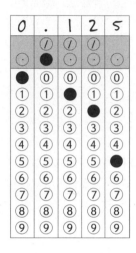

2. **(3)** To calculate the discount, it's easier to change the percentage into a decimal fraction (28% = 0.28) and multiply it by the selling price to arrive at $13.9972. But because this amount is in dollars and cents, the answer would be $14. Notice that you can round $49.99 to $50 to make the calculation simpler.

3. **(3)** If you remember that a fraction becomes larger as the denominator becomes smaller, the question is really "What is the third largest denominator?", which is 7.

4. **(5)** The formula for calculating the volume is $V = lwh$, which is a sequence of multiplications.

5. **(2)** Because multiplying and dividing are opposite operations and addition and subtraction are opposite operations, you would perform the opposite operations in the reverse order to arrive back at the original number—in other words, you would subtract and then divide.

6. **465** To do this calculation, remember the order of operations (BEDMAS). Multiply $36 \times 11 = 396$ first. Then add and subtract in order, left to right, to find the answer, 465. The answer on a standard grid would look like this:

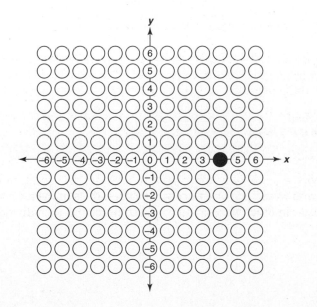

7. **(3)** $24.99 is approximately $25 and six shirts costing $25 each would cost $150 in total.

8. **(4, 0)** The perpendicular line would intersect the x-axis at (4, 0). This would appear on the coordinate-plane grid as follows:

9. **(4)** If you could unfold a die, you would end up with six faces. It would look like this:

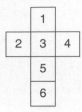

10. **(2)** Substituting in the equation, produces:

$$y = mx + b$$
$$y = \frac{3}{5}x + 8$$
$$5y = 3x + 40$$
$$3x - 5y + 40 = 0$$

11. **(3)** If each tile is 9 inches wide, it would be 0.75 feet wide. To tile the 75-foot side would require 100 tiles. To tile the 28.5-foot side would require 38 tiles. To tile the two sides would require 100 + 38 = 138 tiles. And to tile the four sides would require 138 × 2 = 276 tiles. But that would leave a 9-x-9-inch space at each corner, which would require four more tiles. The total number of tiles required would be 276 + 4 = 280 tiles.

12. **(2)** The meter reads 67,015. To find the total cost, multiply 67,015 × 0.16 to get $10,722.40.

13. **(2)** The area of the larger rug is 10 × 14 = 140 square feet, and the area of the smaller rug is 9 × 12 = 108 square feet. The larger rug will cover 140 − 108 = 32 more square feet.

14. **(4)** The student who stood first (Sam) received 98.2%, and the student who stood fourth (Dave) received 97.6%. The difference is 98.2 − 97.6 = 0.6%.

15. **(4)** The general trend from the chart is that dropout rates have decreased most years, which would mean that more students are staying in school.

16. **(5)** Although there seems to have been a general decline in unemployment rates until 2009, it doesn't match the changes in dropout rates. For example, 2005 shows a rise in dropout rates but a decrease in unemployment rates. Common knowledge may be that people who can't find work go back to school for further education or training, but that is not demonstrated by the statistics presented in these questions and you can use only the information in the questions to answer them.

17. **$6,967** The top salesperson sold $33,444 and the bottom salesperson sold $26,478 in this period. If Salesperson 3 could increase his sales by $6,966, his sales would be equal. In order to exceed it by $1, he would have to sell $6,967. This would be recorded on a standard grid as follows:

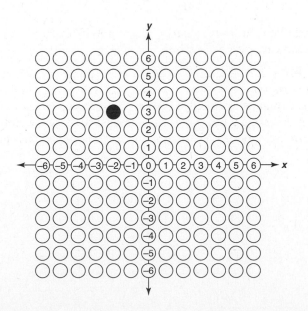

18. **(5)** There is not enough information to draw a conclusion. If the price of regular gas and diesel fuel had been included, a conclusion might be possible.

19. **(4)** Rachel read an average of 529 pages, which is 67 pages more than the average of the averages.

20. **(3)** Equations read like sentences. Choice 3 reads that the number of miles driven by Don is twice the number of miles driven by George plus 36 miles, which is what was asked.

21. **(−2, 3)** To find the value of x, substitute in the equation $y = mx + b$. Then $3 = \frac{5}{2}x + 8$ or $x = -2$. The point is (−2, 3). The coordinate-plane grid would look like this:

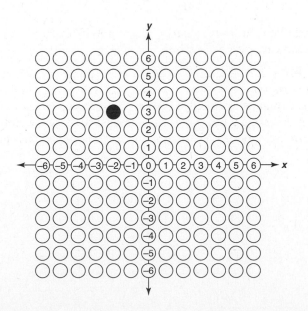

22. (5) The volume of a cone is $\frac{1}{3}\pi r^2 h$, or $0.3333 \times 3.14 \times 1.5 \times 1.5 \times 5 = 11.77$, or 11.8 to one decimal point.

23. (2) Substituting the values into the equation $K = \frac{n}{r(n-r)}$ produces $K = \frac{12}{8(12-8)} = \frac{3}{8}$.

24. (3) Subtract the two equations. We get $x = \frac{1}{2}$, implying $y = \frac{9}{8}$.

25. (5) Doubling the value of a and substituting in the equation would produce $N = \sqrt{25 - 96}$, which would require finding the square root of a negative number, which can't be calculated.

Reading Comprehension Strategies

Reading comprehension questions can be found on three of the five GED subject tests: Social Studies, Science, and Language Arts, Reading. You'll be asked to read text passages and then answer questions about what you've read. This appendix outlines some strategies to help you prepare for this prevalent question type.

Determining the Reliability of Information Presented in the Questions

Your first task when presented with a question based on a statement that is *supposedly* factual is to determine if that question's statement is accurate. In real life, you can go to other sources and verify the facts and ensure that the material you're using is accurate. On a test or exam, you don't have this luxury. If a statement is made, you have no way of verifying it except from your basic knowledge and outside reading.

For example, if you were presented with a question asking if Christopher Columbus made his voyages during Lincoln's term of office as president, your experience and background knowledge would tell you that this is inaccurate because Columbus's exploration took place before there was a country where Lincoln could be elected president. In other words, don't automatically assume that such a statement is true. Use common sense and the knowledge that you bring with you to the test.

Using Data to Answer Questions

In this modern age of computers, applications are programs that enable you to perform a task with a computer. For the purposes of the GED, *application* means how a particular theory might be used. For example, to create a map, you have to begin with a survey to measure the distances between objects or defined locations. In this case, the measurements are the data, and the map is the application of the data. On the GED, you may be asked to use data presented in the reading passage to answer a question. Note that a question might be based on data that is *not* presented in the reading passage.

EXAMPLE:

Christopher Columbus

Christopher Columbus was born in Genoa, Italy, in 1451, to a poor but proud family of five children. He had a limited education but began his seagoing adventures when he was 16. In 1467, Columbus traveled to Iceland and continued his seafaring days as a privateer, plundering ships belonging to the Moors. In one of these battles, off the coast of Portugal, his ship was sunk, but he survived by swimming to shore.

One year later, Columbus began working with his brother, Bartholomew, a cartographer. He married into a wealthy Portuguese family and inherited his father-in-law's maps of the Portuguese possessions in the Atlantic. In 1484, with his maps and experience, Columbus approached the king of Portugal for money to find a fast trade route to the Indies but was turned down.

> Why was Columbus turned down in his appeal for money to find a fast route to the Indies?
>
> (1) He was born to a poor family.
> (2) He had been a pirate.
> (3) He had little education.
> (4) He married into a wealthy Portuguese family.
> (5) No relevant information supplied.

The correct answer is **(5)**. All the answers are present in the passage, but none is connected to the king's refusal. Although a lot of information is presented, in order to apply the information to the question, the information must be relevant and related. As you answer the questions on the GED, make sure that you use the information in a way that answers the question.

Breaking Down Information into Understandable Chunks

Sometimes, information in a question is presented in a large bundle, but in order to answer the questions based on the information, you have to divide it into small parcels.

EXAMPLE:

Can You Feel the Earth Move?

The Earth is not a still, unmoving object. It may feel that way when you stand on it, but there is a lot going on under your feet. The Earth is divided into layers, one of which is the lithosphere, which exists as separate tectonic plates. These plates or surfaces sit on a visco-elastic solid layer called the asthenosphere, which allows them to move very slowly. Although you can't feel the Earth move, it is moving—just very slowly.

> What causes the Earth to move?
>
> (1) Movement of the atmosphere
> (2) Loose sand under the surface
> (3) Movement of the lithoshere
> (4) Poor shoes
> (5) Plane tectonics

The correct answer is **(3)**. This is the best answer although it's not the most complete one. To answer this question, you have to break down the information given. The actual name for this movement is plate tectonics, but that is not mentioned in the passage. Instead, there is information about the lithosphere and how it is composed of plates, which can move on a visco-elastic solid layer. Choice (5) is a spelling mistake and is wrong.

Determining the Meaning of a Word

Comprehension questions test your ability to understand the material presented. This can depend on the material or the words used in presenting the passage and the questions. You often can figure out the meaning of a word you don't understand by the sentence it appears in.

EXAMPLE:

MASH in Korea

There are casualties in every war. The ideal situation is to be able to treat the injuries before they claim the lives of the injured. During the Korean War, a new concept in field emergency care was developed. The United Nations forces developed mobile army surgical hospitals with 150 to 200 beds to treat those requiring surgical care. These hospitals were initially developed to treat casualties requiring surgical services, but the hospital staff quickly saw the need for treating medical as well as surgical patients. With the limited number of beds in each MASH unit and the constant flow of the wounded, it became necessary to develop a plan of airborne evacuation to take the wounded, once stabilized, to more remote hospitals.

During the Korean War, a MASH unit was:

(1) A military assistants survival hospital.
(2) A minor accident survival hospital.
(3) A mobile army surgical hospital.
(4) A movable accident support hospital.
(5) A mobile accident support hospital.

The correct answer is **(3)**. There is a lot of information in this passage, but the best answer to the meaning of the acronym *MASH* is mobile army surgical hospital. The other answers would fit the initials, but the actual words are spelled out in the passage in the fourth sentence. In addition, the passage mentions that these were surgical units that later began to treat medical emergencies.

Recognizing Biases, Inferences, and Effects

Biases, inferences, and effects all have an influence on the passages that you read.

Biases

If the passage contains only primary information, all you'll read is raw information. If the information has been analyzed or interpreted, then you should look for the bias of the author. If the author believes that the needs of large corporation should take precedence over the wants and needs of the people around the plant, then a passage on industrial pollution by the manager of the plant may greatly differ from what an environmentalist would write. The bias of the author is important in understanding the passage in sufficient detail to answer questions about it.

EXAMPLE:

An Interview

INTERVIEWER: Welcome, Mr. Georges, to "Green Earth," the program that concerns itself with the environment.

MR. GEORGES: Thank you for having me.

INTERVIEWER: Let's start with an item that's been in the news lately.

MR. GEORGES: Fine. What's that?

INTERVIEWER: Your company has been criticized for the amount of particulates you release into the air from your new plant.

MR. GEORGES: Did I mention how many new jobs were created in that new plant?

INTERVIEWER: Since the plant opened, there has been a steady rise in lung ailments and a steady decline in air quality.

MR. GEORGES: We have brought a million dollars into the local economy since we opened. That's pretty significant.

INTERVIEWER: But we have complaints about the constant illness facing many families living near the plant.

MR. GEORGES: Which is worse—starving because there are no jobs or a little hacking cough?

How do you know from this passage that Mr. Georges is willing to accept pollution and illness for the sake of his factory?

(1) He says that he has brought a great deal of money into the local economy.

(2) He is proud of creating new jobs.

(3) He is proud of the look of his new building.

(4) He says that a hacking cough is better than unemployment.

(5) He is proud of his rise to the top of the company.

The correct answer is **(4)**. The final sentence in the passage sums up the way that Mr. Georges feels about pollution and the trade-offs he is willing to make. Choices (1) and (2) are mentioned in the passage but have little to do with pollution or Mr. George's bias. Choices (3) and (5) are just irrelevant information.

Inferences

If you can draw a conclusion that is not exactly stated by the words in the passage, then you're inferring that conclusion. You might be asked to answer a question that is based not on what is said in the passage but on what is inferred—implied—in the passage.

EXAMPLE:

VQZ Corporation Newsletter: New CEO at the Helm

VQZ Enterprises, Ltd., is pleased to announce the appointment of Hachim Oliveston as our new CEO. Mr. Oliveston is leaving a very prestigious appointment as financial advisor to the president of the United States. During his term as financial advisor, he was able to propose three reductions in corporate income tax and an easing of the rules for off-shore deposits of capital. We know that with Mr. Oliveston at the helm of VQZ Enterprises, Ltd., we will benefit from his vast experience in financial matters. Welcome aboard, Hachim.

What is the major implication of this appointment?

(1)   The new CEO can influence the president.
(2)   The new CEO can balance the books at VQZ Enterprises, Ltd.
(3)   The new CEO can captain a large ship.
(4)   The new CEO will be friendly with the senior staff.
(5)   The new CEO will understand the Income Tax Act.

The correct answer is **(1).** From the passage, the implication is made that, because he was a senior advisor to the president, Oliveston would still be able to influence him. Nowhere does the passage explicitly state this, but the implication is there. The other answers do not indicate how this appointment could help the company.

Effects

An effect is a result of something else and may have to be deduced or inferred from the passage presented. Read passages carefully, remembering to look for a cause if an effect is asked for.

EXAMPLE:

A Message from Your Mayor

Fellow citizens, we are facing a crisis of epic proportions. We are running out of money, and you have indicated to me on many occasions that you do not want a tax hike. My staff and I have gone over the city's budget with a fine-tooth comb. Social services cannot be touched; they are mandated by higher levels of government. We can hope and pray for a mild winter, but it would be a huge error to reduce the street clearing budget to zero. If we did that and it snowed or the leaves fell from the trees, the roads would remain untouched, and you all know what an uproar that would cause. That only leaves one option, and I only hope that you can learn to live with potholes.

Based on this speech, what item must be left out of the budget?

(1)   School maintenance
(2)   Refreshments at meetings
(3)   Street cleaning
(4)   Road repair
(5)   The mayor's salary

The correct answer is **(4).** The cause is the lack of money and the fact that certain city services cannot be dropped because they are mandated or would cause a political backlash. The only area that is seen to be possible to not fund is road repair. This is based on his comment about potholes.

Interpreting Questions Based on Opinion, not Fact

A fact has actually happened or is something based on irrefutable proof. An opinion is what someone thinks about it. For example, consider the question: if no one was in the forest when a tree fell, would it make a noise? We are sure that if a tree fell, there would be a noise, but if no one were there to witness the event, could we ever be sure that this was not an exception? This question would be a basis for speculation and opinion but difficult to answer based on fact.

EXAMPLE:

A Message from a Politician

As your representative and a politician from the inner core of this great city, I truly believe that the only answer to moving large numbers of people efficiently is the subway. We all understand that transportation is a vital necessity in a crowded city, but buses only add to that congestion. We have to keep the public people movers underground to leave our streets free and clear for cars and bicycles.

According to the passage, the only solution to moving large numbers of people efficiently is the:

(1) Car.
(2) Bicycle.
(3) Subway.
(4) Bus.
(5) Train.

The correct answer is **(3).** The opinion of the speaker is that subways are best for this purpose. He or she has not presented any facts to back up this opinion. Answers (1), (2), and (4) are mentioned but not as a solution to the problem. Answer (5) may be correct, but it is not mentioned in the passage; thus, for the purposes of answering this question, it's incorrect.

Answering Questions Based on Generalizations

If you're presented with a series of facts, statements, or opinions and asked to summarize the facts, statements, or opinions without altering the main meaning or implication of all the information given, then you are generalizing.

EXAMPLE:

Selling the Car

SALESPERSON: Look at this car. It's all electric. That means it uses no gas at all.
CUSTOMER: Sounds great.
SALESPERSON: Think about how much money you could save!
CUSTOMER: But how far can I go before I have to fill up?
SALESPERSON: Since the Electro Special runs on electricity, you never have to fill up.
CUSTOMER: How far can I go before I have to do something like plug it in?
SALESPERSON: Well, if you drive carefully, you could go about 70 miles before you have to plug it in.
CUSTOMER: But I work 53 miles from the house and still have to get home.
SALESPERSON: Do you think you could find a job closer to home?

What was the salesperson's goal in this conversation?

(1) To protect the environment
(2) To give the customer a good deal on the car
(3) To sell the car
(4) To satisfy the customer's transportation needs
(5) To find a suitable color to match the customer's clothes

The correct answer is **(3).** The salesperson is obviously only interested in selling the car. When an objection is raised about the distance to and from work, the salesperson's only comment is a suggestion to get a job closer to home. The other answers are interesting but do not answer the question. We're generalizing from the conversation that the salesperson is interested only in selling a car and not saving the planet from pollution, making a good deal for the customer, figuring out the customer's actual transportation needs, or matching the car's color to the customer's wardrobe. The main objective of the salesperson is to sell the car. Because this is not specifically stated in the conversation, we're generalizing.

Recognizing Types of Information

Information can be divided into three main categories:

- **Primary:** Information that is original and has not been analyzed, interpreted, or explained, such as a journal or statistics
- **Secondary:** Information that is developed from primary information and that interprets it, such as a textbook or an article in a newspaper or magazine
- **Tertiary:** Information about information such as a database or dictionary

Primary information is usually regarded as accurate but secondary information may be biased, or even incorrect depending on the degree of interpretation and the bias of the interpreter.

EXAMPLE:

Alice's editor assigns her to do a story about Senator George Geores. To do this, she interviews the senator, talks to his friends, researches him in the library, looks him up on the Internet, and speculates about his motives in proposing a bill to limit the manufacturing of gas-powered trucks.

> Of all her efforts, which would be classified as a primary source?
>
> **(1)** Her speculation about his motives
> **(2)** Her interview with the senator
> **(3)** Her conversations with the senator's friends
> **(4)** Her library research
> **(5)** None of the above

The correct answer is **(2).** An interview is regarded as a primary source of information. Answers (2), (3), and (4) would be secondary sources of information.

Recognizing Value-and-Belief Questions

In order to understand the material on the GED, you need to be able to recognize values and beliefs. A belief is a conviction that people believe true without supporting proof or evidence. A value is a concept that we believe to be important to our lives and how we live them. Values and beliefs color the writings of many people because they are an important part of the person. When you read a passage, try to understand the value and belief system that underlies the words.

EXAMPLE:

The Smithington Family and the Environment

The Smithington family is concerned about their impact on the environment and has decided to do something about it. At a family conference, they decide the following:

- They will sell their family car.
- They will ride bicycles as a mode of transportation.
- They will only buy food grown within a hundred miles of their city.
- They will investigate solar power panels on their roof.
- They will replace all their light bulbs with LEDs.
- They will only do laundry after midnight.
- They will investigate the savings if they reinsulated their home.

Which word or words indicate a possible action that may or may not take place to reduce the Smithington's impact on the environment?

(1) Sell
(2) Buy
(3) Replace
(4) Do laundry
(5) Investigate

The correct answer is **(5).** Although the family obviously has a strong belief that they can do something to reduce their impact on the environment, there seem to be some actions they are willing to take and some they are prepared to consider before making a final decision. The word *investigate* implies an action that will be considered before it is taken.

Understanding Relational, Compare-and-Contrast Questions

If you're asked to compare and contrast two sets of information, you have to look for similarities and differences in the information.

If you're asked to discuss the relationship between two sets of information, you have to look at the two sets and see how they compare with each other. They may have a direct relationship in that one set supports the other. They may have an inverse or negative relationship in that they may be opposite opinions. The relationship may be causal, implying that one set of information causes the second set to happen. There may be a dependent relationship in that one set of information may be dependent on the other. In reading passages, it is important to recognize what type of relationship exists and use that to answer the questions.

EXAMPLE:

Regifting or Buying New

Regifting has gotten a bad reputation. Each holiday season we are faced with a dilemma. What do we buy for each person on our list? Often we have a whole collection of gifts that were given to us and that are sitting in a cupboard waiting to become forgotten or fade away. Yet some of these would be perfect for some of the people on our lists. All we have to do is clean them up, wrap them, and they are ready for a new life as wanted and appreciated gifts.

On the other hand, there are dangers of regifting. If you don't have an excellent memory or a good cataloging system, you might give a gift back to the person who gave it to you. That would be embarrassing. With all the new gadgets coming on the market each season, a regifted item could easily be last year's hot item. You just have to know your friends and take your chances. There is nothing as lonely as a gift hidden away on a shelf, gathering dust, as it sits and waits for someone to appreciate it.

In this passage, what is the strongest argument for NOT regifting?

(1) Some gifts might have become damaged over time.

(2) A gift might be returned to the original giver.

(3) Older gifts get dusty.

(4) Some gifts get lonely.

(5) It is harder to wrap an old gift.

The correct answer is **(2).** The passage states that giving a gift back to the person who gave it to you could prove embarrassing. This passage is a good example of compare and contrast in that it presents both sides of an argument and asks a question about one side. A second question might ask about the advantages of regifting or how regifting might be environmentally friendly. With this type of passage, you have to read carefully to see which side of the argument you are being questioned about.

Interpreting Strategy Questions

When someone develops a plan of action to reach a particular goal, he is said to have developed a strategy. In some questions' reading passages, especially those about military operations, the strategy developed is an important part of understanding the text.

EXAMPLE:

Custer's Last Stand

The Battle of the Little Big Horn was fought between the combined forces of four native tribes and the 7th Calvary Regiment of the United States Army. The fighting took place near the Little Bighorn River in Montana. The Calvary Regiment was led by George Armstrong Custer who entered battle assuming that the native army was small and, thus, could be easily defeated. This information was provided by the Indian agents in the territory who based their information on false assumptions.

Custer based his plans on his wish to contain the native soldiers rather that fight and possibly kill them. The battle was to begin early in the morning, because Custer believed that all the natives would still be asleep. Looking over the village preparing for the day, Custer assumed that when he began firing the rifles, any nearby units would come to their aid. He was wrong, and the battle was disastrous for the American Calvary, resulting in 268 casualties and 55 soldiers being wounded. One of the casualties was George Armstrong Custer.

What assumptions did Custer make in preparing for battle?

(1) That the native army was small
(2) That the native army would be asleep early in the morning
(3) That Custer could contain the native army because of his superior numbers
(4) That nearby army units would come to his aid quickly
(5) All of the above

The correct answer is **(5)**. Reading the passage, you can see that answers (1), (2), (3), and (4) were part of Custer's plan or strategy for this battle. His complete strategy may have been more complex, but you can only answer the question with the best answer based on the passage.

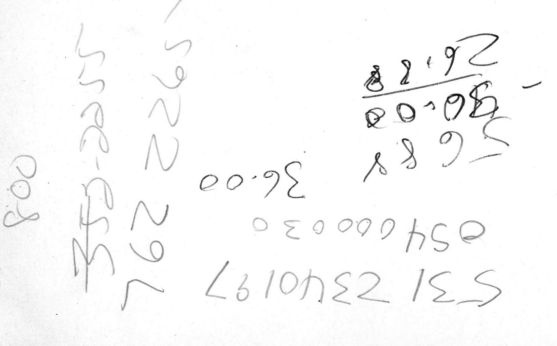